PIECES OF A SPIRAL

Vol. 3

By Kaimu Tachibana

PIECES OF A SPIRAL

CAST OF CHARACTERS

RUKI
DEMON WHO REVERES AND IDOLIZES BISHU. AIDING SAKUYA.

GARAI
BISHU'S FATHER AND LORD OF ALL DEMONS. PRISONER WITHIN MASAYUKI.

BISHU
BORN OF DEMON FATHER AND HUMAN MOTHER. POSSESSES TREMENDOUS POWER.

KAZUKI OKINO
REINCARNATED WITH BISHU'S BODY AND VOICE.

TAGI
RUKI'S FRIEND. BLIND BUT WIELDS POWERFUL MAGIC.

TAKAKO
BISHU'S MOTHER WHO FOR SOME REASON WANTS TO KILL HIM. HAS TAKEN POSSESSION OF WAKYO.

MASAYUKI KAGA
KAZUKI'S BEST FRIEND. BISHU'S REINCARNATION, BUT DOESN'T REMEMBER THE LAST WORLD.

MAKOTO IMAIZUMI
REINCARNATED WITH BISHU'S BODY AND VIOLET EYES.

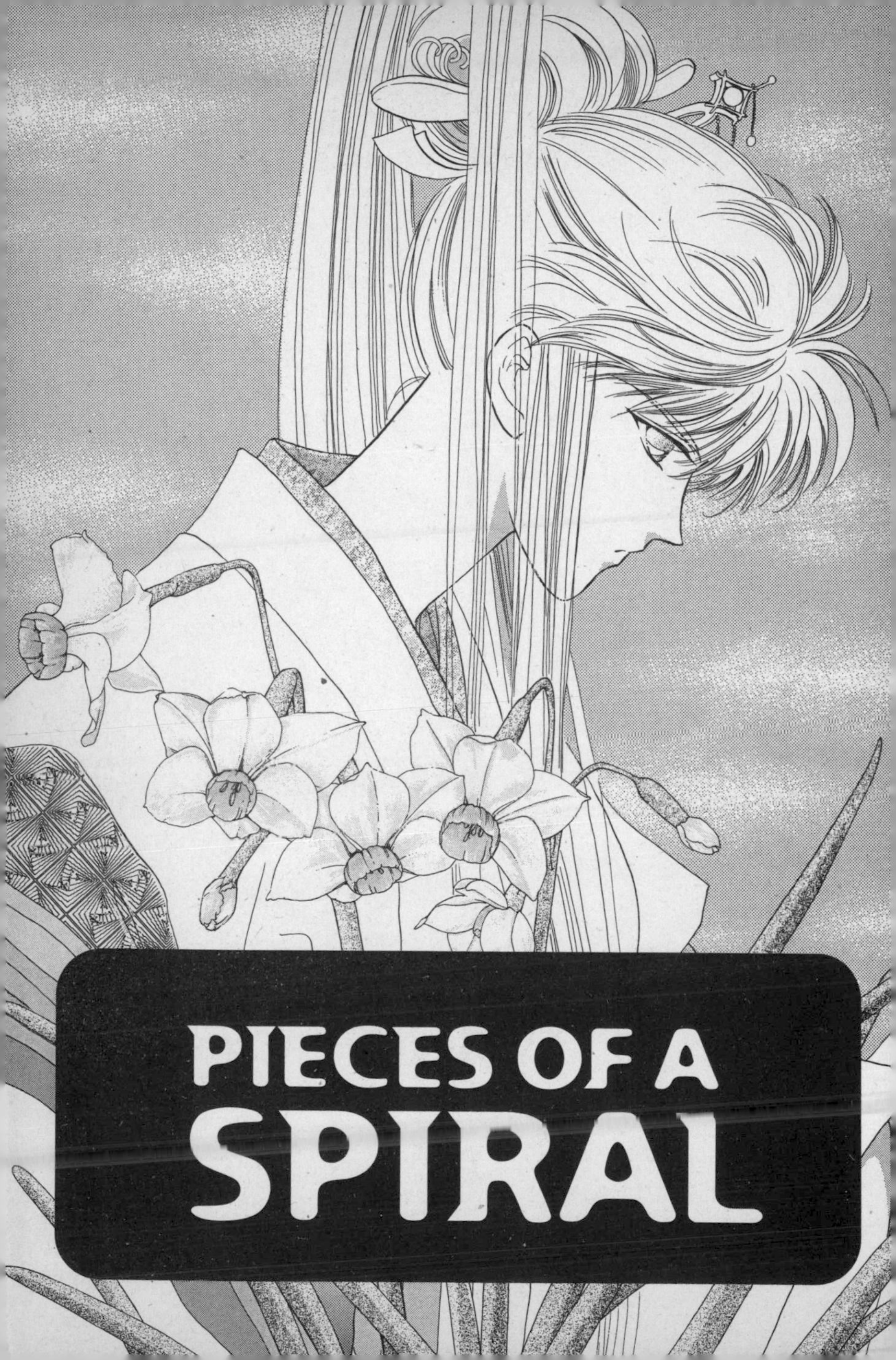
PIECES OF A
SPIRAL

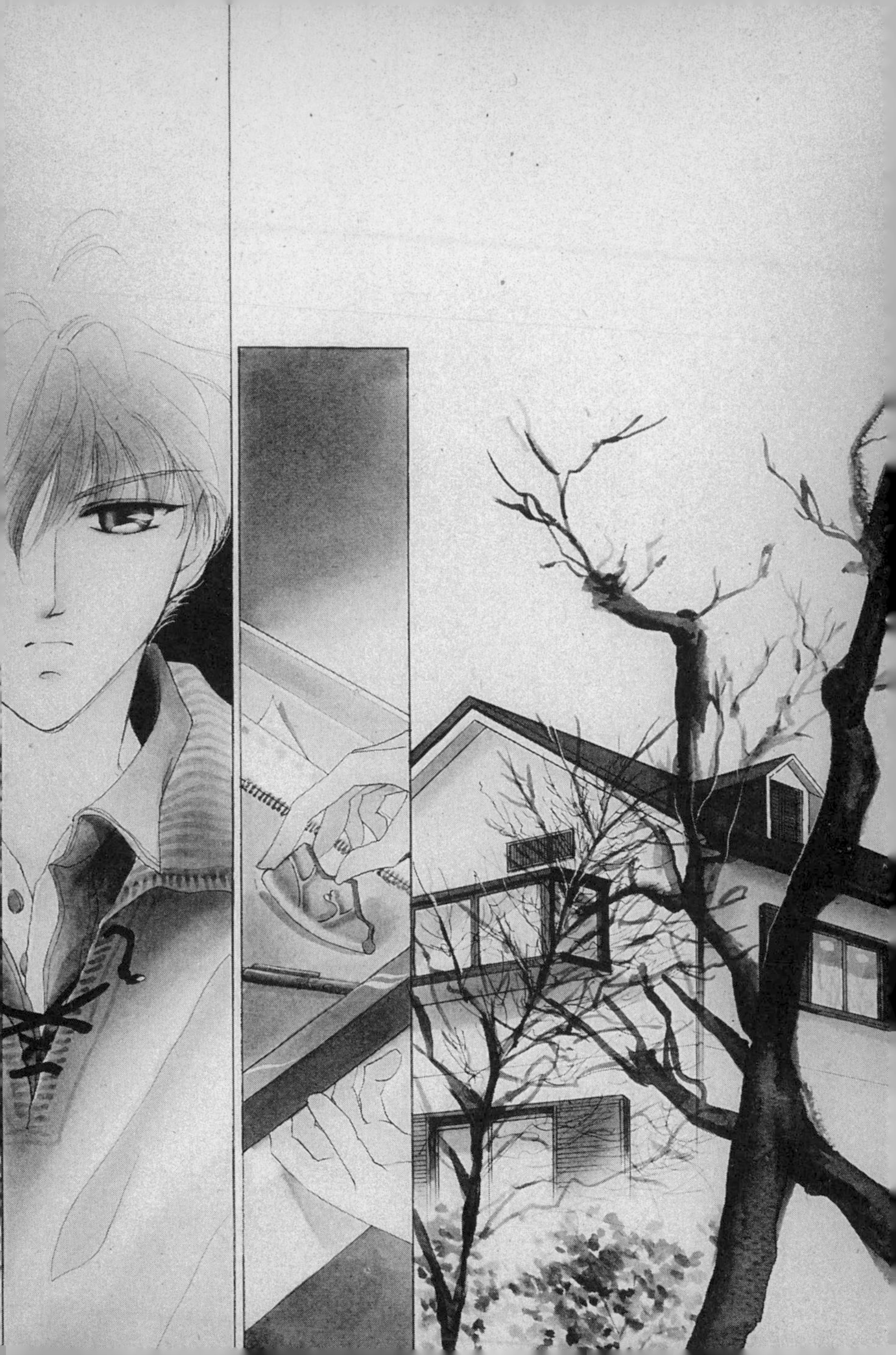

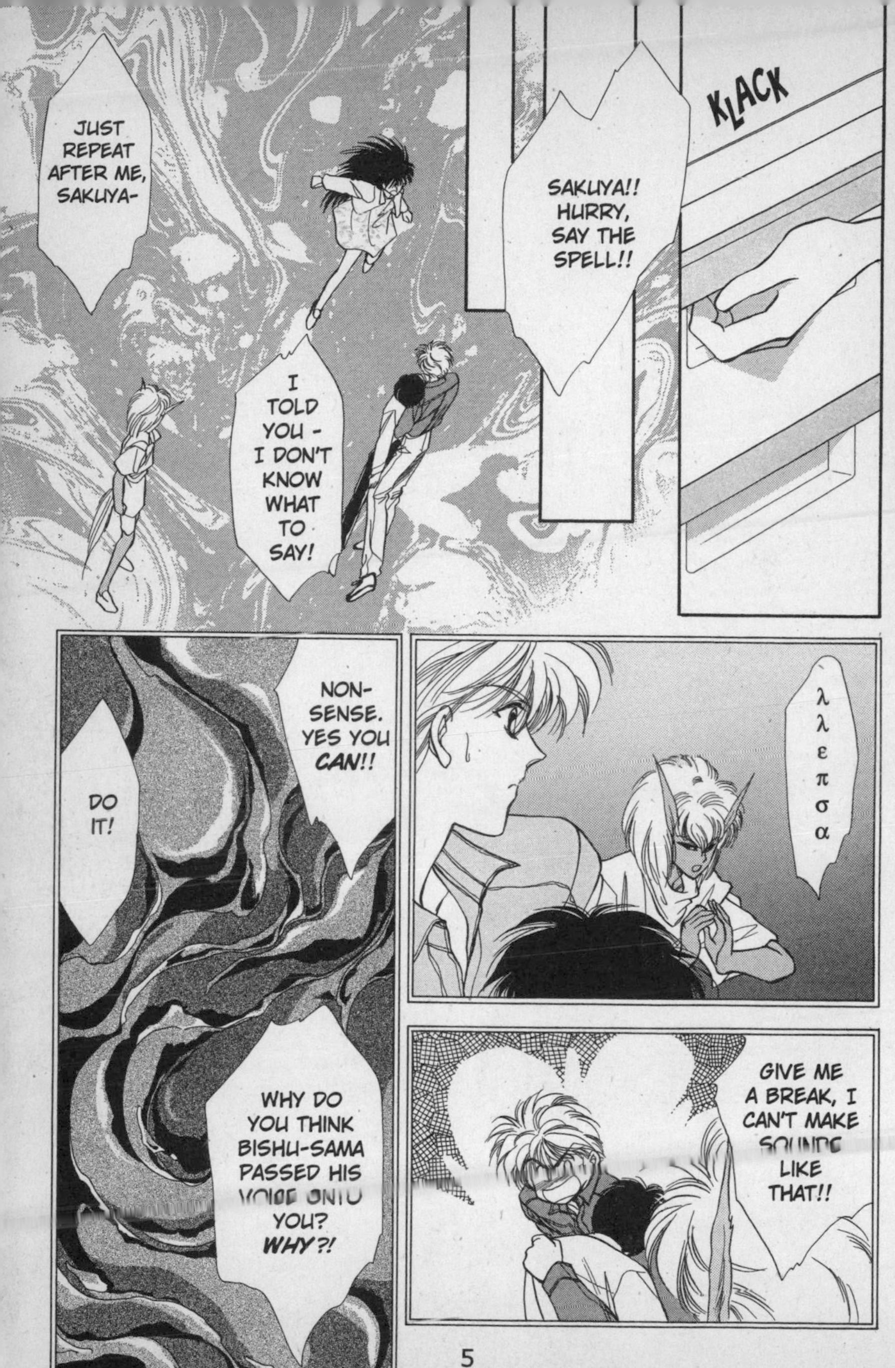
KLACK
SAKUYA!! HURRY, SAY THE SPELL!!
JUST REPEAT AFTER ME, SAKUYA-
I TOLD YOU - I DON'T KNOW WHAT TO SAY!
λλεπσα
GIVE ME A BREAK, I CAN'T MAKE SOUNDS LIKE THAT!!
NON-SENSE. YES YOU *CAN*!!
DO IT!
WHY DO YOU THINK BISHU-SAMA PASSED HIS VOICE ONTO YOU? *WHY*?!

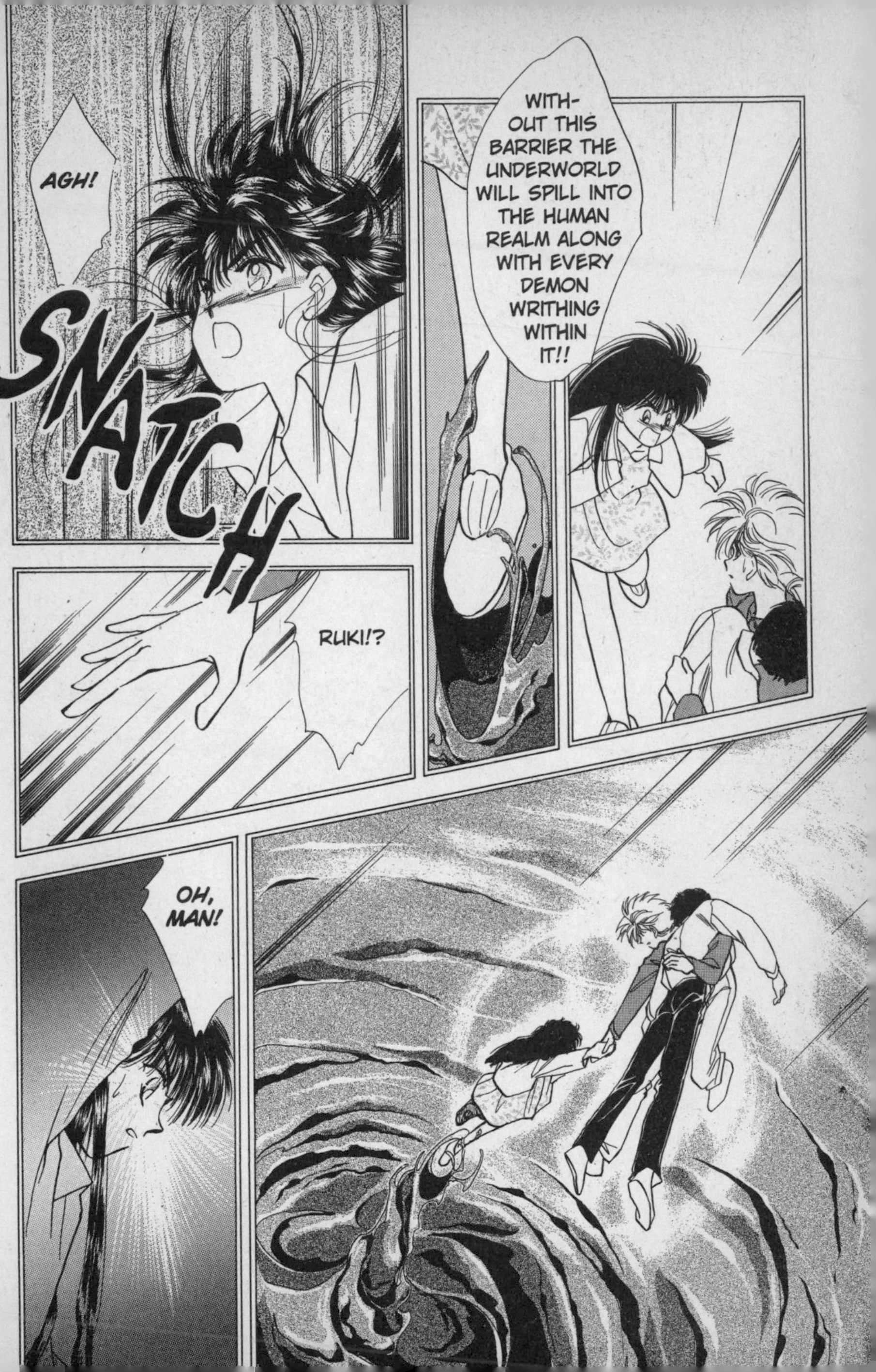
WITH-OUT THIS BARRIER THE UNDERWORLD WILL SPILL INTO THE HUMAN REALM ALONG WITH EVERY DEMON WRITHING WITHIN IT!!
AGH!
SNATCH
RUKI!?
OH, MAN!

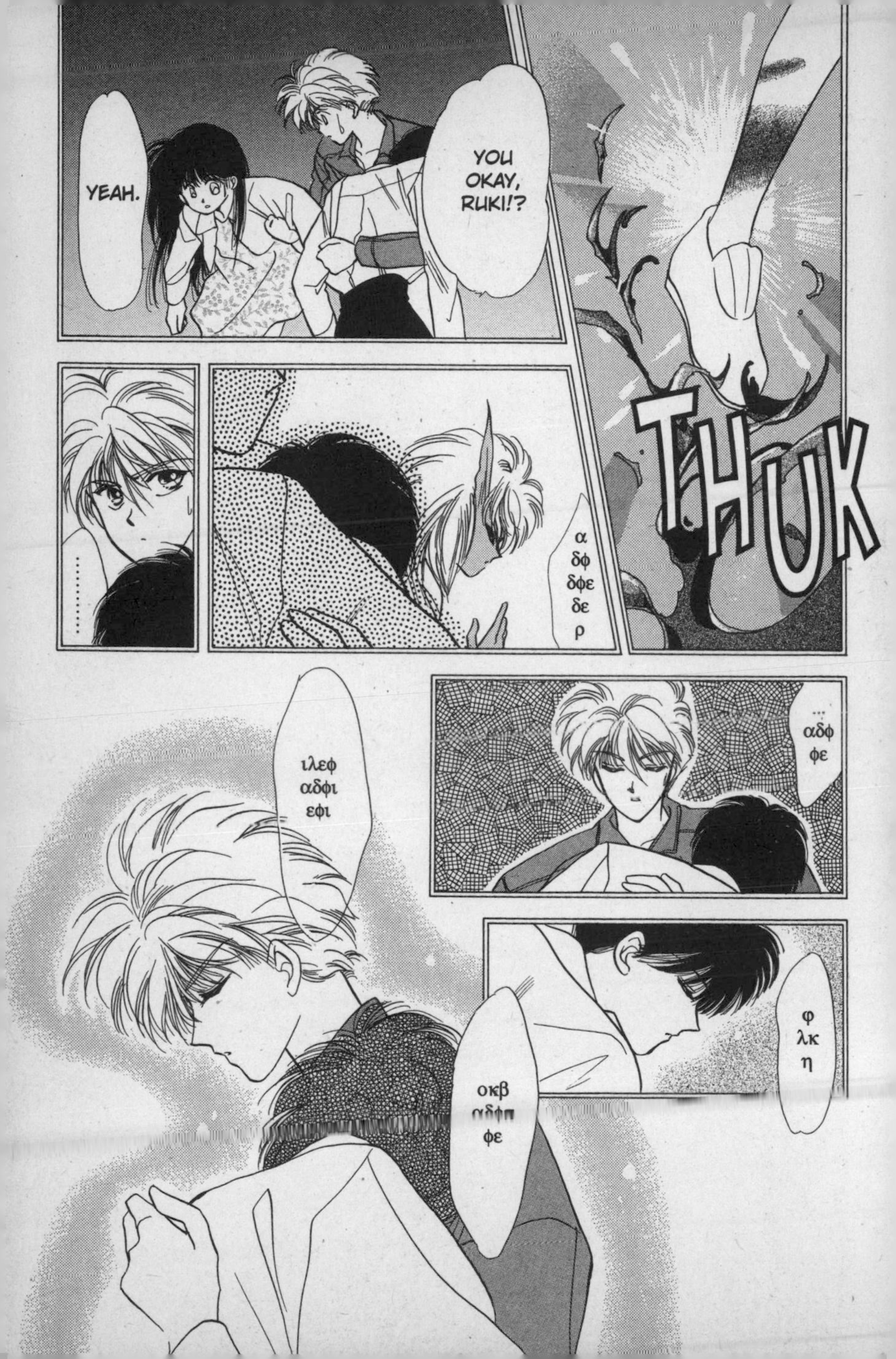
THUK
YOU OKAY, RUKI!?
YEAH.
α δφ δφε δε ρ
……
... αδφ φε
φ λκ η
ιλεφ αδφι εφι
οκβ φε

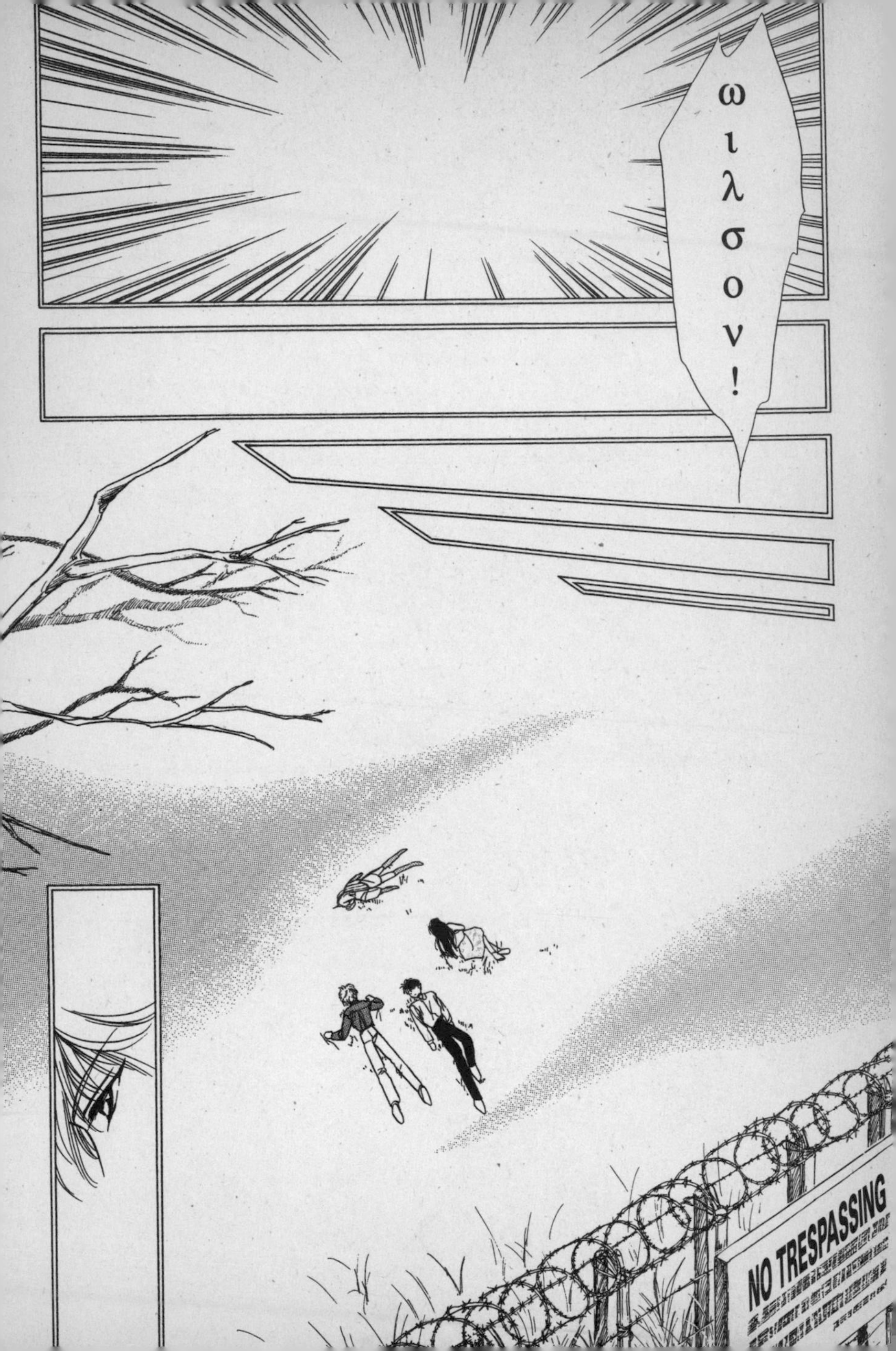
ωιλσον!
NO TRESPASSING

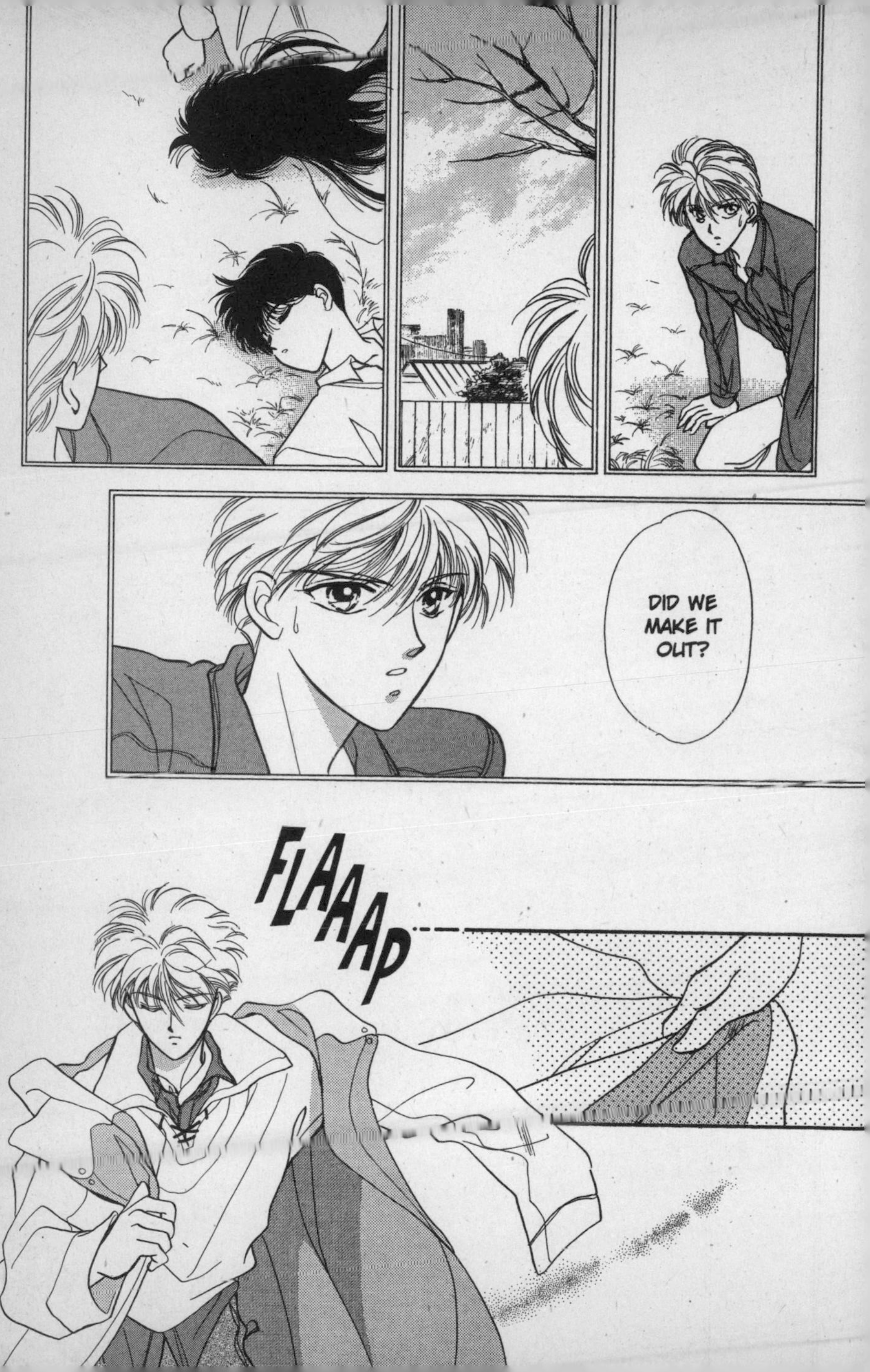
DID WE MAKE IT OUT?
FLAAAP

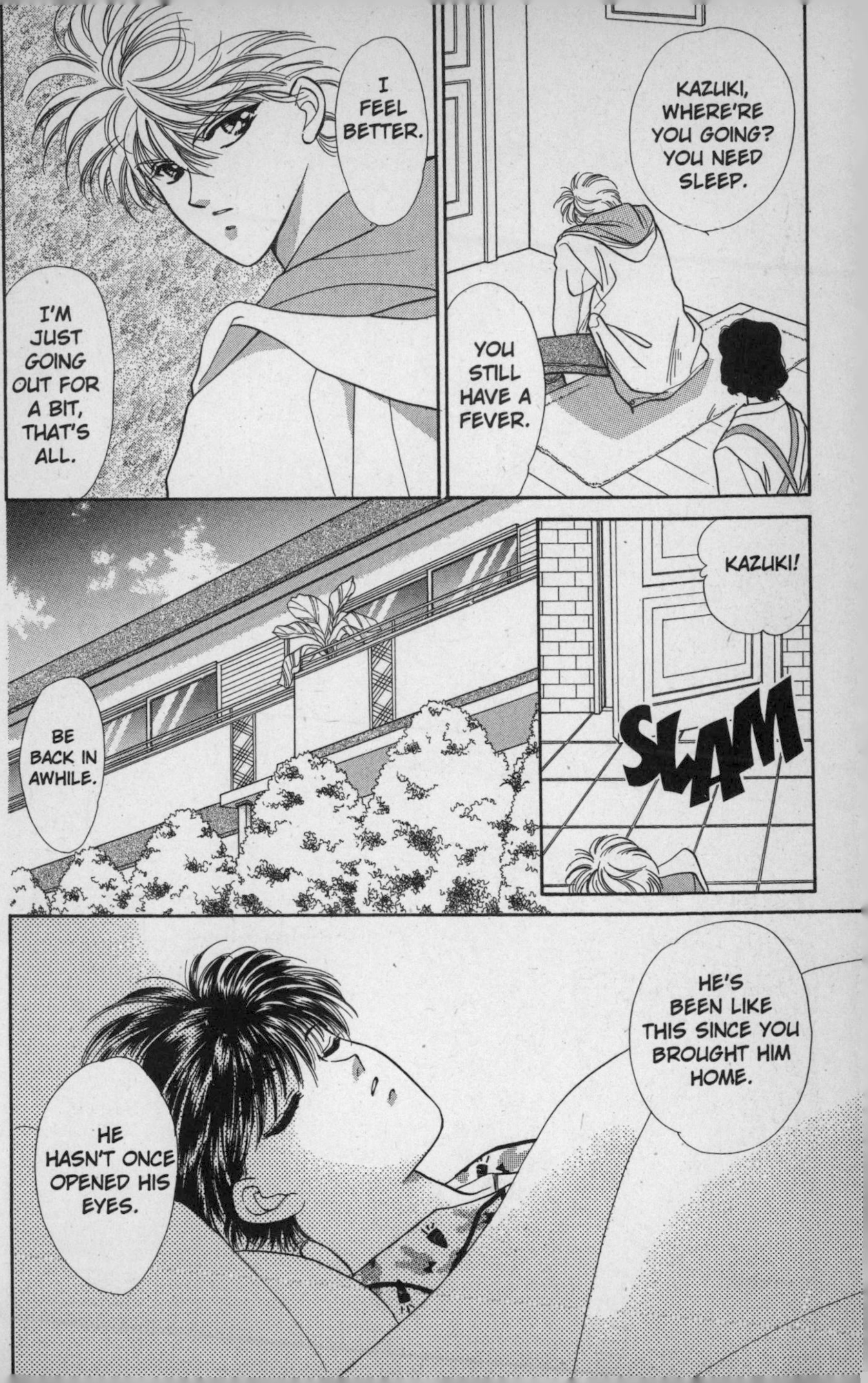
KAZUKI, WHERE'RE YOU GOING? YOU NEED SLEEP.
YOU STILL HAVE A FEVER.
I FEEL BETTER.
I'M JUST GOING OUT FOR A BIT, THAT'S ALL.
KAZUKI!
SLAM
BE BACK IN AWHILE.
HE'S BEEN LIKE THIS SINCE YOU BROUGHT HIM HOME.
HE HASN'T ONCE OPENED HIS EYES.

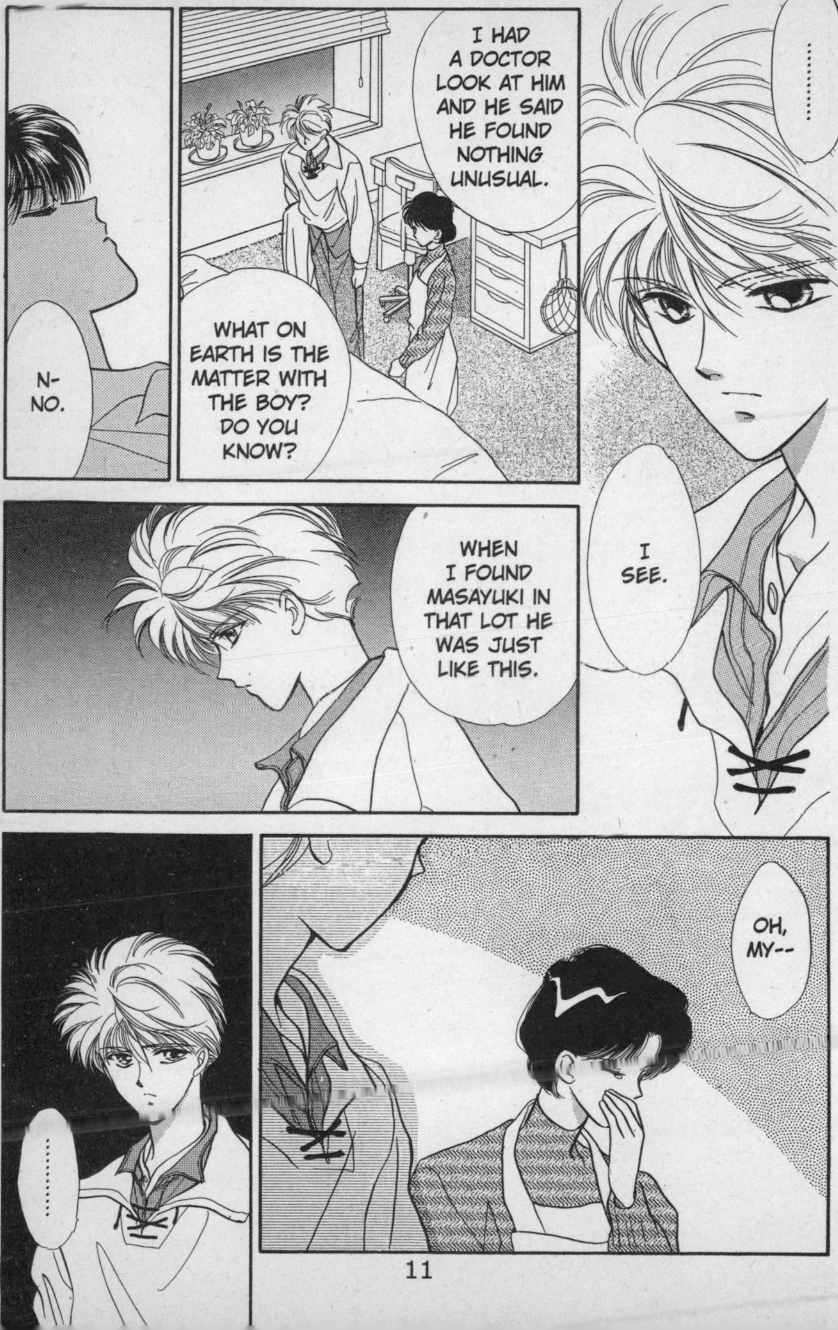

......
I SEE.
I HAD A DOCTOR LOOK AT HIM AND HE SAID HE FOUND NOTHING UNUSUAL.
WHAT ON EARTH IS THE MATTER WITH THE BOY? DO YOU KNOW?
N-NO.
WHEN I FOUND MASAYUKI IN THAT LOT HE WAS JUST LIKE THIS.
OH, MY--
......

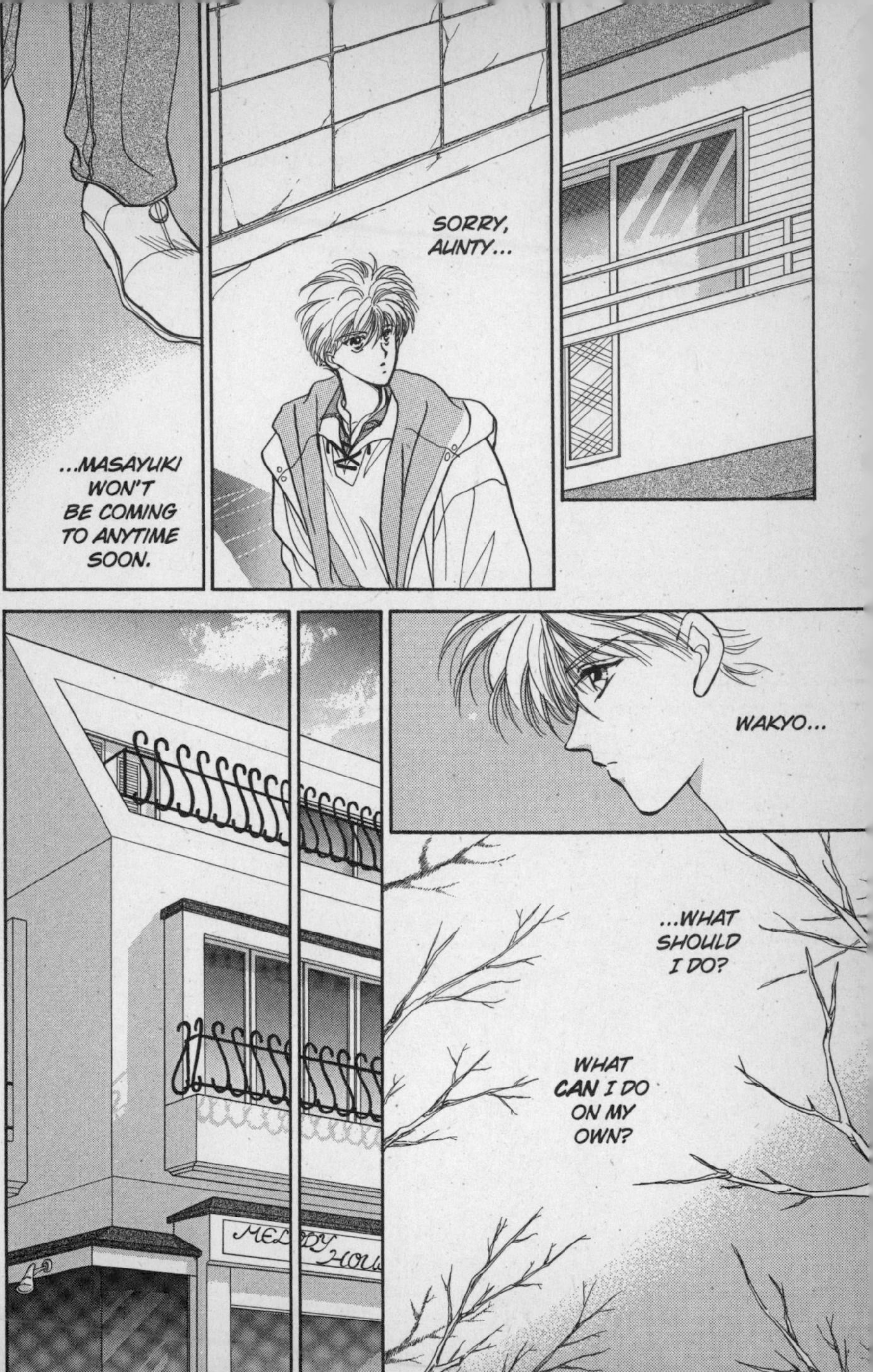
SORRY, AUNTY...
...MASAYUKI WON'T BE COMING TO ANYTIME SOON.
WAKYO...
...WHAT SHOULD I DO?
WHAT CAN I DO ON MY OWN?

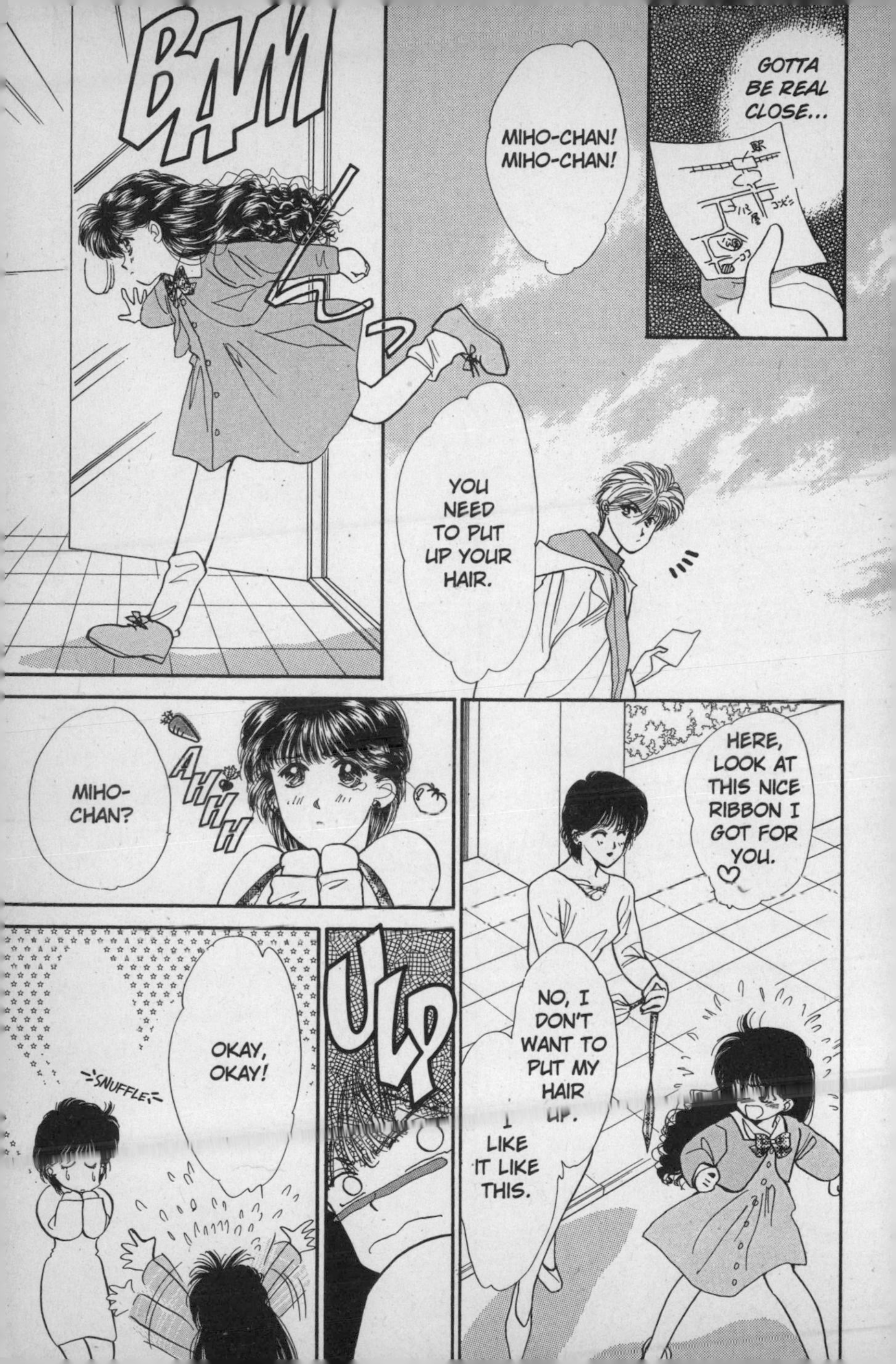

GOTTA BE REAL CLOSE...
MIHO-CHAN! MIHO-CHAN!
YOU NEED TO PUT UP YOUR HAIR.
BAM
HERE, LOOK AT THIS NICE RIBBON I GOT FOR YOU. ♡
NO, I DON'T WANT TO PUT MY HAIR UP.
I LIKE IT LIKE THIS.
AHHHH
MIHO-CHAN?
ULP
OKAY, OKAY!
SNUFFLE

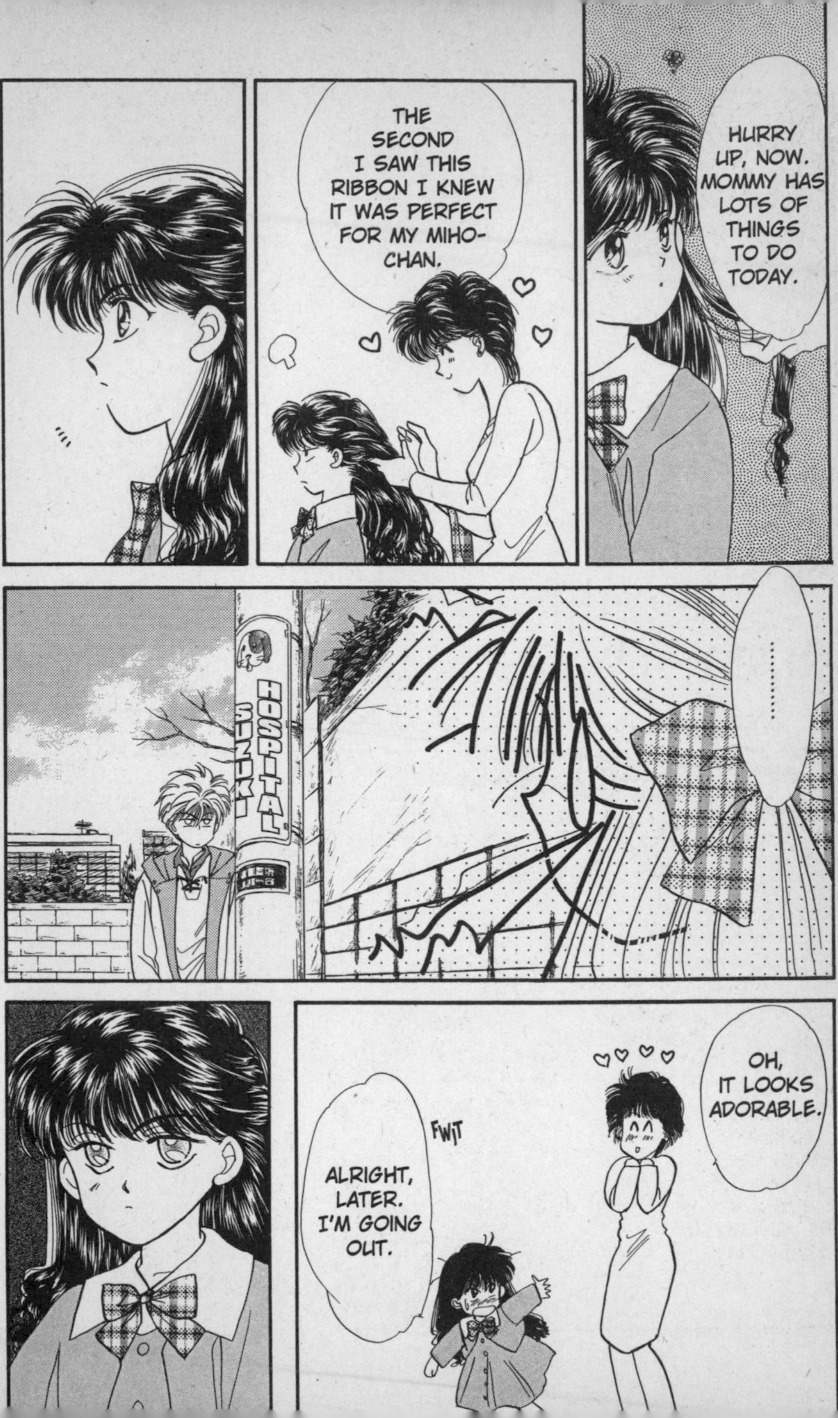
HURRY UP, NOW. MOMMY HAS LOTS OF THINGS TO DO TODAY.
THE SECOND I SAW THIS RIBBON I KNEW IT WAS PERFECT FOR MY MIHO-CHAN.
......
HOSPITAL
SUZUKI
OH, IT LOOKS ADORABLE.
FWIT
ALRIGHT, LATER. I'M GOING OUT.

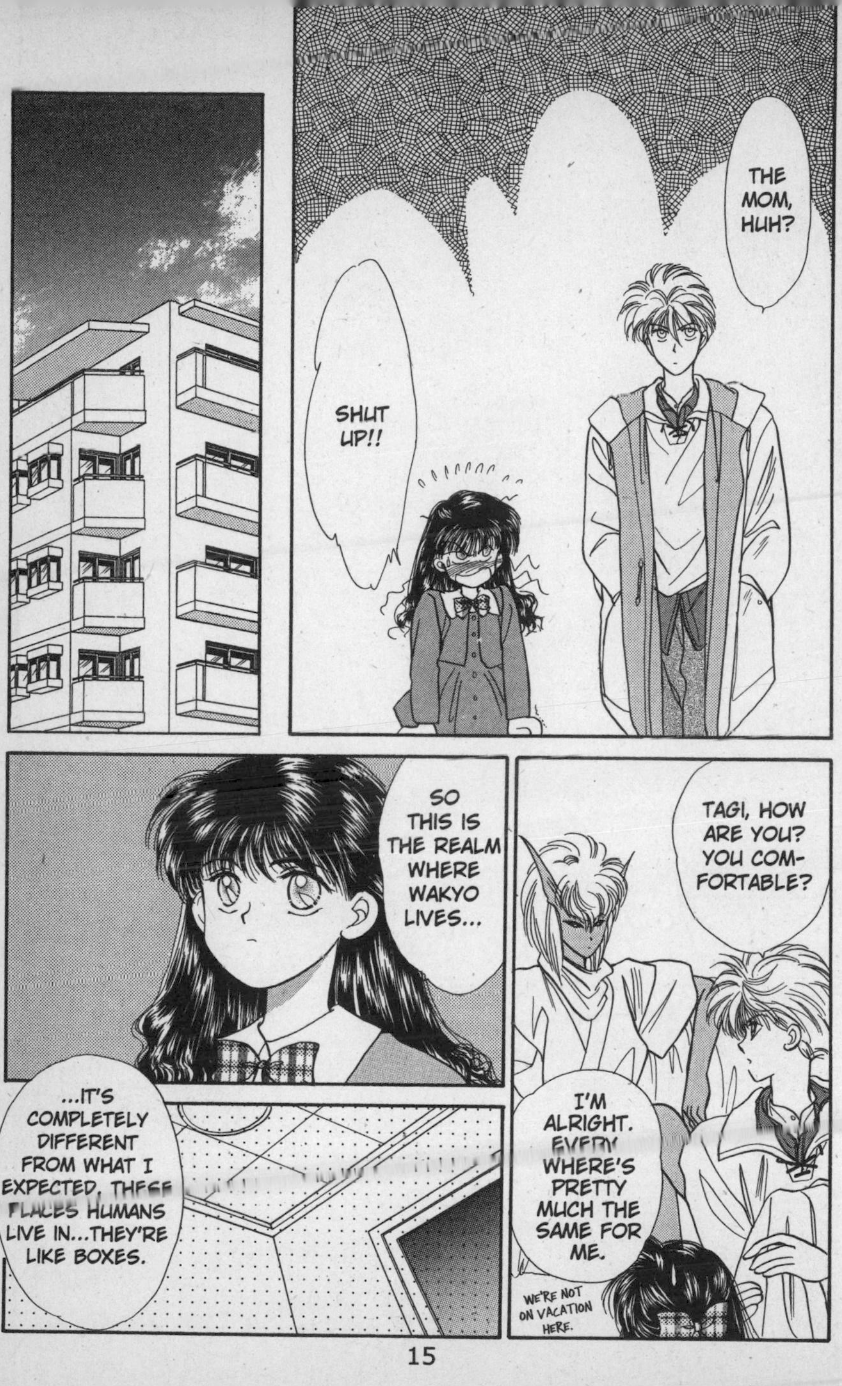

THE MOM, HUH?
SHUT UP!!
TAGI, HOW ARE YOU? YOU COM-FORTABLE?
I'M ALRIGHT. EVERY WHERE'S PRETTY MUCH THE SAME FOR ME.
WE'RE NOT ON VACATION HERE.
SO THIS IS THE REALM WHERE WAKYO LIVES...
...IT'S COMPLETELY DIFFERENT FROM WHAT I EXPECTED. THESE PLACES HUMANS LIVE IN...THEY'RE LIKE BOXES.

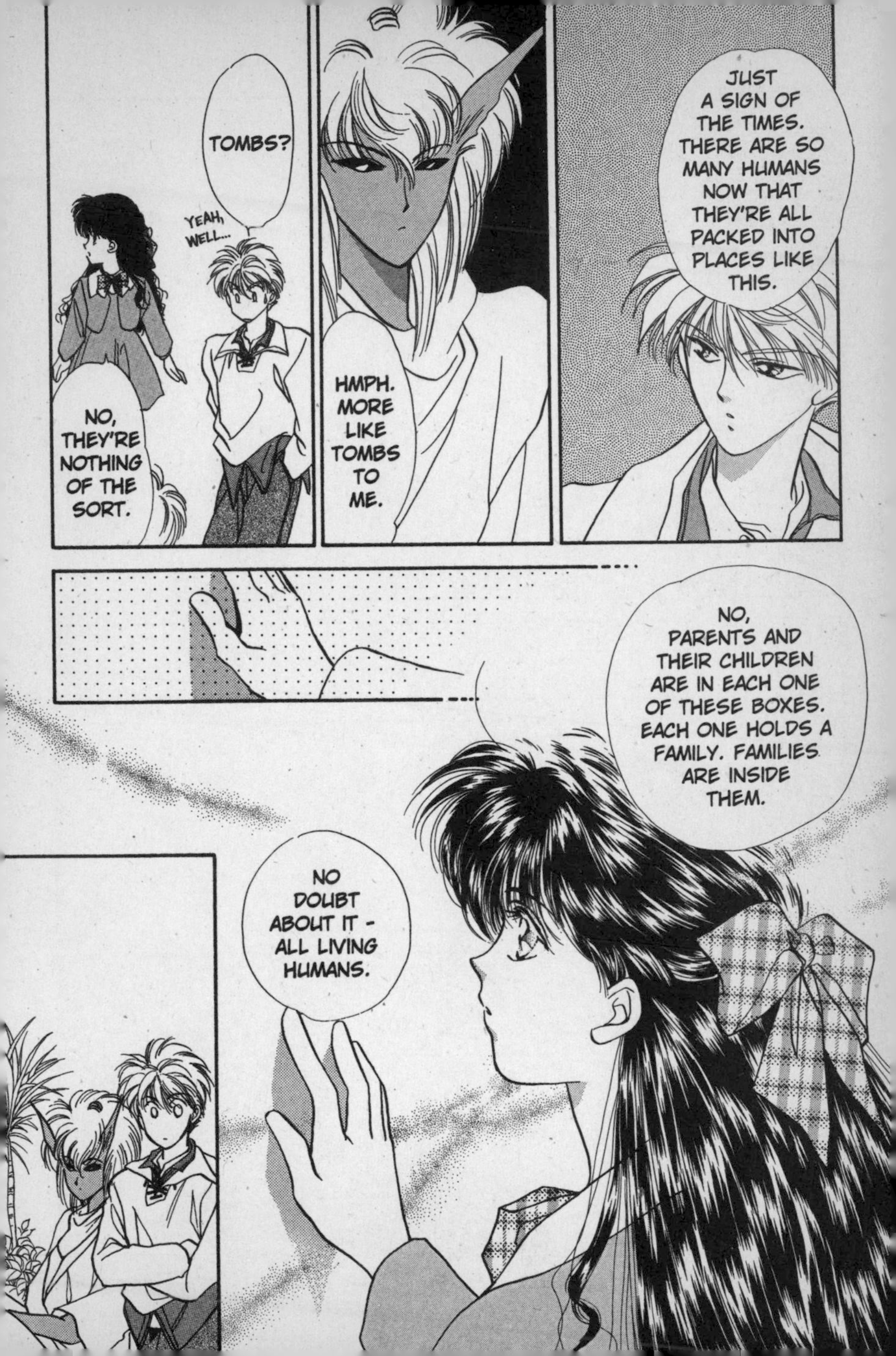
JUST A SIGN OF THE TIMES. THERE ARE SO MANY HUMANS NOW THAT THEY'RE ALL PACKED INTO PLACES LIKE THIS.
HMPH. MORE LIKE TOMBS TO ME.
TOMBS?
YEAH, WELL...
NO, THEY'RE NOTHING OF THE SORT.
NO, PARENTS AND THEIR CHILDREN ARE IN EACH ONE OF THESE BOXES. EACH ONE HOLDS A FAMILY. FAMILIES ARE INSIDE THEM.
NO DOUBT ABOUT IT - ALL LIVING HUMANS.

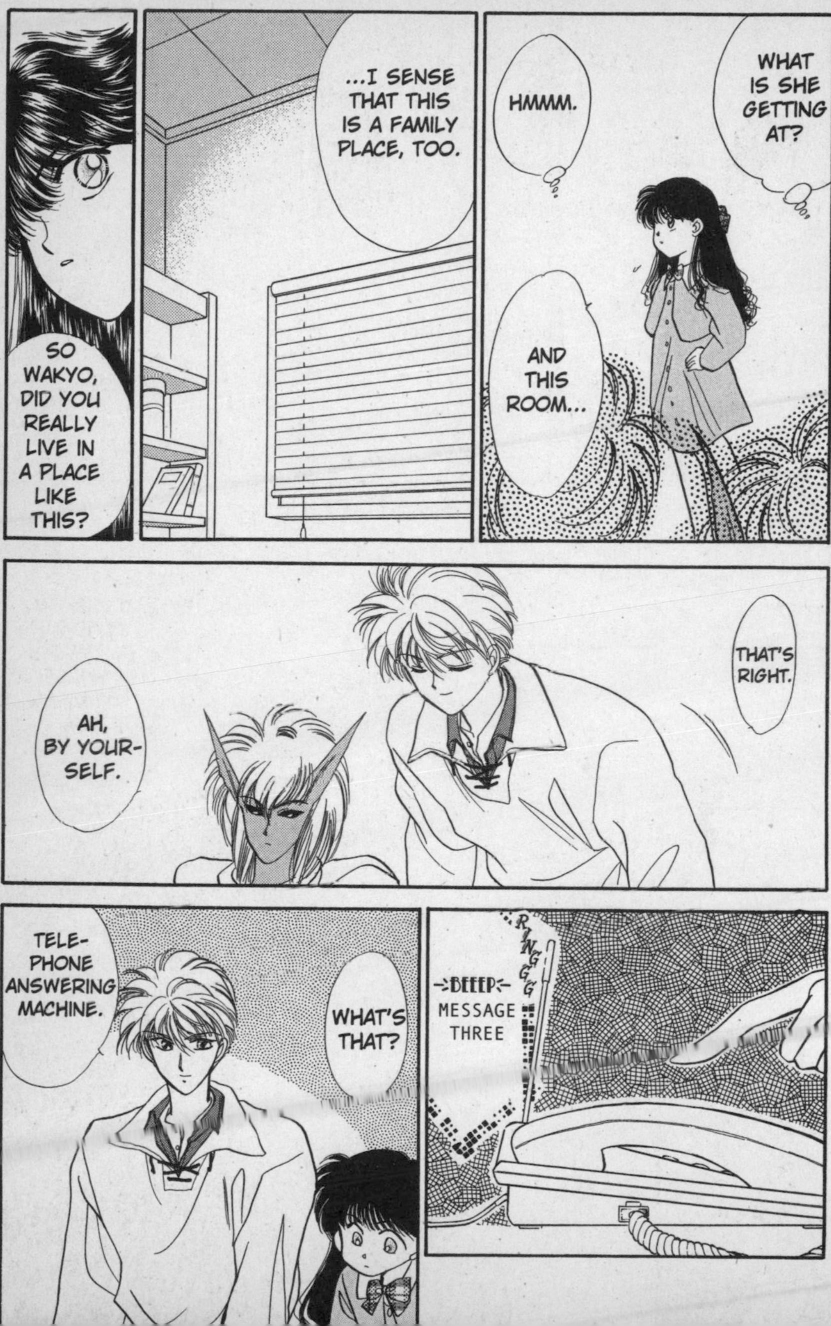
WHAT IS SHE GETTING AT?
HMMM.
AND THIS ROOM...
...I SENSE THAT THIS IS A FAMILY PLACE, TOO.
SO WAKYO, DID YOU REALLY LIVE IN A PLACE LIKE THIS?
THAT'S RIGHT.
AH, BY YOURSELF.
RINGG
BEEEP
MESSAGE THREE
WHAT'S THAT?
TELEPHONE ANSWERING MACHINE.

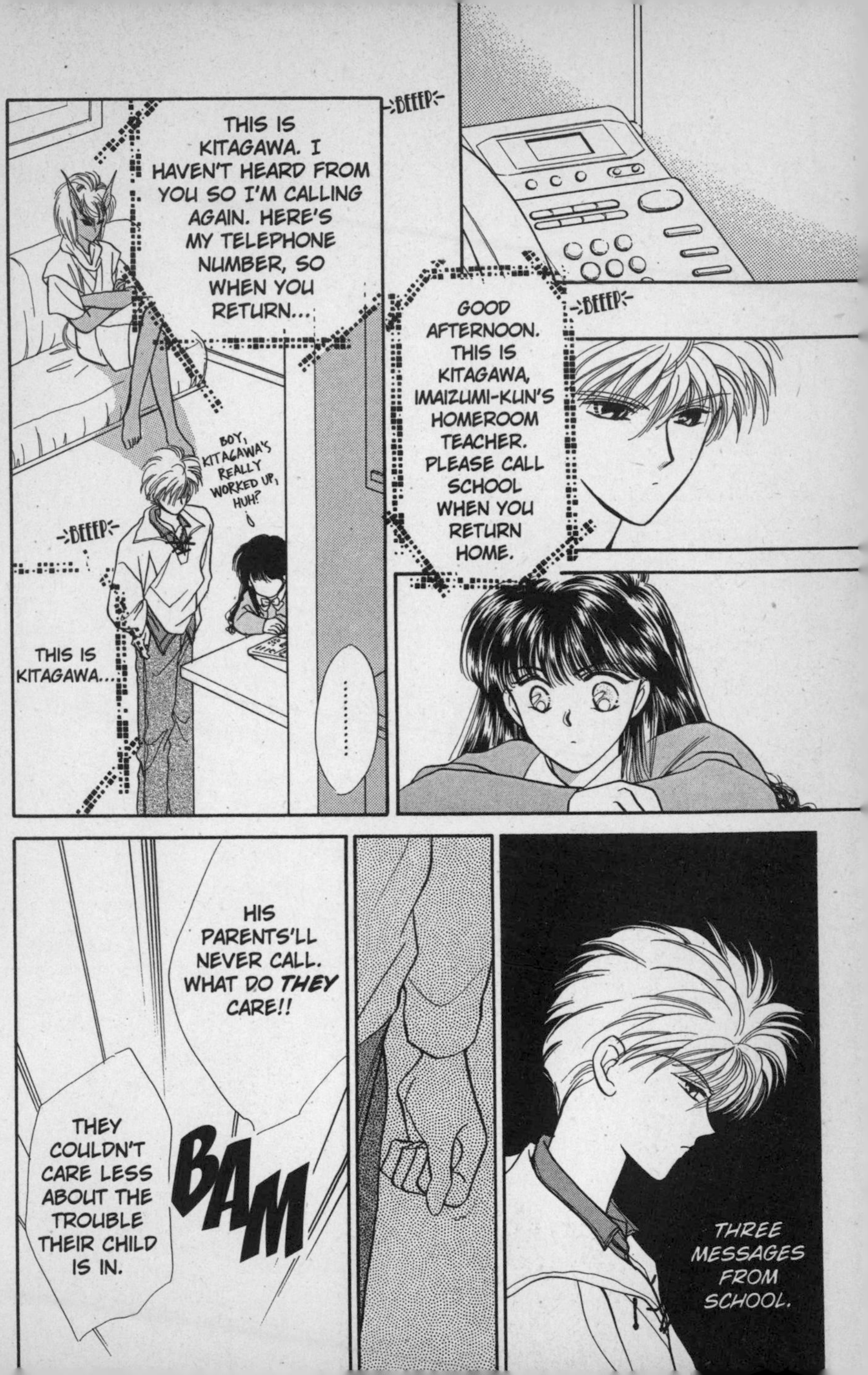

-BEEEP-
-BEEEP-
GOOD AFTERNOON. THIS IS KITAGAWA, IMAIZUMI-KUN'S HOMEROOM TEACHER. PLEASE CALL SCHOOL WHEN YOU RETURN HOME.
THIS IS KITAGAWA. I HAVEN'T HEARD FROM YOU SO I'M CALLING AGAIN. HERE'S MY TELEPHONE NUMBER, SO WHEN YOU RETURN...
BOY, KITAGAWA'S REALLY WORKED UP, HUH?
-BEEEP-
THIS IS KITAGAWA...
......
THREE MESSAGES FROM SCHOOL.
HIS PARENTS'LL NEVER CALL. WHAT DO *THEY* CARE!!
THEY COULDN'T CARE LESS ABOUT THE TROUBLE THEIR CHILD IS IN.
BAM

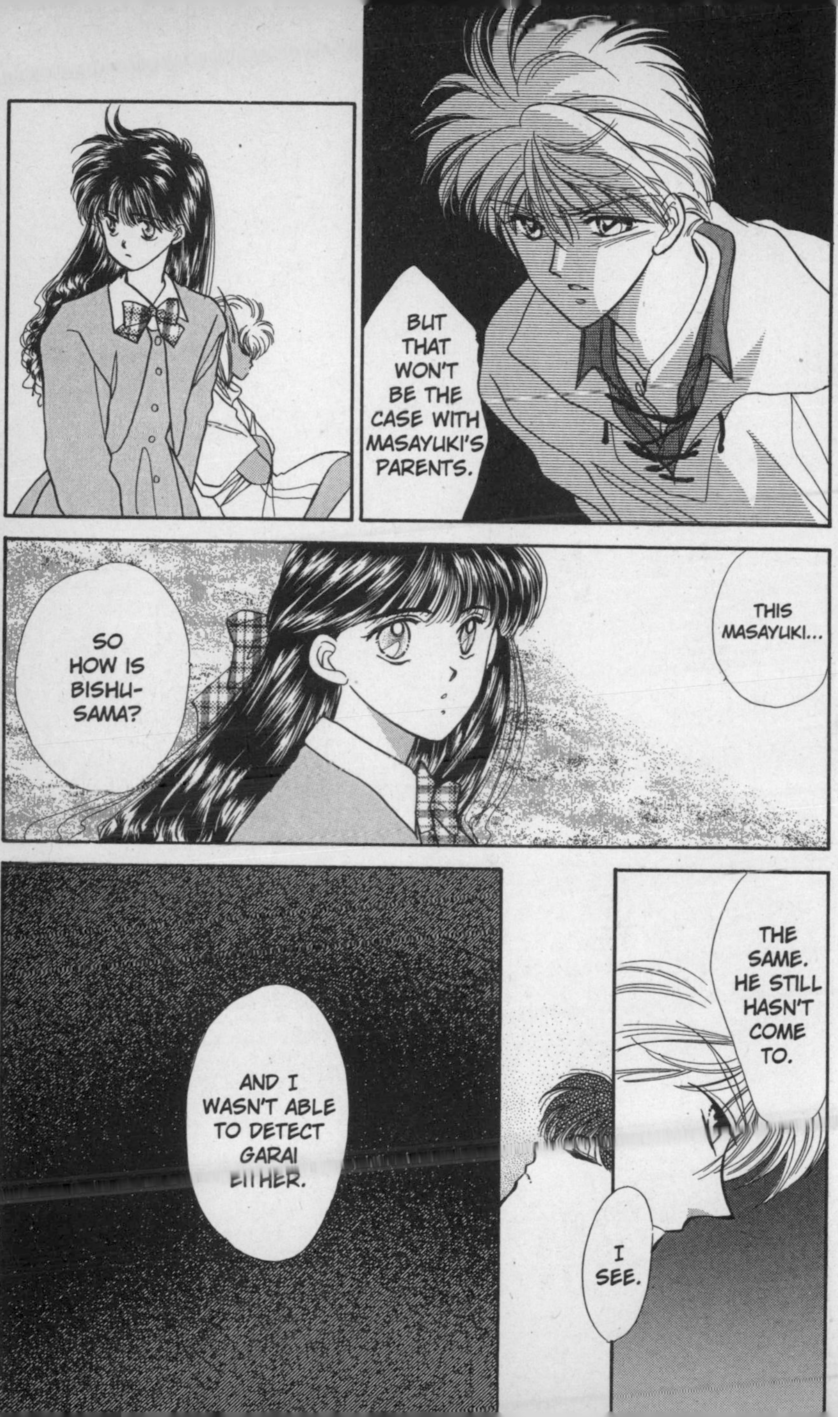
BUT THAT WON'T BE THE CASE WITH MASAYUKI'S PARENTS.
THIS MASAYUKI...
SO HOW IS BISHU-SAMA?
THE SAME. HE STILL HASN'T COME TO.
I SEE.
AND I WASN'T ABLE TO DETECT GARAI EITHER.

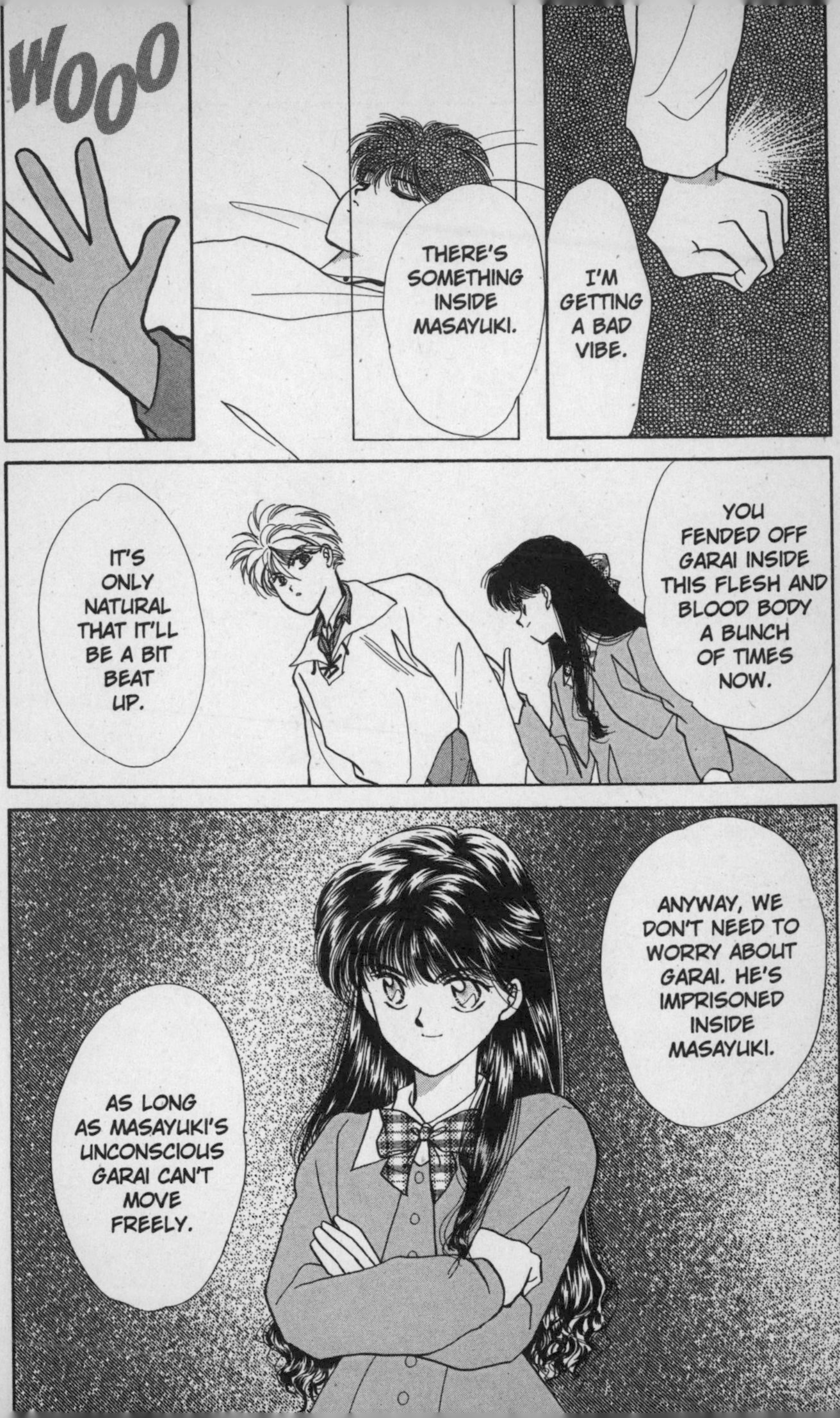
I'M GETTING A BAD VIBE.
THERE'S SOMETHING INSIDE MASAYUKI.
WOOO
YOU FENDED OFF GARAI INSIDE THIS FLESH AND BLOOD BODY A BUNCH OF TIMES NOW.
IT'S ONLY NATURAL THAT IT'LL BE A BIT BEAT UP.
ANYWAY, WE DON'T NEED TO WORRY ABOUT GARAI. HE'S IMPRISONED INSIDE MASAYUKI.
AS LONG AS MASAYUKI'S UNCONSCIOUS GARAI CAN'T MOVE FREELY.

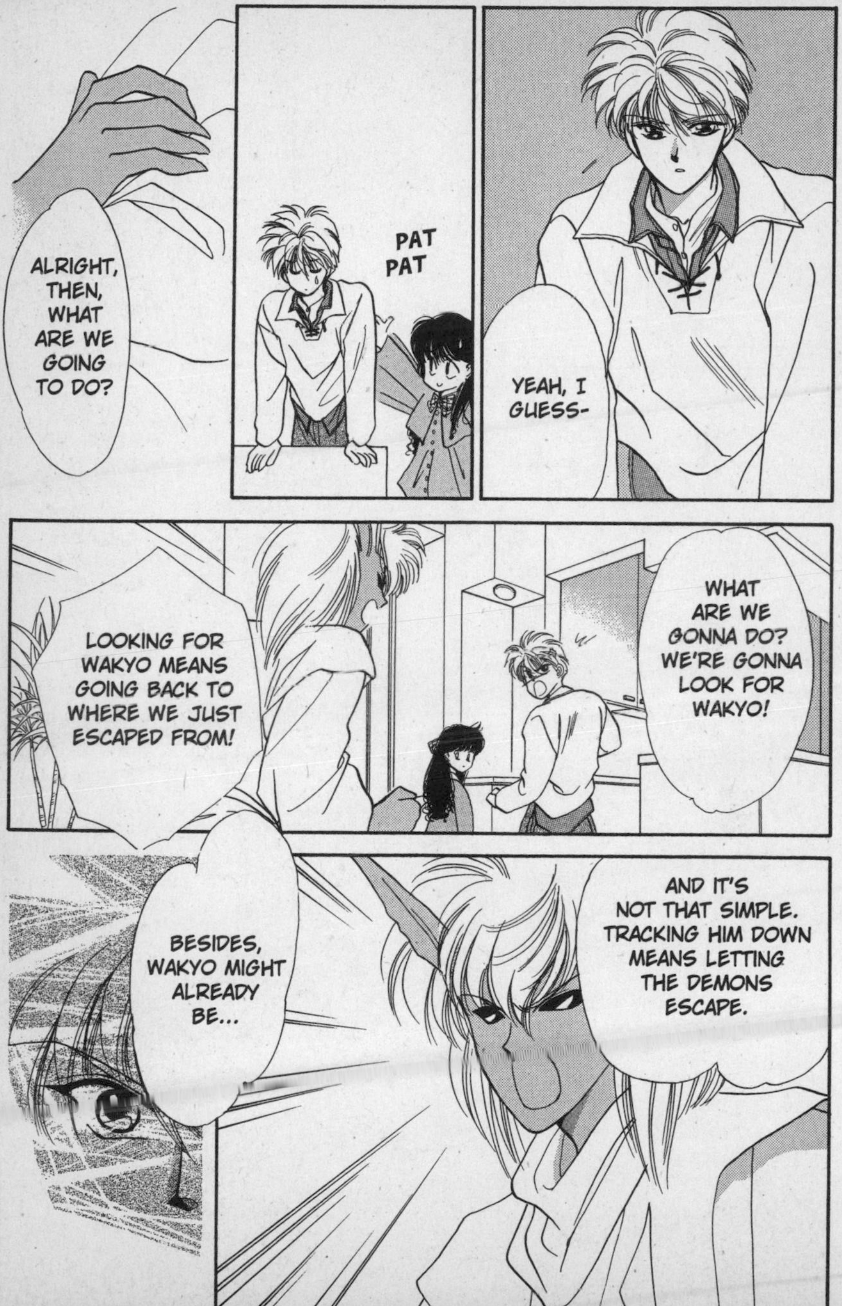
YEAH, I GUESS-
PAT PAT
ALRIGHT, THEN, WHAT ARE WE GOING TO DO?
WHAT ARE WE GONNA DO? WE'RE GONNA LOOK FOR WAKYO!
LOOKING FOR WAKYO MEANS GOING BACK TO WHERE WE JUST ESCAPED FROM!
AND IT'S NOT THAT SIMPLE. TRACKING HIM DOWN MEANS LETTING THE DEMONS ESCAPE.
BESIDES, WAKYO MIGHT ALREADY BE...

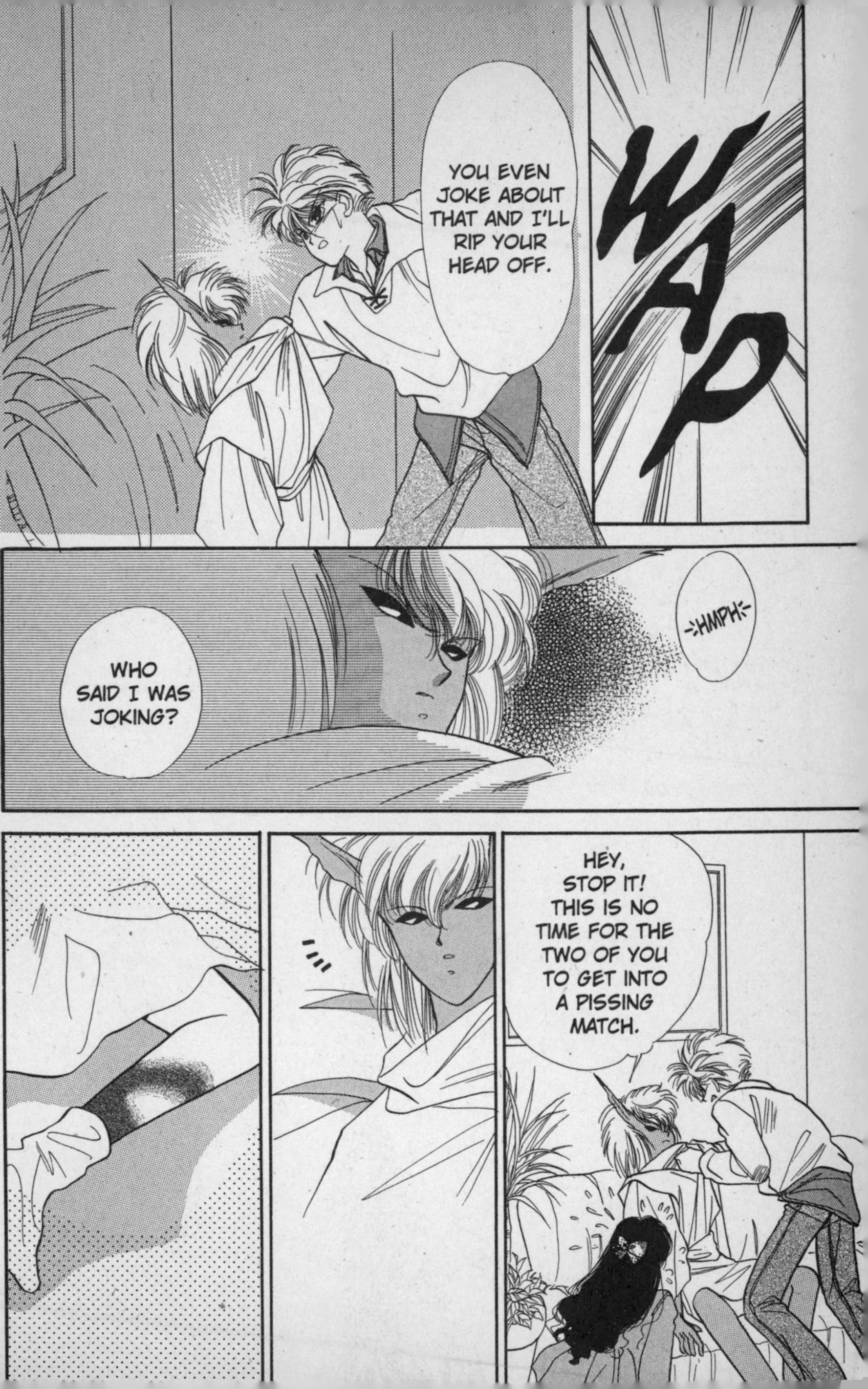
WAP
YOU EVEN JOKE ABOUT THAT AND I'LL RIP YOUR HEAD OFF.
HMPH
WHO SAID I WAS JOKING?
HEY, STOP IT! THIS IS NO TIME FOR THE TWO OF YOU TO GET INTO A PISSING MATCH.

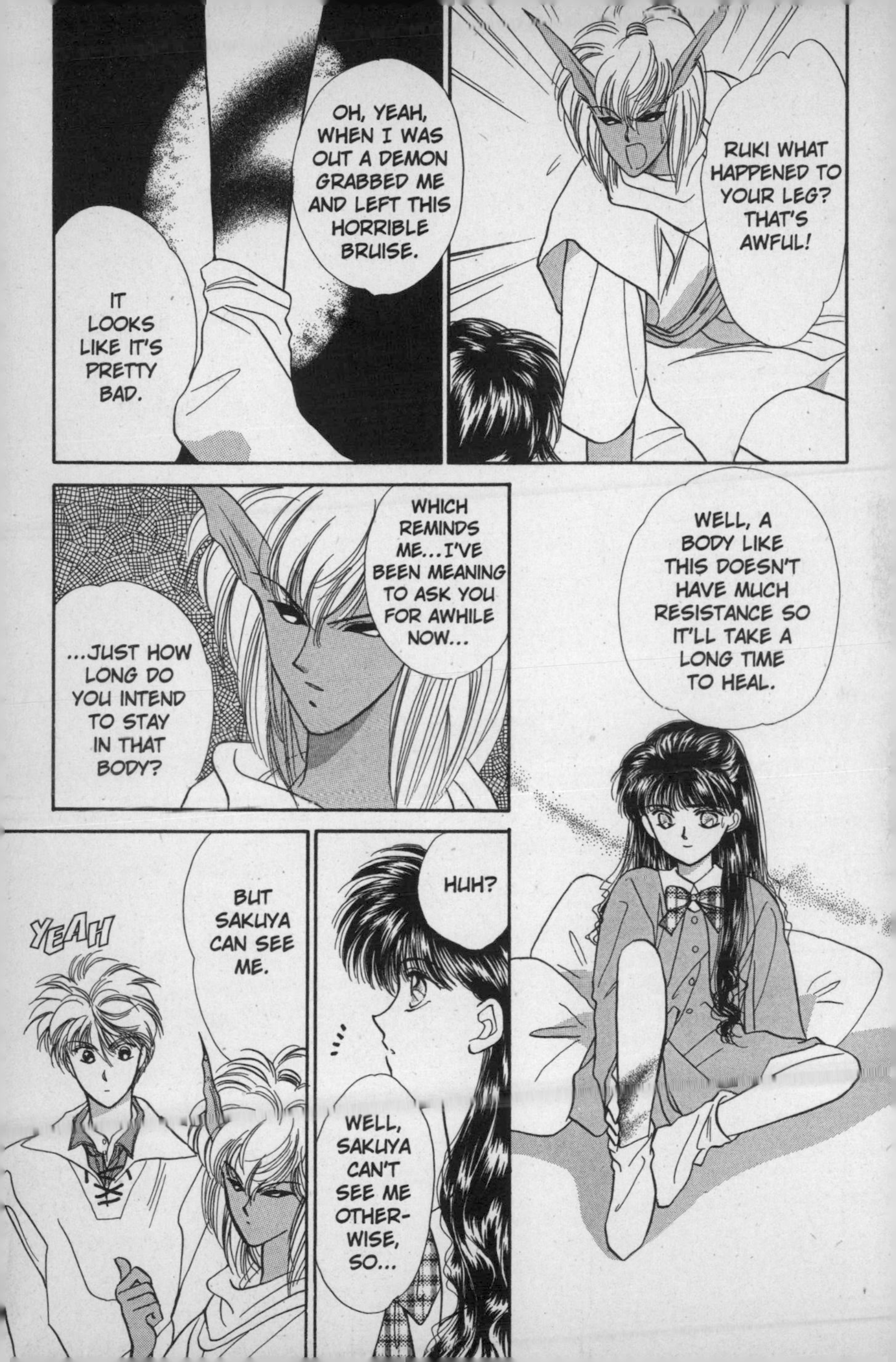
RUKI WHAT HAPPENED TO YOUR LEG? THAT'S AWFUL!
OH, YEAH, WHEN I WAS OUT A DEMON GRABBED ME AND LEFT THIS HORRIBLE BRUISE.
IT LOOKS LIKE IT'S PRETTY BAD.
WELL, A BODY LIKE THIS DOESN'T HAVE MUCH RESISTANCE SO IT'LL TAKE A LONG TIME TO HEAL.
WHICH REMINDS ME...I'VE BEEN MEANING TO ASK YOU FOR AWHILE NOW...
...JUST HOW LONG DO YOU INTEND TO STAY IN THAT BODY?
HUH?
WELL, SAKUYA CAN'T SEE ME OTHER-WISE, SO...
BUT SAKUYA CAN SEE ME.
YEAH

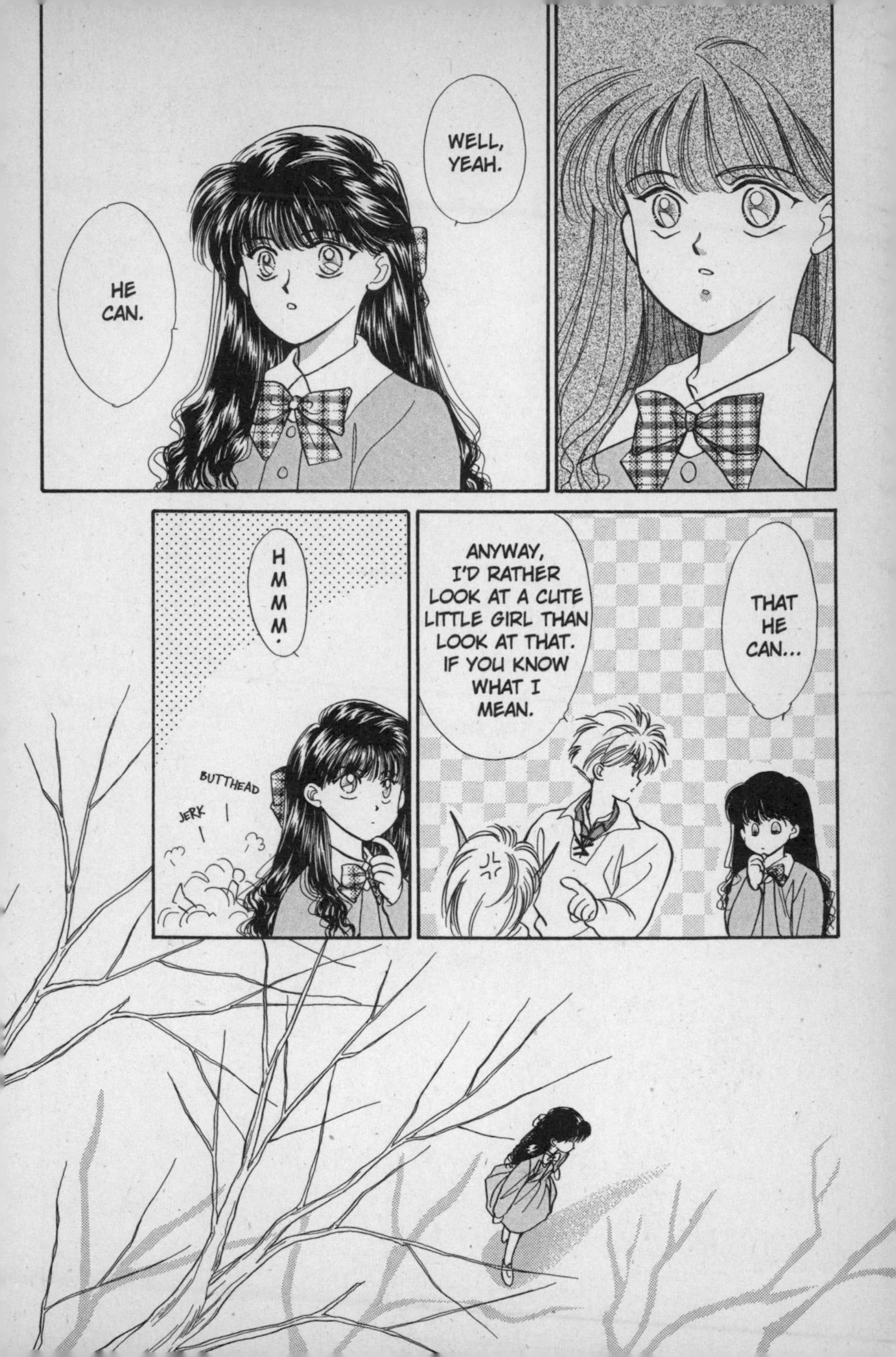
WELL, YEAH.
HE CAN.
THAT HE CAN...
ANYWAY, I'D RATHER LOOK AT A CUTE LITTLE GIRL THAN LOOK AT THAT. IF YOU KNOW WHAT I MEAN.
HMMM.
BUTTHEAD
JERK

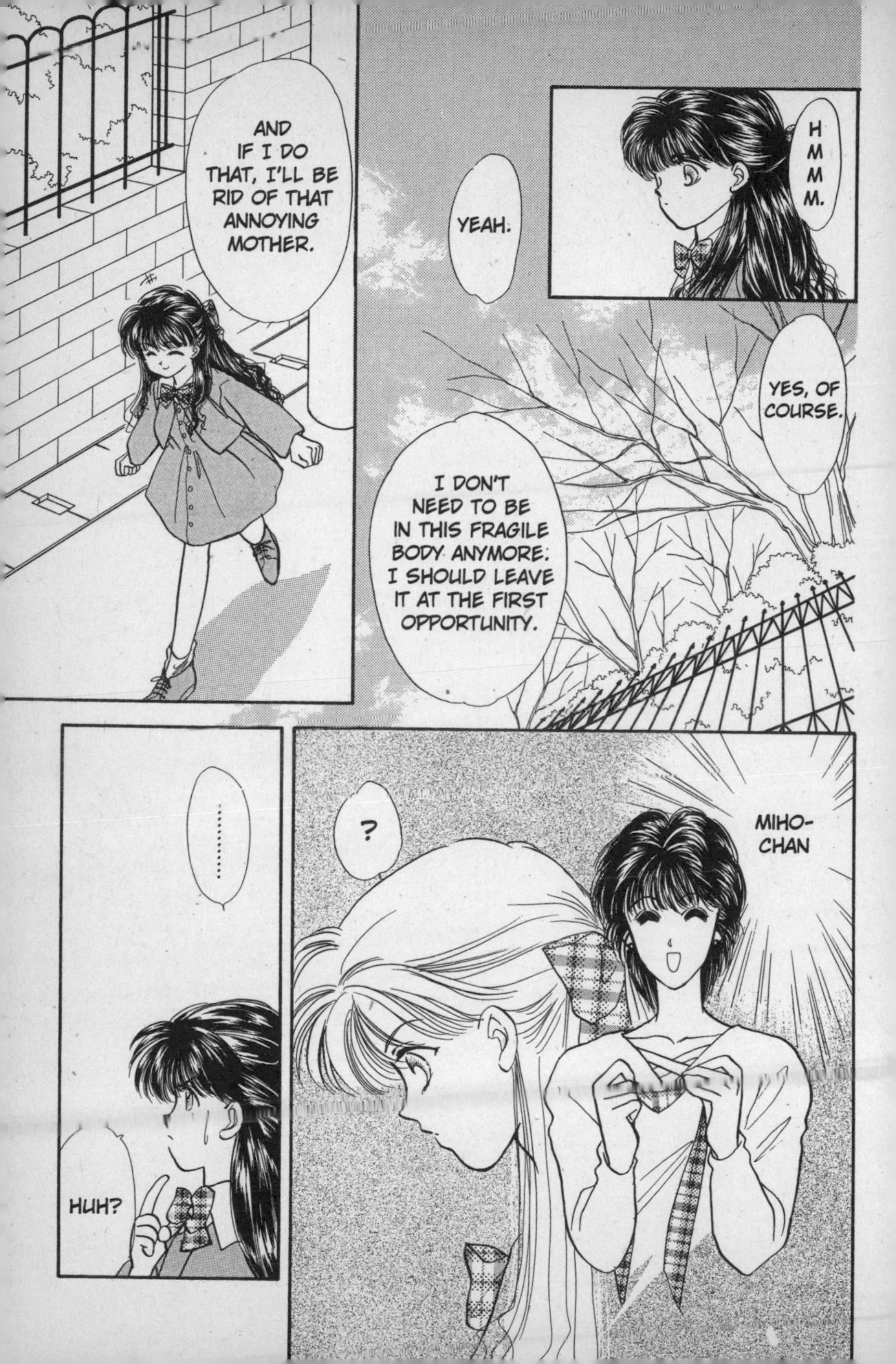
HMMM.
YEAH.
YES, OF COURSE.
I DON'T NEED TO BE IN THIS FRAGILE BODY ANYMORE. I SHOULD LEAVE IT AT THE FIRST OPPORTUNITY.
AND IF I DO THAT, I'LL BE RID OF THAT ANNOYING MOTHER.
MIHO-CHAN
?
......
HUH?

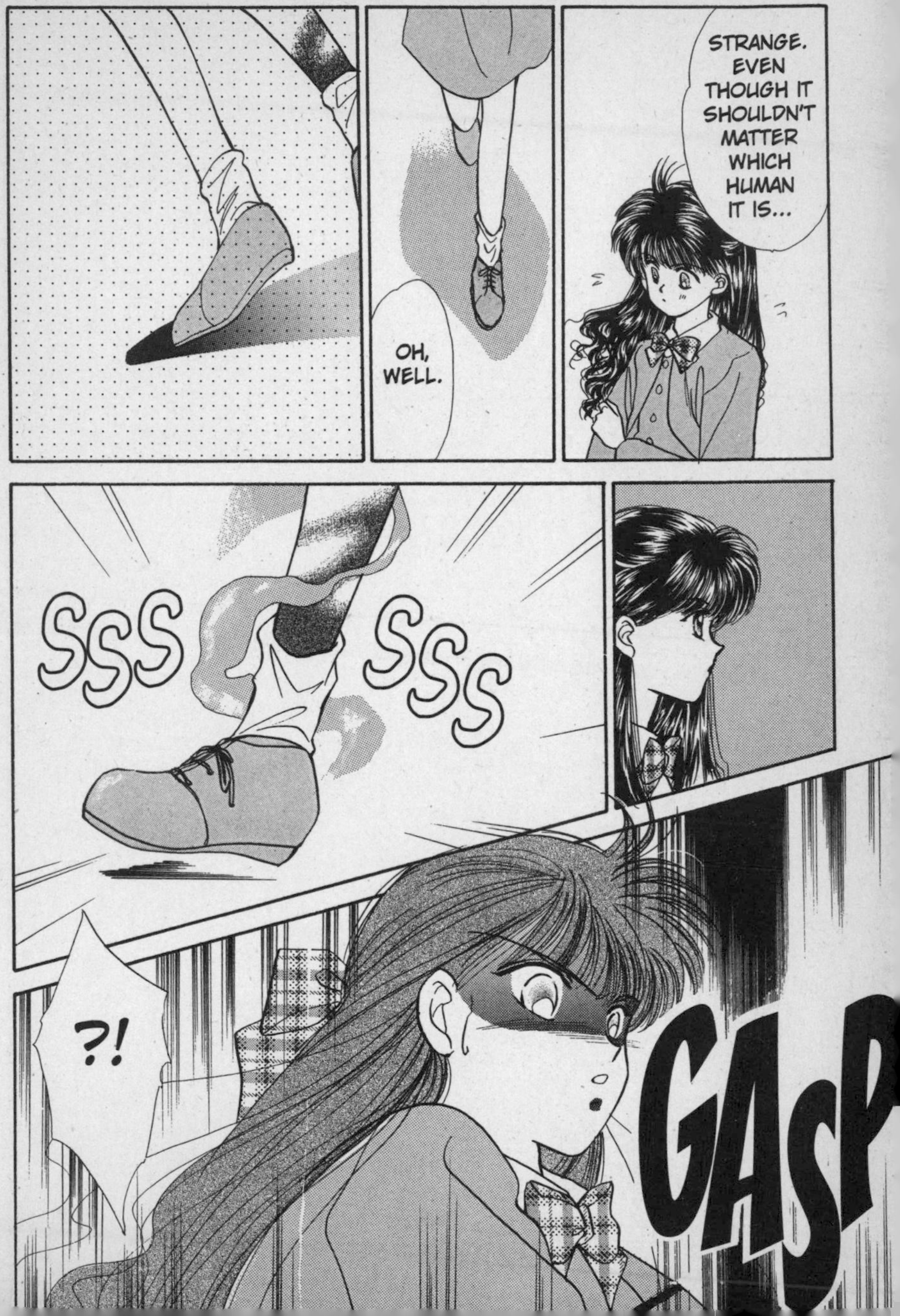
STRANGE. EVEN THOUGH IT SHOULDN'T MATTER WHICH HUMAN IT IS...
OH, WELL.
SSS SSS
GASP
?!

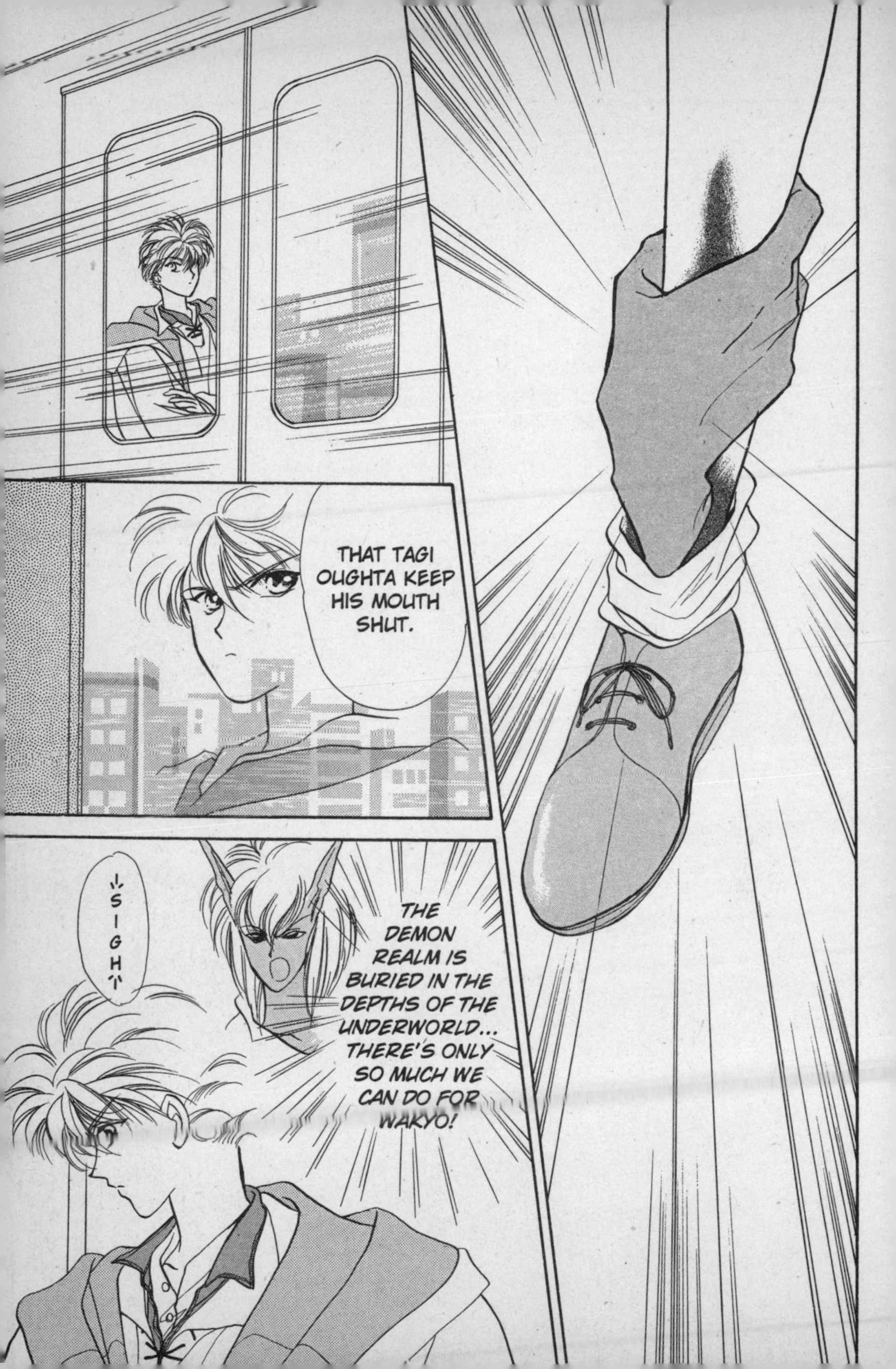
THAT TAGI OUGHTA KEEP HIS MOUTH SHUT.
THE DEMON REALM IS BURIED IN THE DEPTHS OF THE UNDERWORLD... THERE'S ONLY SO MUCH WE CAN DO FOR WAKYO!
SIGH

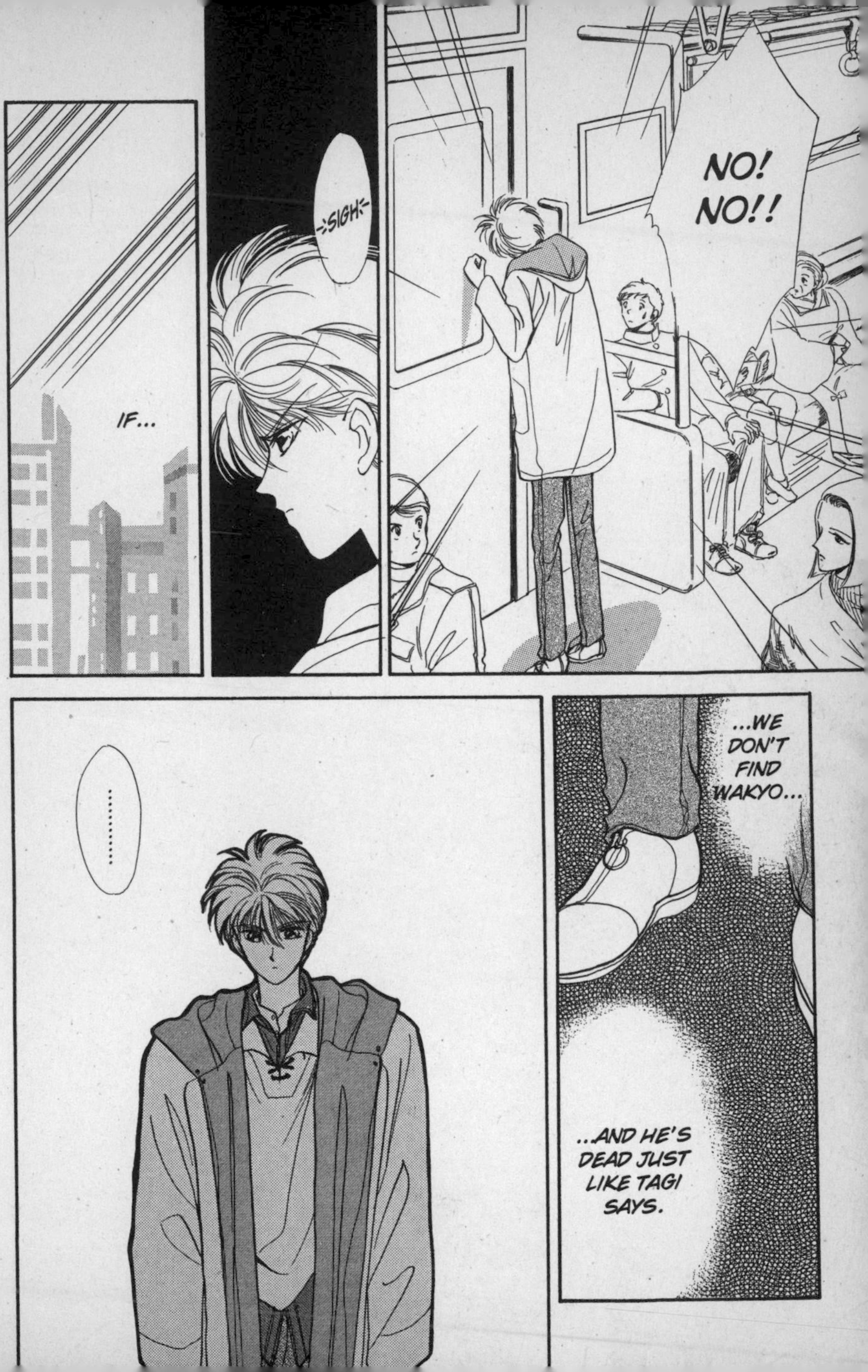
NO! NO!!
-SIGH-
IF...
...WE DON'T FIND WAKYO...
...AND HE'S DEAD JUST LIKE TAGI SAYS.
....

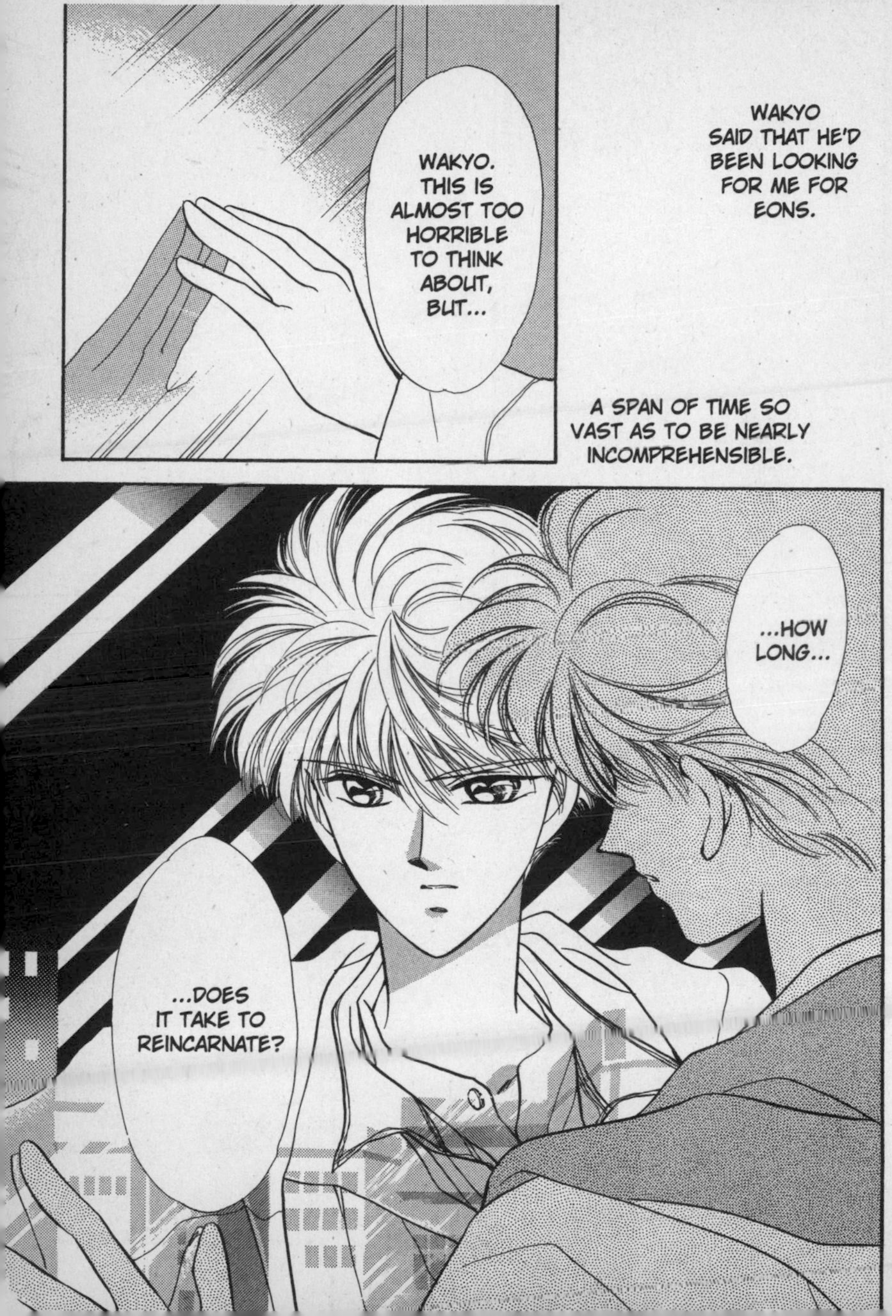
WAKYO SAID THAT HE'D BEEN LOOKING FOR ME FOR EONS.
A SPAN OF TIME SO VAST AS TO BE NEARLY INCOMPREHENSIBLE.
WAKYO. THIS IS ALMOST TOO HORRIBLE TO THINK ABOUT, BUT...
...HOW LONG...
...DOES IT TAKE TO REINCARNATE?

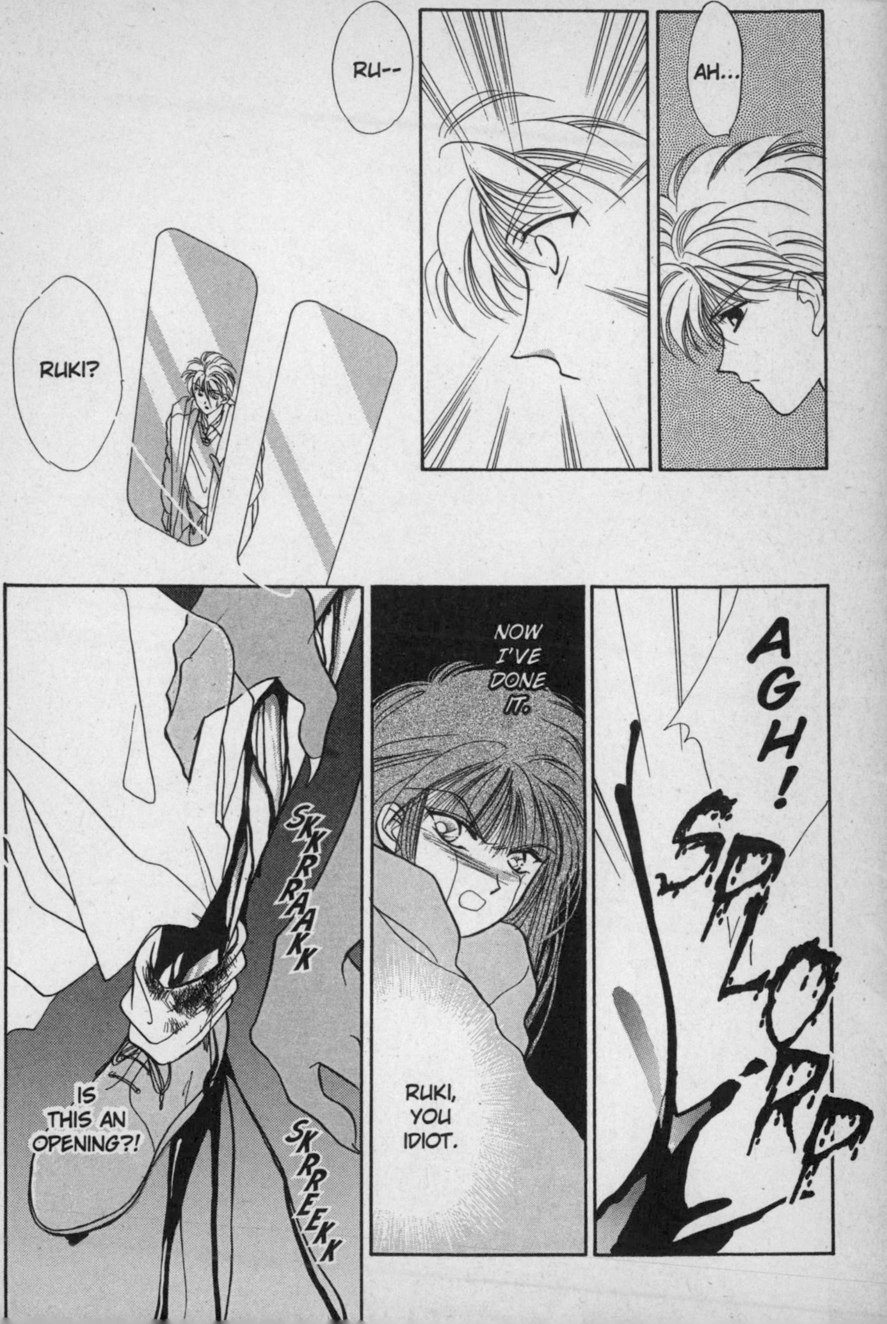
AH...
RU--
RUKI?
AGH!
SPLORP
NOW I'VE DONE IT.
RUKI, YOU IDIOT.
SKKRRAAKK
SKRREEKK
IS THIS AN OPENING?!

AN OPENING TO THE DEMON REALM IN THE LOWER DEPTHS?!
WHAT AM I GONNA DO?
SHOULD I JUST LEAVE THE LEG BEHIND?
I CAN'T HOLD OUT.
I'M LOSING STRENGTH... FEEL WEAK...
AH, C'MON RUKI, YOU CAN DO BETTER THAN THIS.

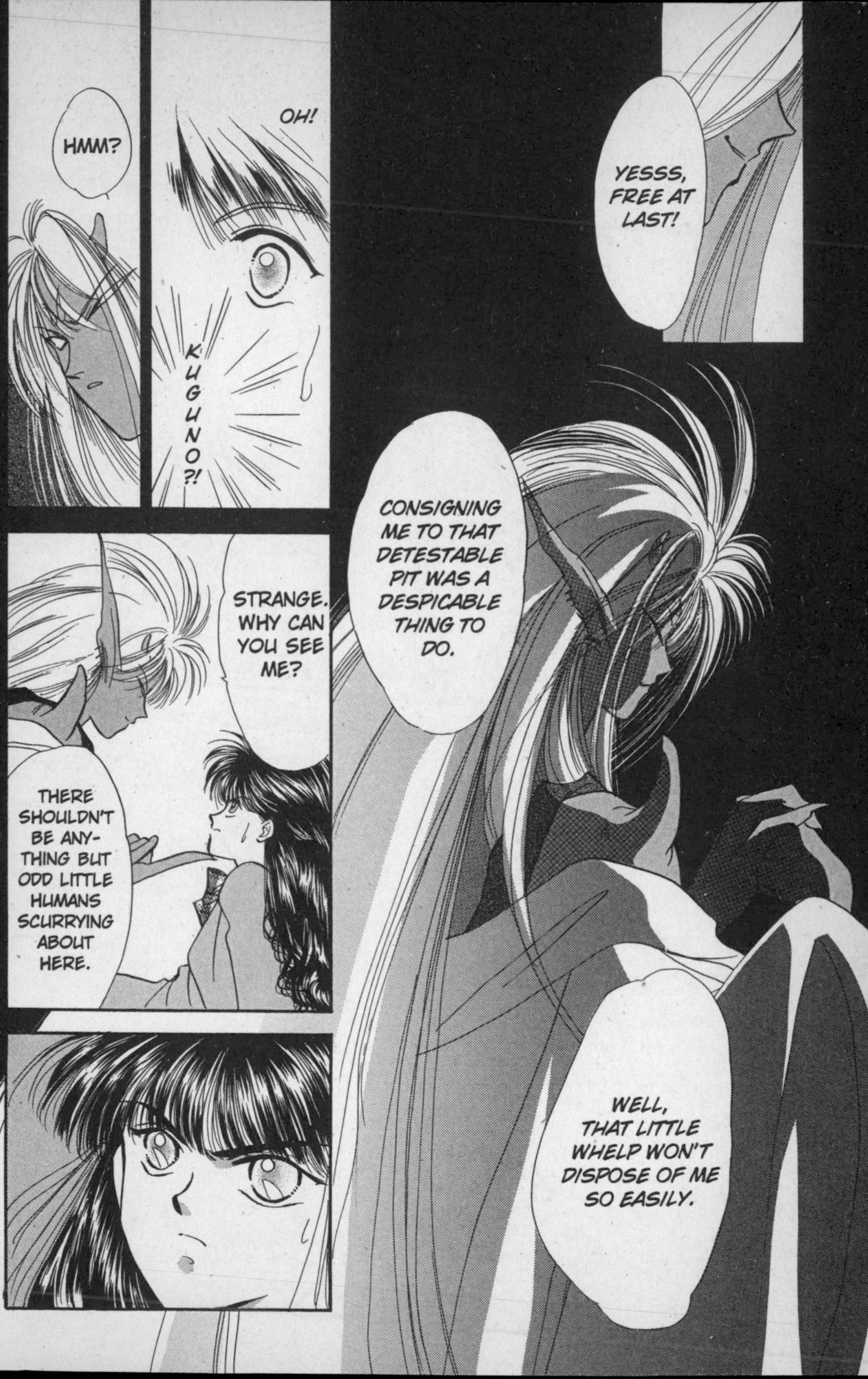
YESSS, FREE AT LAST!
CONSIGNING ME TO THAT DETESTABLE PIT WAS A DESPICABLE THING TO DO.
WELL, THAT LITTLE WHELP WON'T DISPOSE OF ME SO EASILY.
OH!
KUGUNO?!
HMM?
STRANGE. WHY CAN YOU SEE ME?
THERE SHOULDN'T BE ANY-THING BUT ODD LITTLE HUMANS SCURRYING ABOUT HERE.

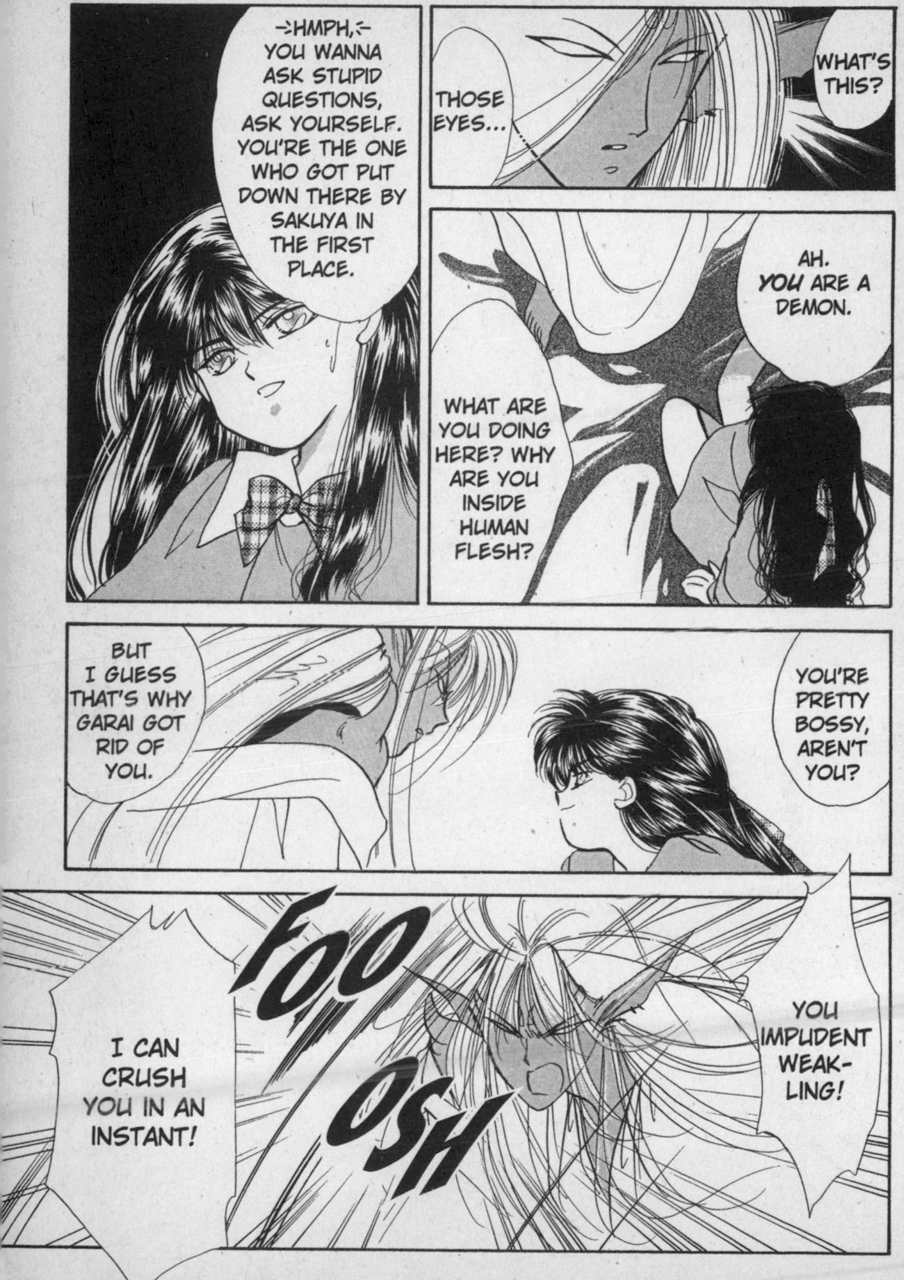
WHAT'S THIS?
THOSE EYES...
AH. *YOU* ARE A DEMON.
WHAT ARE YOU DOING HERE? WHY ARE YOU INSIDE HUMAN FLESH?
HMPH, YOU WANNA ASK STUPID QUESTIONS, ASK YOURSELF. YOU'RE THE ONE WHO GOT PUT DOWN THERE BY SAKUYA IN THE FIRST PLACE.
YOU'RE PRETTY BOSSY, AREN'T YOU?
BUT I GUESS THAT'S WHY GARAI GOT RID OF YOU.
YOU IMPUDENT WEAK-LING!
FOOOSH
I CAN CRUSH YOU IN AN INSTANT!

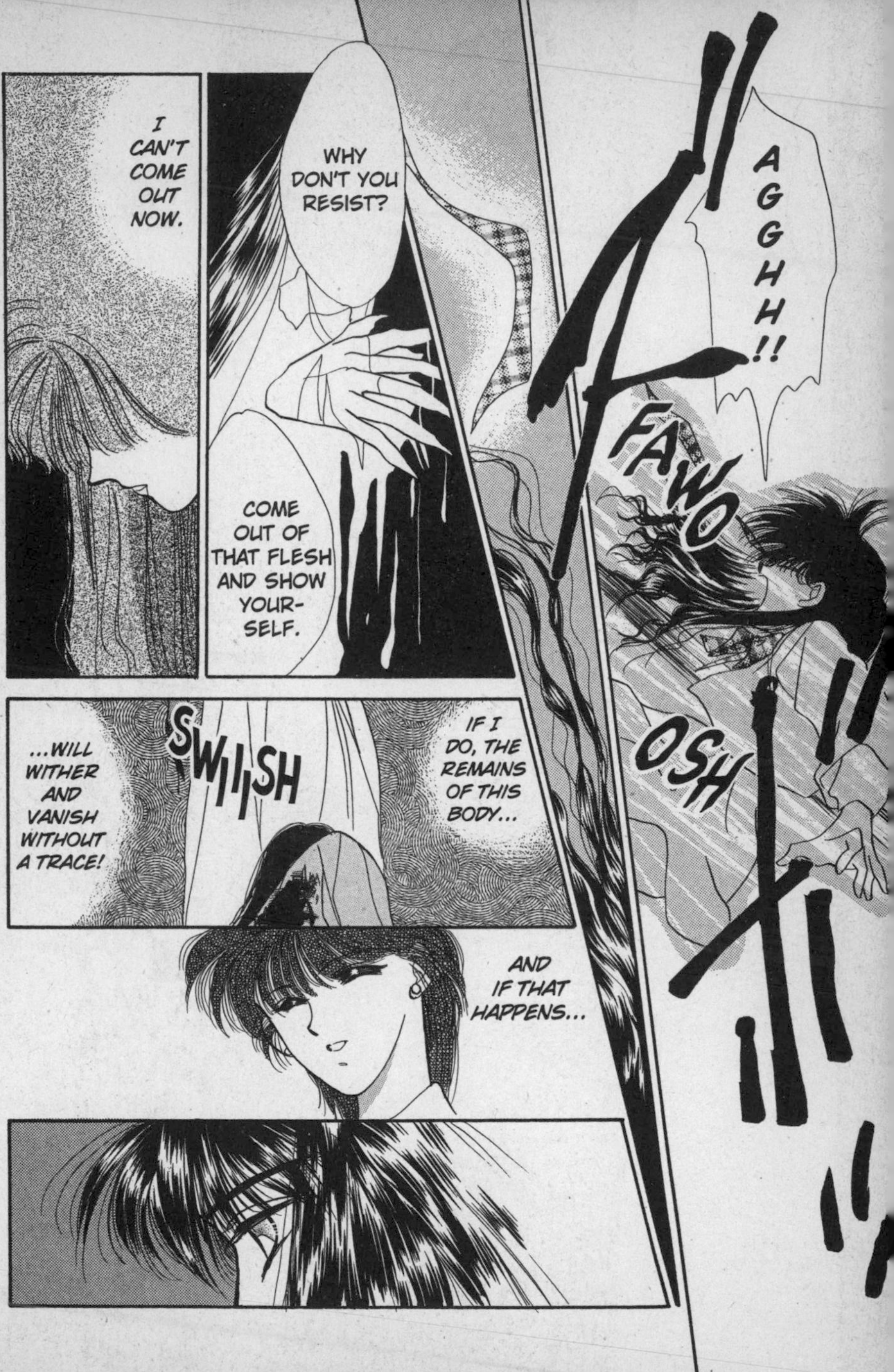
AGGGHH!!
FAWOOSH
WHY DON'T YOU RESIST?
COME OUT OF THAT FLESH AND SHOW YOURSELF.
I CAN'T COME OUT NOW.
IF I DO, THE REMAINS OF THIS BODY...
SWIIISH
...WILL WITHER AND VANISH WITHOUT A TRACE!
AND IF THAT HAPPENS...

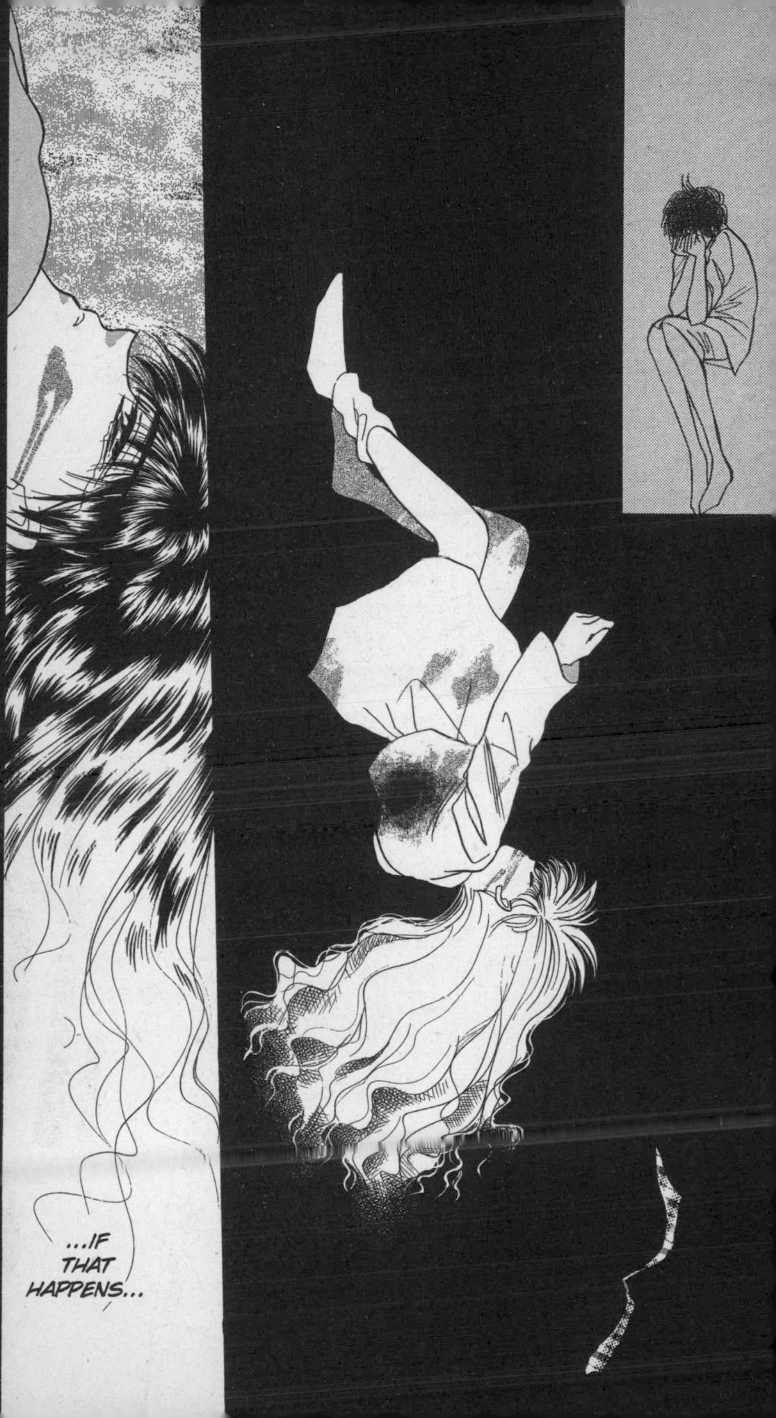
...IF THAT HAPPENS...

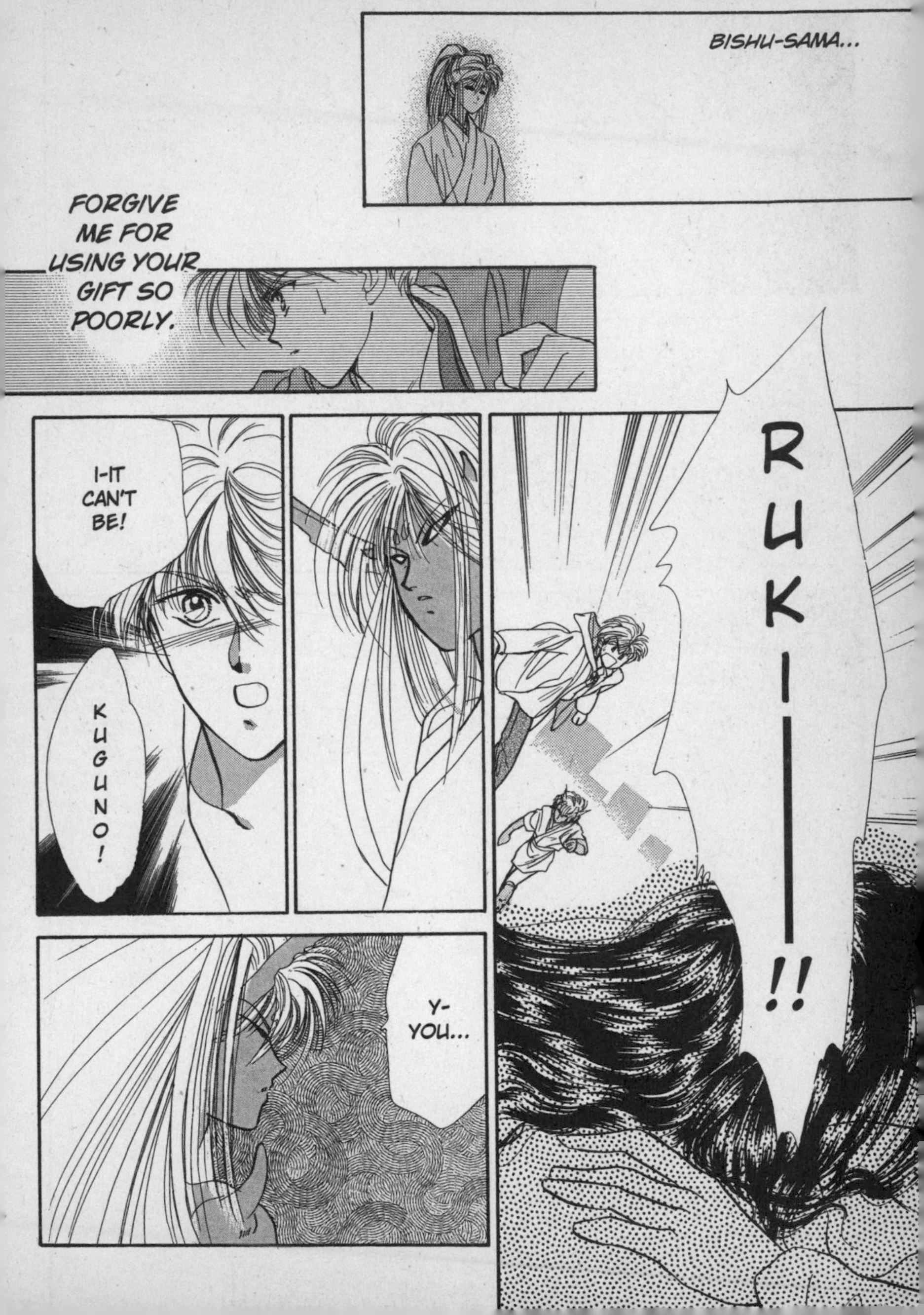
BISHU-SAMA...
FORGIVE ME FOR USING YOUR GIFT SO POORLY.
RUKI—!!
I-IT CAN'T BE!
KUGUNO!
Y-YOU...

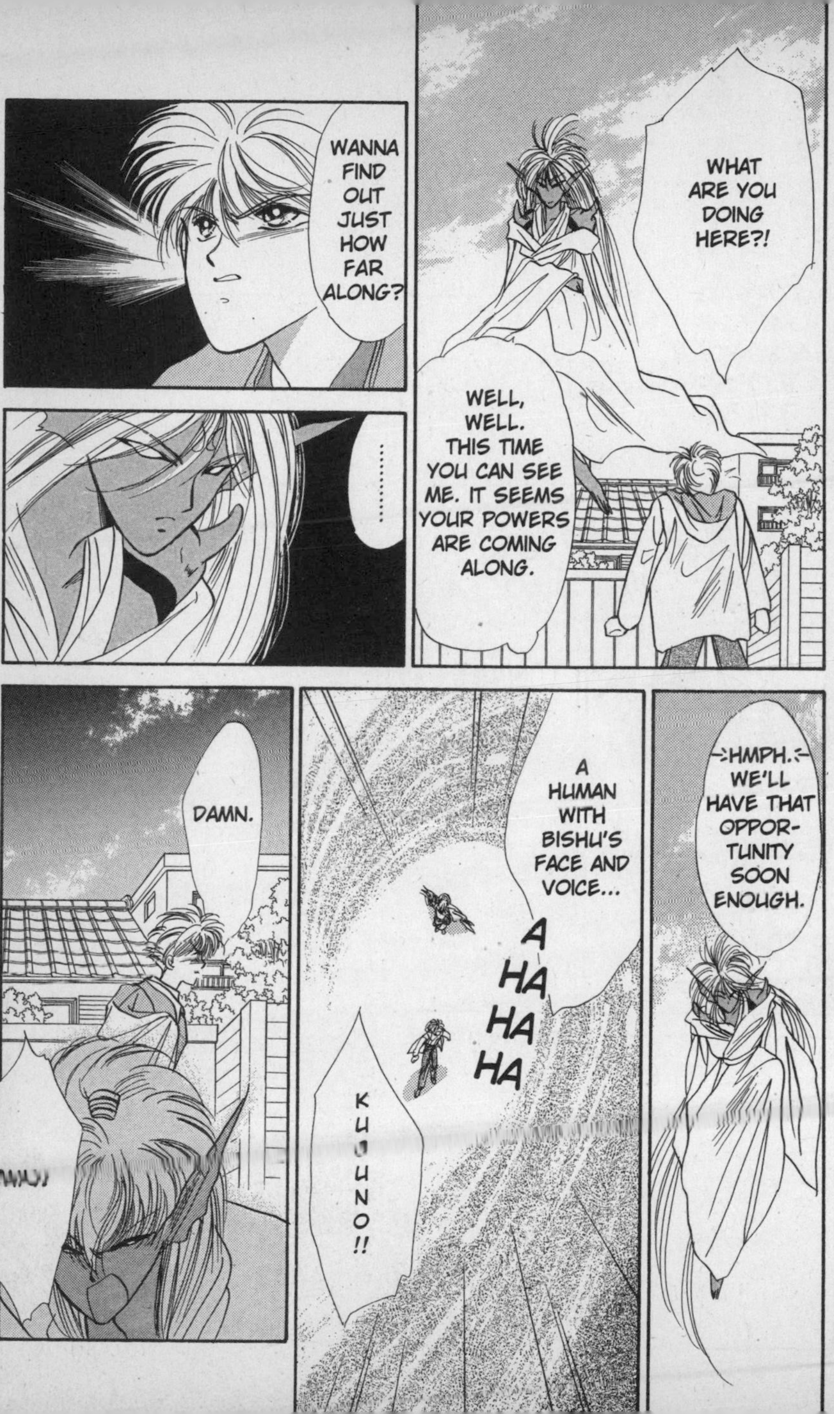

WHAT ARE YOU DOING HERE?!
WELL, WELL. THIS TIME YOU CAN SEE ME. IT SEEMS YOUR POWERS ARE COMING ALONG.
WANNA FIND OUT JUST HOW FAR ALONG?
......
HMPH. WE'LL HAVE THAT OPPORTUNITY SOON ENOUGH.
A HUMAN WITH BISHU'S FACE AND VOICE...
A HA HA HA
KUSUNO!!
DAMN.

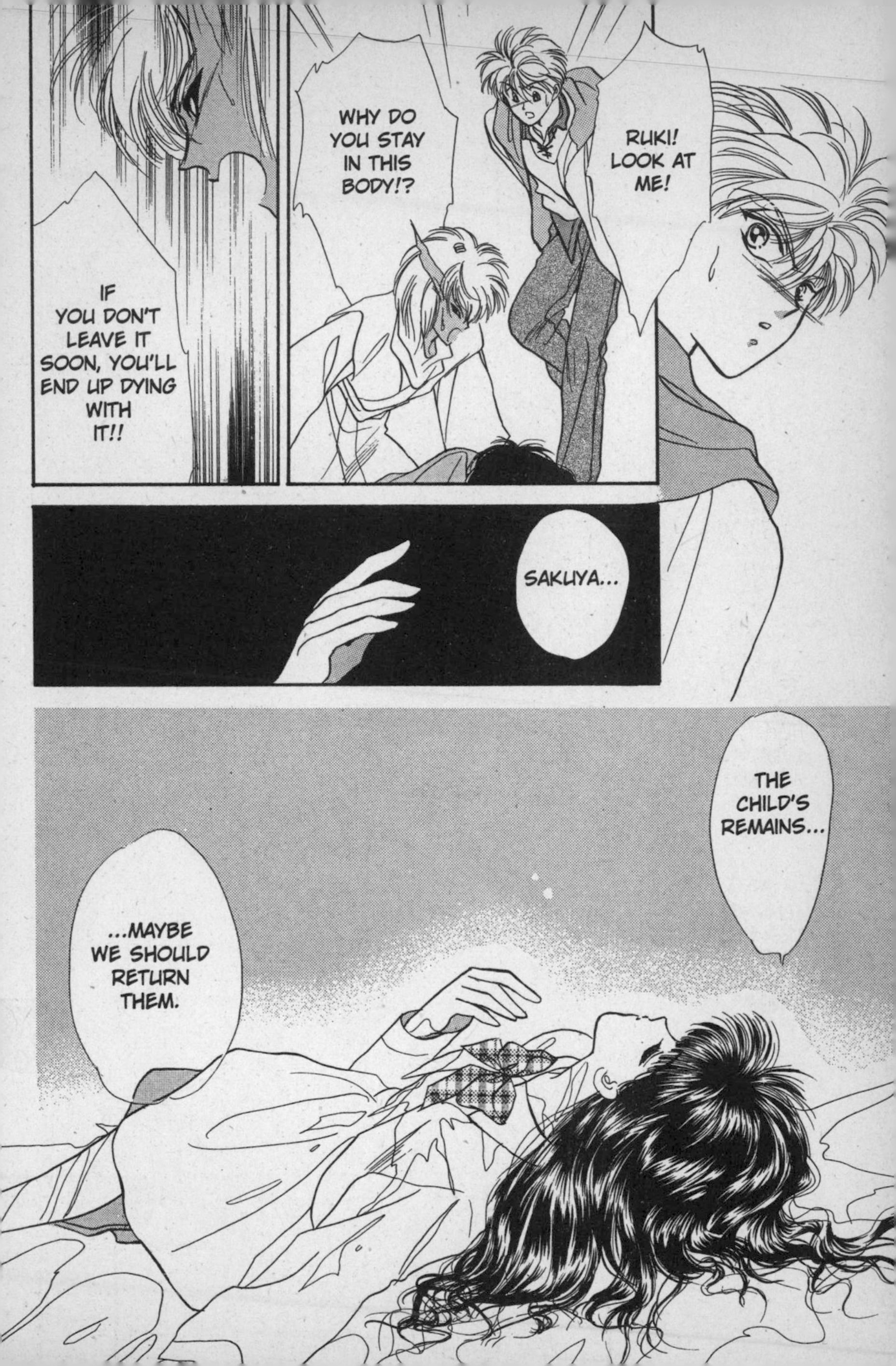
RUKI! LOOK AT ME!
WHY DO YOU STAY IN THIS BODY!?
IF YOU DON'T LEAVE IT SOON, YOU'LL END UP DYING WITH IT!!
SAKUYA...
THE CHILD'S REMAINS...
...MAYBE WE SHOULD RETURN THEM.

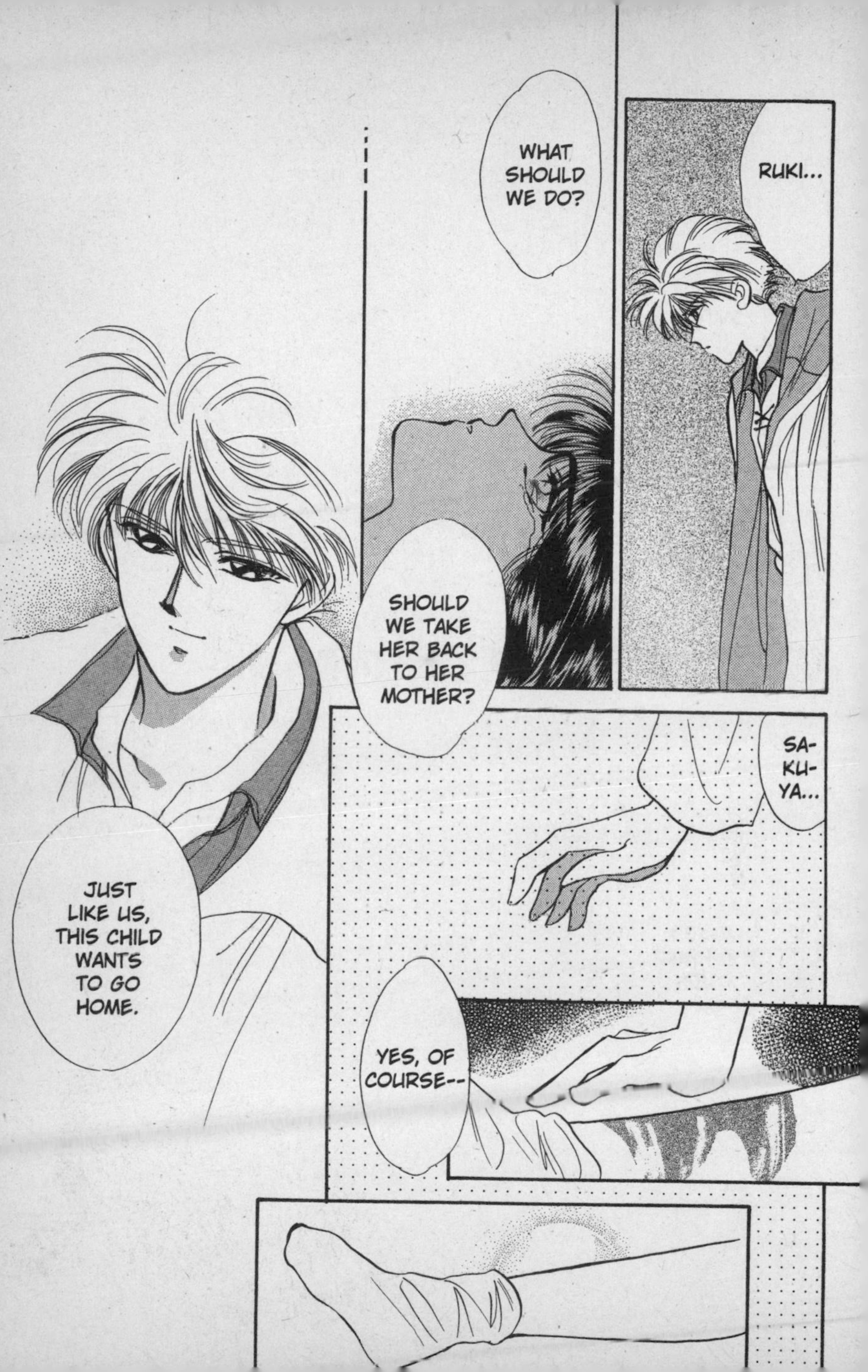
RUKI...
WHAT SHOULD WE DO?
SHOULD WE TAKE HER BACK TO HER MOTHER?
SA-KU-YA...
YES, OF COURSE--
JUST LIKE US, THIS CHILD WANTS TO GO HOME.

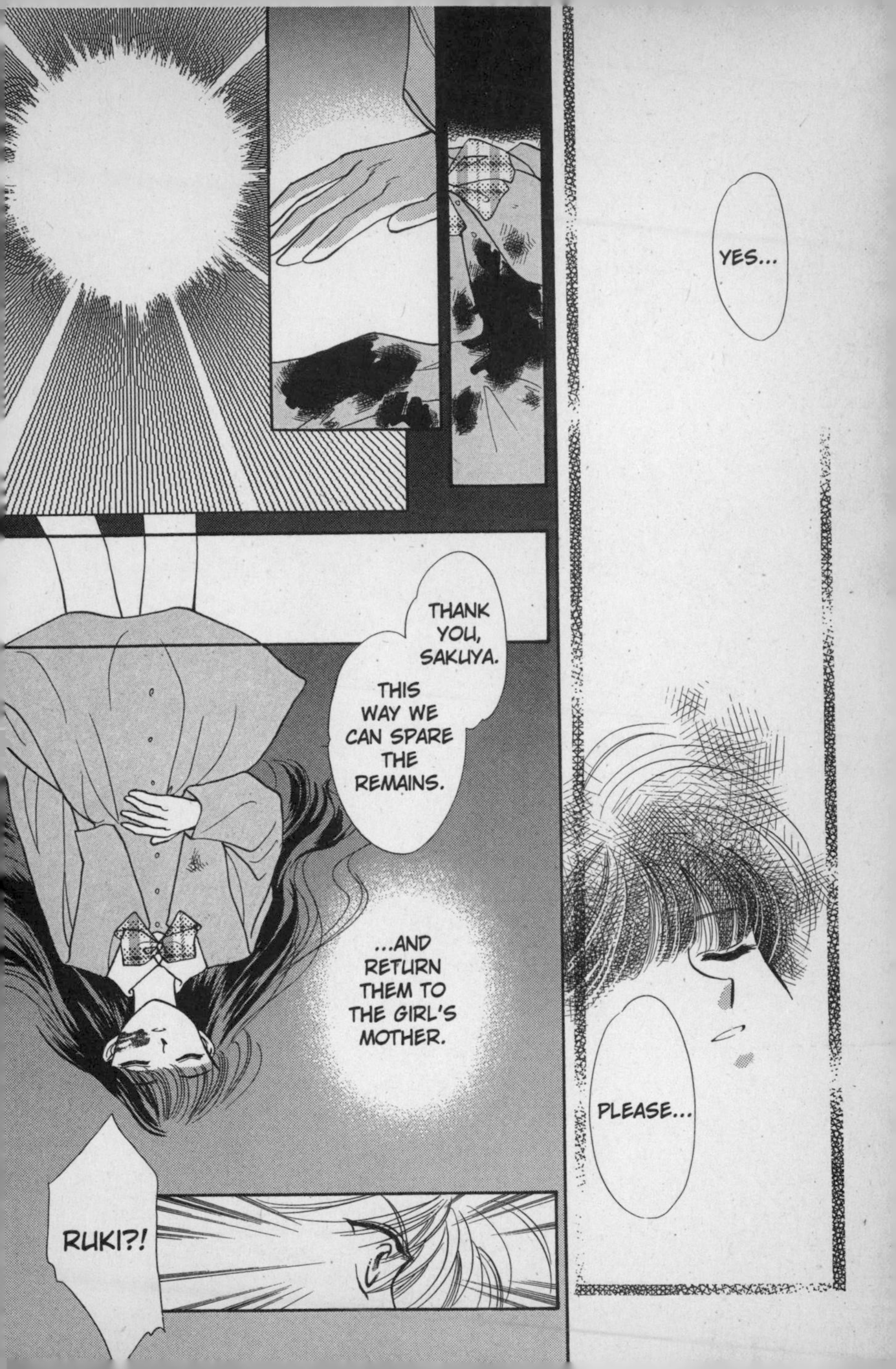
YES...
PLEASE...
THANK YOU, SAKUYA.
THIS WAY WE CAN SPARE THE REMAINS.
...AND RETURN THEM TO THE GIRL'S MOTHER.
RUKI?!

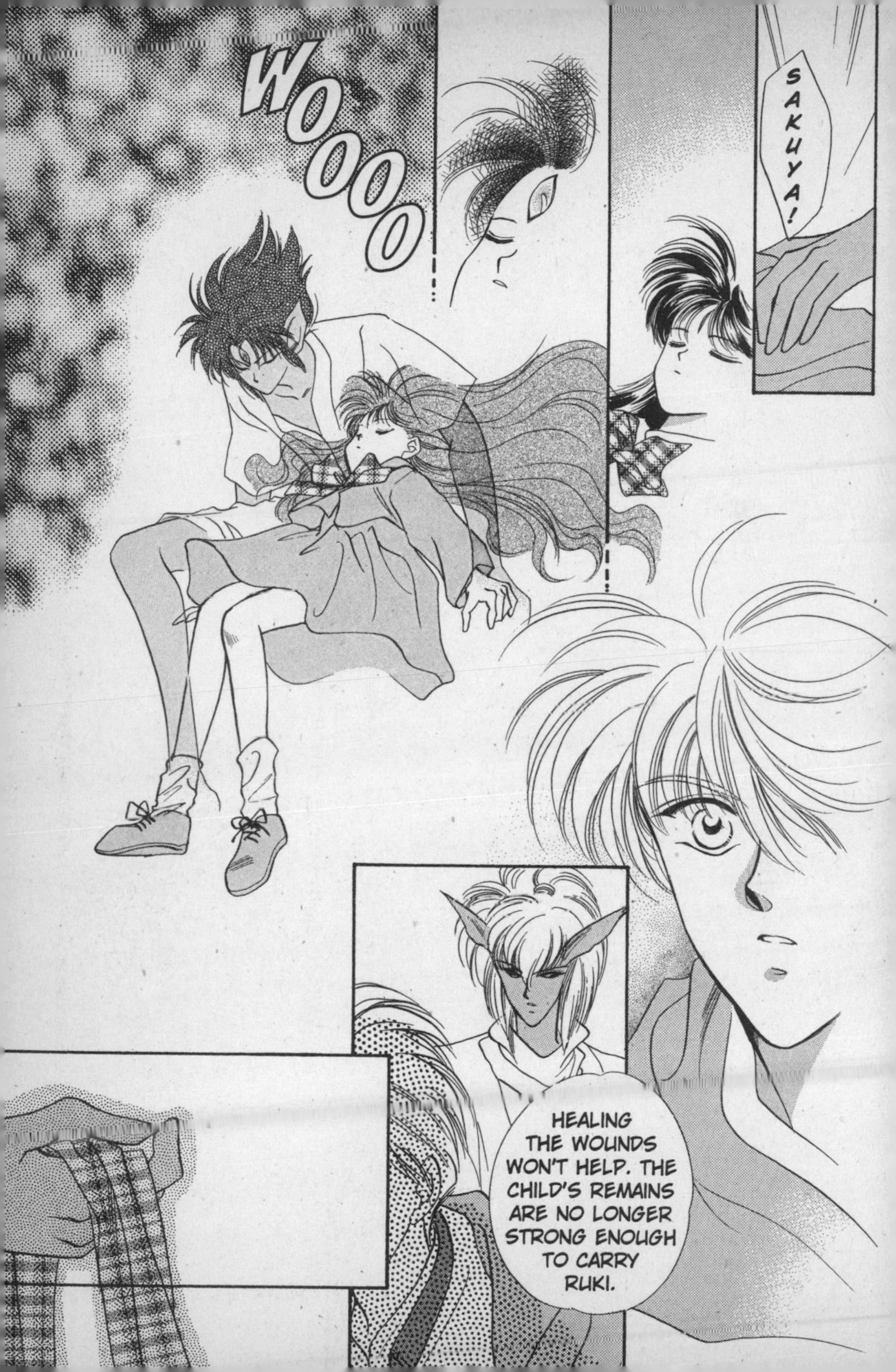
SAKUYA!
WOOOO
HEALING THE WOUNDS WON'T HELP. THE CHILD'S REMAINS ARE NO LONGER STRONG ENOUGH TO CARRY RUKI.

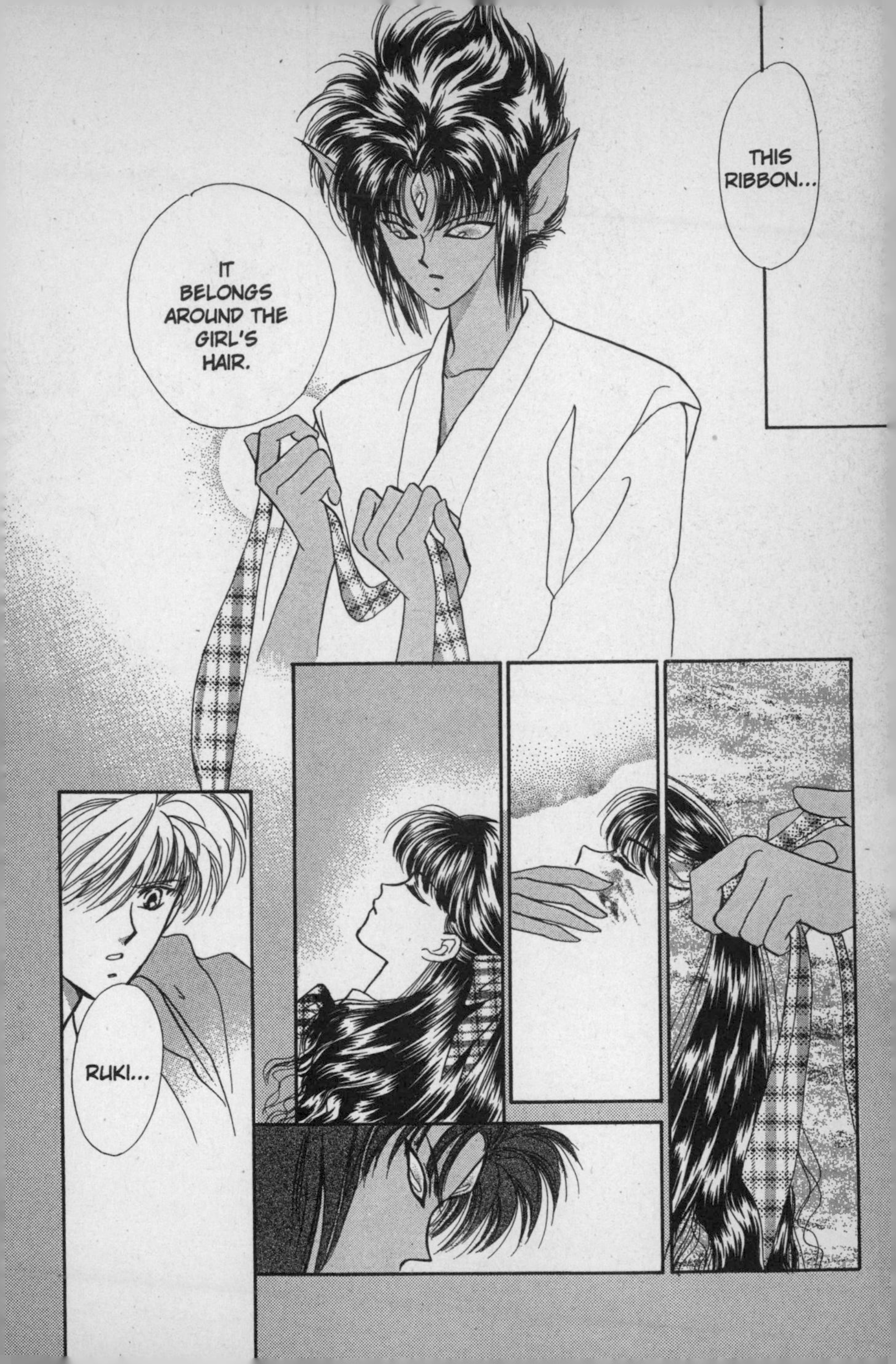
THIS RIBBON...
IT BELONGS AROUND THE GIRL'S HAIR.
RUKI...

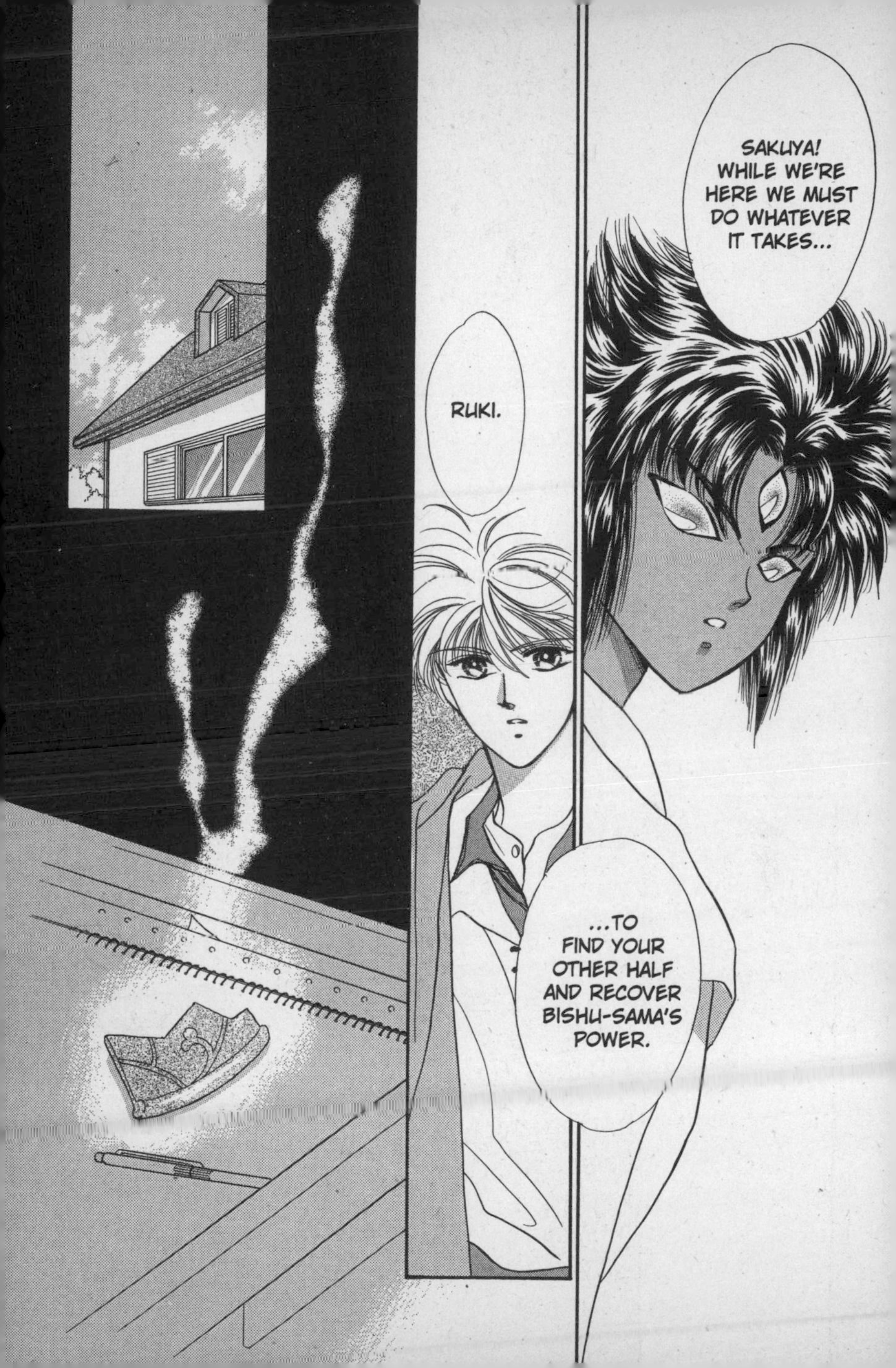
SAKUYA! WHILE WE'RE HERE WE MUST DO WHATEVER IT TAKES...
RUKI.
...TO FIND YOUR OTHER HALF AND RECOVER BISHU-SAMA'S POWER.

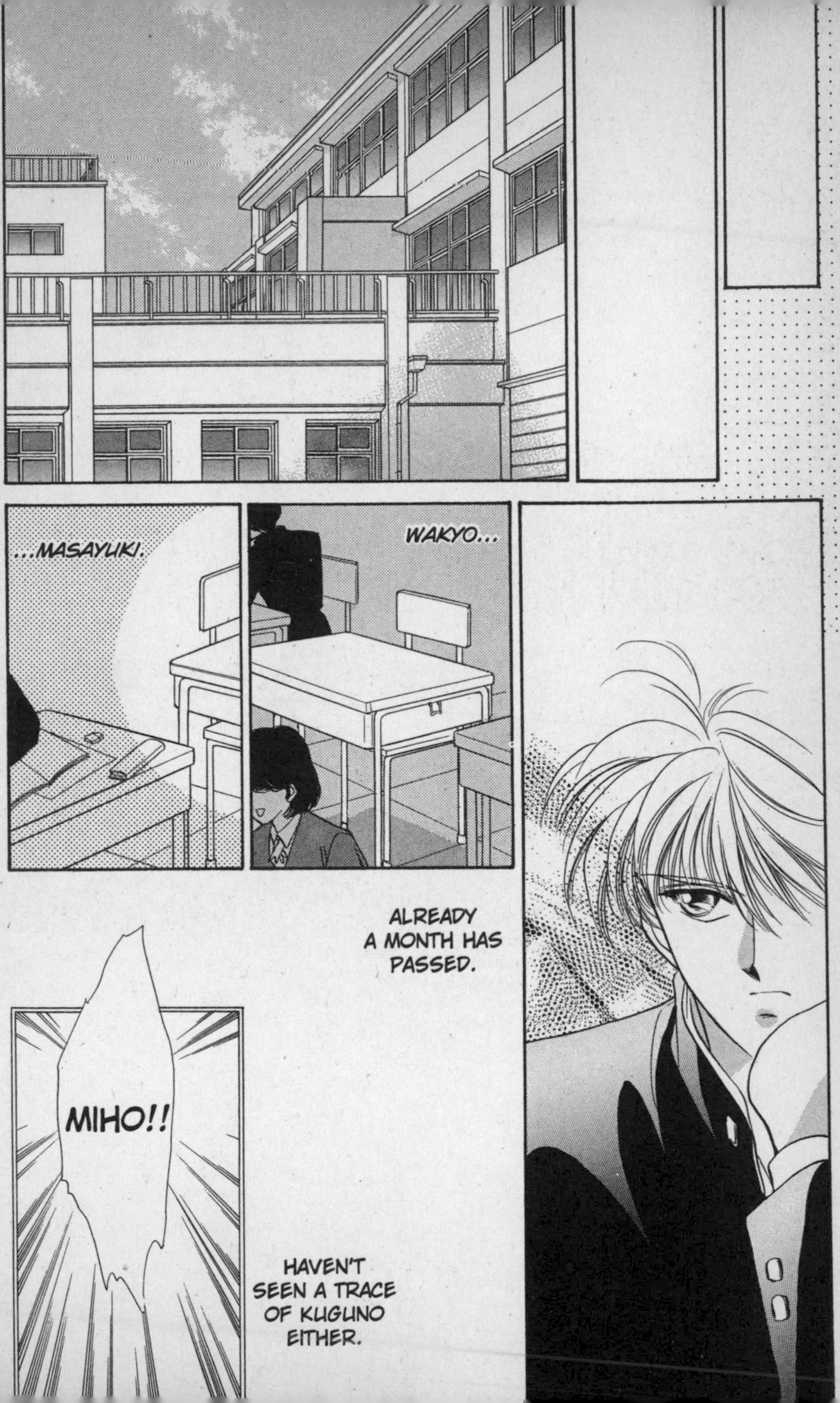
ALREADY A MONTH HAS PASSED.
HAVEN'T SEEN A TRACE OF KUGUNO EITHER.
WAKYO...
...MASAYUKI.
MIHO!!

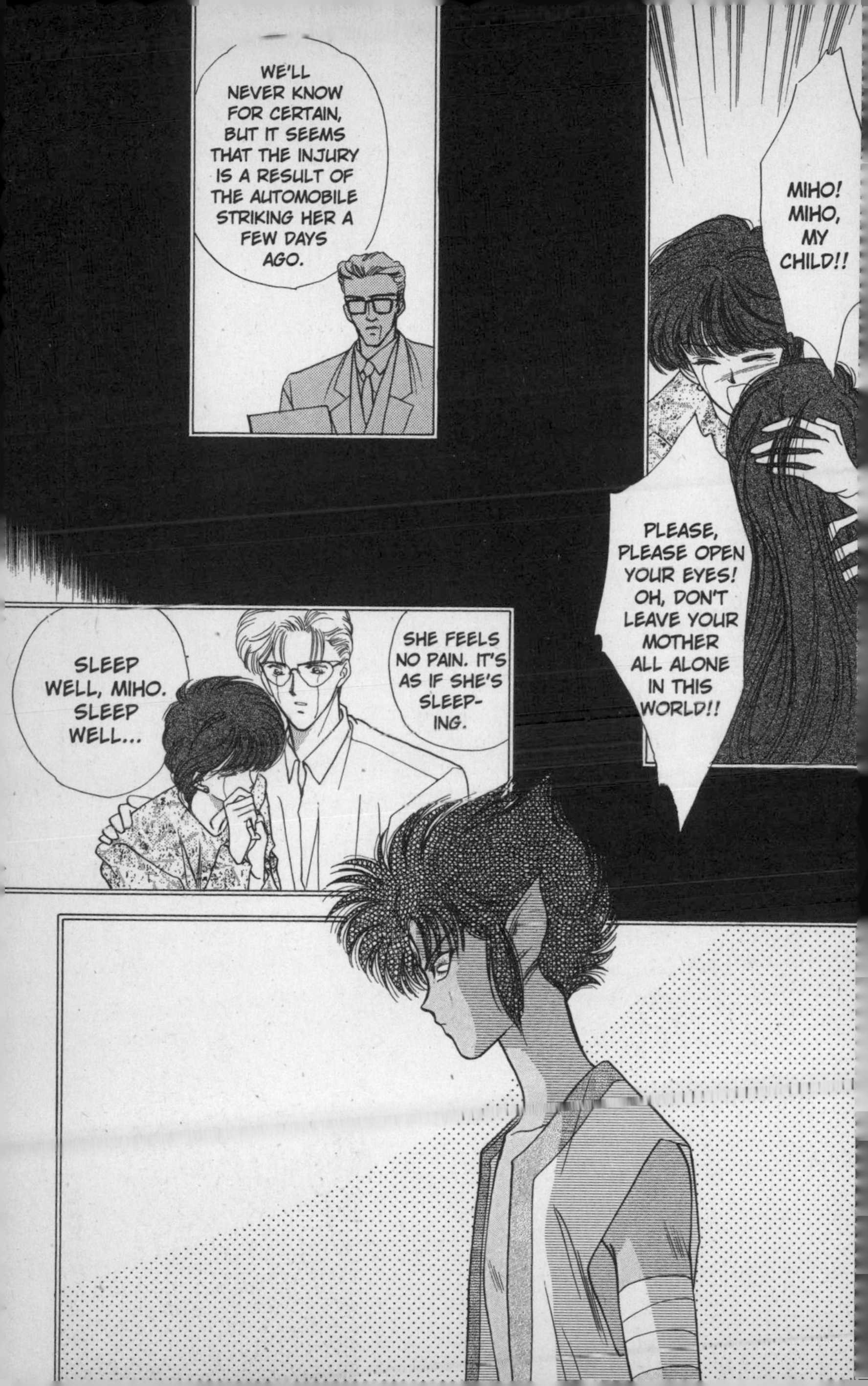
MIHO! MIHO, MY CHILD!!
PLEASE, PLEASE OPEN YOUR EYES! OH, DON'T LEAVE YOUR MOTHER ALL ALONE IN THIS WORLD!!
WE'LL NEVER KNOW FOR CERTAIN, BUT IT SEEMS THAT THE INJURY IS A RESULT OF THE AUTOMOBILE STRIKING HER A FEW DAYS AGO.
SHE FEELS NO PAIN. IT'S AS IF SHE'S SLEEP-ING.
SLEEP WELL, MIHO. SLEEP WELL...

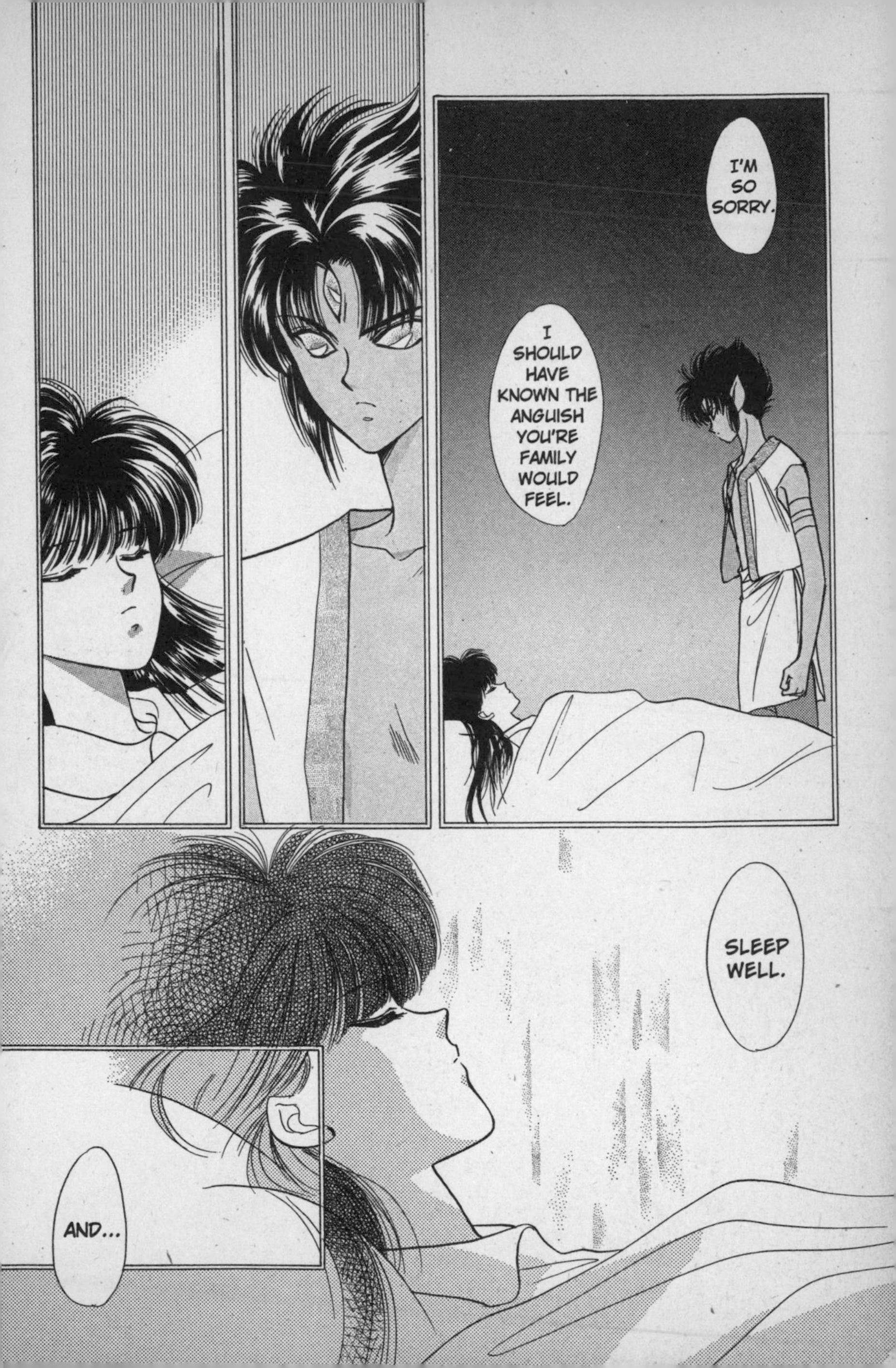
I'M SO SORRY.
I SHOULD HAVE KNOWN THE ANGUISH YOU'RE FAMILY WOULD FEEL.
SLEEP WELL.
AND...

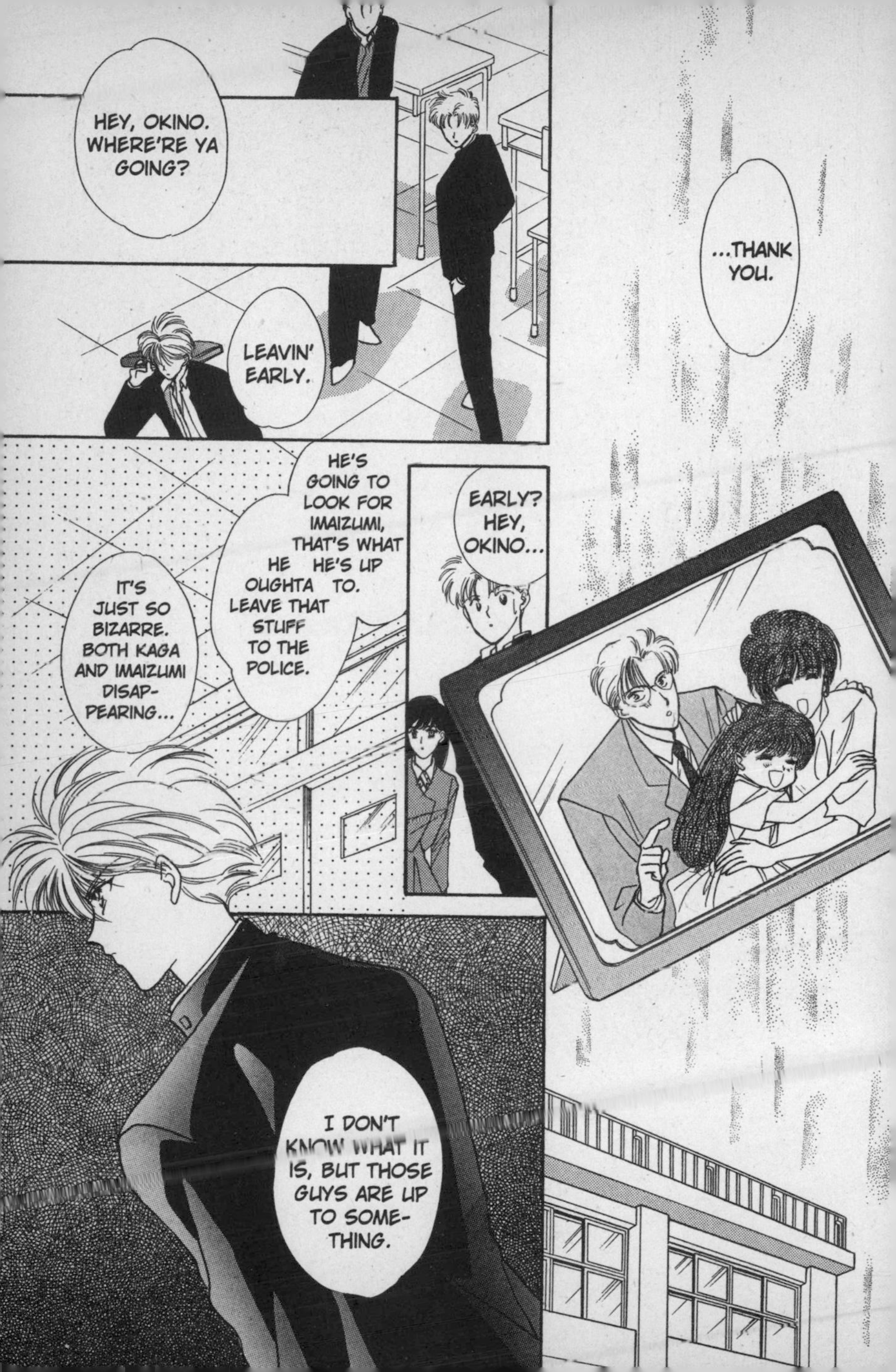
...THANK YOU.
HEY, OKINO. WHERE'RE YA GOING?
LEAVIN' EARLY.
EARLY? HEY, OKINO...
HE'S GOING TO LOOK FOR IMAIZUMI, THAT'S WHAT HE'S UP TO.
HE OUGHTA LEAVE THAT STUFF TO THE POLICE.
IT'S JUST SO BIZARRE. BOTH KAGA AND IMAIZUMI DISAP-PEARING...
I DON'T KNOW WHAT IT IS, BUT THOSE GUYS ARE UP TO SOME-THING.

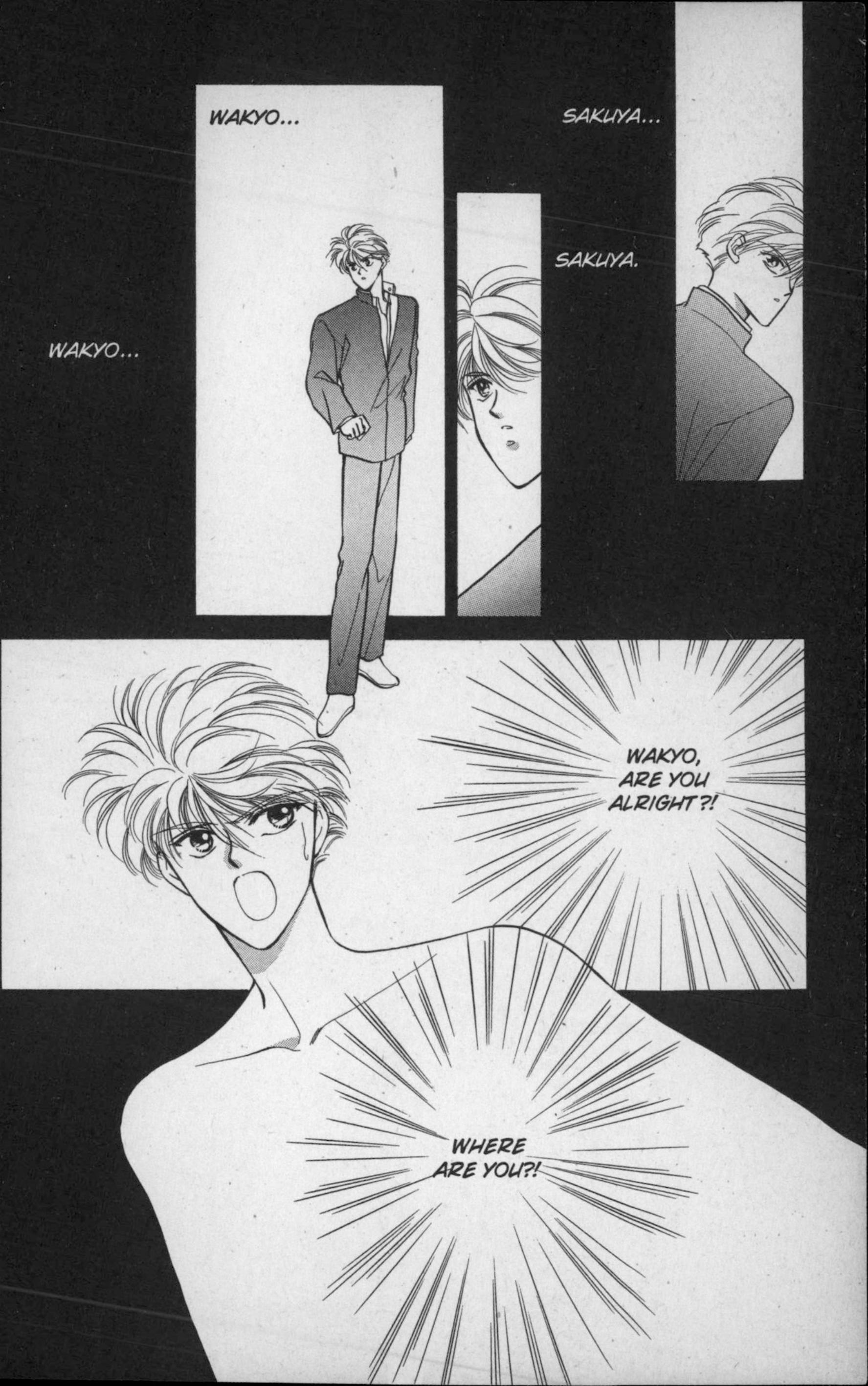
SAKUYA...
SAKUYA.
WAKYO...
WAKYO...
WAKYO, ARE YOU ALRIGHT?!
WHERE ARE YOU?!

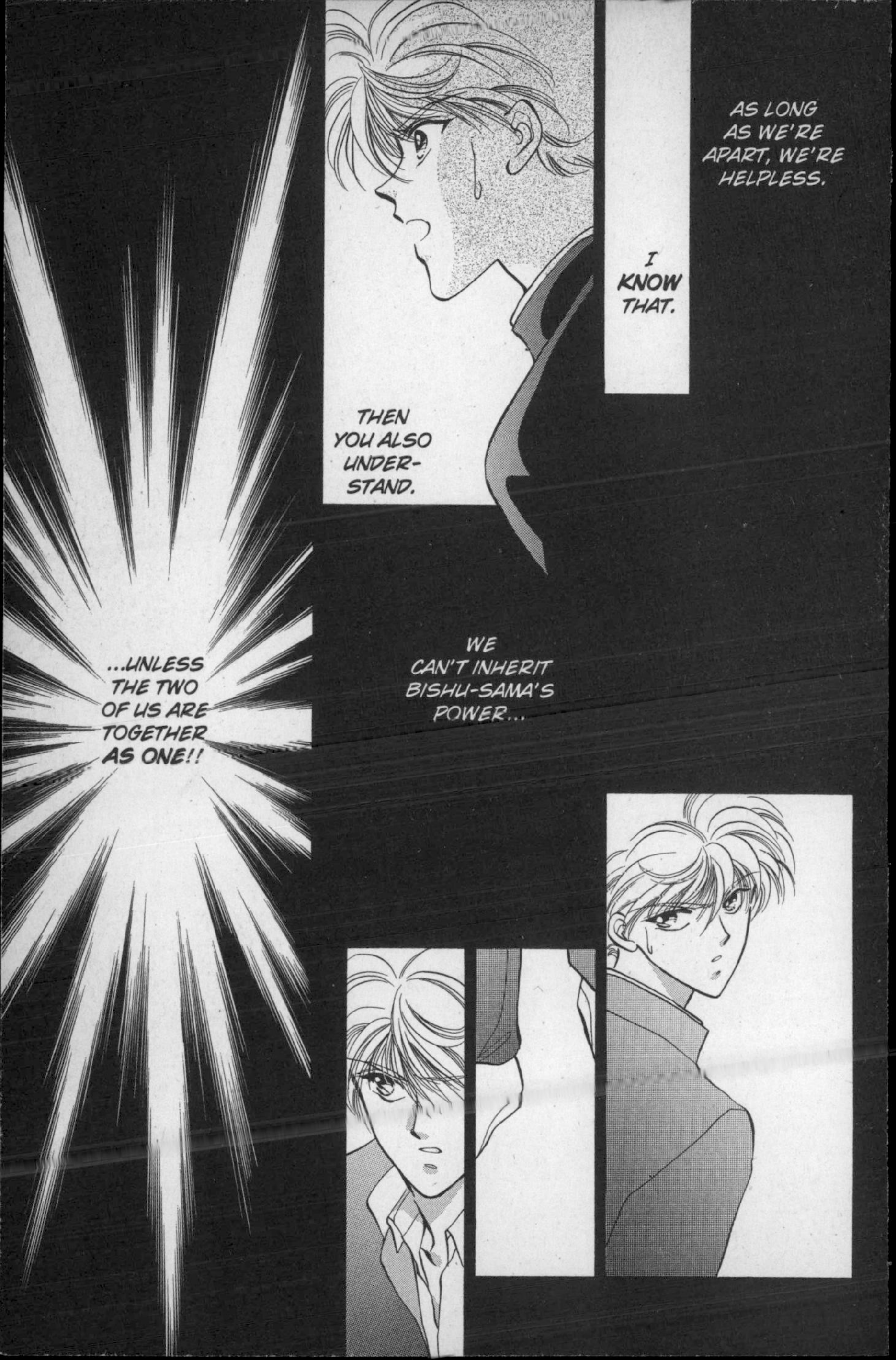
AS LONG AS WE'RE APART, WE'RE HELPLESS.
I KNOW THAT.
THEN YOU ALSO UNDERSTAND.
WE CAN'T INHERIT BISHU-SAMA'S POWER...
...UNLESS THE TWO OF US ARE TOGETHER AS ONE!!

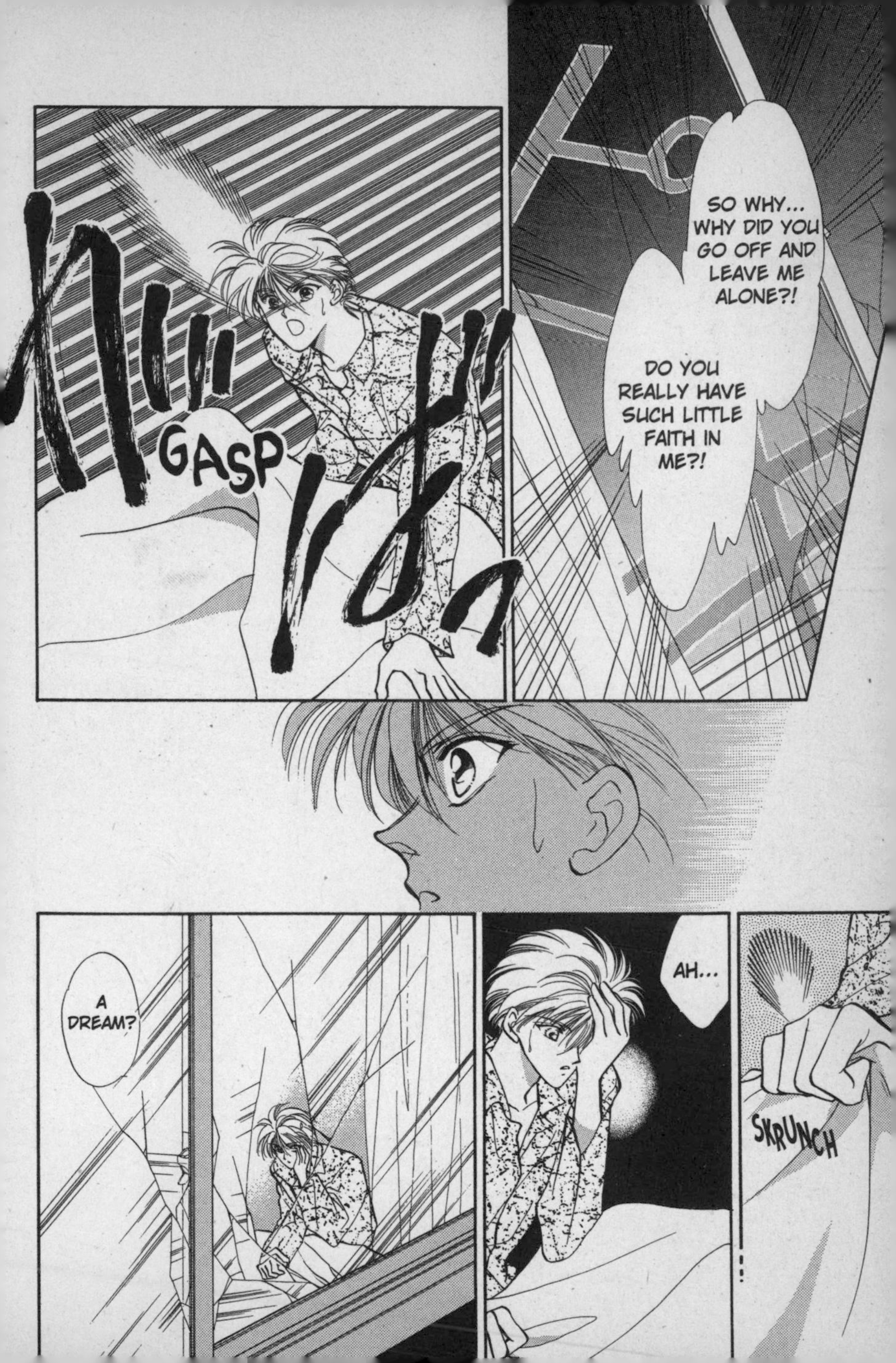
SO WHY... WHY DID YOU GO OFF AND LEAVE ME ALONE?!
DO YOU REALLY HAVE SUCH LITTLE FAITH IN ME?!
GASP
SKRUNCH
AH...
A DREAM?

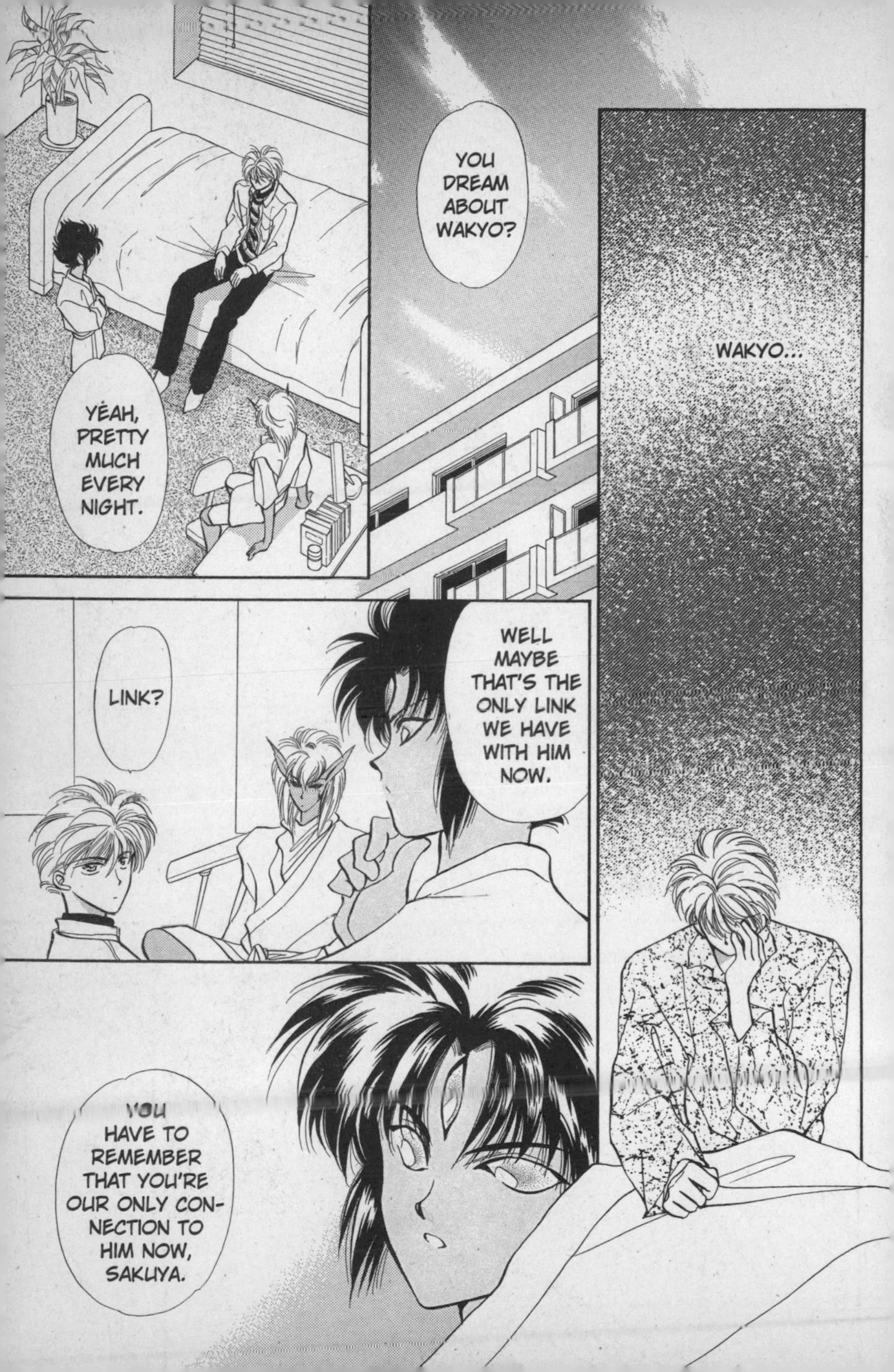
YOU DREAM ABOUT WAKYO?
YEAH, PRETTY MUCH EVERY NIGHT.
WAKYO...
WELL MAYBE THAT'S THE ONLY LINK WE HAVE WITH HIM NOW.
LINK?
YOU HAVE TO REMEMBER THAT YOU'RE OUR ONLY CONNECTION TO HIM NOW, SAKUYA.

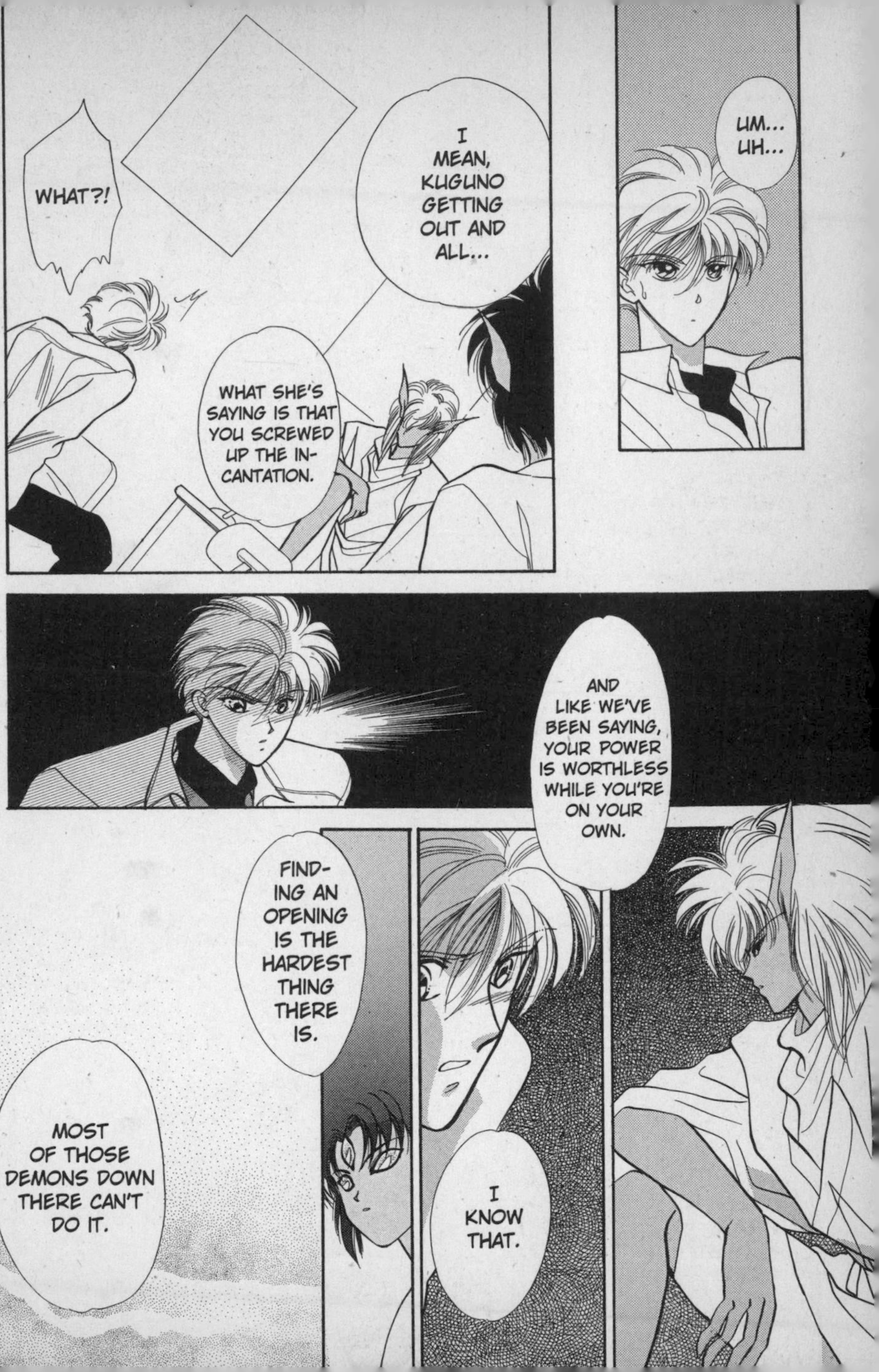
UM... UH...
I MEAN, KUGUNO GETTING OUT AND ALL...
WHAT?!
WHAT SHE'S SAYING IS THAT YOU SCREWED UP THE IN-CANTATION.
AND LIKE WE'VE BEEN SAYING, YOUR POWER IS WORTHLESS WHILE YOU'RE ON YOUR OWN.
I KNOW THAT.
FIND-ING AN OPENING IS THE HARDEST THING THERE IS.
MOST OF THOSE DEMONS DOWN THERE CAN'T DO IT.

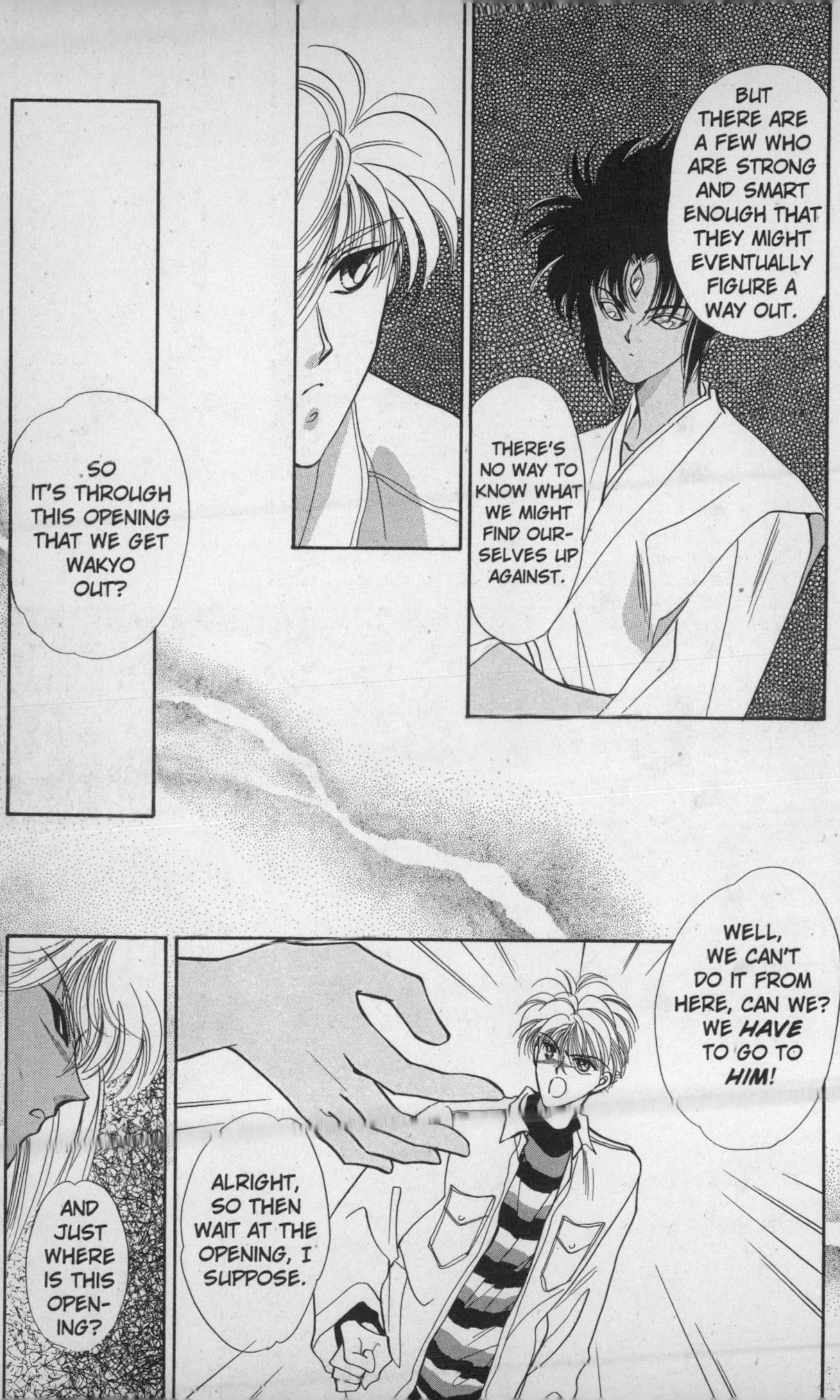
BUT THERE ARE A FEW WHO ARE STRONG AND SMART ENOUGH THAT THEY MIGHT EVENTUALLY FIGURE A WAY OUT.
THERE'S NO WAY TO KNOW WHAT WE MIGHT FIND OUR-SELVES UP AGAINST.
SO IT'S THROUGH THIS OPENING THAT WE GET WAKYO OUT?
WELL, WE CAN'T DO IT FROM HERE, CAN WE? WE *HAVE* TO GO TO *HIM*!
ALRIGHT, SO THEN WAIT AT THE OPENING, I SUPPOSE.
AND JUST WHERE IS THIS OPEN-ING?

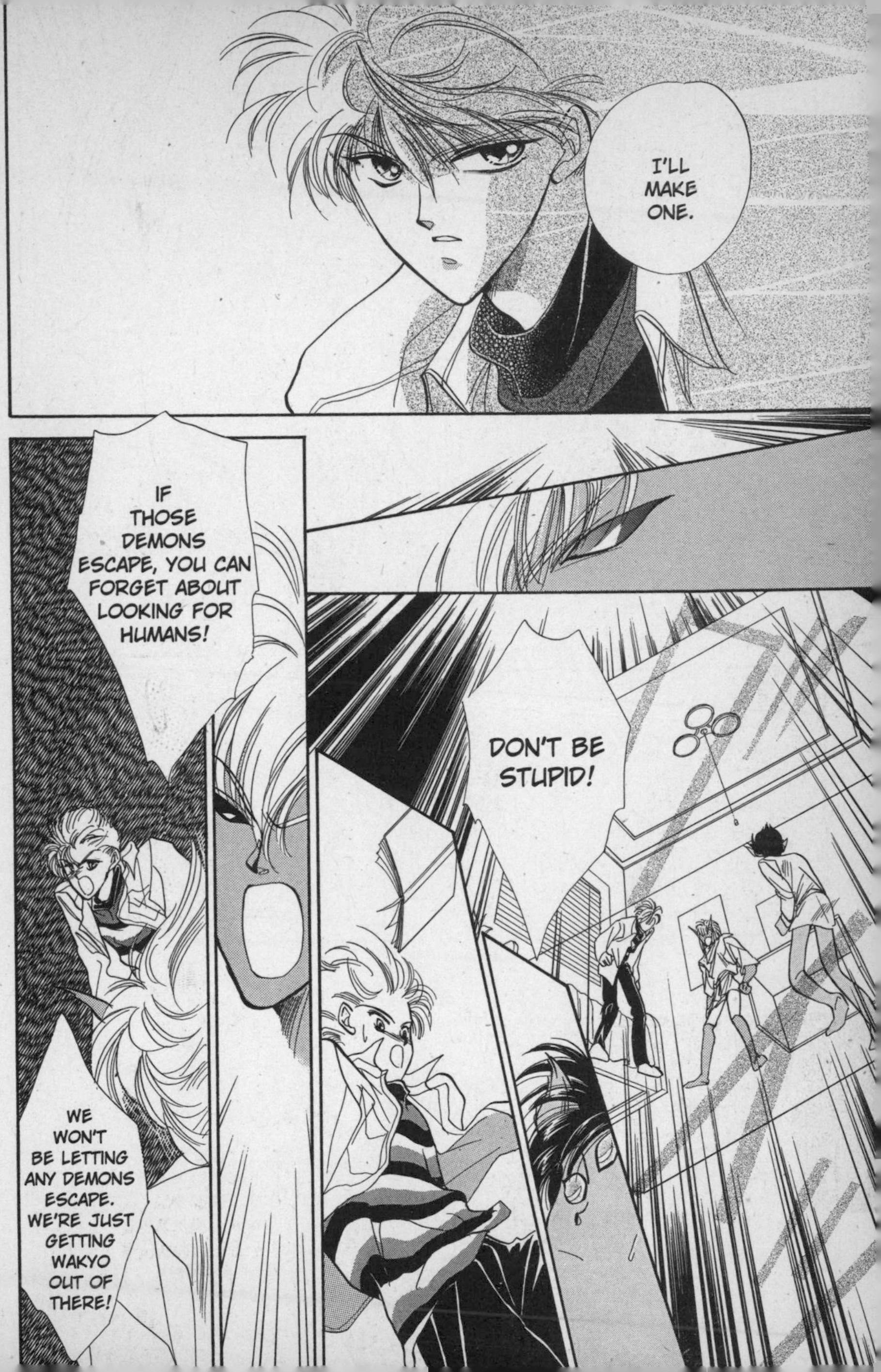
I'LL MAKE ONE.
DON'T BE STUPID!
IF THOSE DEMONS ESCAPE, YOU CAN FORGET ABOUT LOOKING FOR HUMANS!
WE WON'T BE LETTING ANY DEMONS ESCAPE. WE'RE JUST GETTING WAKYO OUT OF THERE!

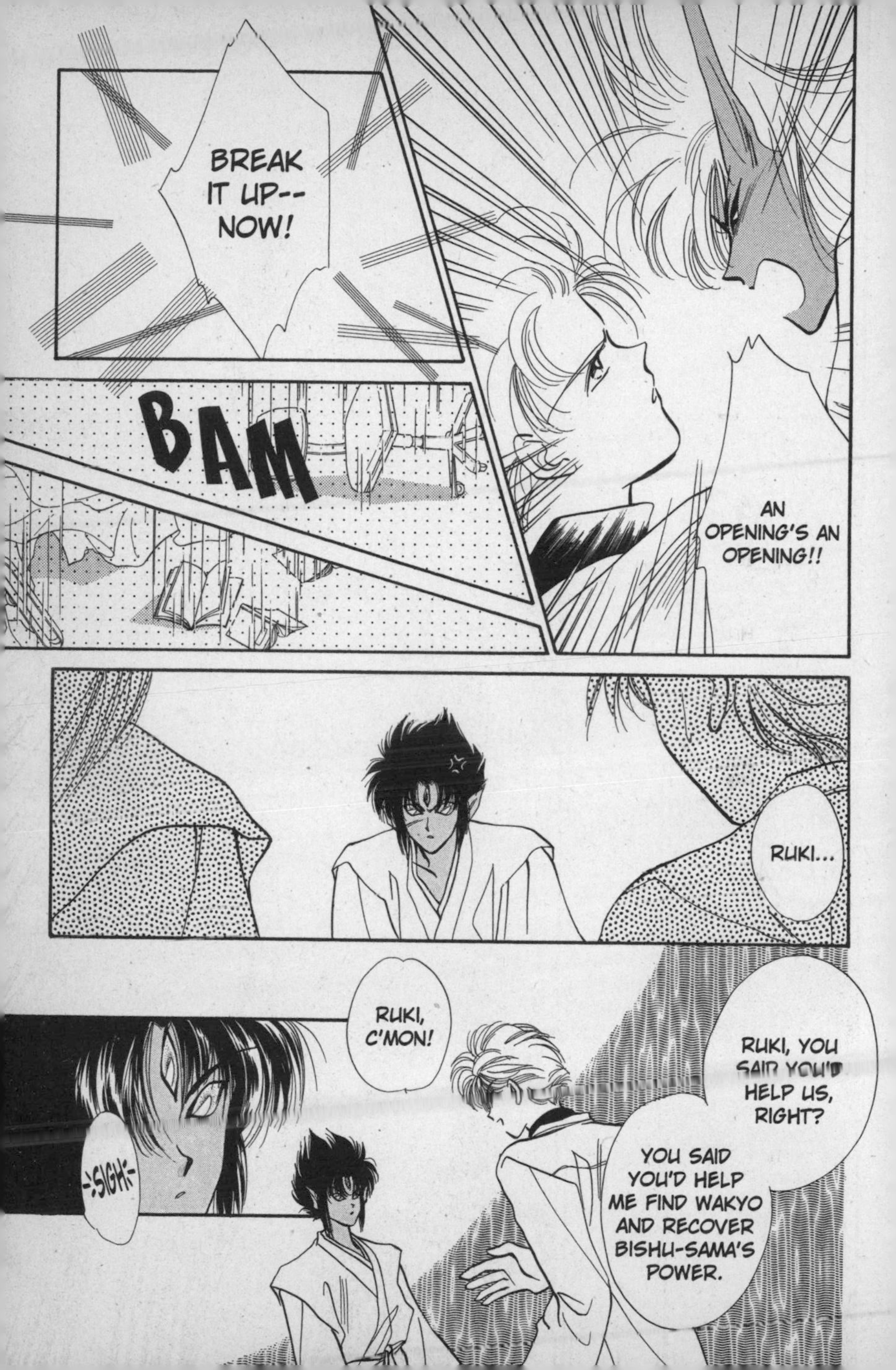
AN OPENING'S AN OPENING!!
BREAK IT UP-- NOW!
BAM
RUKI...
RUKI, YOU SAID YOU'D HELP US, RIGHT?
YOU SAID YOU'D HELP ME FIND WAKYO AND RECOVER BISHU-SAMA'S POWER.
RUKI, C'MON!
-SIGH-

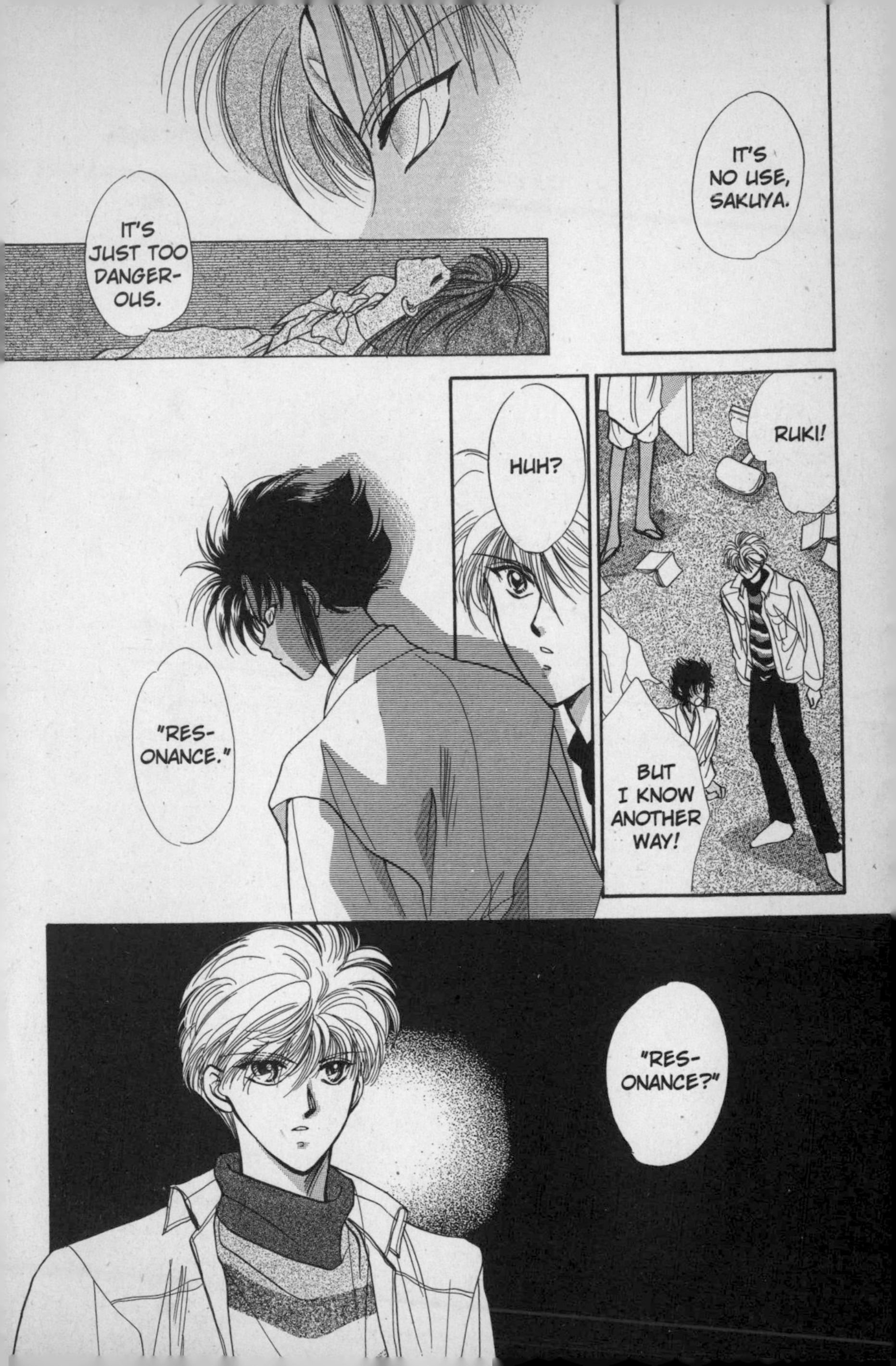
IT'S NO USE, SAKUYA.
IT'S JUST TOO DANGER-OUS.
RUKI!
BUT I KNOW ANOTHER WAY!
HUH?
"RES-ONANCE."
"RES-ONANCE?"

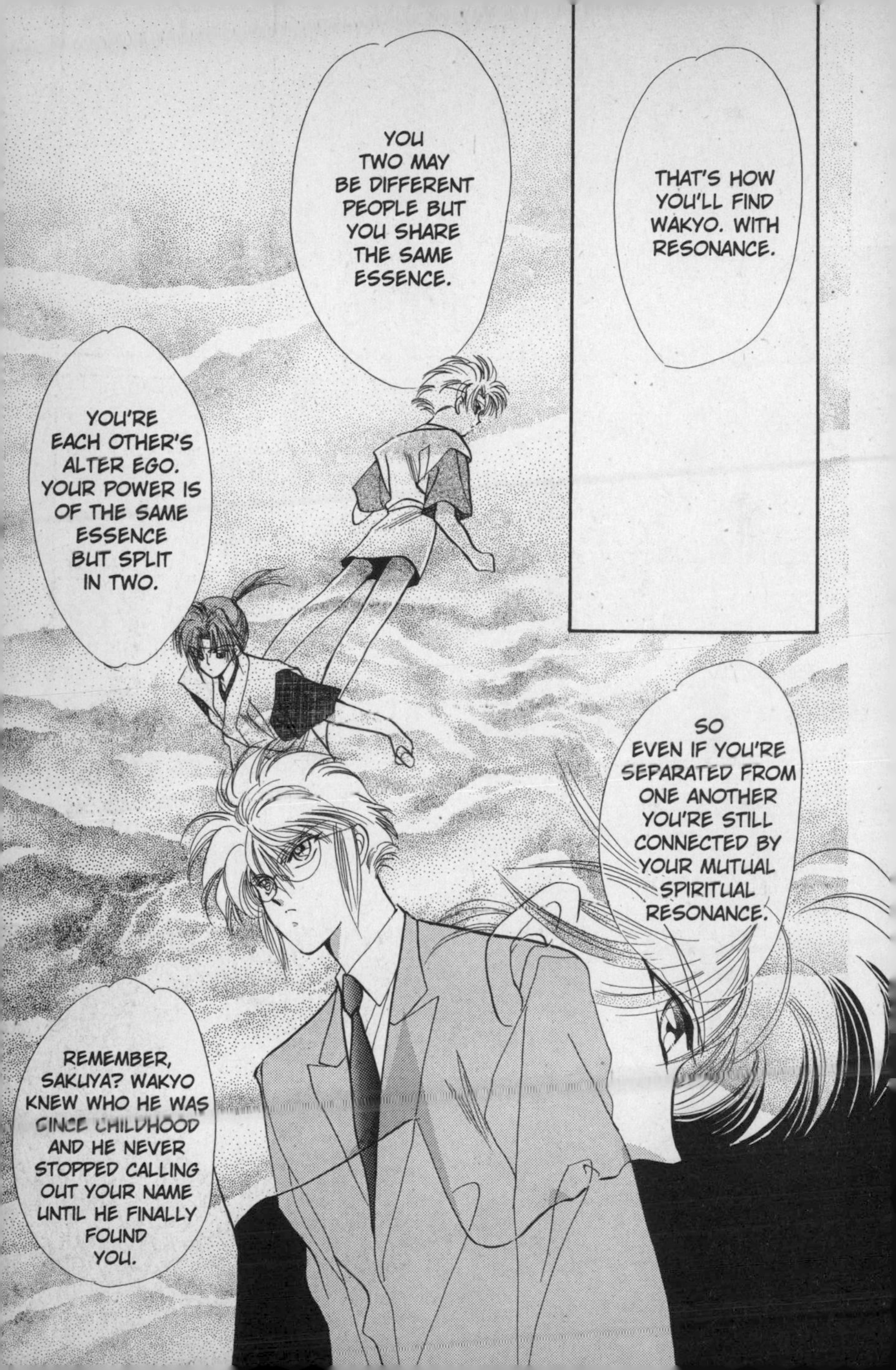
THAT'S HOW YOU'LL FIND WAKYO. WITH RESONANCE.
YOU TWO MAY BE DIFFERENT PEOPLE BUT YOU SHARE THE SAME ESSENCE.
YOU'RE EACH OTHER'S ALTER EGO. YOUR POWER IS OF THE SAME ESSENCE BUT SPLIT IN TWO.
SO EVEN IF YOU'RE SEPARATED FROM ONE ANOTHER YOU'RE STILL CONNECTED BY YOUR MUTUAL SPIRITUAL RESONANCE.
REMEMBER, SAKUYA? WAKYO KNEW WHO HE WAS SINCE CHILDHOOD AND HE NEVER STOPPED CALLING OUT YOUR NAME UNTIL HE FINALLY FOUND YOU.

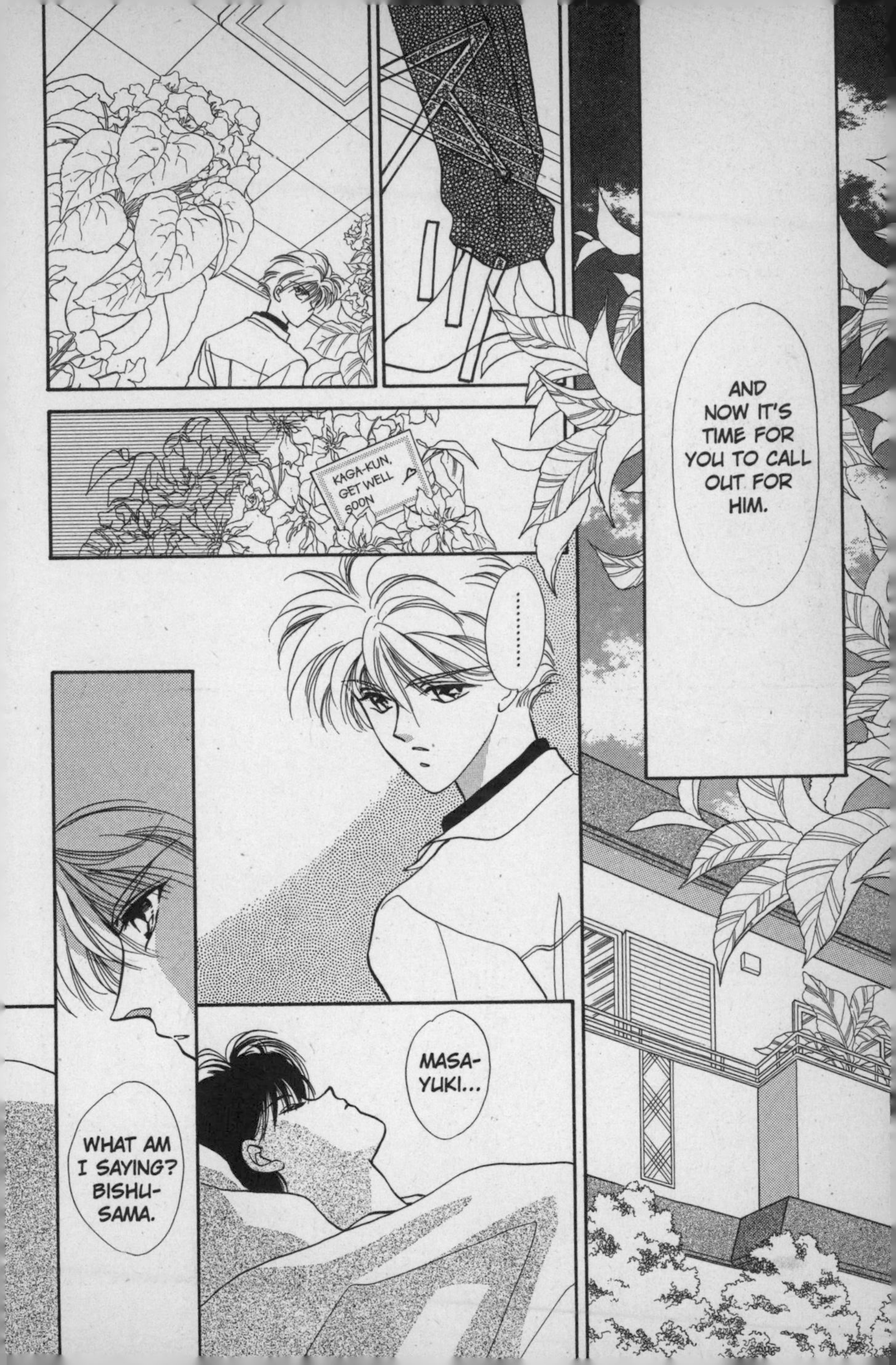
AND NOW IT'S TIME FOR YOU TO CALL OUT FOR HIM.
KAGA-KUN, GET WELL SOON
......
MASA-YUKI...
WHAT AM I SAYING? BISHU-SAMA.

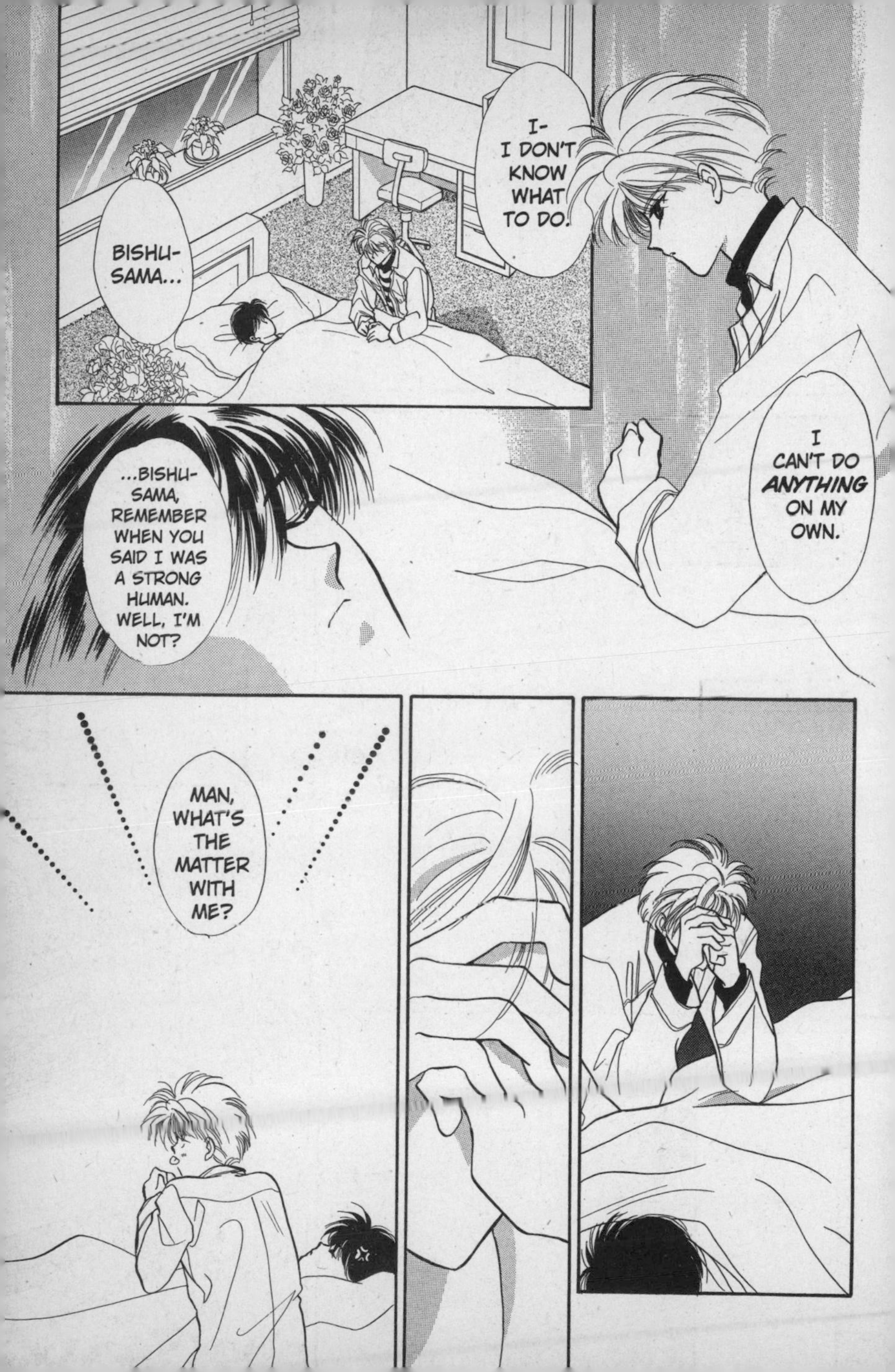
I- I DON'T KNOW WHAT TO DO.
I CAN'T DO *ANYTHING* ON MY OWN.
BISHU-SAMA...
...BISHU-SAMA, REMEMBER WHEN YOU SAID I WAS A STRONG HUMAN. WELL, I'M NOT?
MAN, WHAT'S THE MATTER WITH ME?

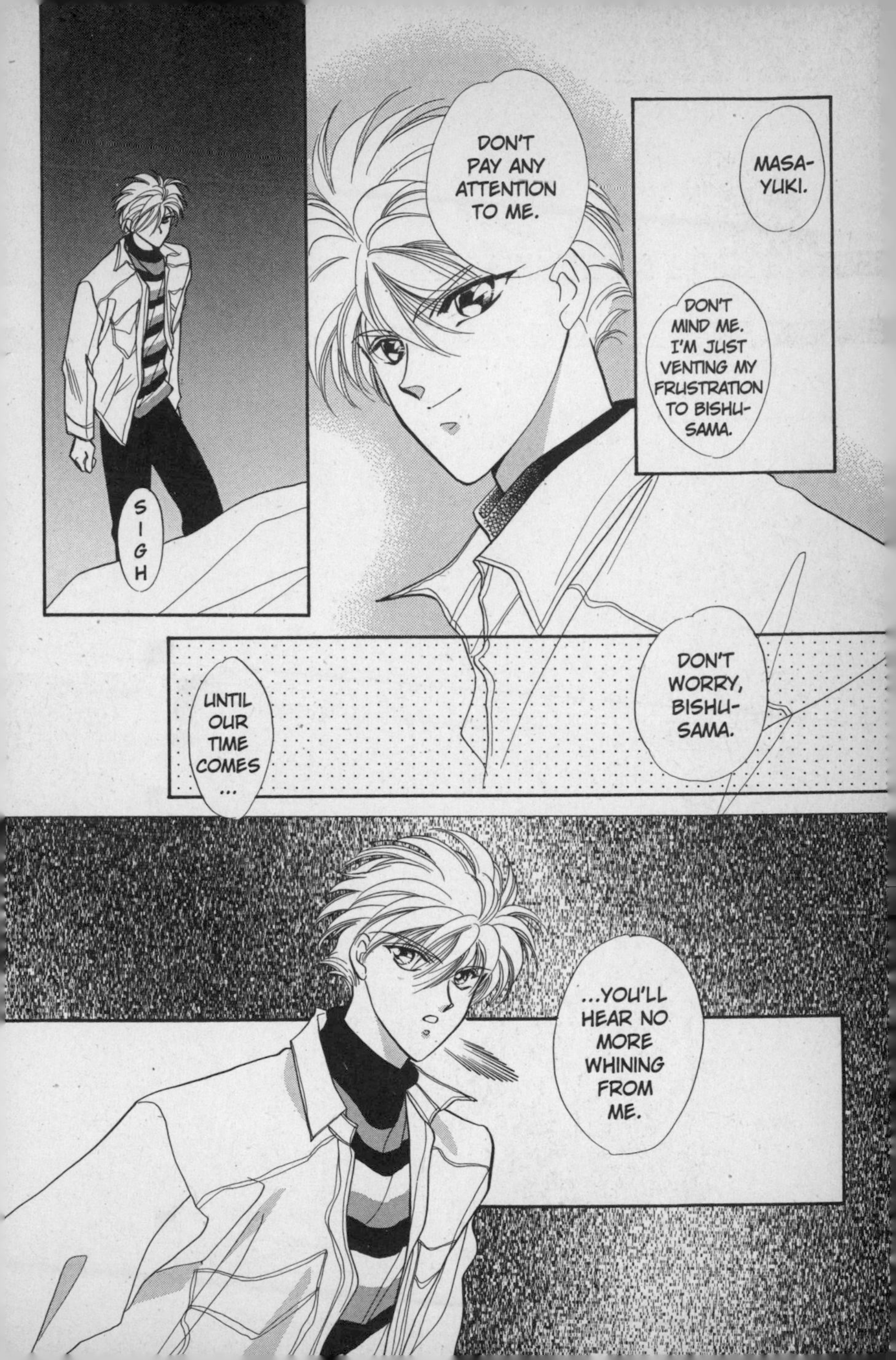
MASA-YUKI.
DON'T MIND ME. I'M JUST VENTING MY FRUSTRATION TO BISHU-SAMA.
DON'T PAY ANY ATTENTION TO ME.
SIGH
DON'T WORRY, BISHU-SAMA.
UNTIL OUR TIME COMES ...
...YOU'LL HEAR NO MORE WHINING FROM ME.

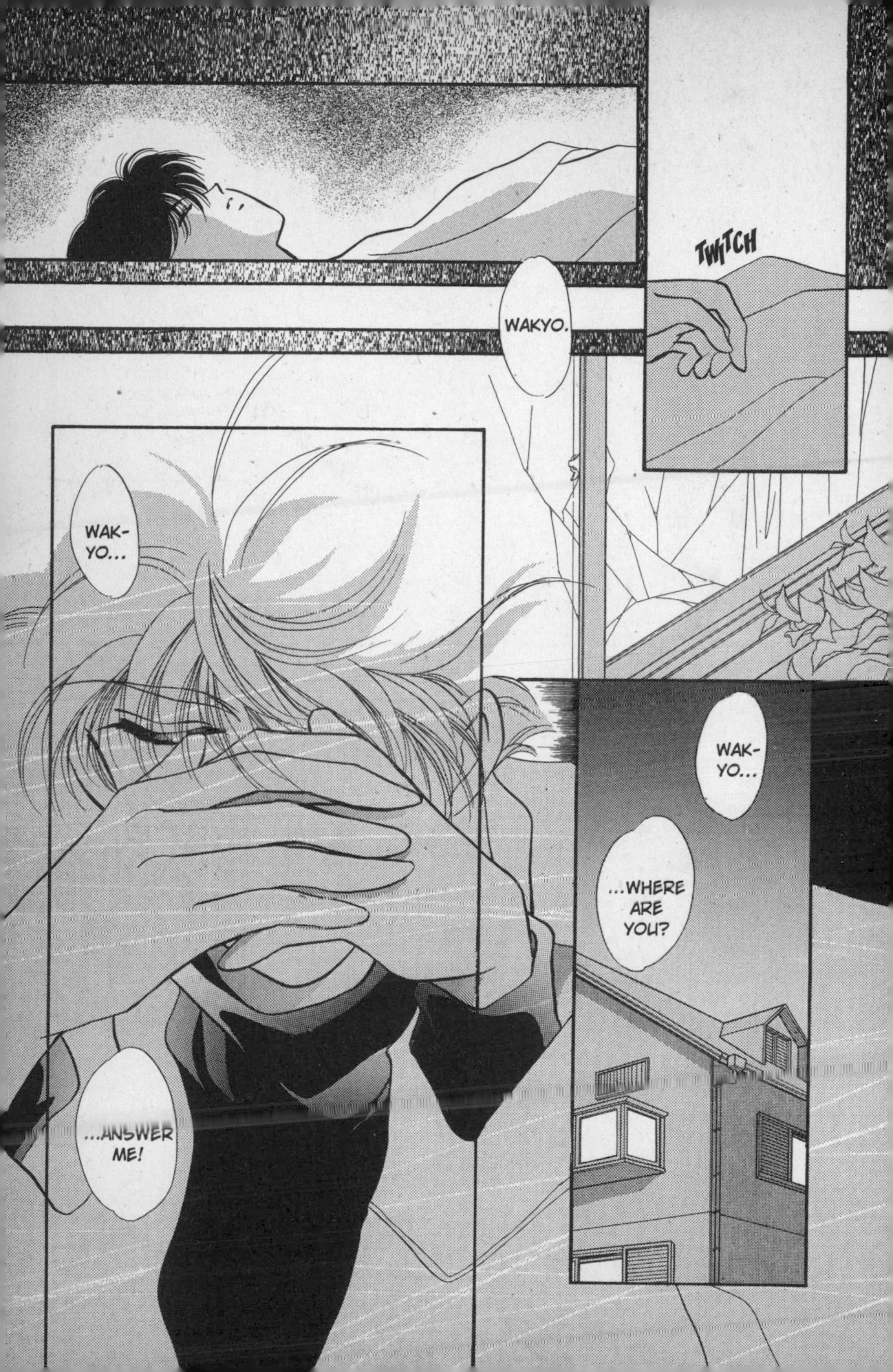
TWITCH
WAKYO.
WAK-YO...
...WHERE ARE YOU?
WAK-YO...
...ANSWER ME!

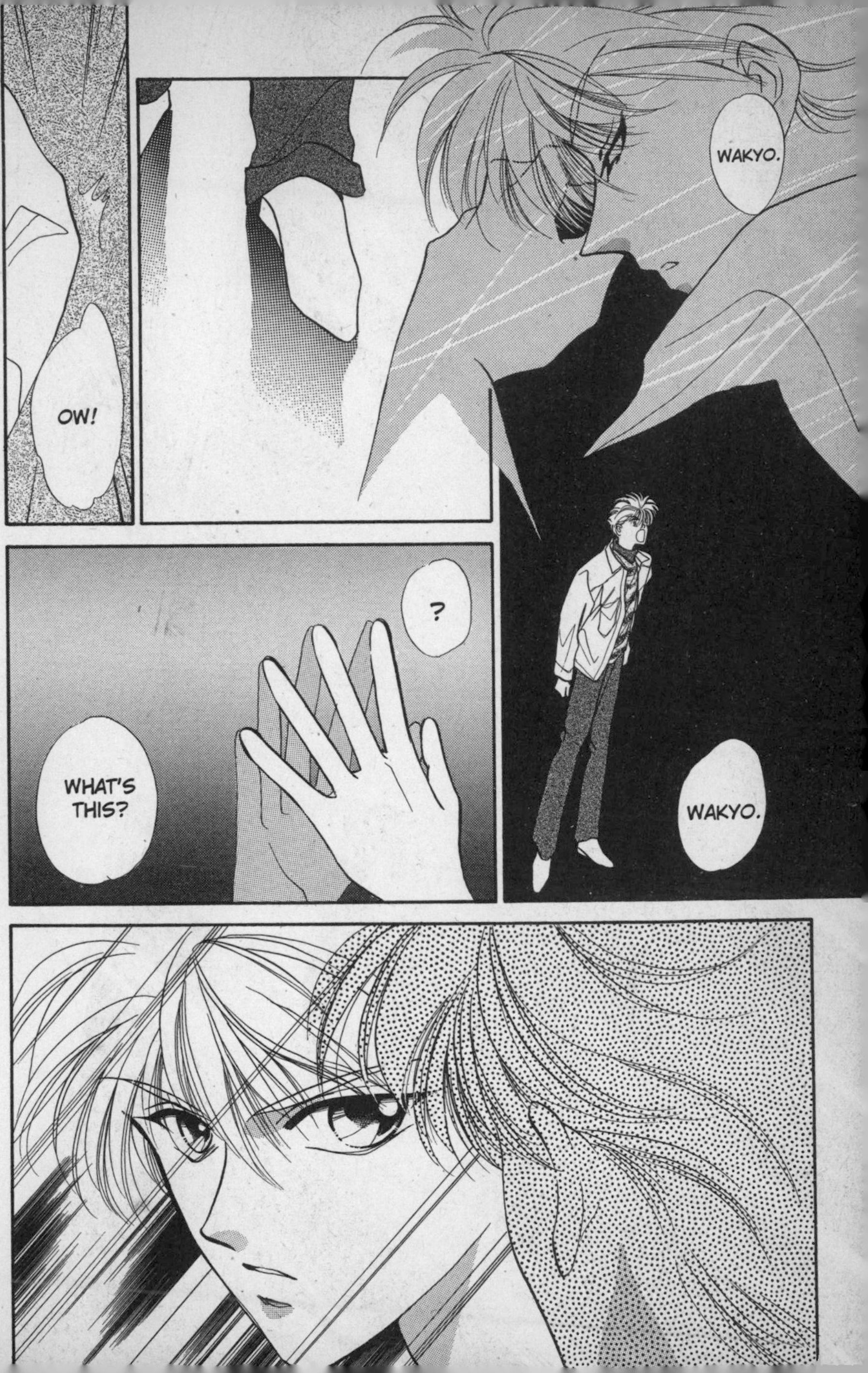
WAKYO.
WAKYO.
OW!
?
WHAT'S THIS?

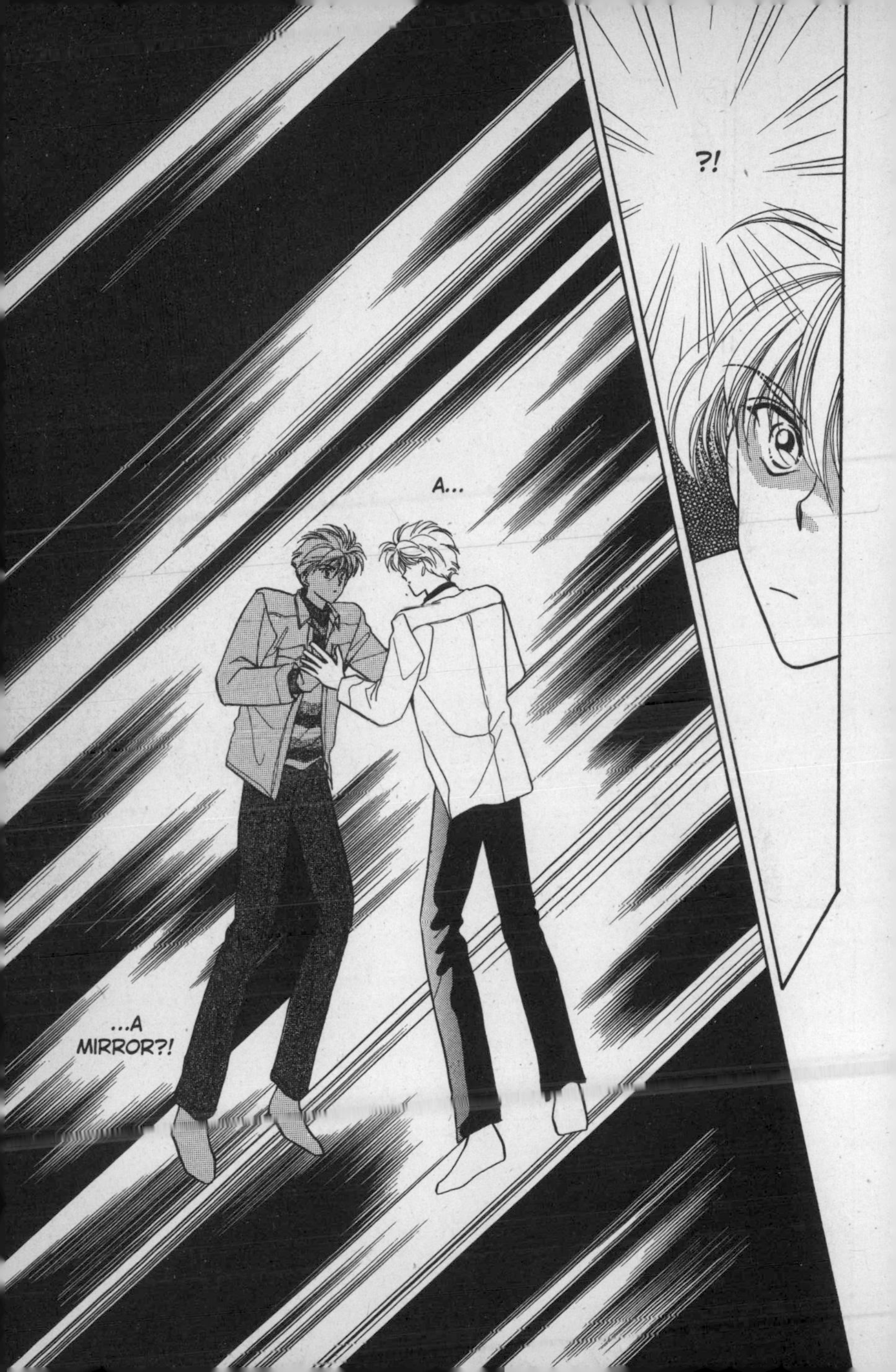
?!
A...
...A
MIRROR?!

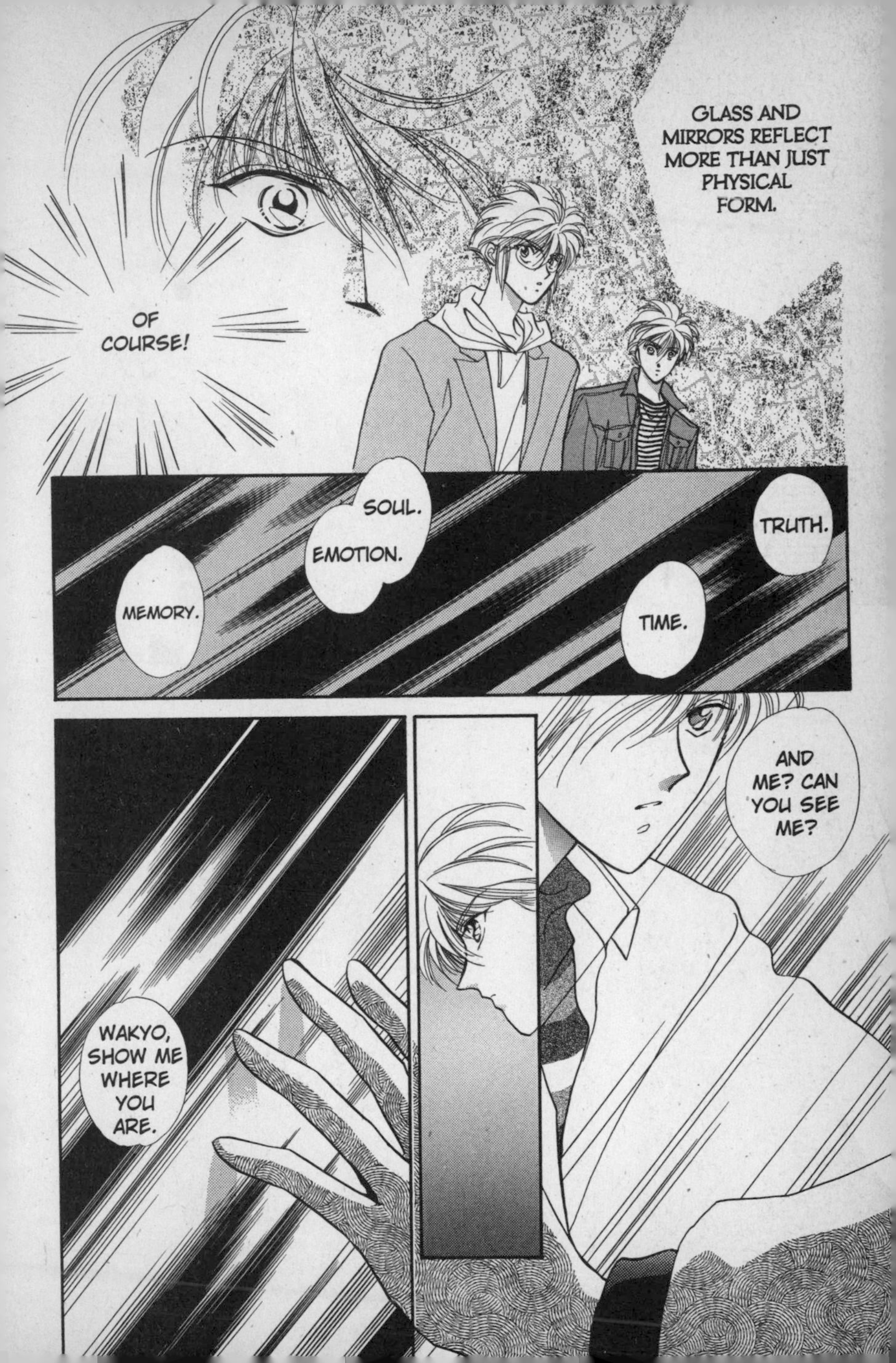
GLASS AND MIRRORS REFLECT MORE THAN JUST PHYSICAL FORM.
OF COURSE!
TRUTH.
TIME.
SOUL.
EMOTION.
MEMORY.
AND ME? CAN YOU SEE ME?
WAKYO, SHOW ME WHERE YOU ARE.

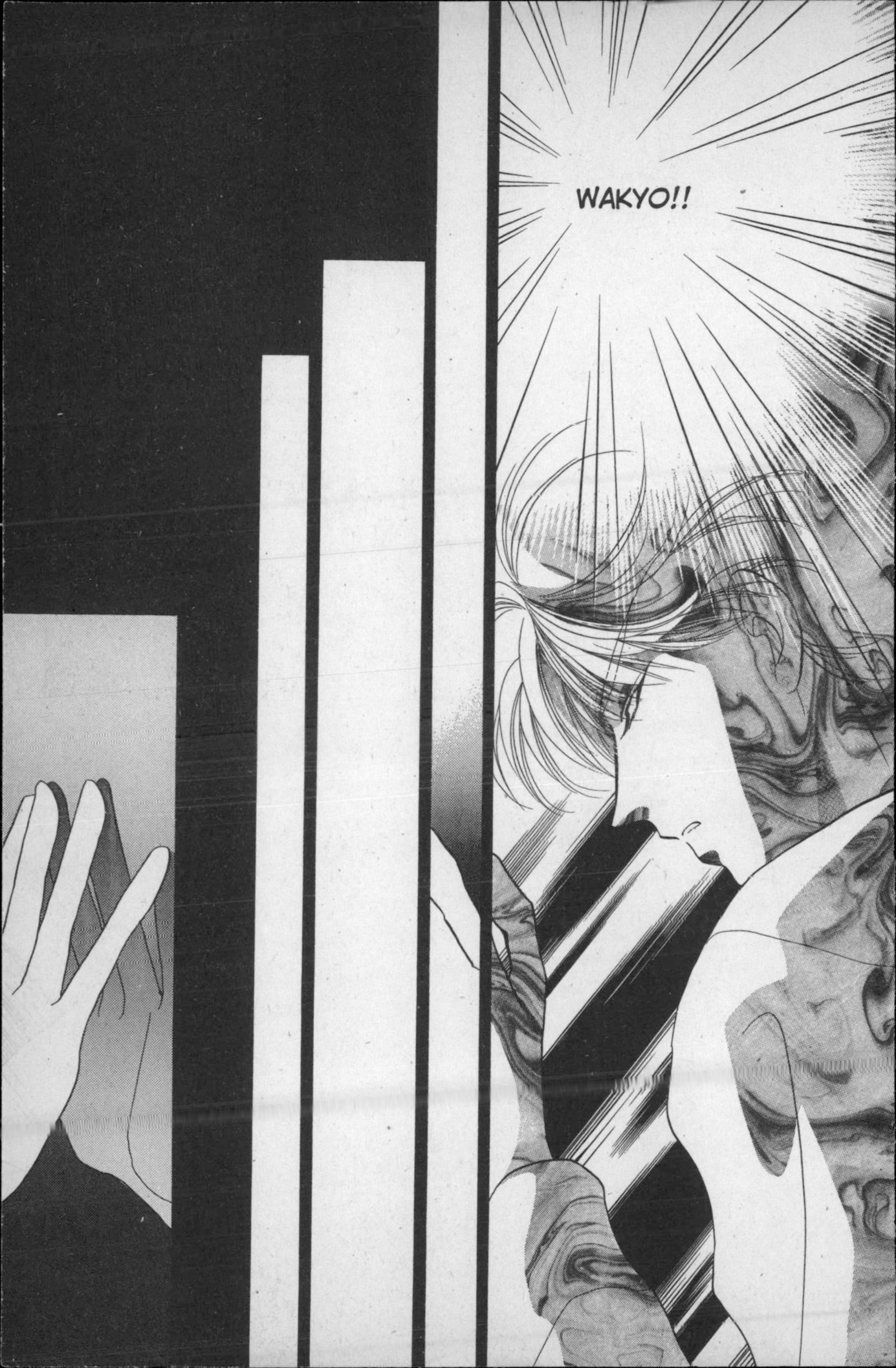
WAKYO!!

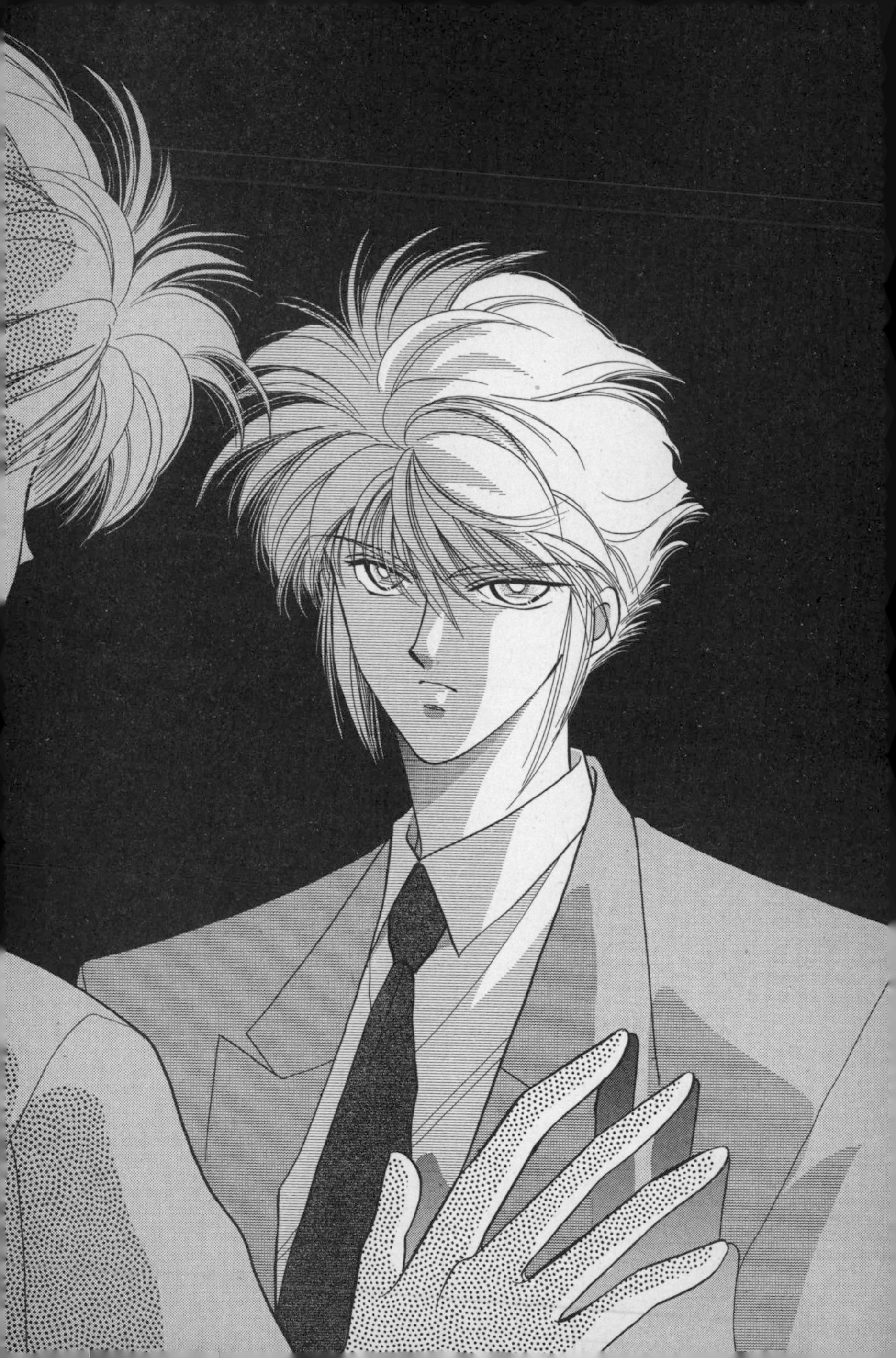

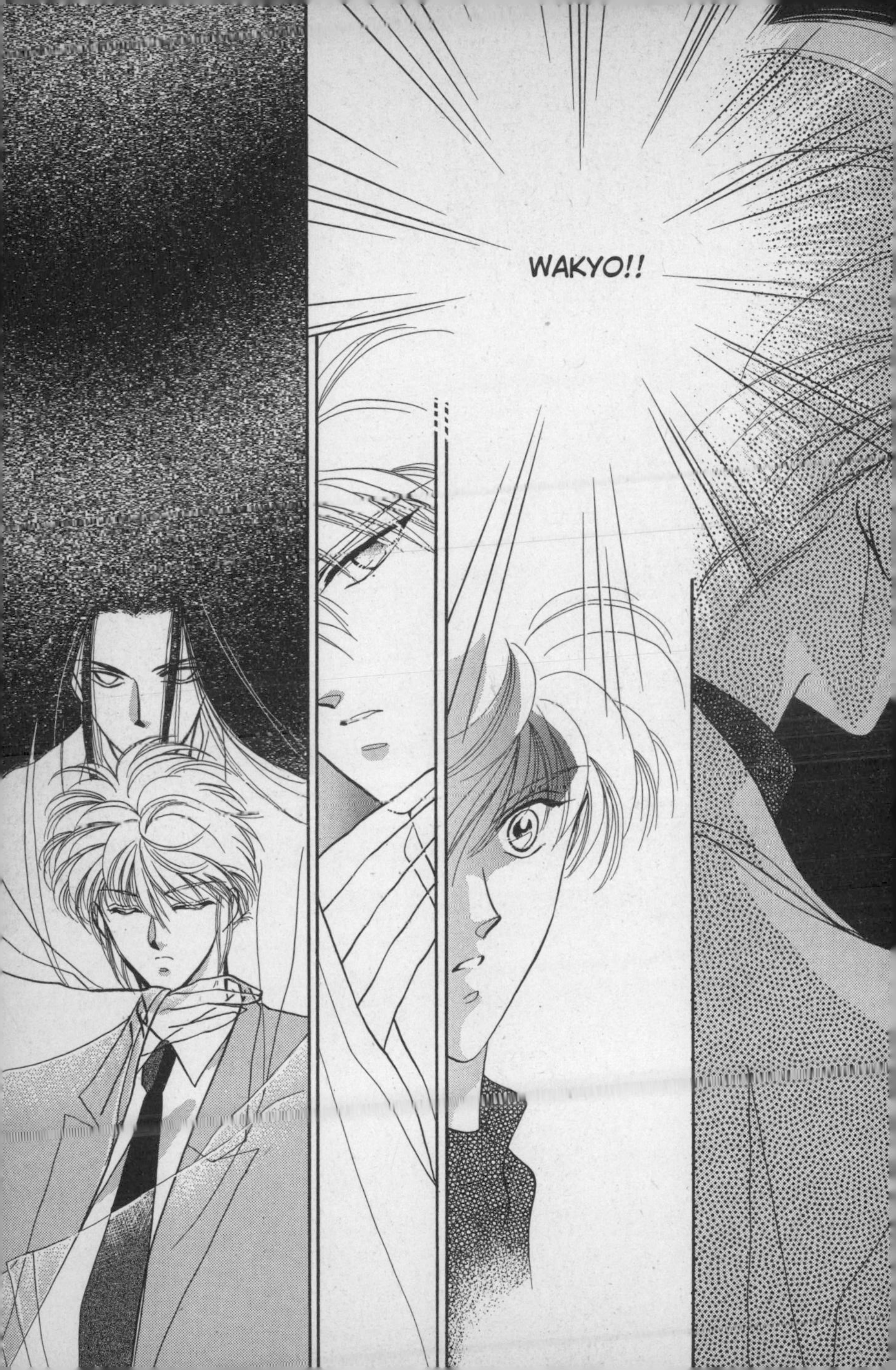
WAKYO!!

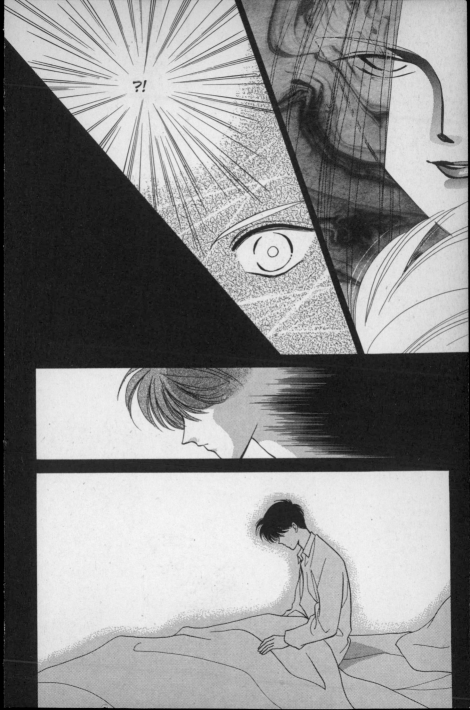

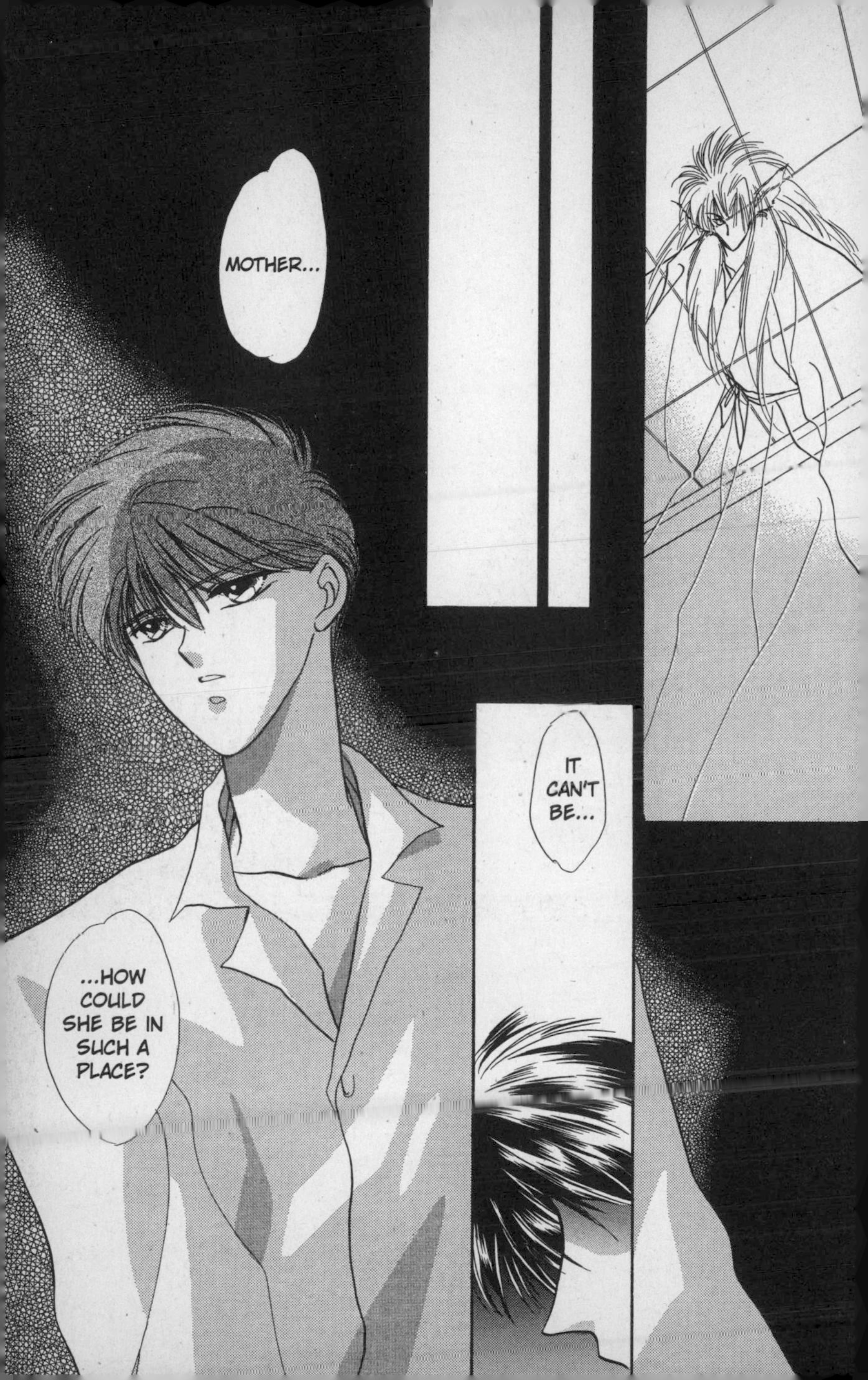
IT CAN'T BE...
MOTHER...
...HOW COULD SHE BE IN SUCH A PLACE?

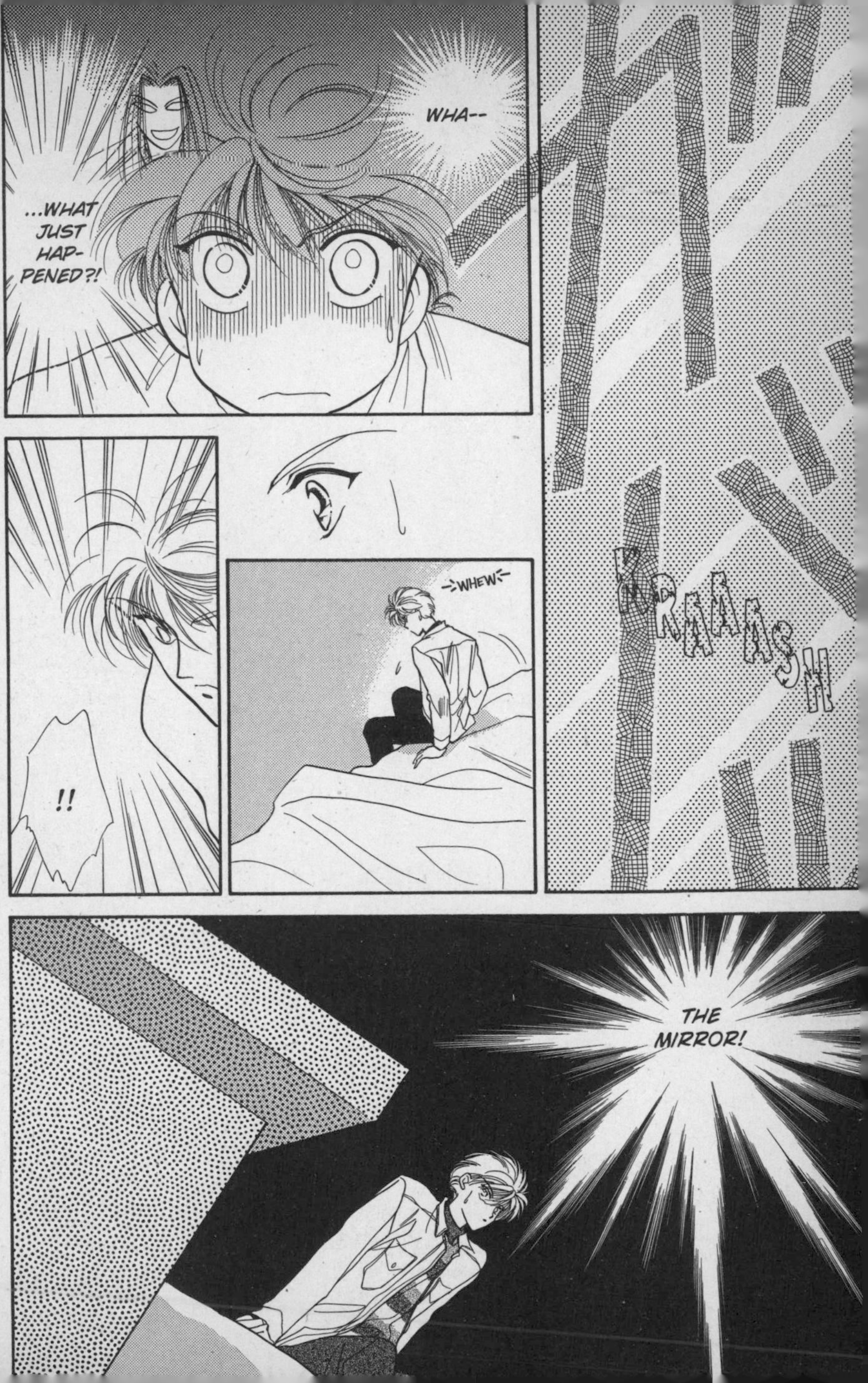
KRRAAASH
WHA--
...WHAT JUST HAPPENED?!
WHEW
!!
THE MIRROR!

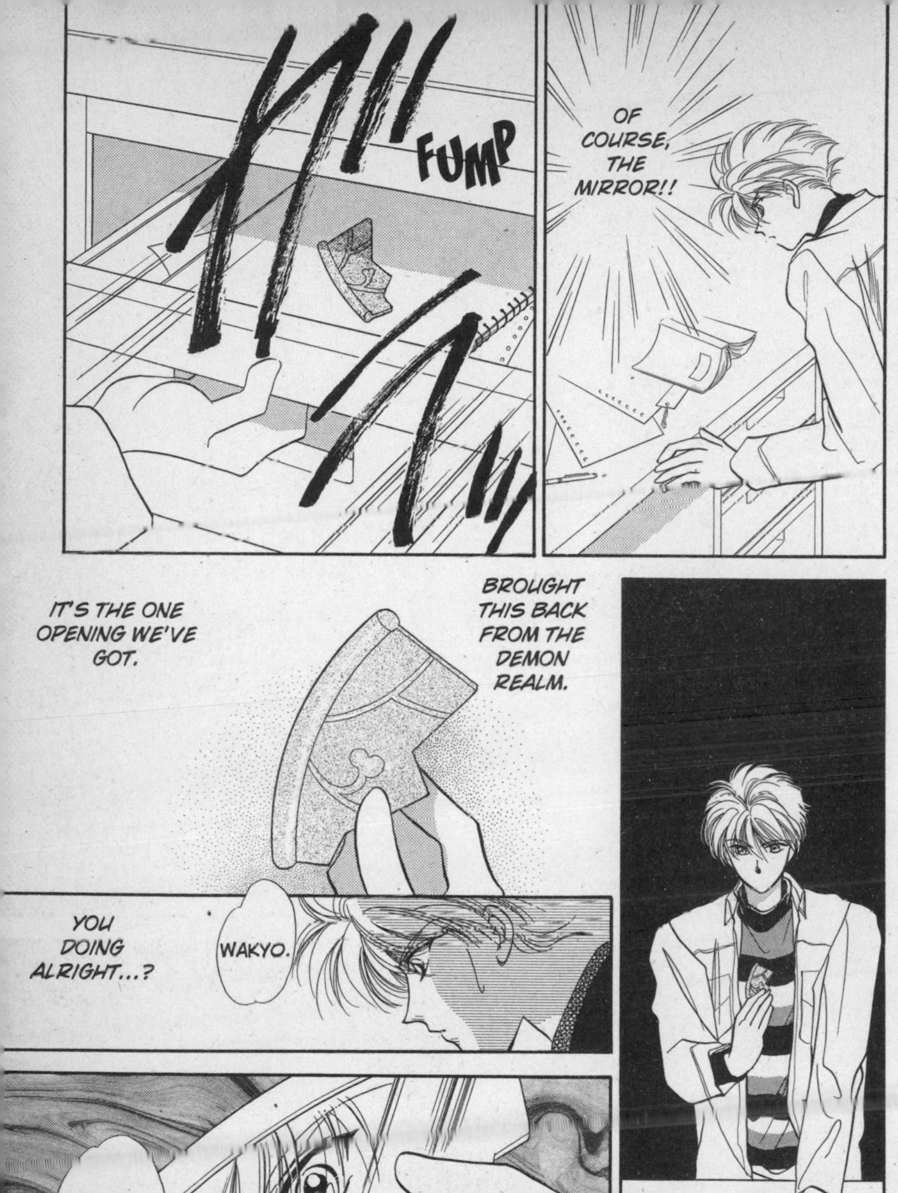
OF COURSE, THE MIRROR!!
FUMP
BROUGHT THIS BACK FROM THE DEMON REALM.
IT'S THE ONE OPENING WE'VE GOT.
WAKYO.
YOU DOING ALRIGHT...?
CAN YOU HEAR MY VOICE?

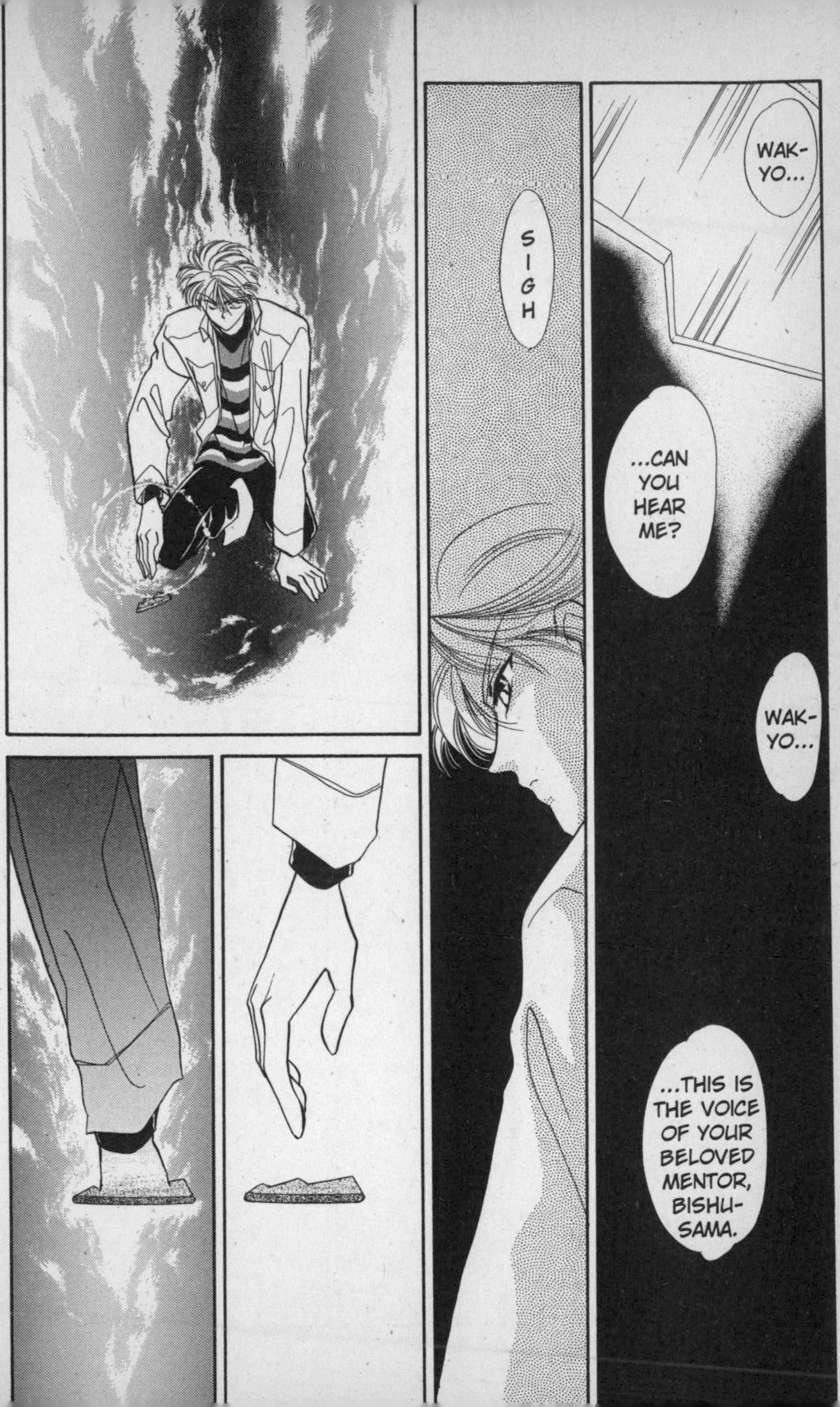
WAK-YO...
...CAN YOU HEAR ME?
WAK-YO...
...THIS IS THE VOICE OF YOUR BELOVED MENTOR, BISHU-SAMA.
SIGH

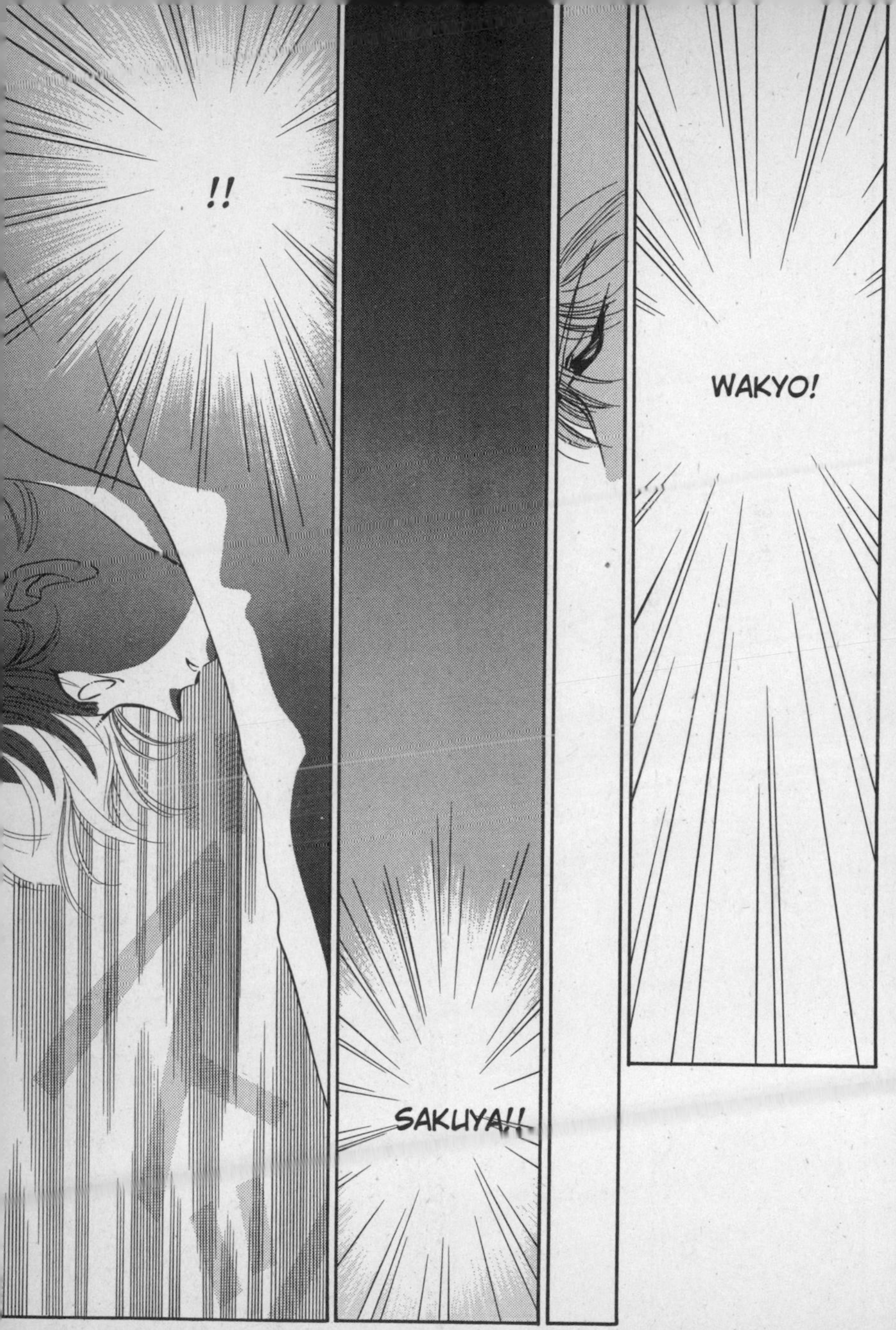
WAKYO!
SAKUYA!!
!!

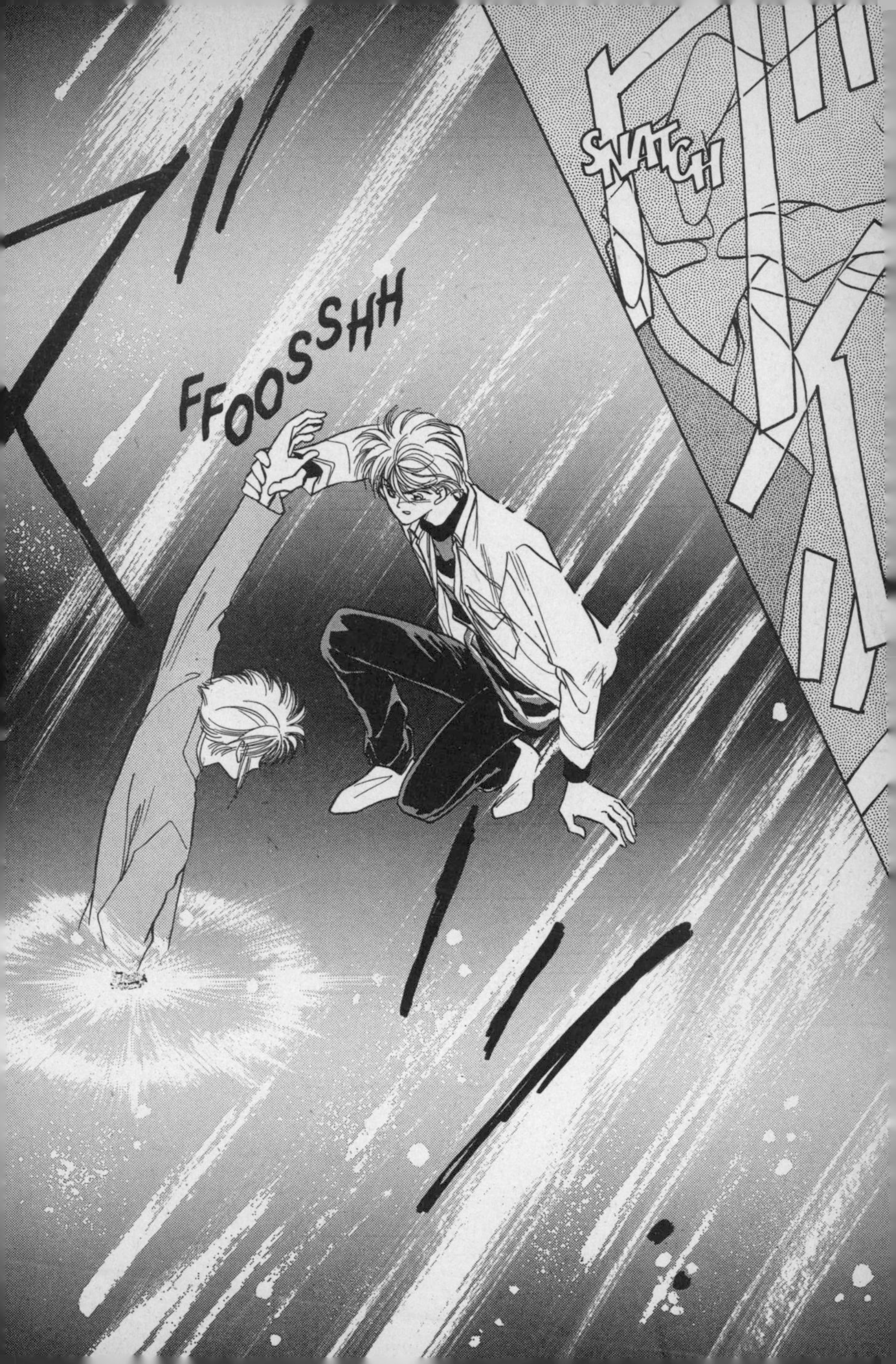
SNATCH
FFOOSSHH

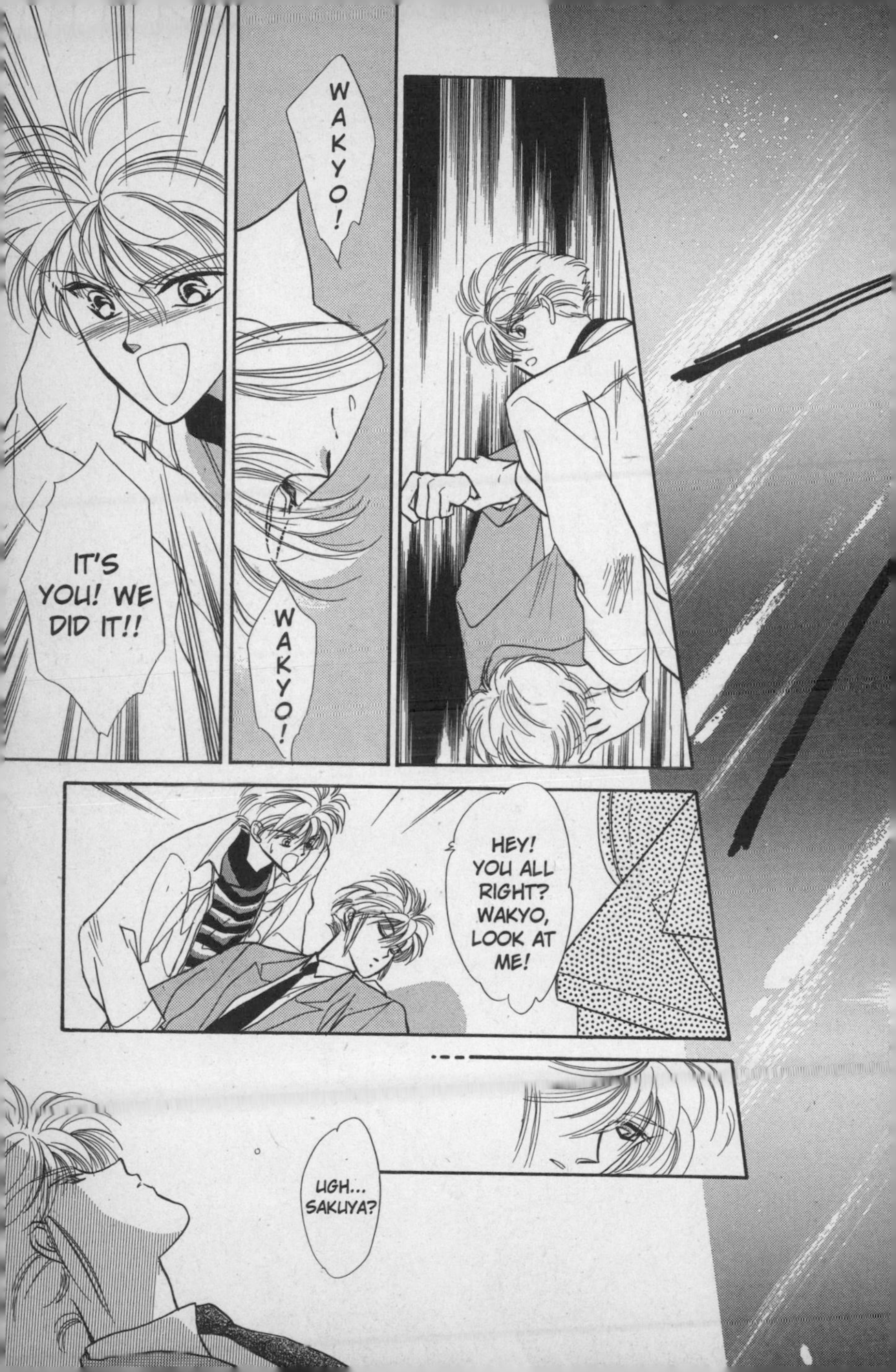
WAKYO!
WAKYO!
IT'S YOU! WE DID IT!!
HEY! YOU ALL RIGHT? WAKYO, LOOK AT ME!
UGH... SAKUYA?

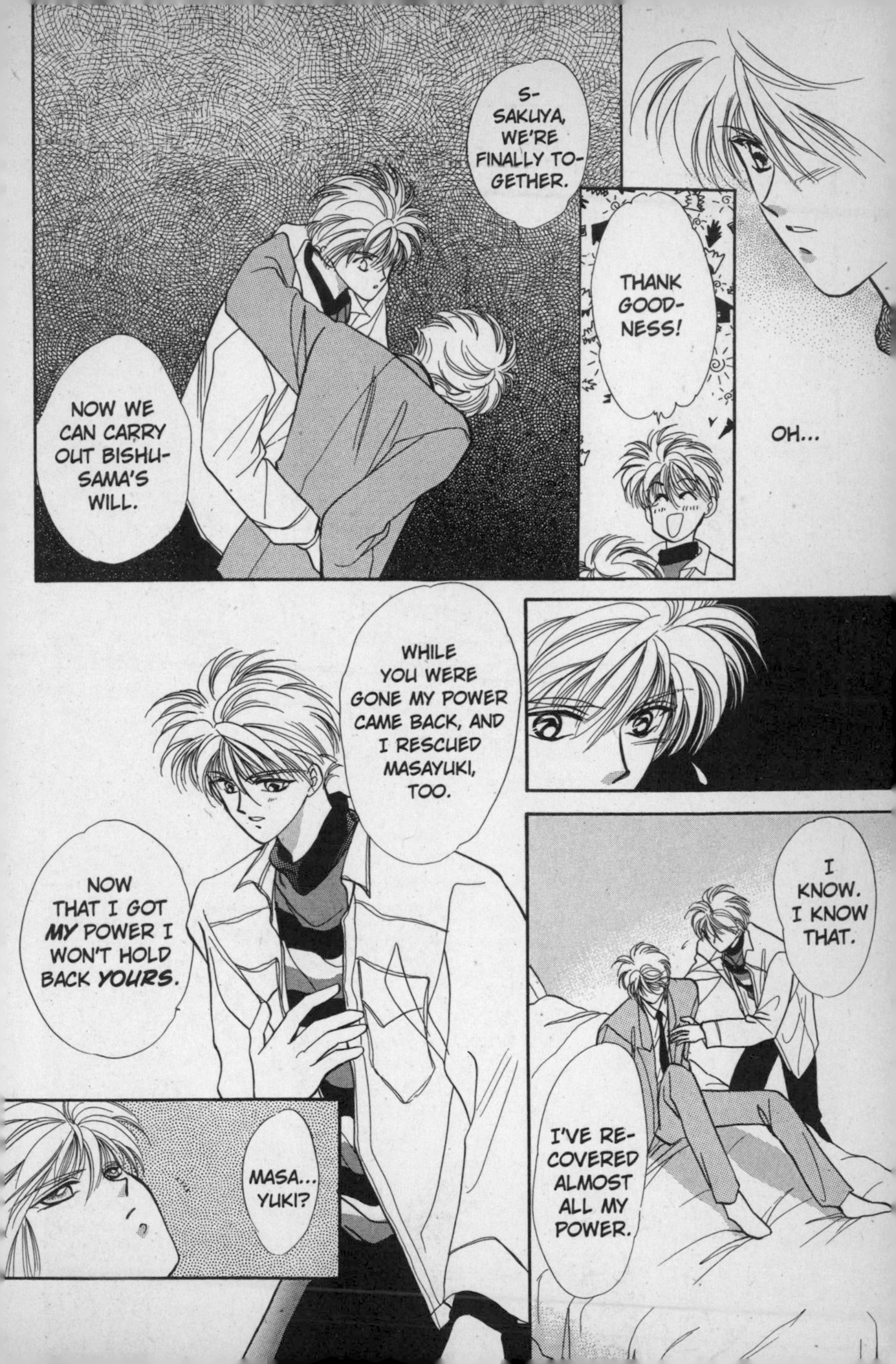
THANK GOODNESS!
OH...
S-SAKUYA, WE'RE FINALLY TOGETHER.
NOW WE CAN CARRY OUT BISHU-SAMA'S WILL.
WHILE YOU WERE GONE MY POWER CAME BACK, AND I RESCUED MASAYUKI, TOO.
NOW THAT I GOT *MY* POWER I WON'T HOLD BACK *YOURS*.
I KNOW. I KNOW THAT.
I'VE RECOVERED ALMOST ALL MY POWER.
MASA... YUKI?

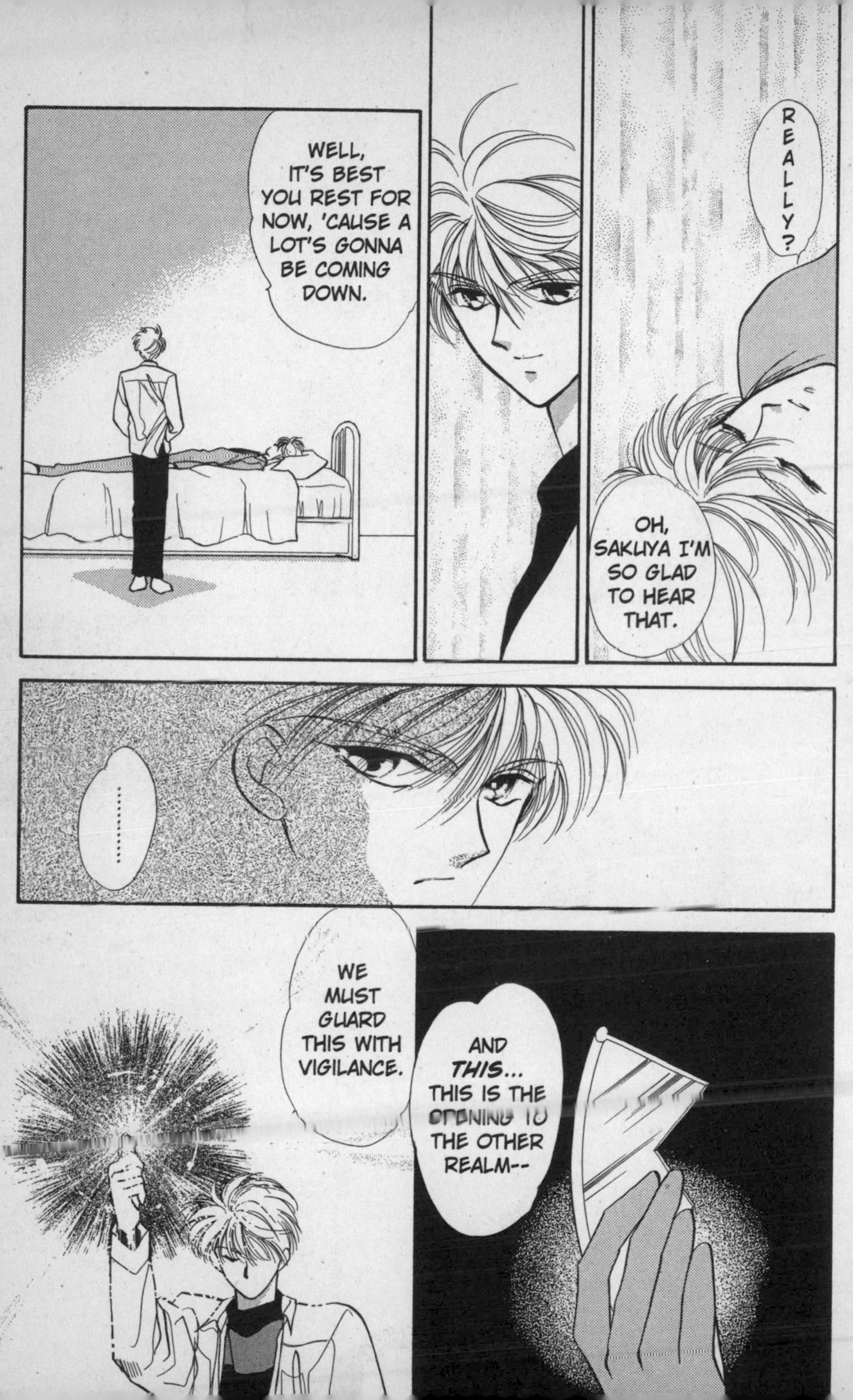
REALLY?
OH, SAKUYA I'M SO GLAD TO HEAR THAT.
WELL, IT'S BEST YOU REST FOR NOW, 'CAUSE A LOT'S GONNA BE COMING DOWN.
......
AND *THIS*... THIS IS THE OPENING TO THE OTHER REALM--
WE MUST GUARD THIS WITH VIGILANCE.

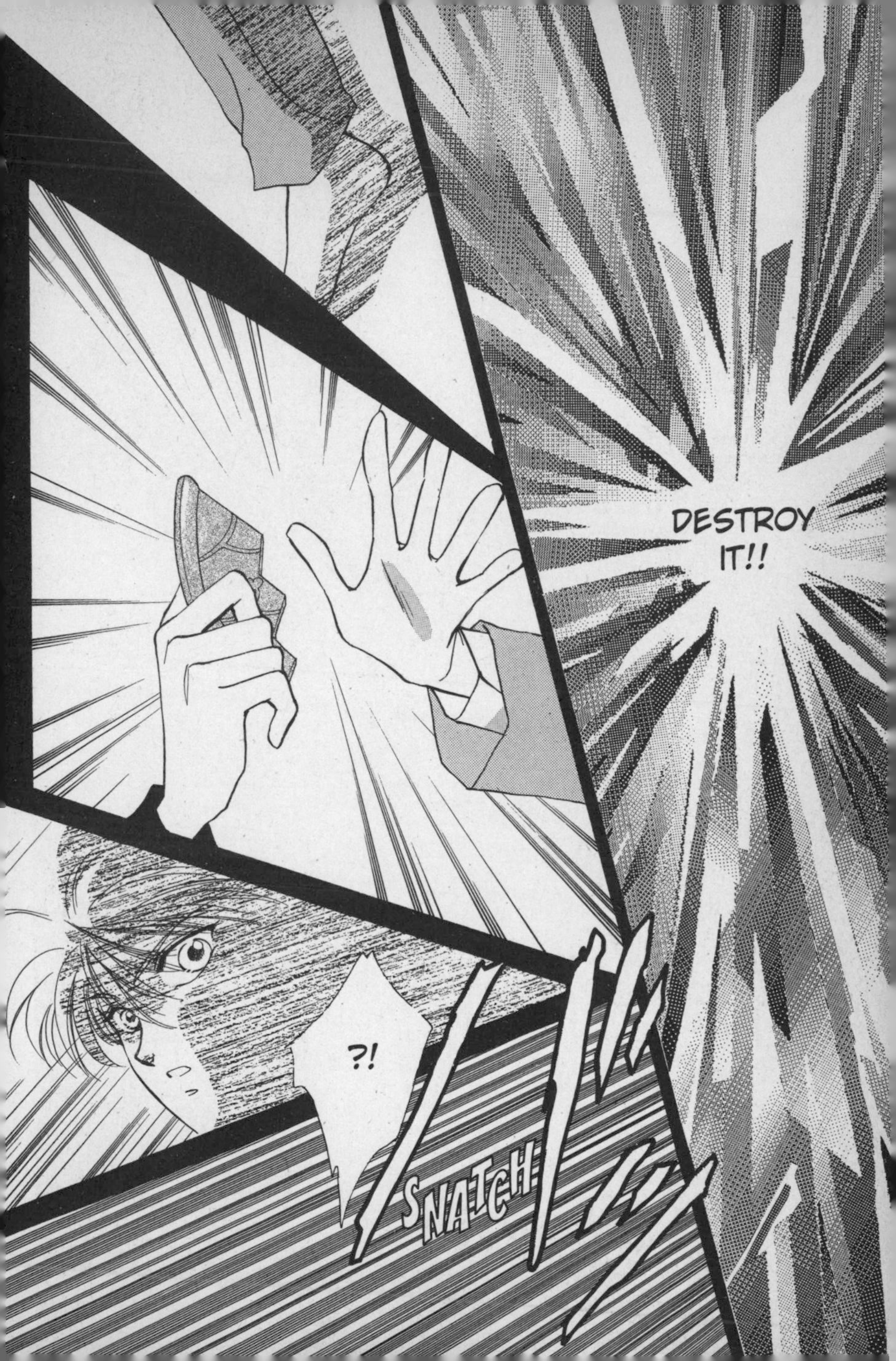
DESTROY IT!!
?!
SNATCH

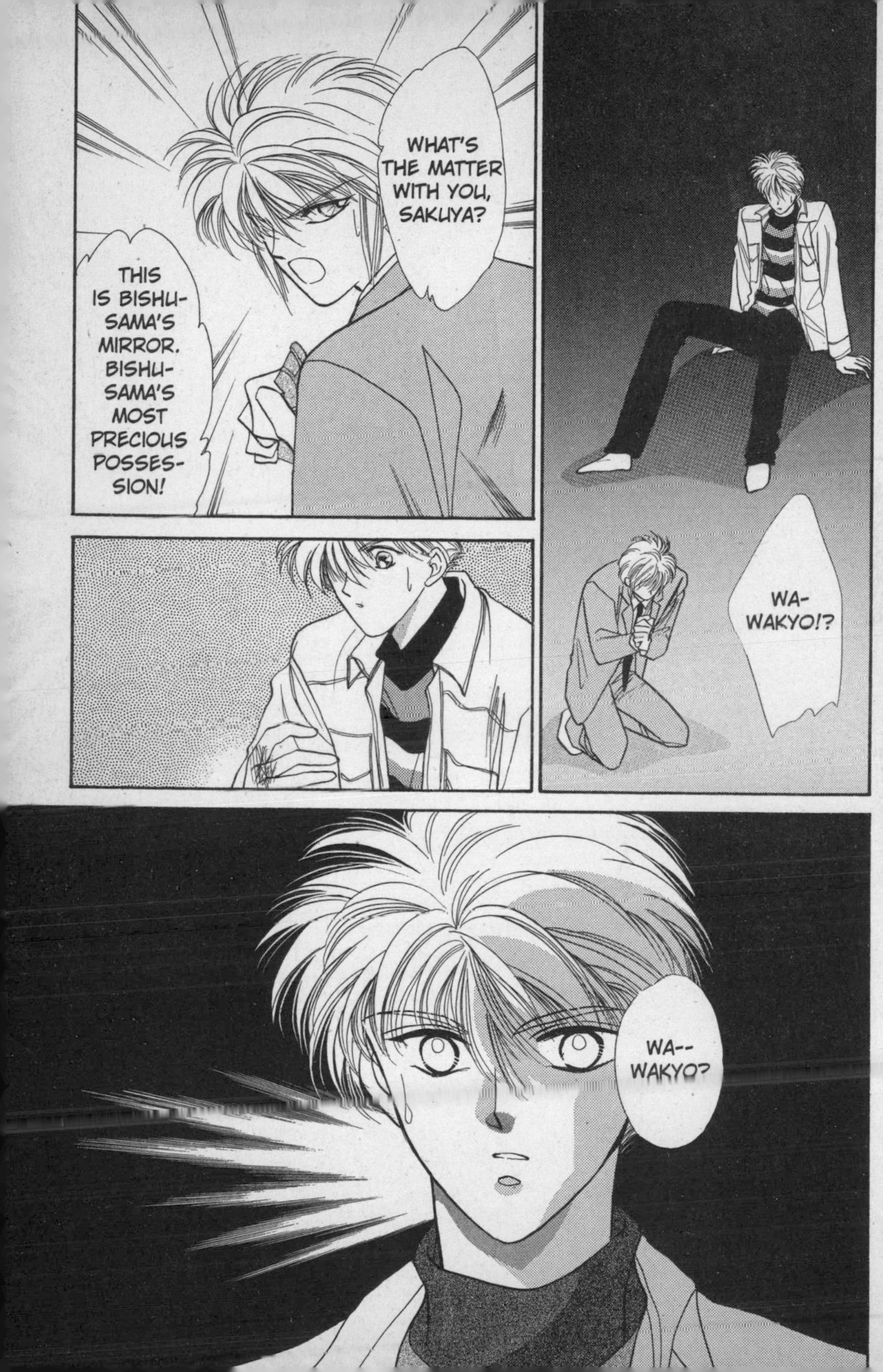
WA-WAKYO!?
WHAT'S THE MATTER WITH YOU, SAKUYA?
THIS IS BISHU-SAMA'S MIRROR. BISHU-SAMA'S MOST PRECIOUS POSSESSION!
WA--WAKYO?

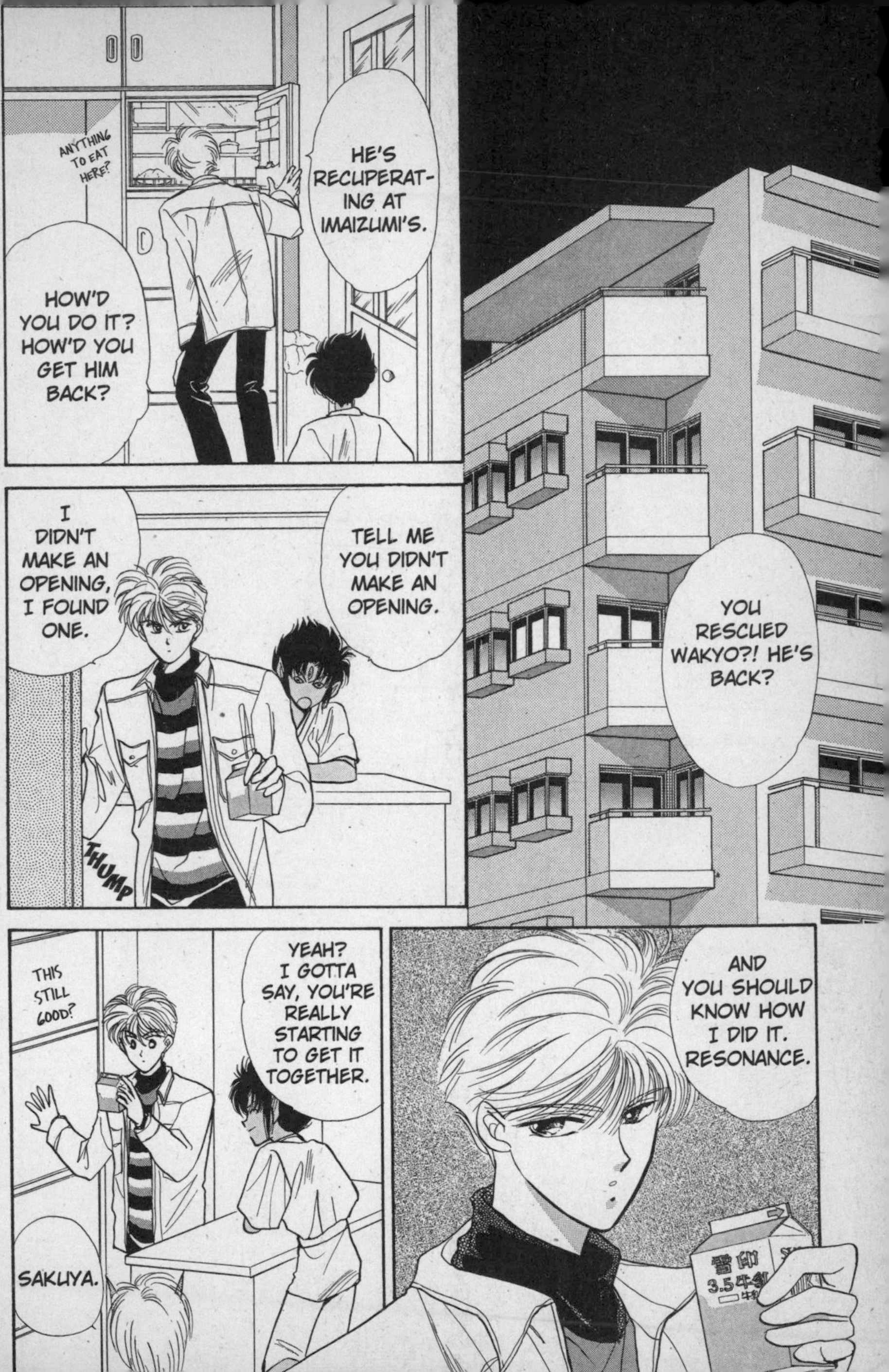
YOU RESCUED WAKYO?! HE'S BACK?
HE'S RECUPERAT-ING AT IMAIZUMI'S.
ANYTHING TO EAT HERE?
HOW'D YOU DO IT? HOW'D YOU GET HIM BACK?
TELL ME YOU DIDN'T MAKE AN OPENING.
I DIDN'T MAKE AN OPENING, I FOUND ONE.
THUMP
AND YOU SHOULD KNOW HOW I DID IT. RESONANCE.
YEAH? I GOTTA SAY, YOU'RE REALLY STARTING TO GET IT TOGETHER.
THIS STILL GOOD?
SAKUYA.

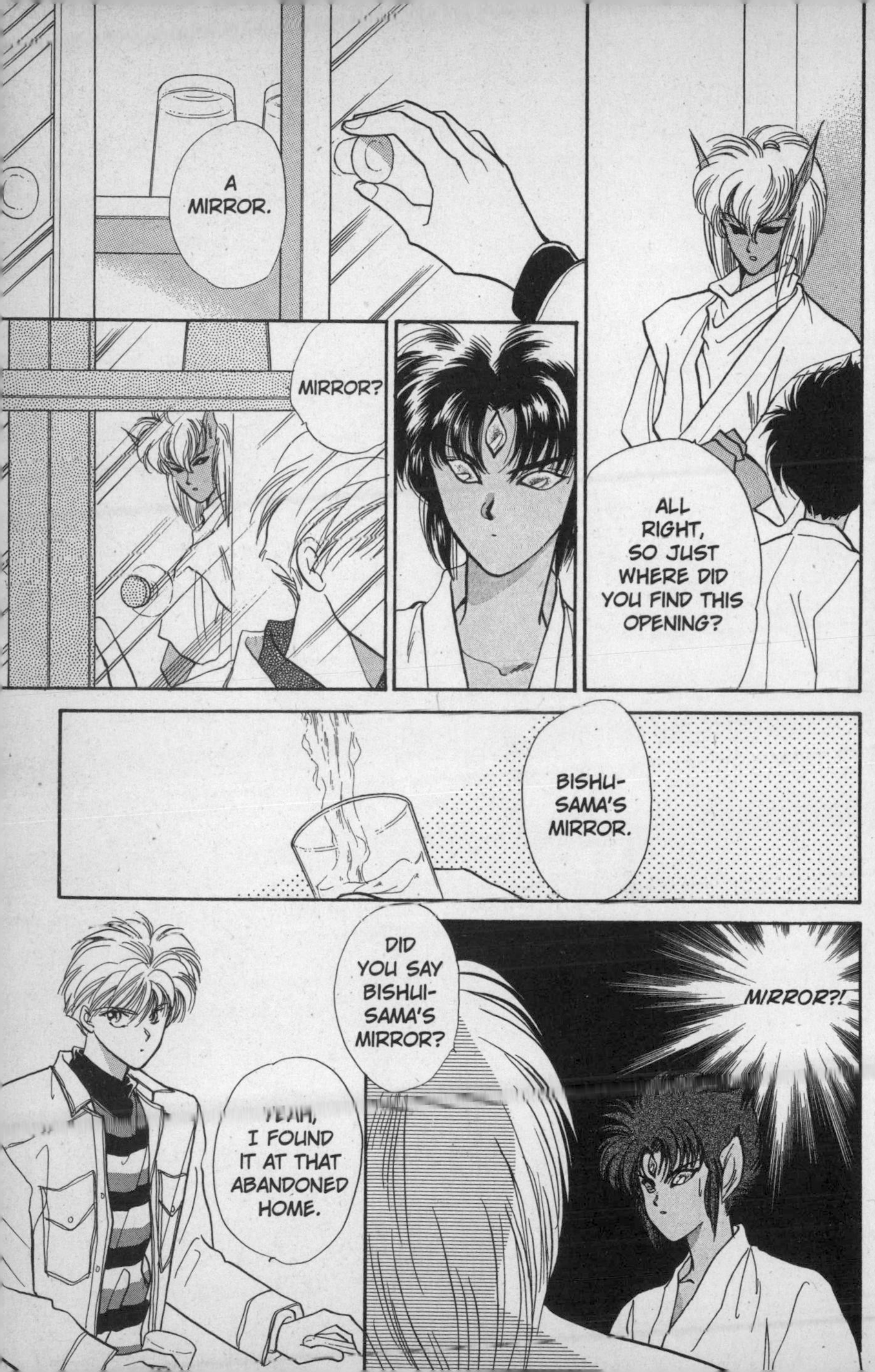
ALL RIGHT, SO JUST WHERE DID YOU FIND THIS OPENING?
A MIRROR.
MIRROR?
BISHU-SAMA'S MIRROR.
MIRROR?!
DID YOU SAY BISHUI-SAMA'S MIRROR?
YEAH, I FOUND IT AT THAT ABANDONED HOME.

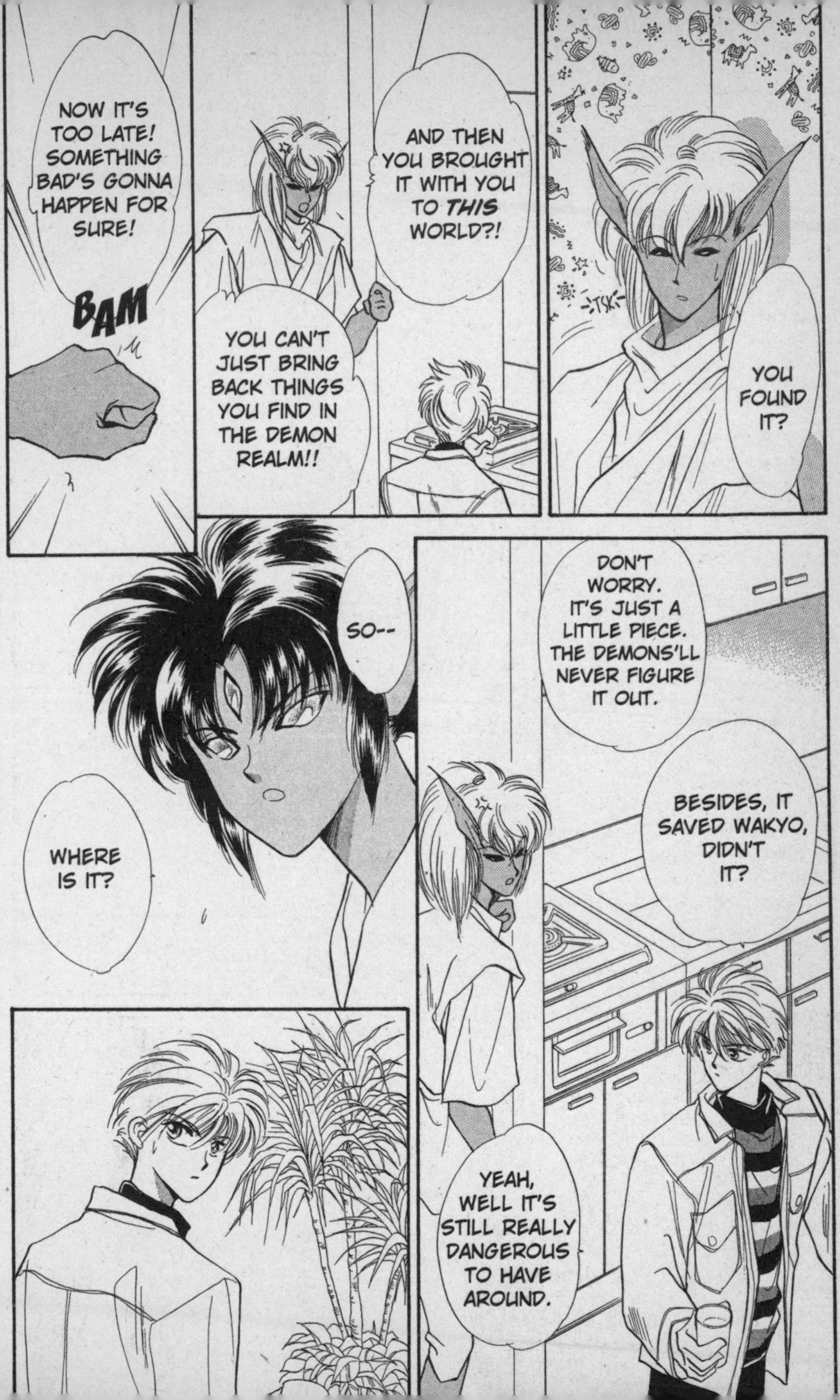
TSK
YOU FOUND IT?
AND THEN YOU BROUGHT IT WITH YOU TO *THIS* WORLD?!
YOU CAN'T JUST BRING BACK THINGS YOU FIND IN THE DEMON REALM!!
NOW IT'S TOO LATE! SOMETHING BAD'S GONNA HAPPEN FOR SURE!
BAM
DON'T WORRY. IT'S JUST A LITTLE PIECE. THE DEMONS'LL NEVER FIGURE IT OUT.
BESIDES, IT SAVED WAKYO, DIDN'T IT?
YEAH, WELL IT'S STILL REALLY DANGEROUS TO HAVE AROUND.
SO--
WHERE IS IT?

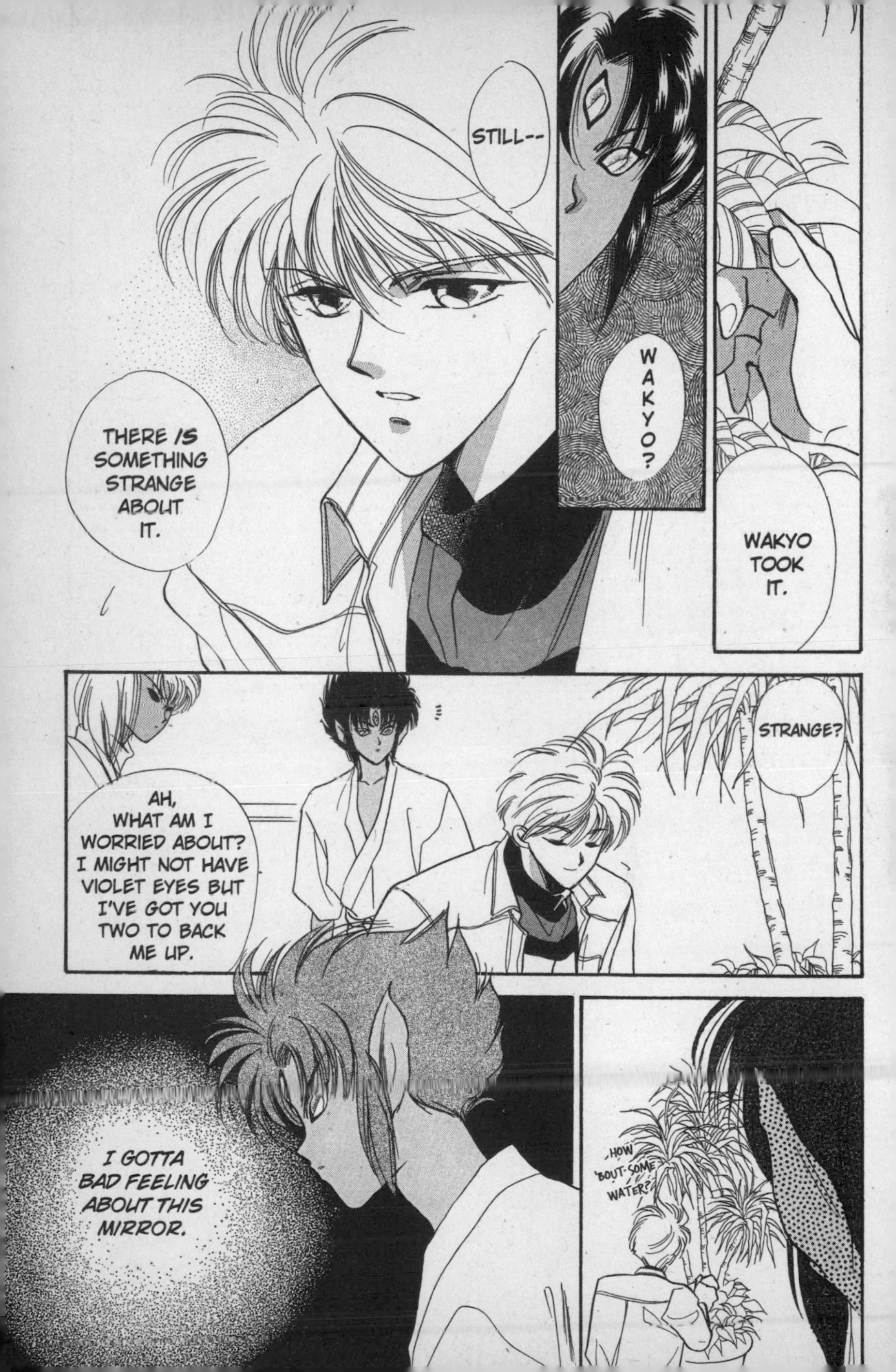
WAKYO TOOK IT.
WAKYO?
STILL--
THERE IS SOMETHING STRANGE ABOUT IT.
STRANGE?
AH, WHAT AM I WORRIED ABOUT? I MIGHT NOT HAVE VIOLET EYES BUT I'VE GOT YOU TWO TO BACK ME UP.
HOW 'BOUT SOME WATER?
I GOTTA BAD FEELING ABOUT THIS MIRROR.

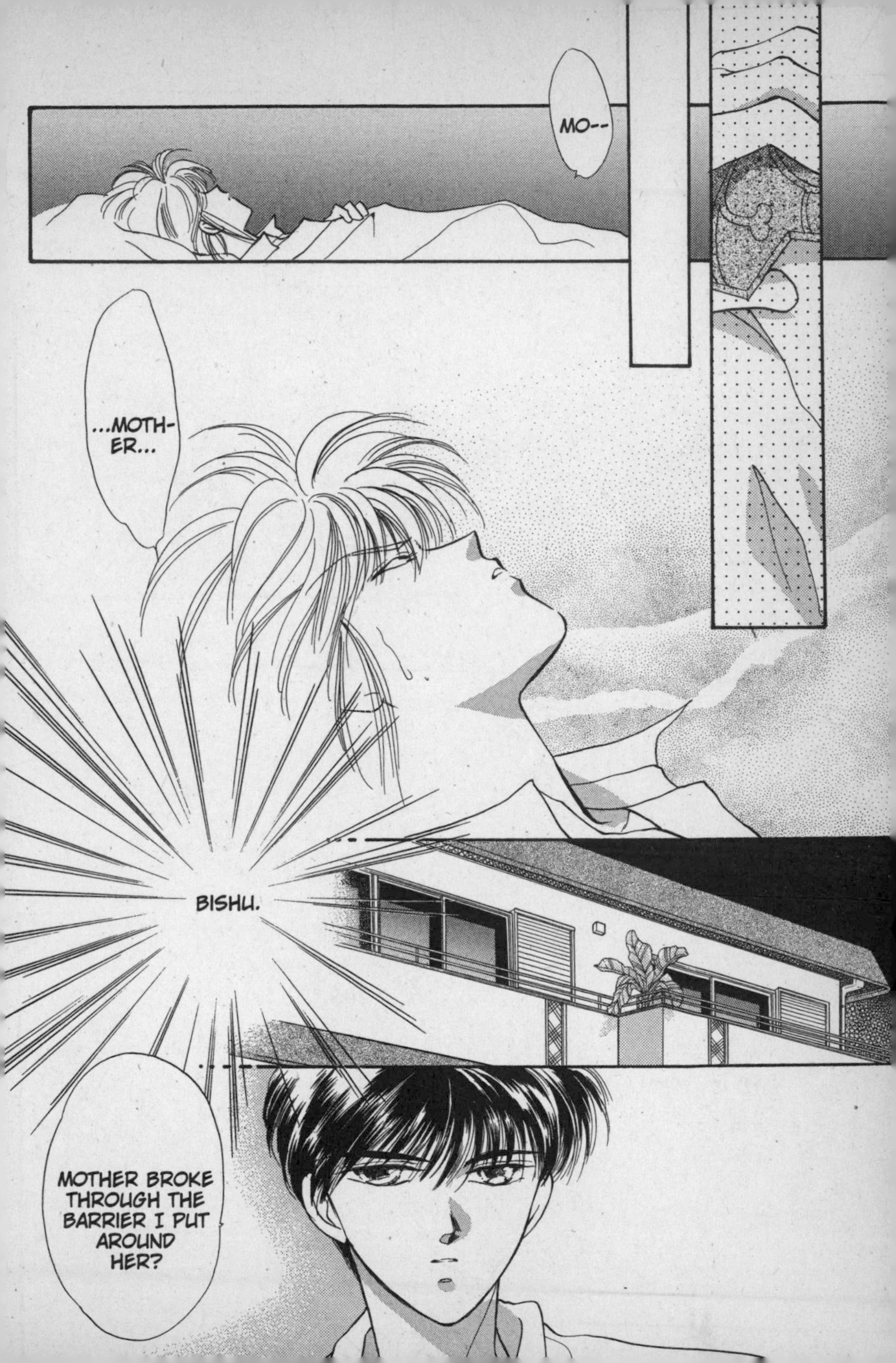
MO--
...MOTH-
ER...
BISHU.
MOTHER BROKE
THROUGH THE
BARRIER I PUT
AROUND
HER?

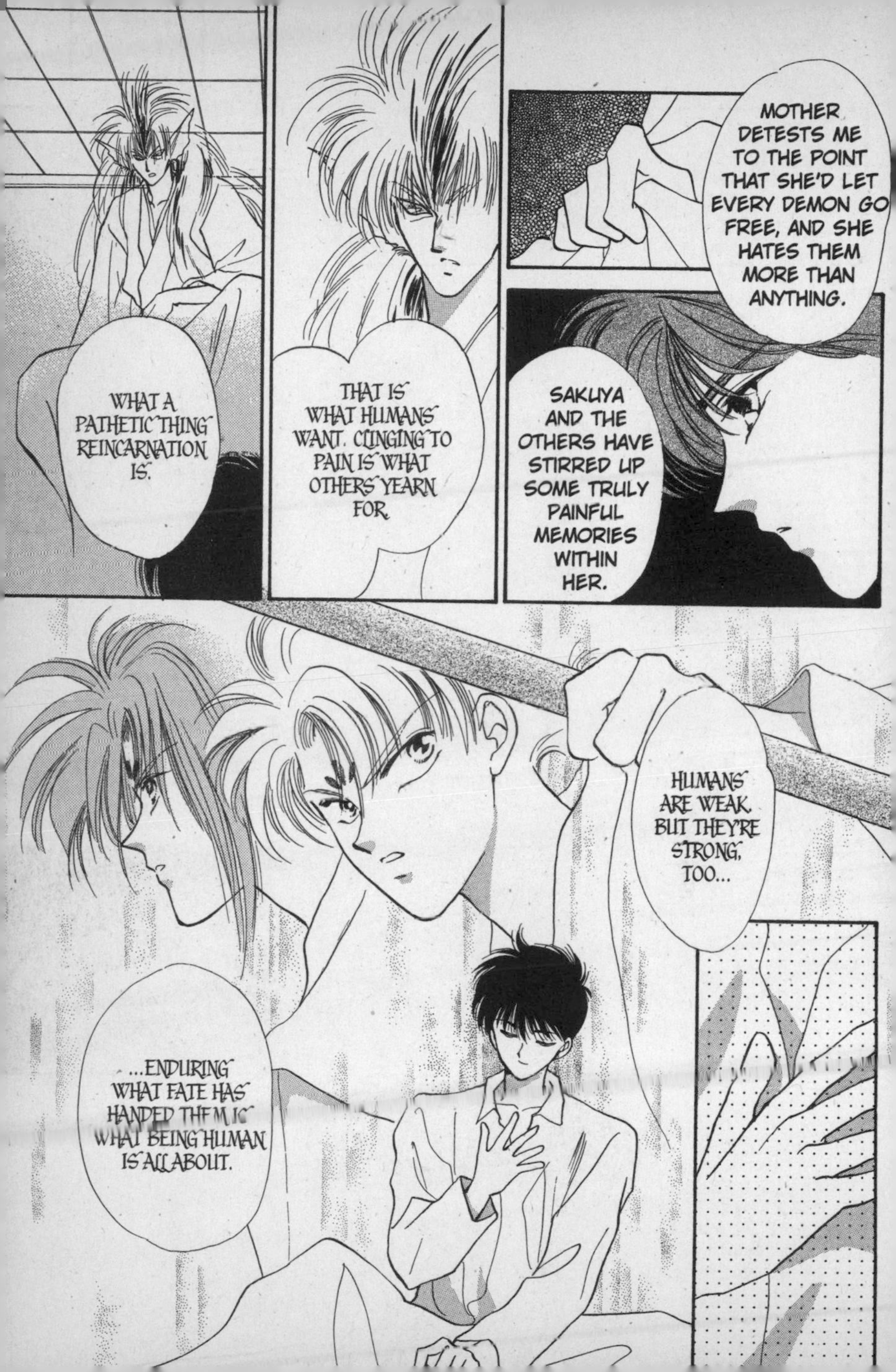
MOTHER DETESTS ME TO THE POINT THAT SHE'D LET EVERY DEMON GO FREE, AND SHE HATES THEM MORE THAN ANYTHING.
SAKUYA AND THE OTHERS HAVE STIRRED UP SOME TRULY PAINFUL MEMORIES WITHIN HER.
THAT IS WHAT HUMANS WANT. CLINGING TO PAIN IS WHAT OTHERS YEARN FOR.
WHAT A PATHETIC THING REINCARNATION IS.
HUMANS ARE WEAK. BUT THEY'RE STRONG, TOO...
...ENDURING WHAT FATE HAS HANDED THEM IS WHAT BEING HUMAN IS ALL ABOUT.

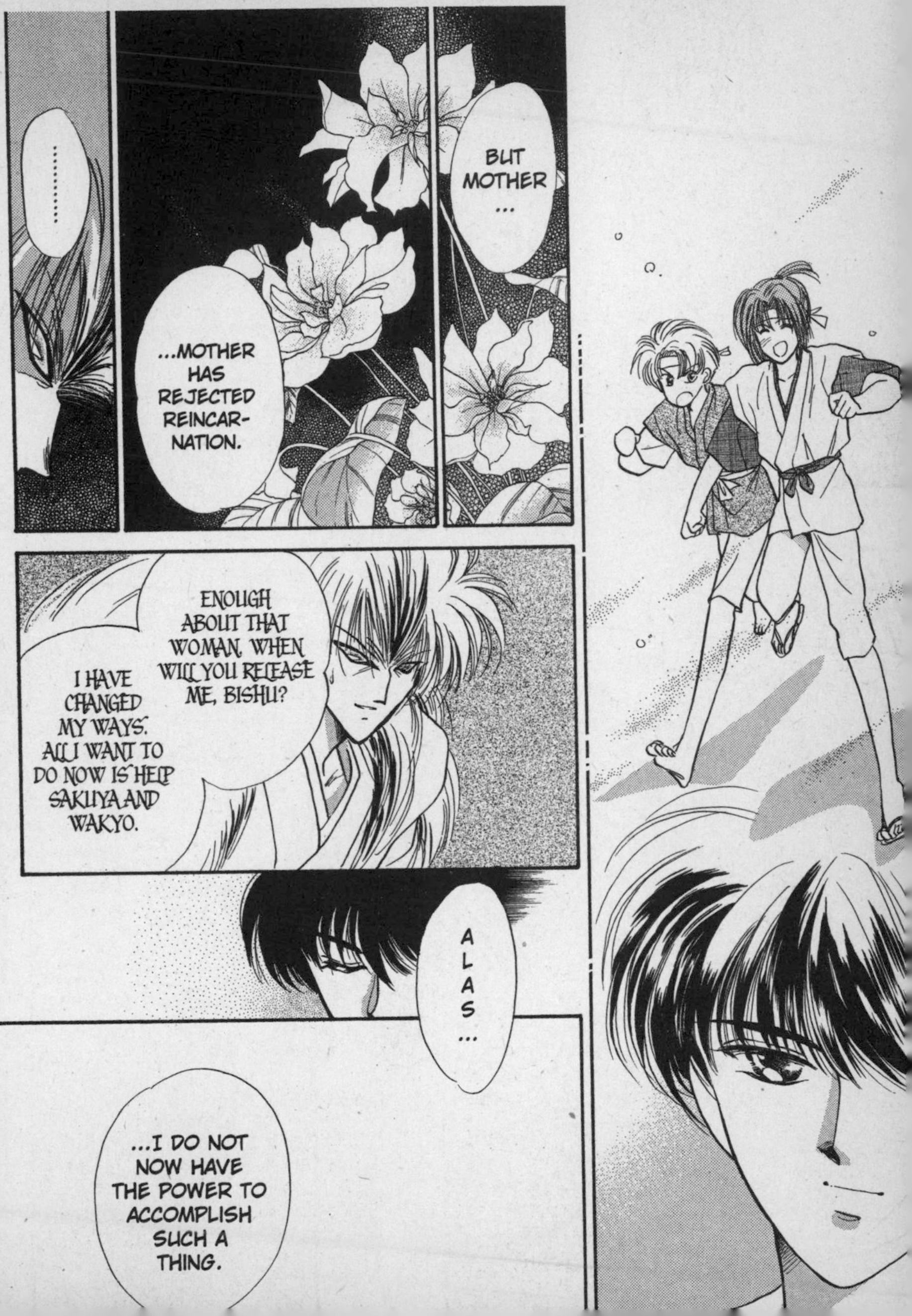
BUT MOTHER ...
...MOTHER HAS REJECTED REINCAR-NATION.
......
ENOUGH ABOUT THAT WOMAN. WHEN WILL YOU RELEASE ME, BISHU?
I HAVE CHANGED MY WAYS. ALL I WANT TO DO NOW IS HELP SAKUYA AND WAKYO.
ALAS ...
...I DO NOT NOW HAVE THE POWER TO ACCOMPLISH SUCH A THING.

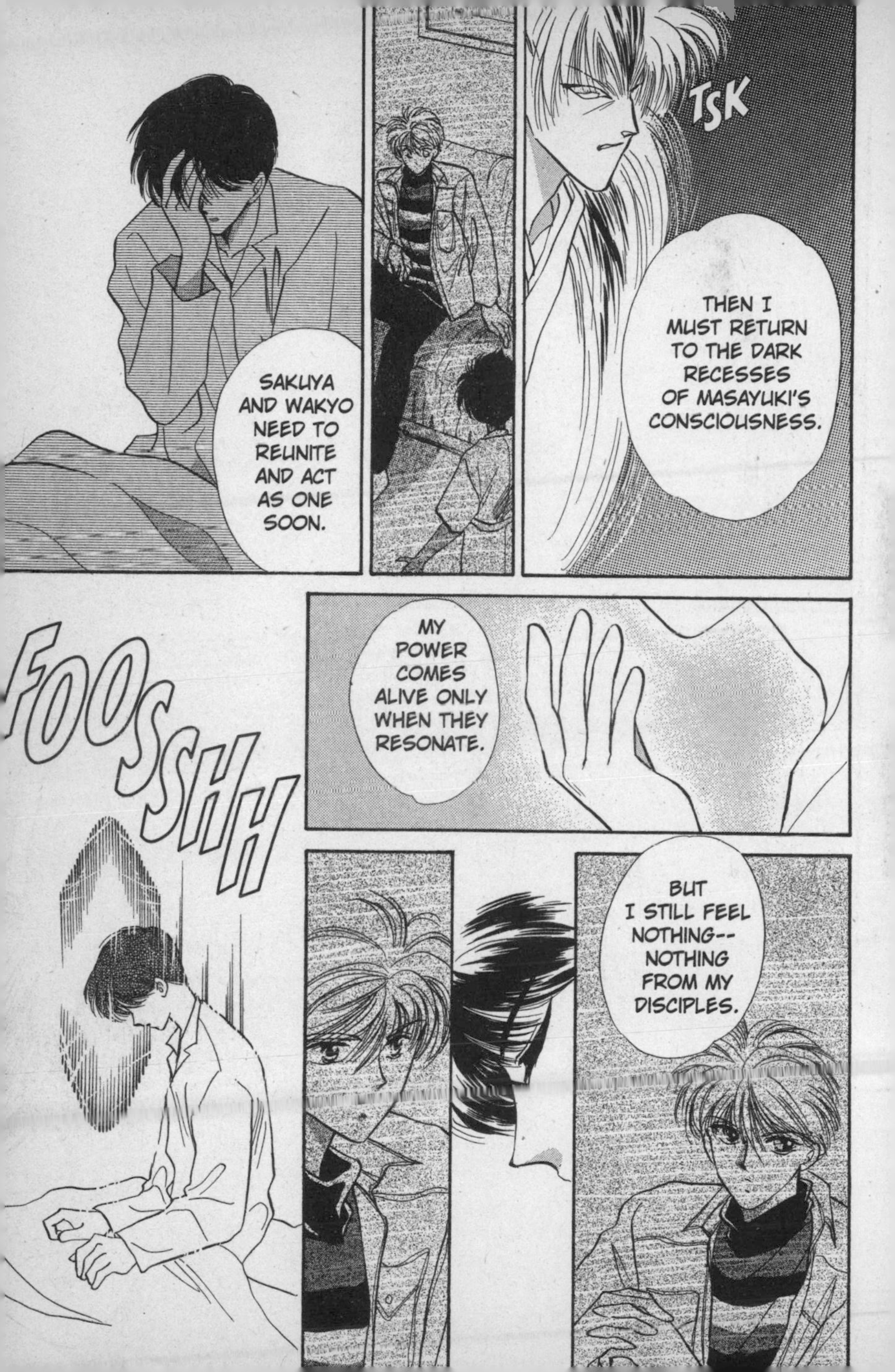
TSK
THEN I MUST RETURN TO THE DARK RECESSES OF MASAYUKI'S CONSCIOUSNESS.
SAKUYA AND WAKYO NEED TO REUNITE AND ACT AS ONE SOON.
MY POWER COMES ALIVE ONLY WHEN THEY RESONATE.
BUT I STILL FEEL NOTHING-- NOTHING FROM MY DISCIPLES.
FOOSSHH

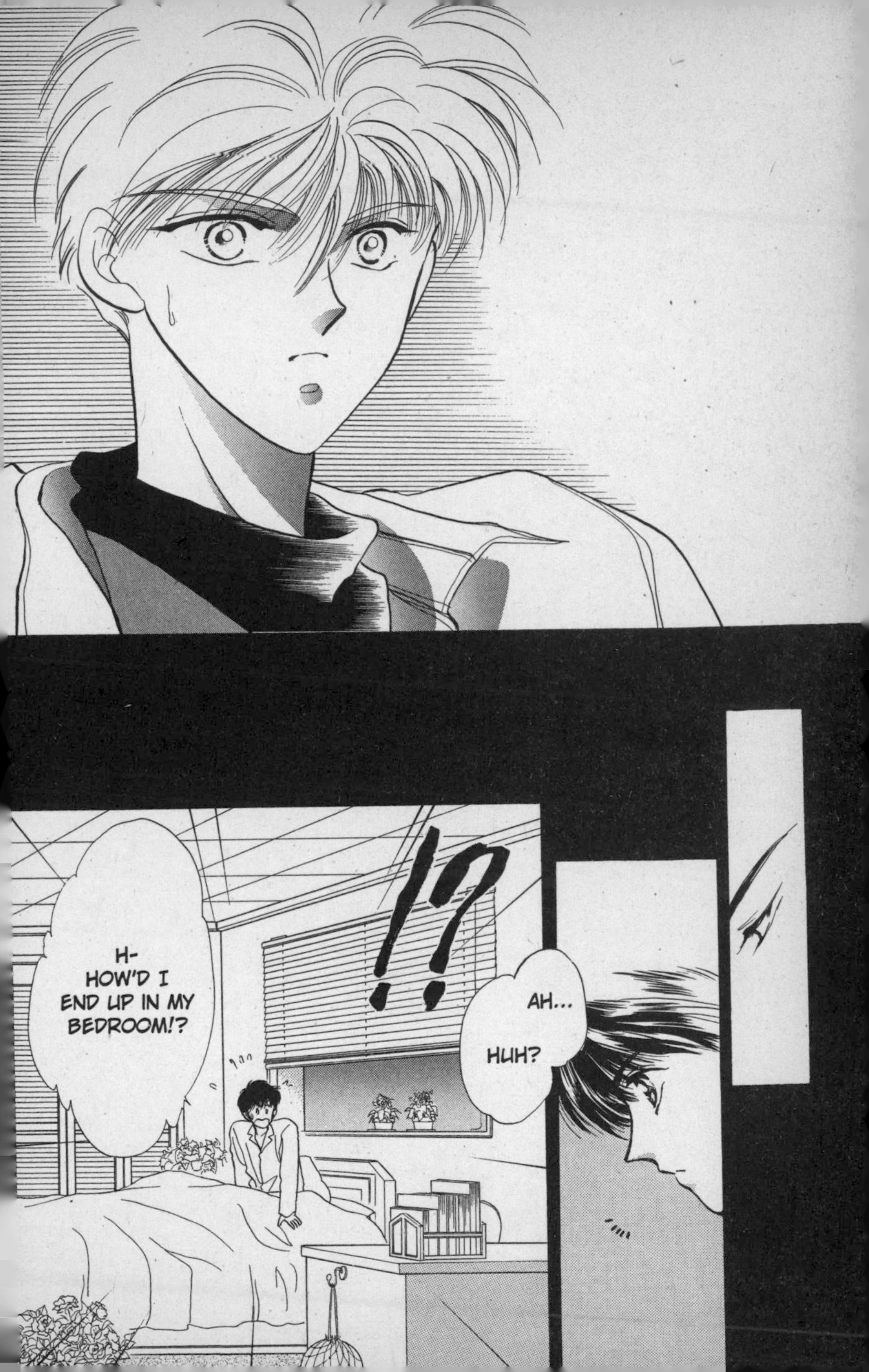
AH...
HUH?
!?
H- HOW'D I END UP IN MY BEDROOM!?

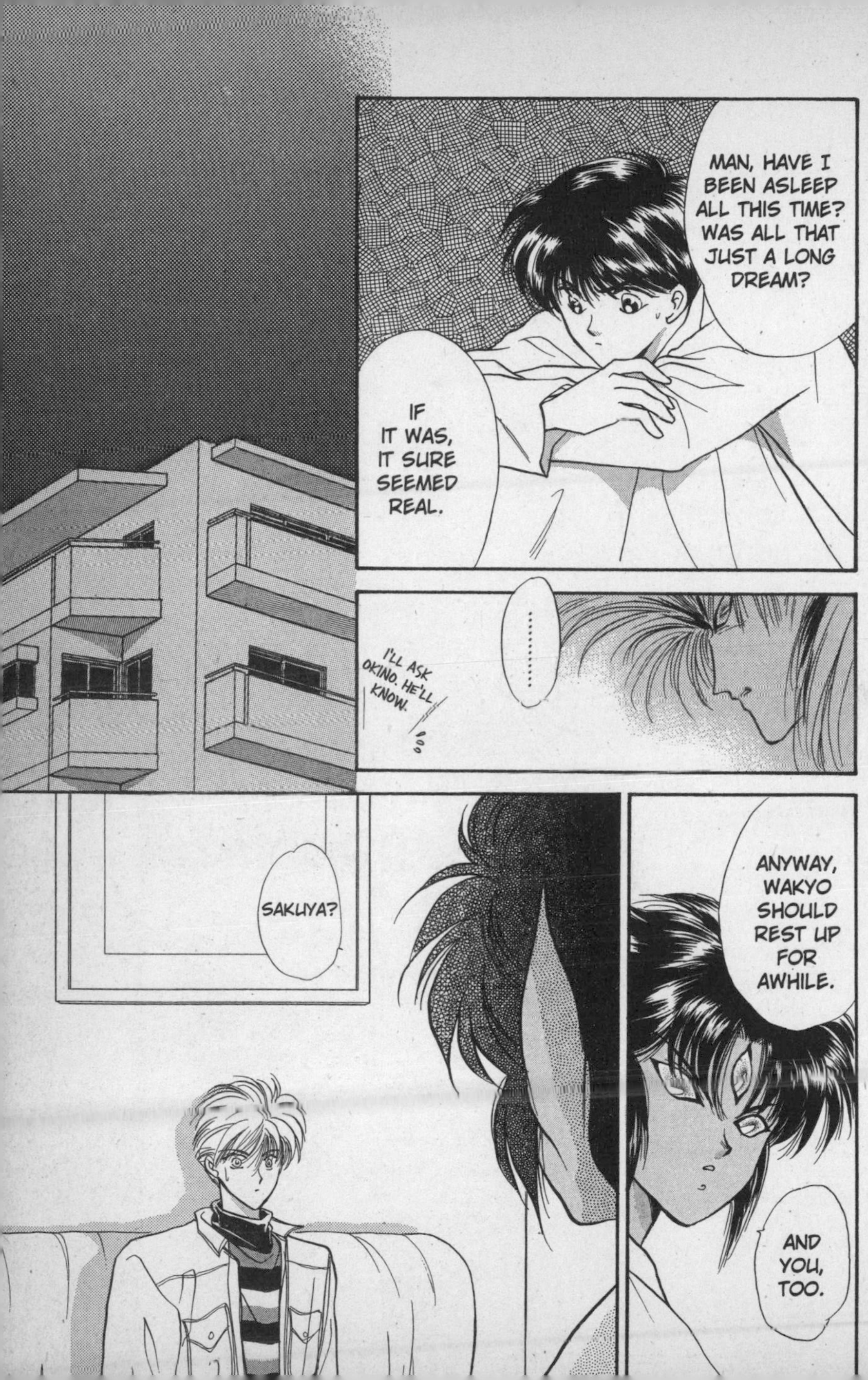
MAN, HAVE I BEEN ASLEEP ALL THIS TIME? WAS ALL THAT JUST A LONG DREAM?
IF IT WAS, IT SURE SEEMED REAL.
......
I'LL ASK OKINO. HE'LL KNOW.
ANYWAY, WAKYO SHOULD REST UP FOR AWHILE.
AND YOU, TOO.
SAKUYA?

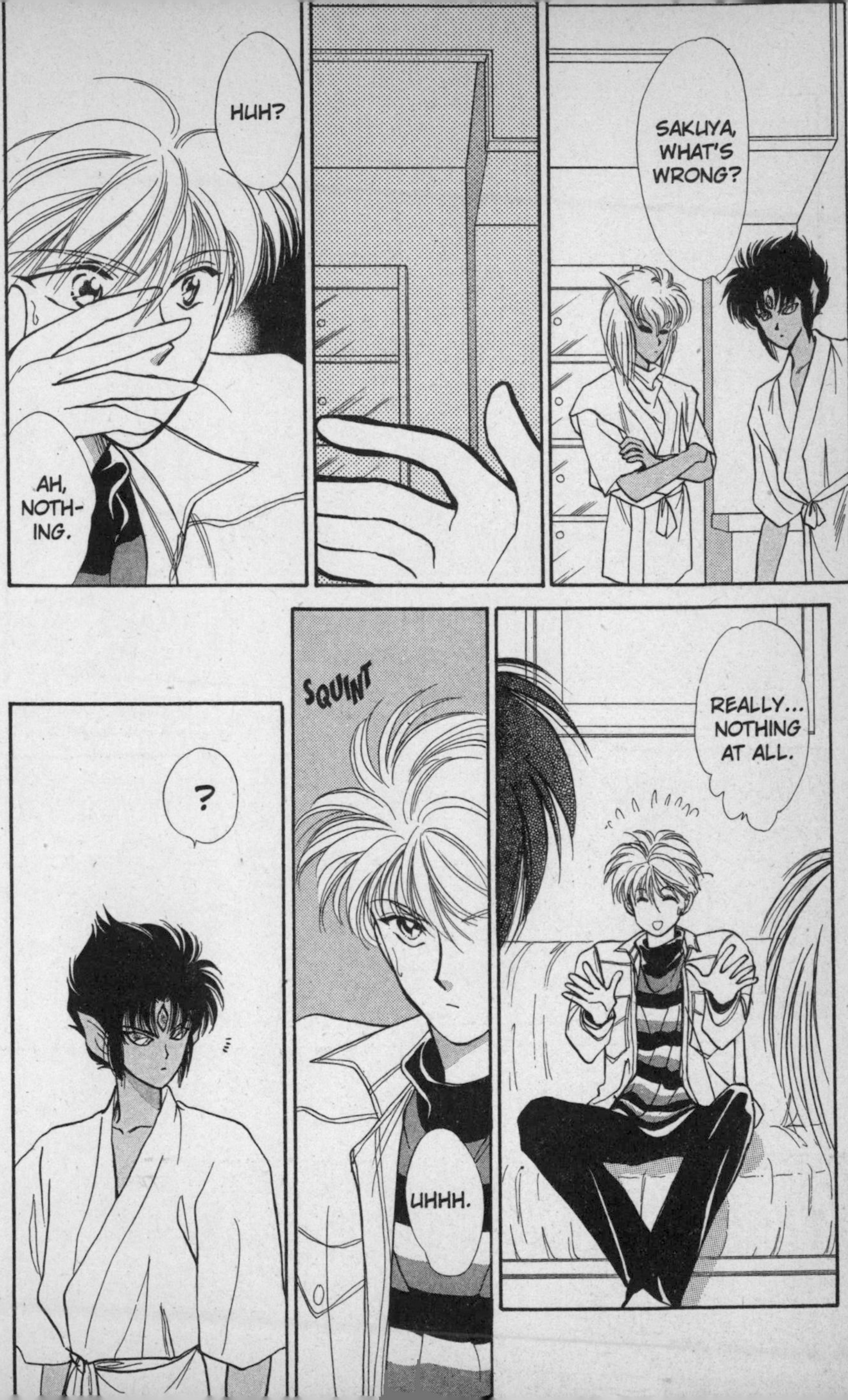
SAKUYA, WHAT'S WRONG?
HUH?
AH, NOTH-ING.
REALLY... NOTHING AT ALL.
SQUINT
UHHH.
?

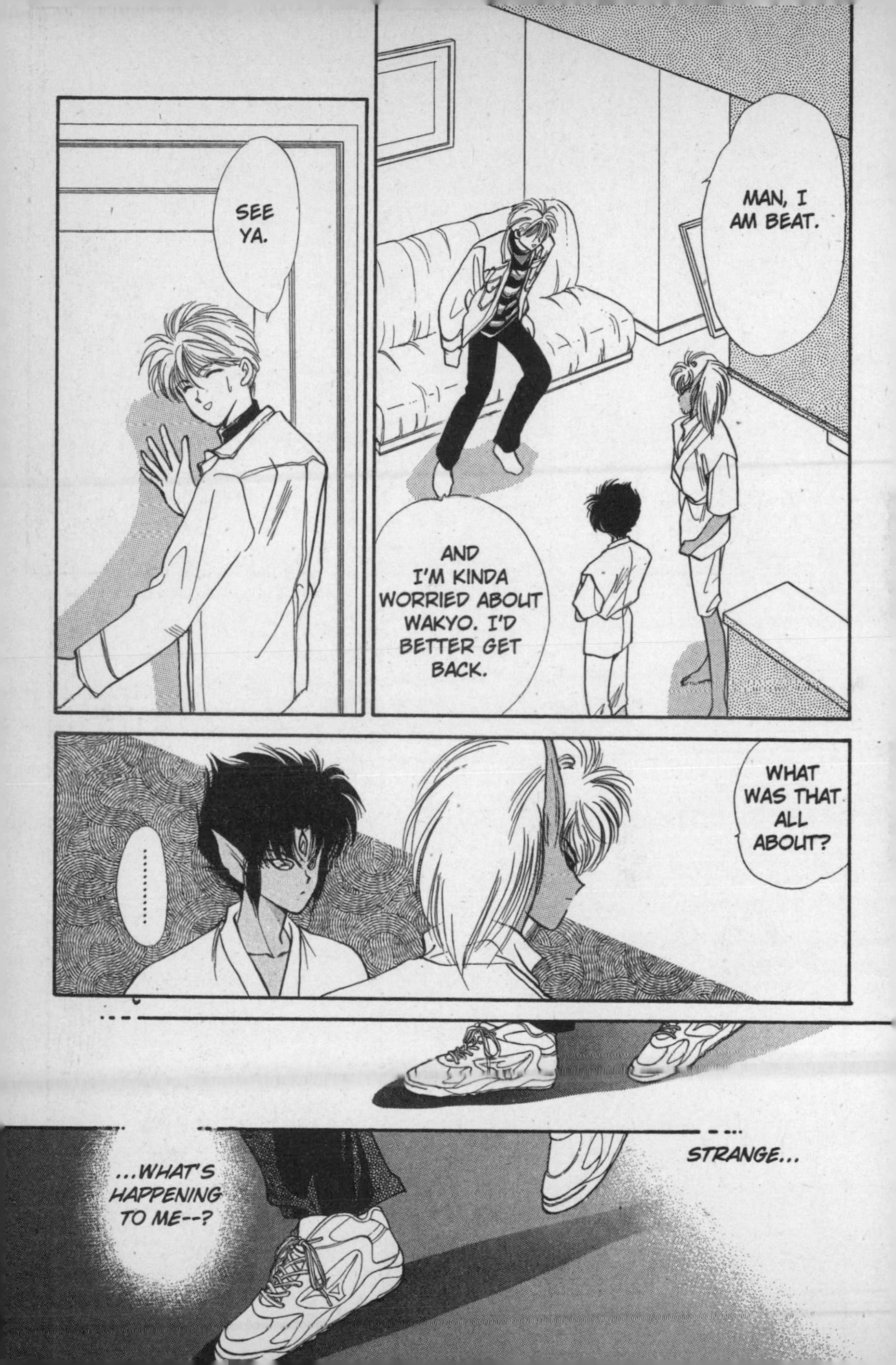

MAN, I AM BEAT.
AND I'M KINDA WORRIED ABOUT WAKYO. I'D BETTER GET BACK.
SEE YA.
WHAT WAS THAT ALL ABOUT?
......
STRANGE...
...WHAT'S HAPPENING TO ME--?

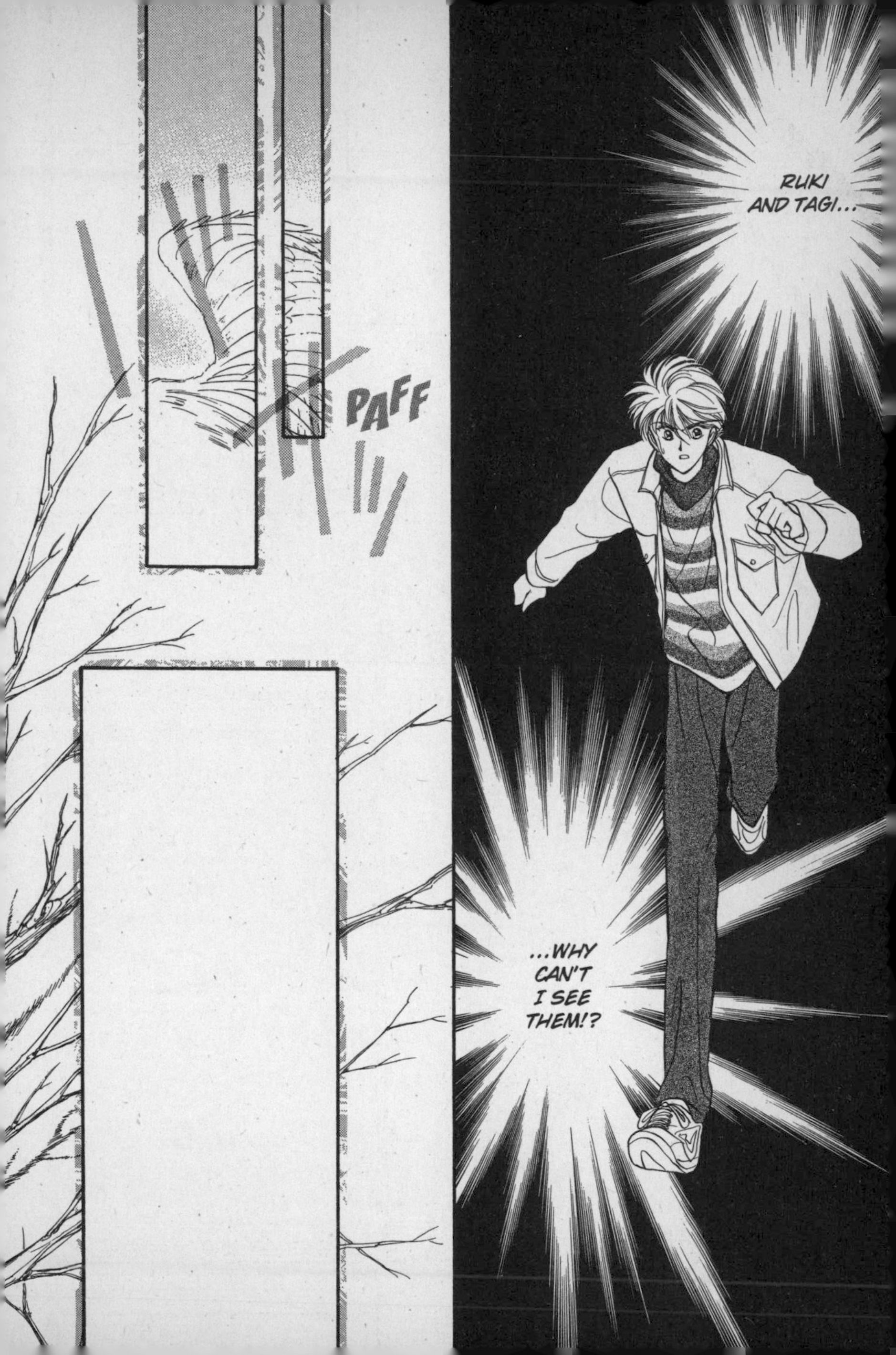
RUKI AND TAGI...
...WHY CAN'T I SEE THEM!?
PAFF

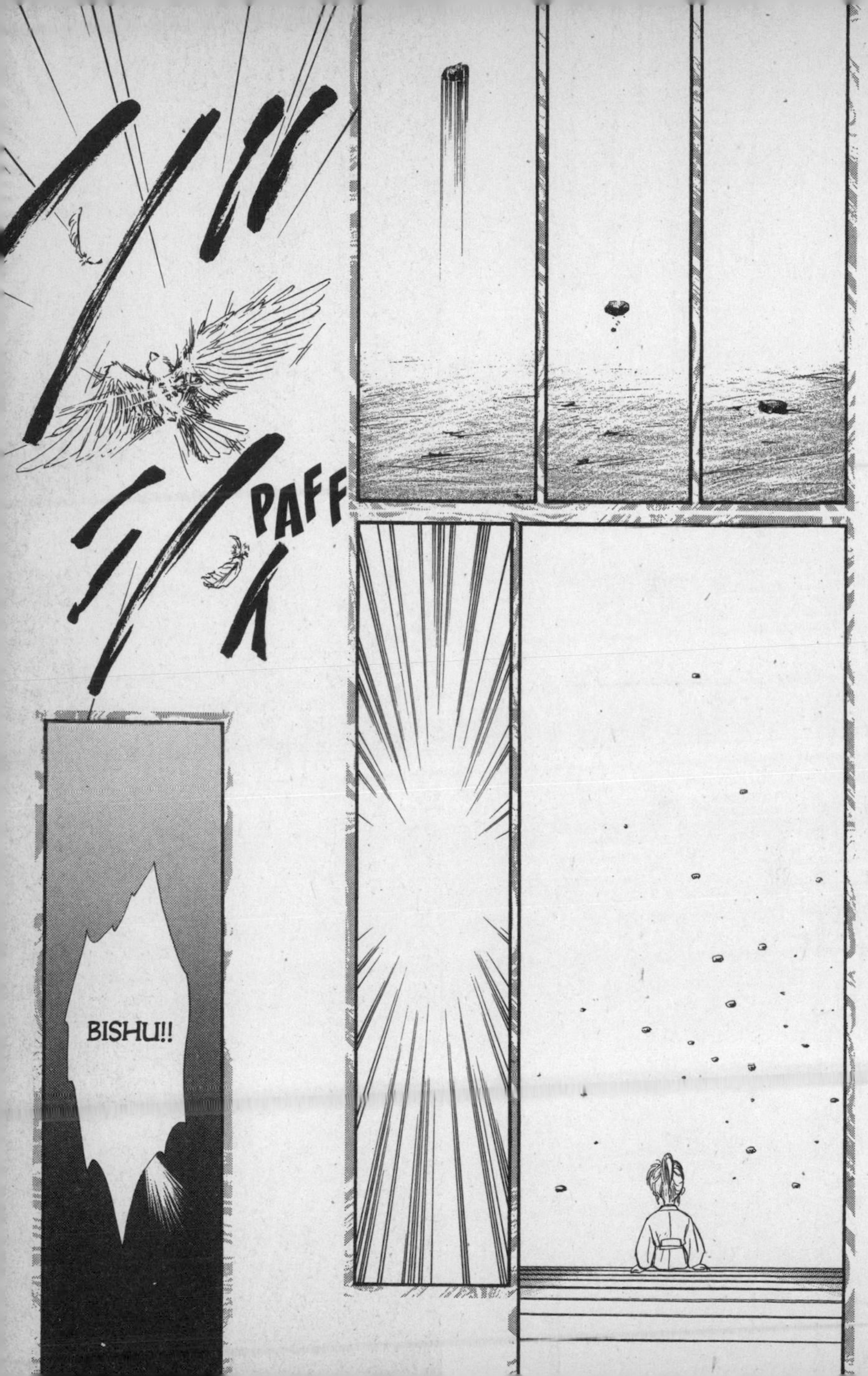
PAFF
BISHU!!

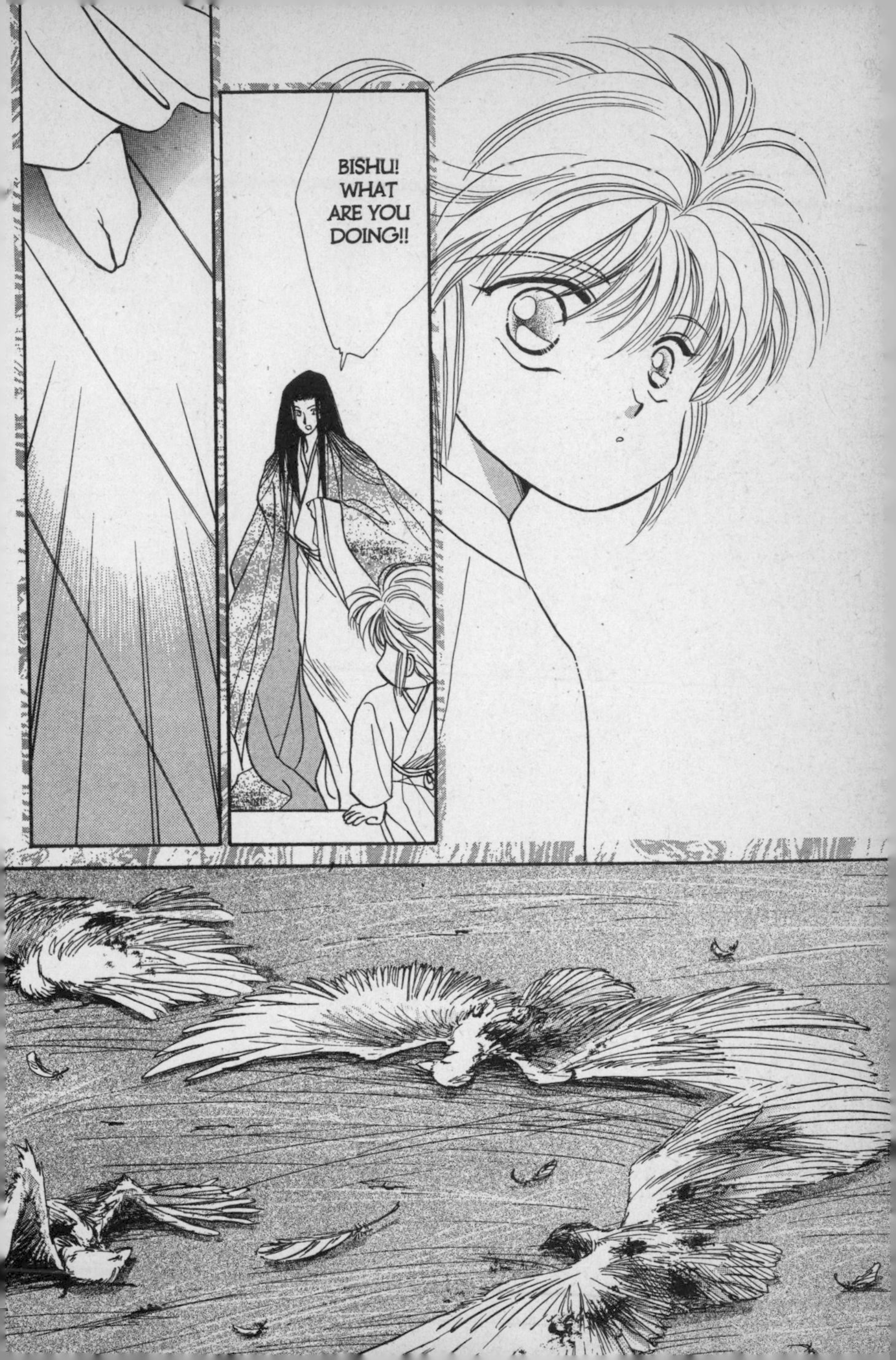
BISHU! WHAT ARE YOU DOING!!

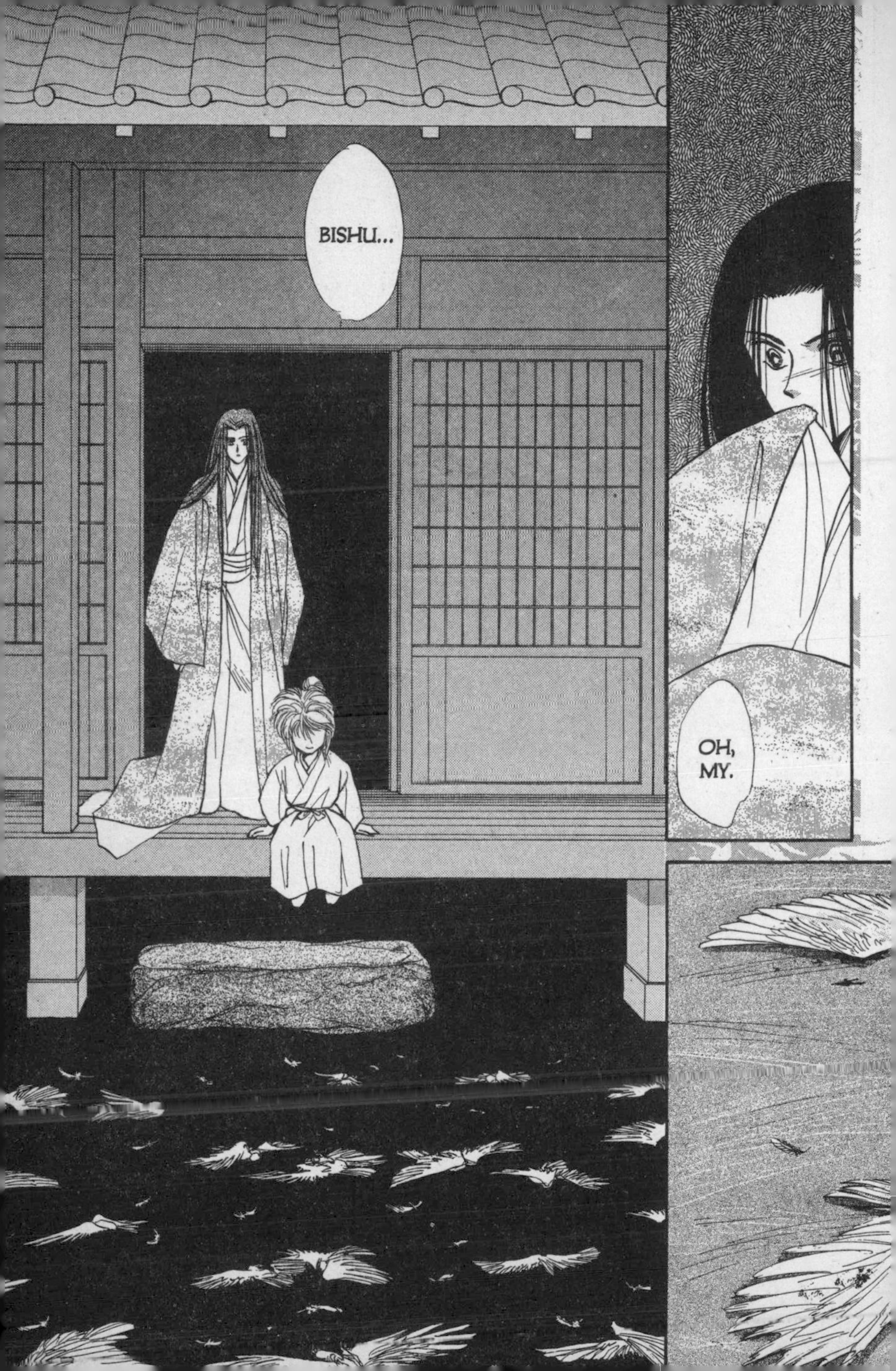
OH, MY.
BISHU...

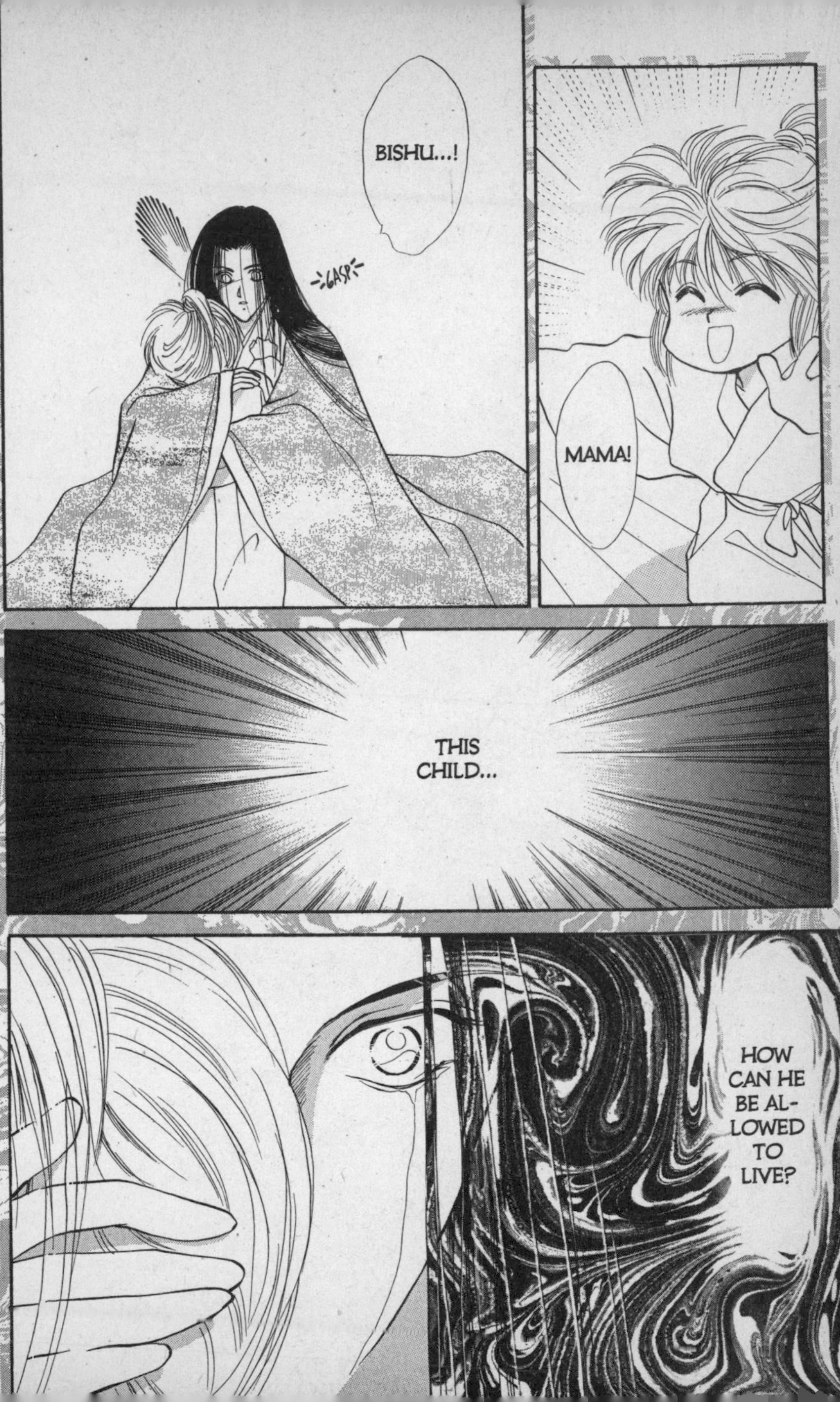
MAMA!
BISHU...!
GASP
THIS CHILD...
HOW CAN HE BE AL-LOWED TO LIVE?

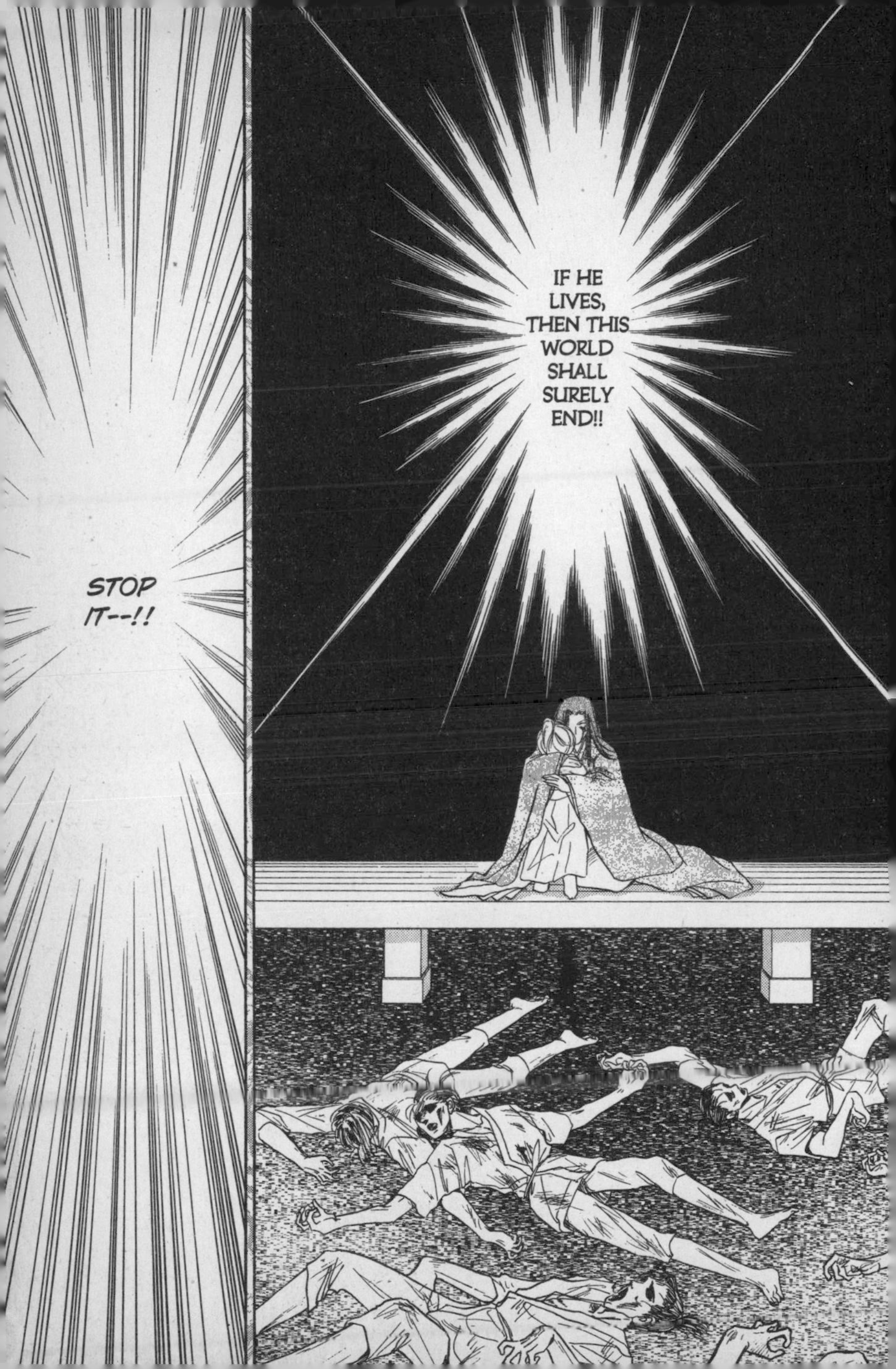
IF HE LIVES, THEN THIS WORLD SHALL SURELY END!!
STOP IT--!!

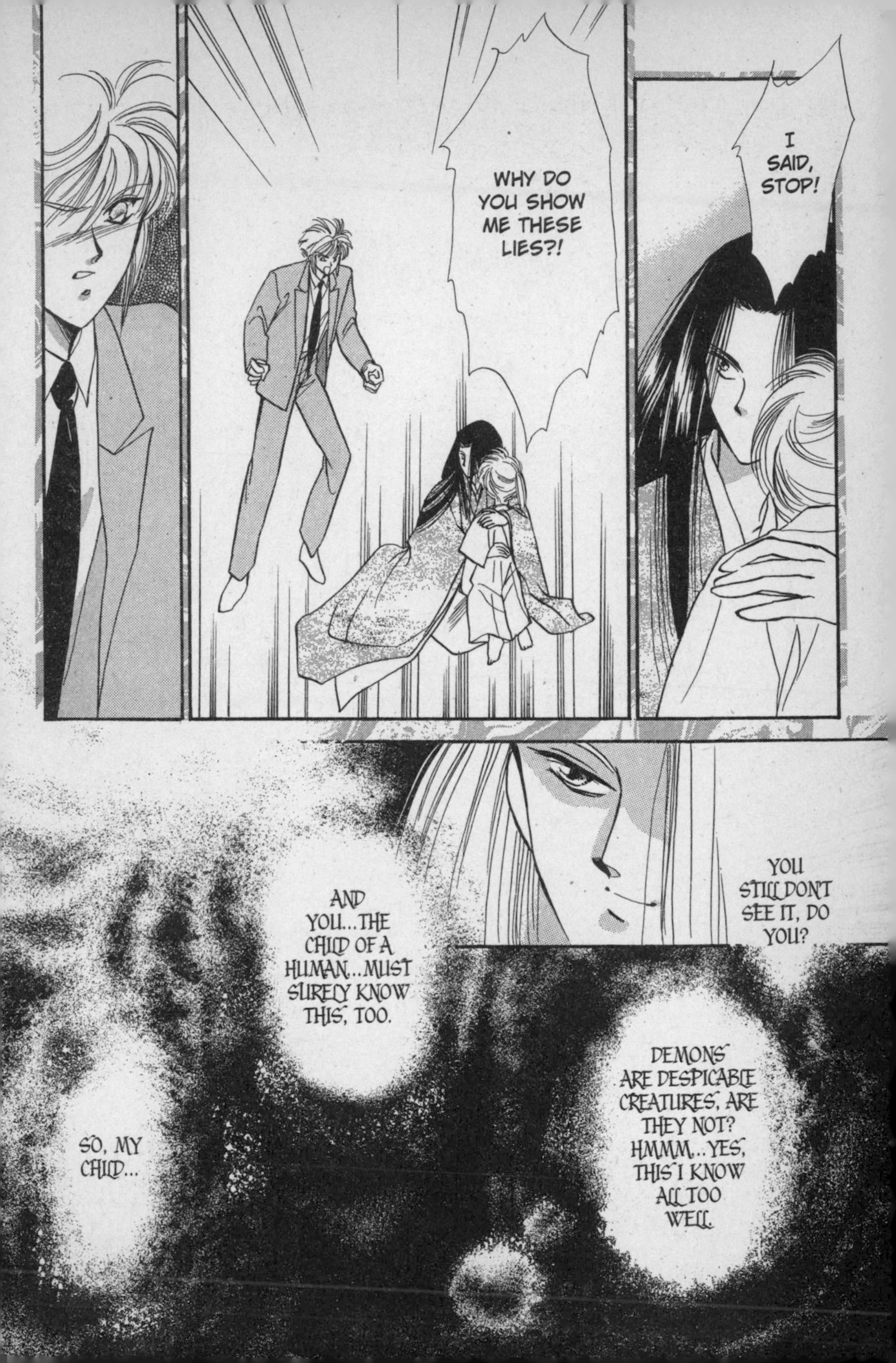
I SAID, STOP!
WHY DO YOU SHOW ME THESE LIES?!
YOU STILL DON'T SEE IT, DO YOU?
DEMONS ARE DESPICABLE CREATURES, ARE THEY NOT? HMMM...YES, THIS I KNOW ALL TOO WELL.
AND YOU...THE CHILD OF A HUMAN...MUST SURELY KNOW THIS, TOO.
SO, MY CHILD...

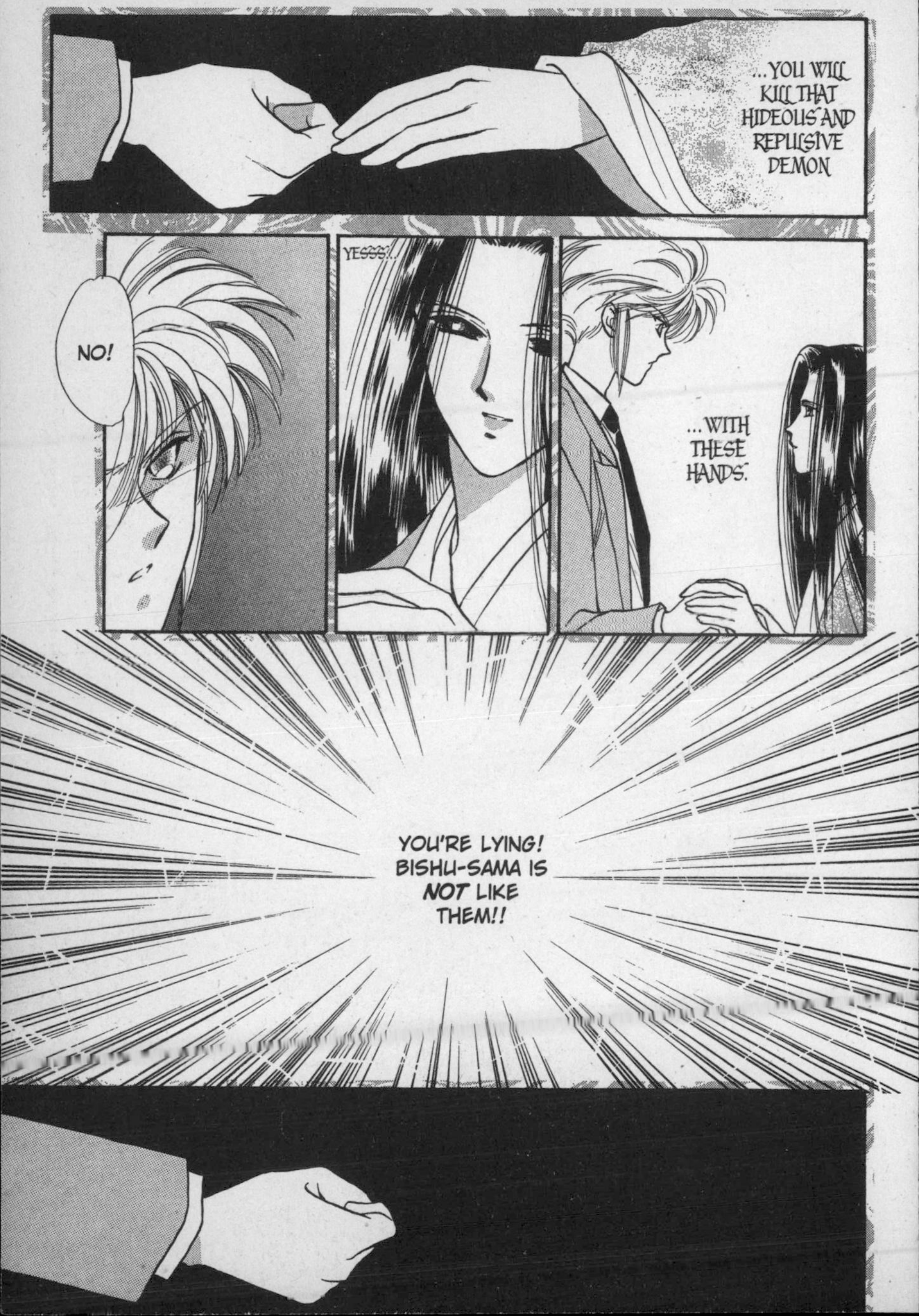
...YOU WILL KILL THAT HIDEOUS AND REPULSIVE DEMON
...WITH THESE HANDS.
YESSS!..
NO!
YOU'RE LYING! BISHU-SAMA IS *NOT* LIKE THEM!!

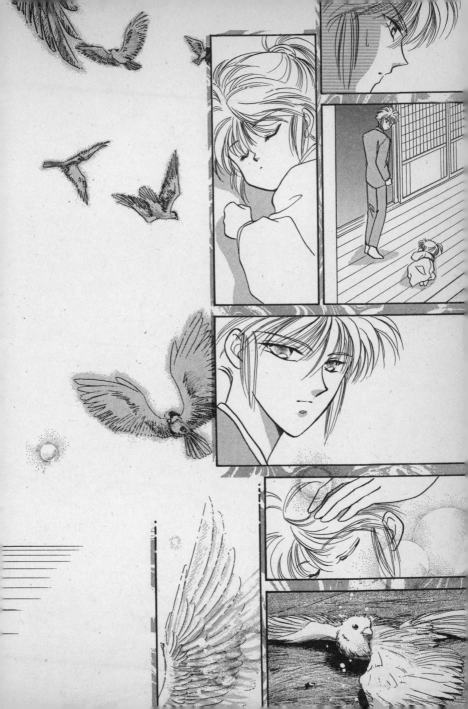

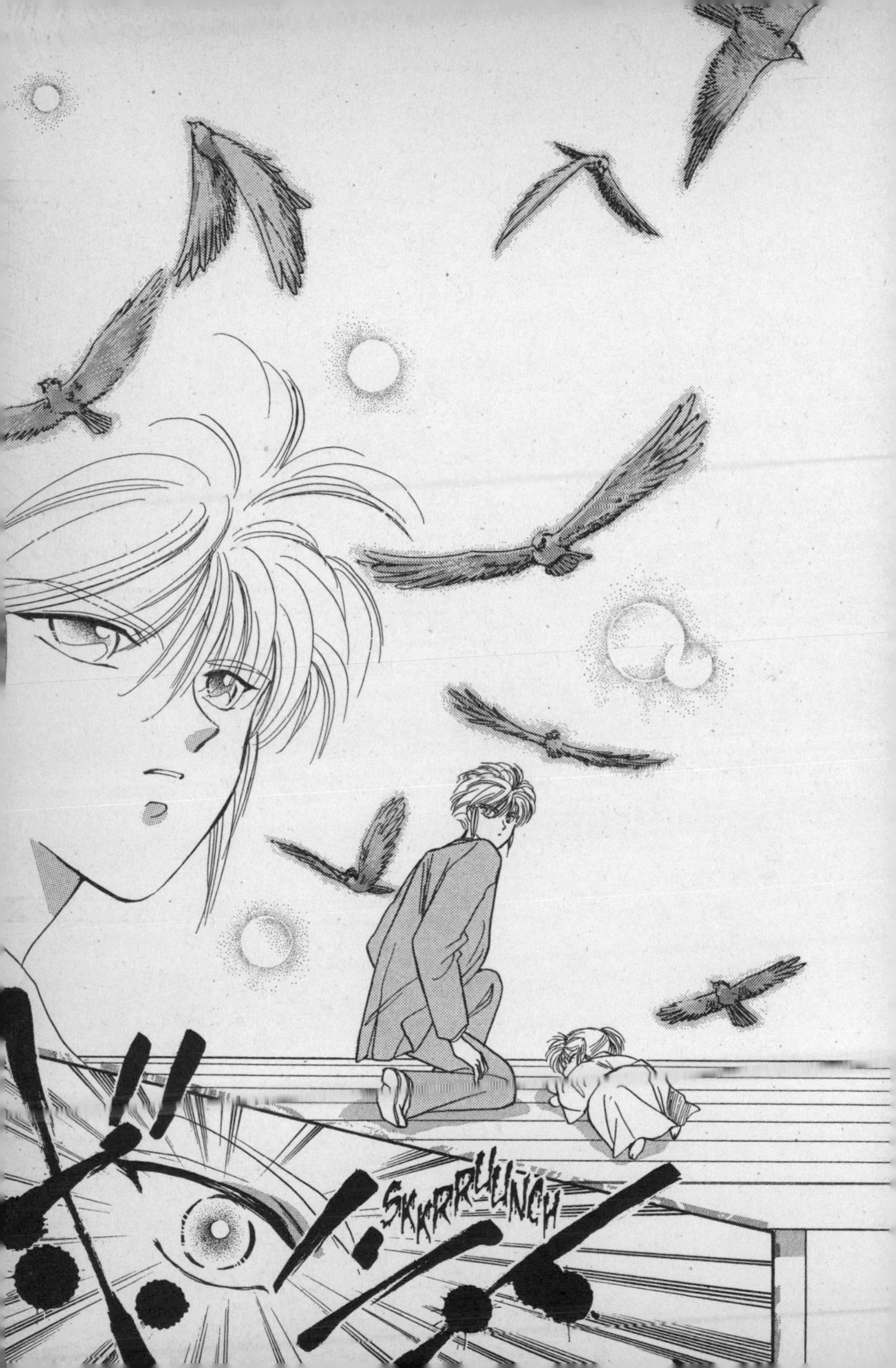
SKKRRUUNCH

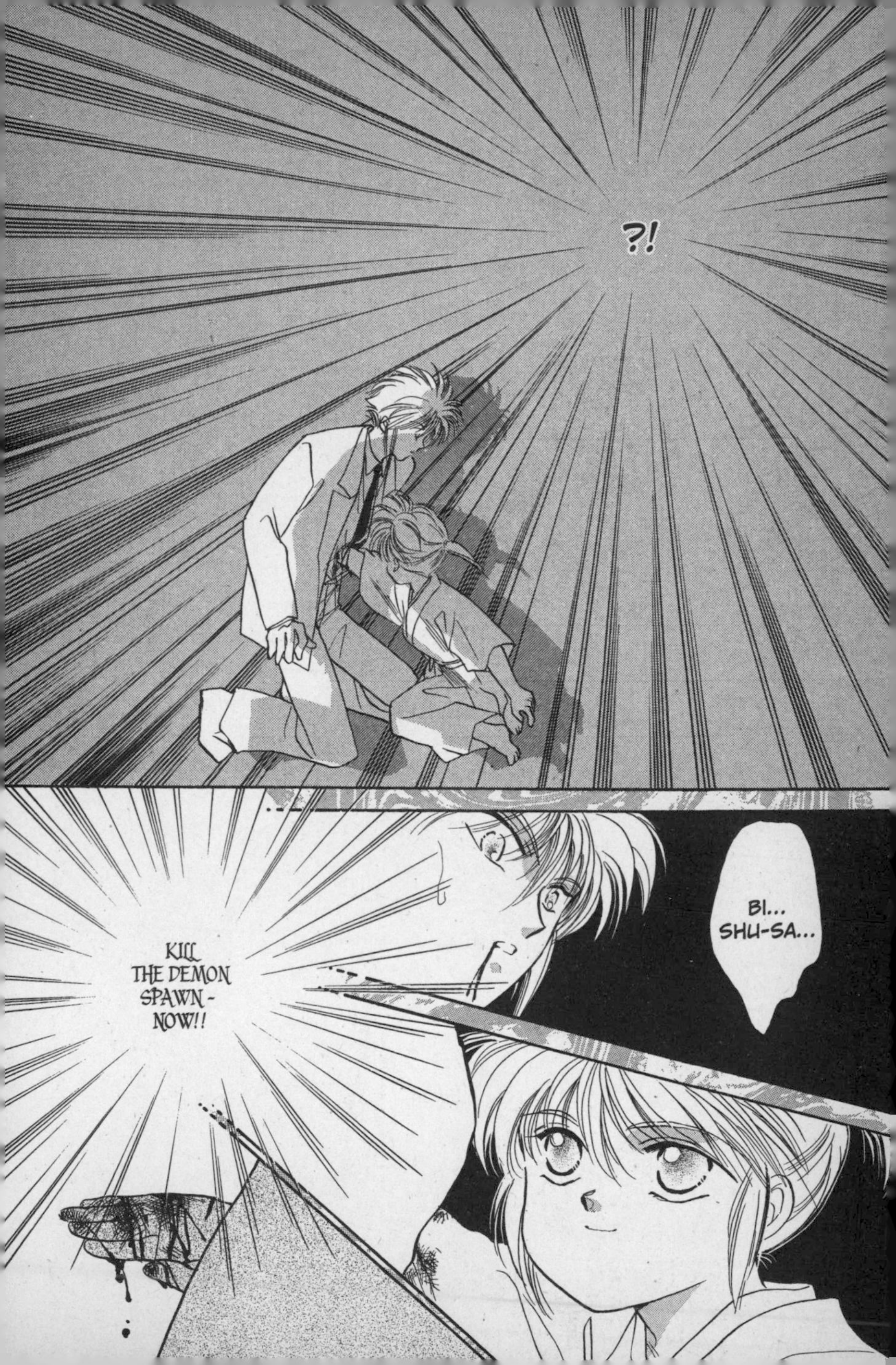
?!
BI... SHU-SA...
KILL THE DEMON SPAWN - NOW!!

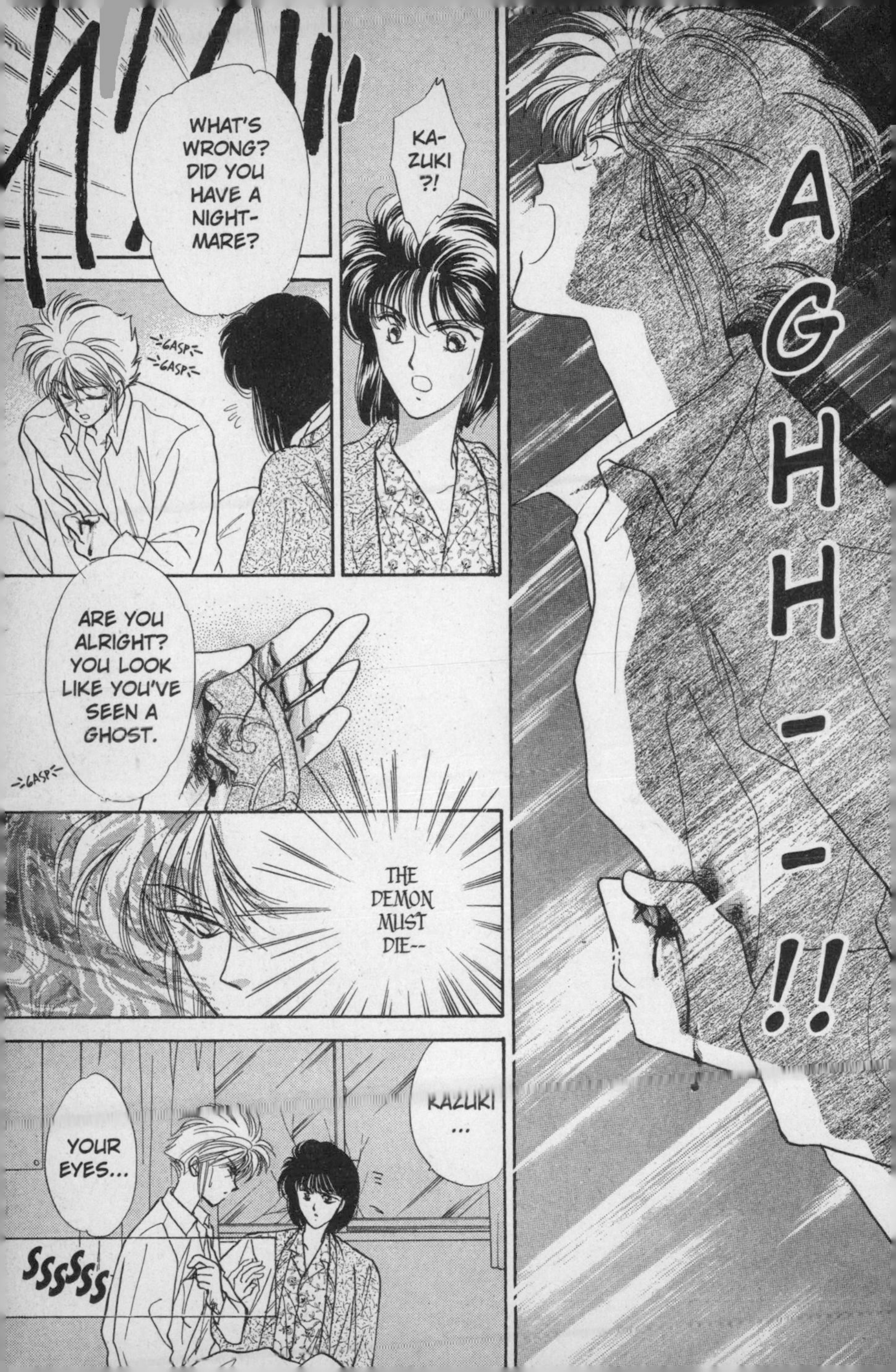

AGHH--!!
KA-ZUKI?!
WHAT'S WRONG? DID YOU HAVE A NIGHT-MARE?
GASP
GASP
ARE YOU ALRIGHT? YOU LOOK LIKE YOU'VE SEEN A GHOST.
GASP
THE DEMON MUST DIE--
KAZUKI...
YOUR EYES...
SSSSSS

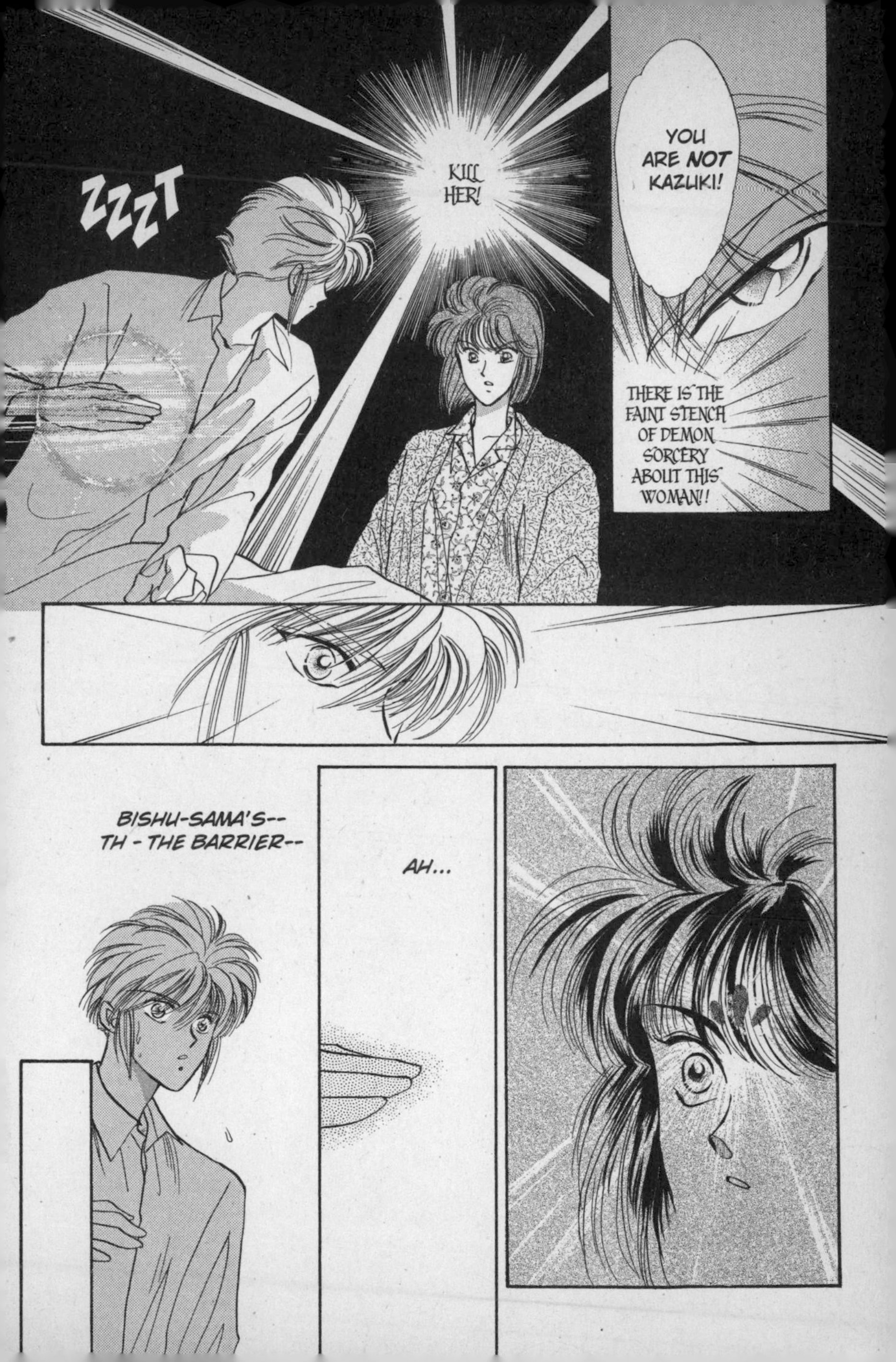
YOU ARE NOT KAZUKI!
THERE IS THE FAINT STENCH OF DEMON SORCERY ABOUT THIS WOMAN!!
KILL HER!
ZZZT
AH...
BISHU-SAMA'S-- TH - THE BARRIER--

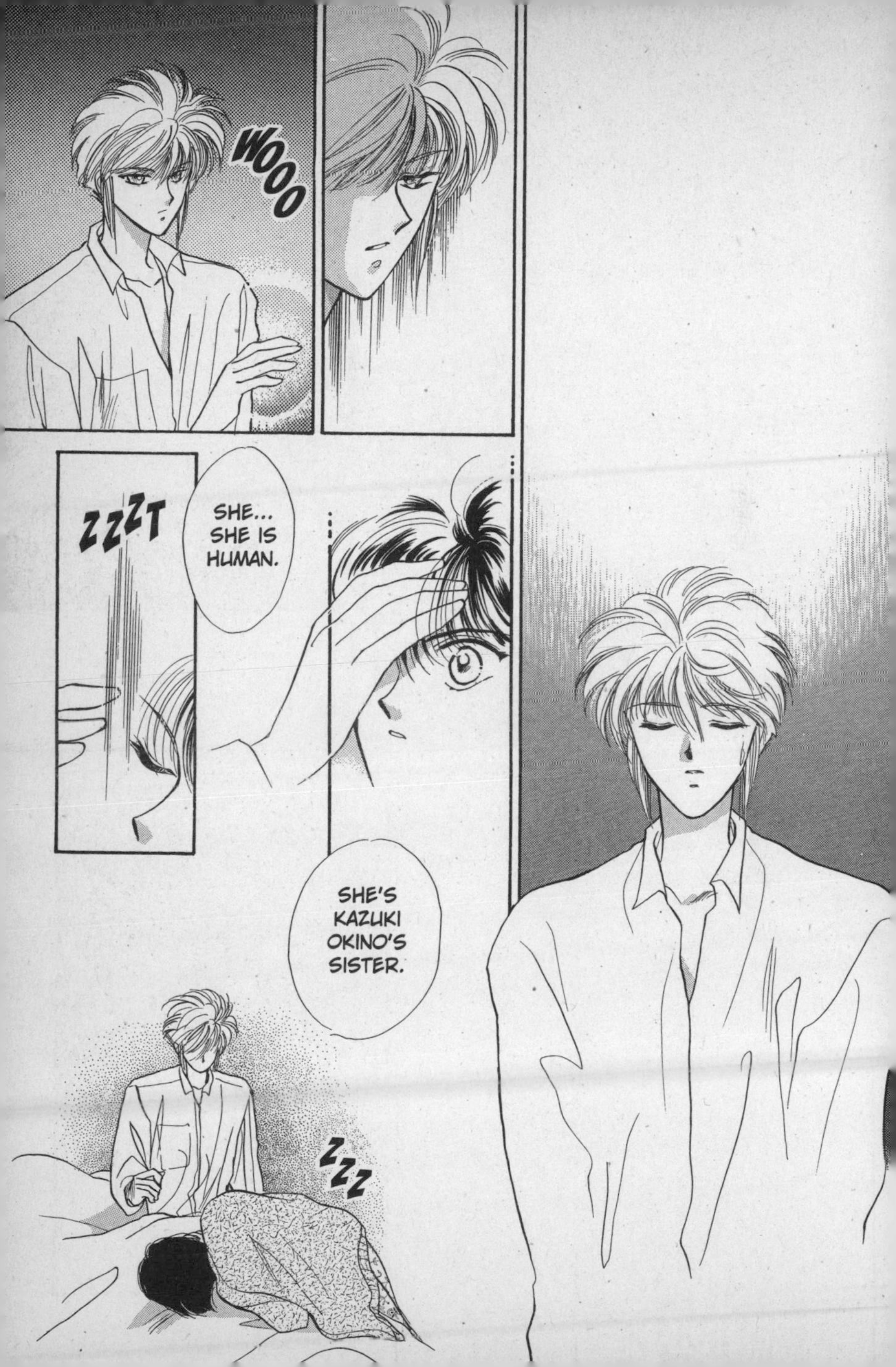
WOOO
SHE... SHE IS HUMAN.
ZZZT
SHE'S KAZUKI OKINO'S SISTER.
ZZZ

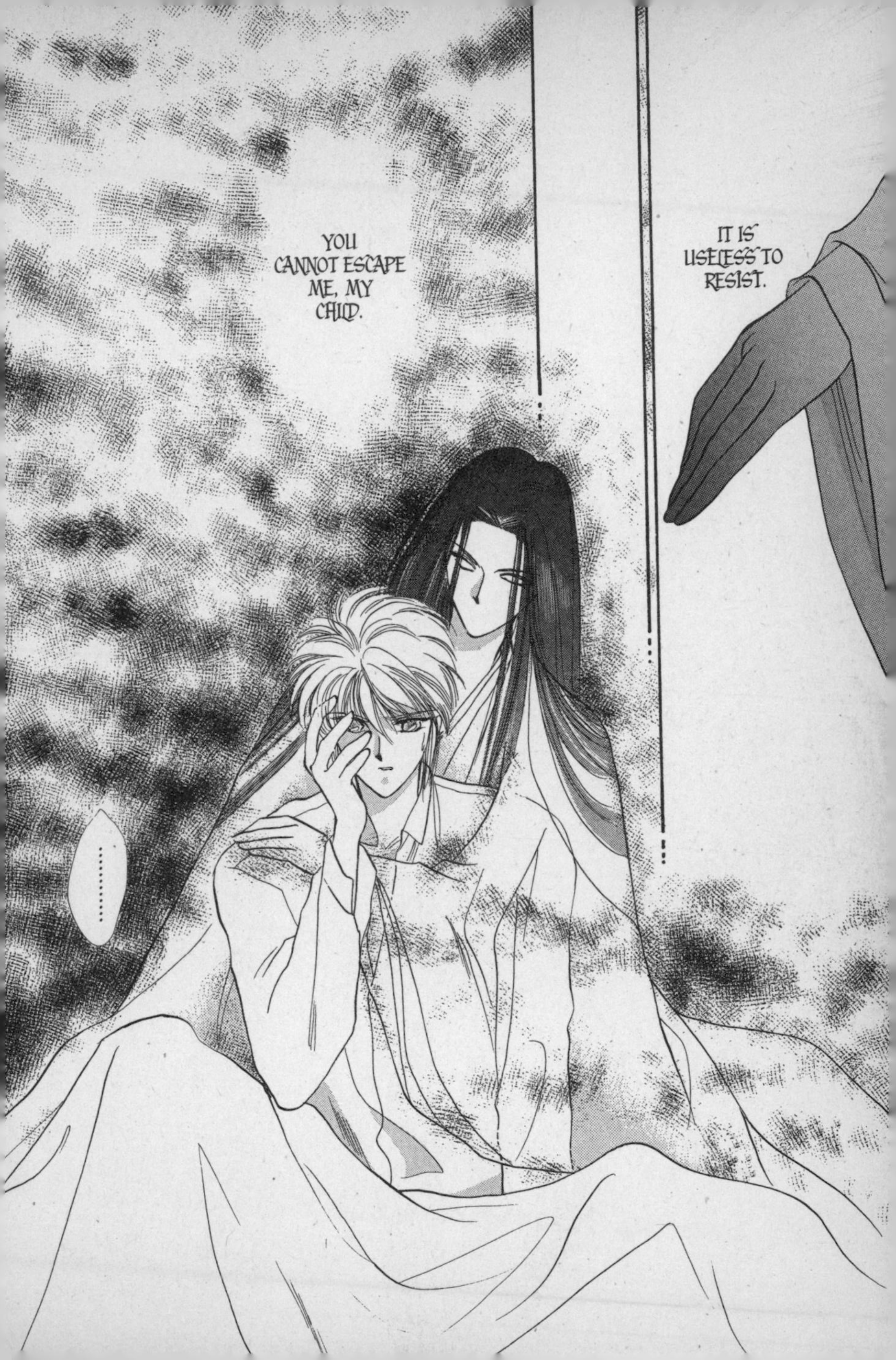
IT IS USELESS TO RESIST.
YOU CANNOT ESCAPE ME, MY CHILD.
......

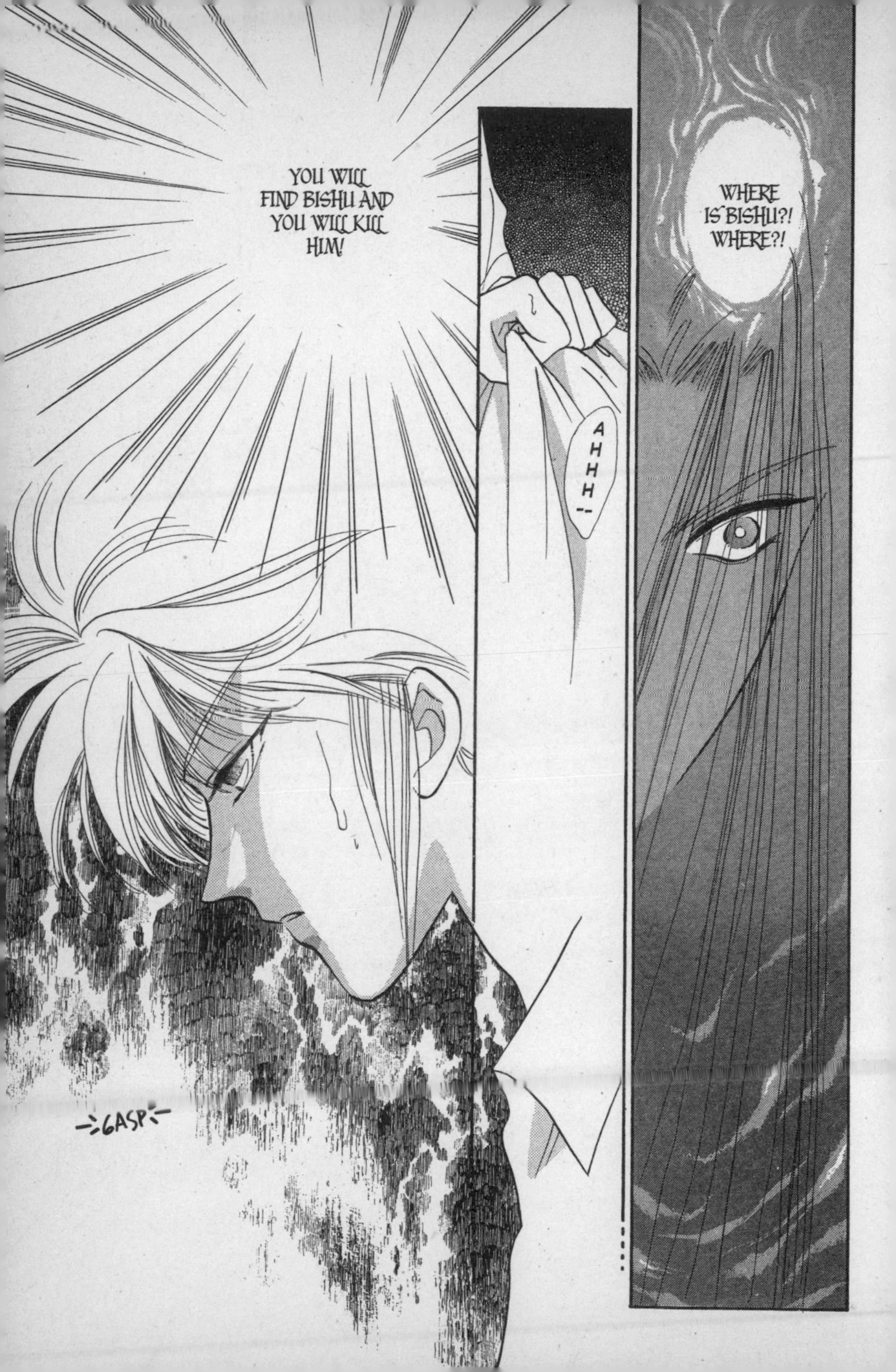
WHERE IS BISHU?! WHERE?!
AHHH--
YOU WILL FIND BISHU AND YOU WILL KILL HIM!
-GASP-

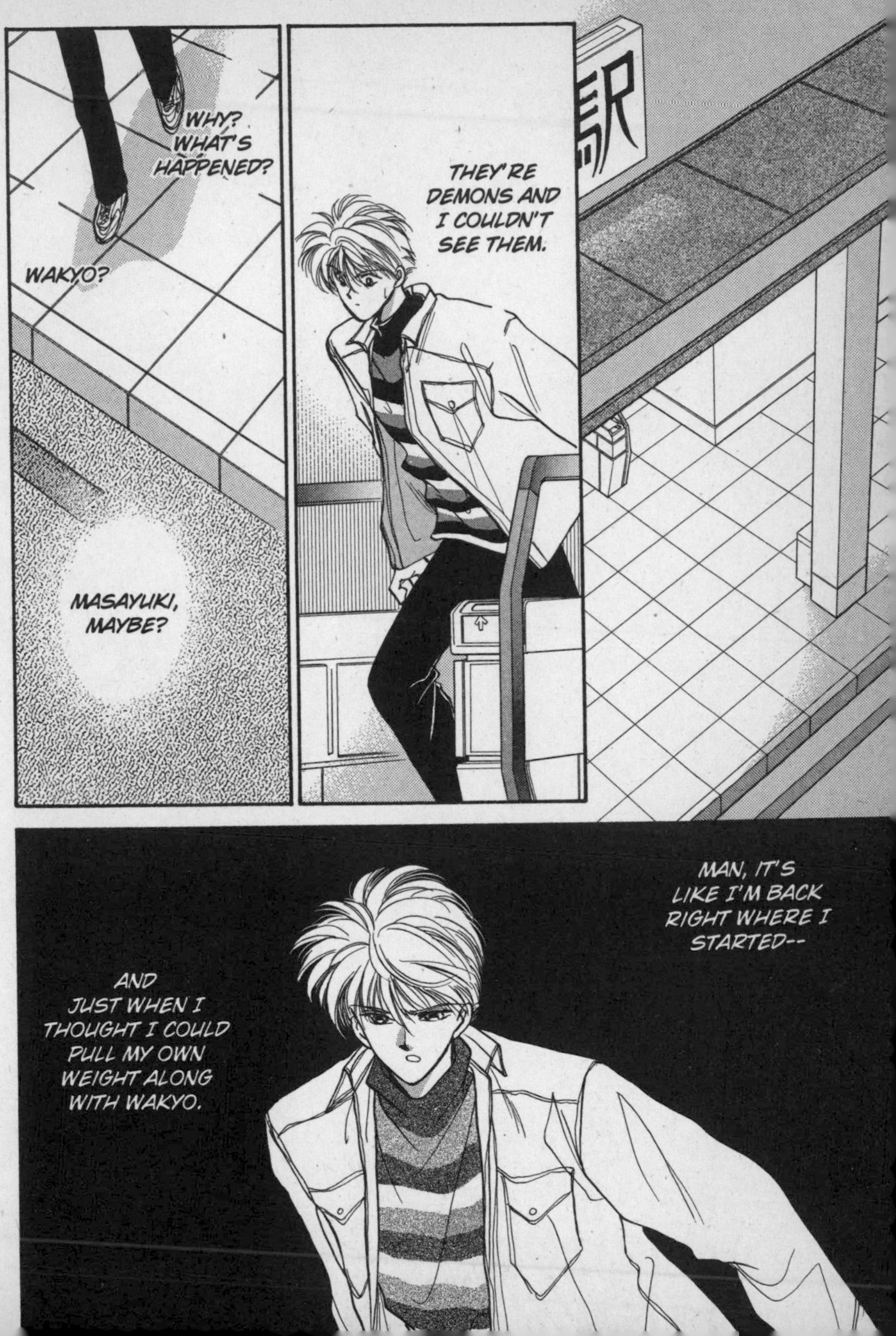
駅
THEY'RE DEMONS AND I COULDN'T SEE THEM.
WHY? WHAT'S HAPPENED?
WAKYO?
MASAYUKI, MAYBE?
MAN, IT'S LIKE I'M BACK RIGHT WHERE I STARTED--
AND JUST WHEN I THOUGHT I COULD PULL MY OWN WEIGHT ALONG WITH WAKYO.

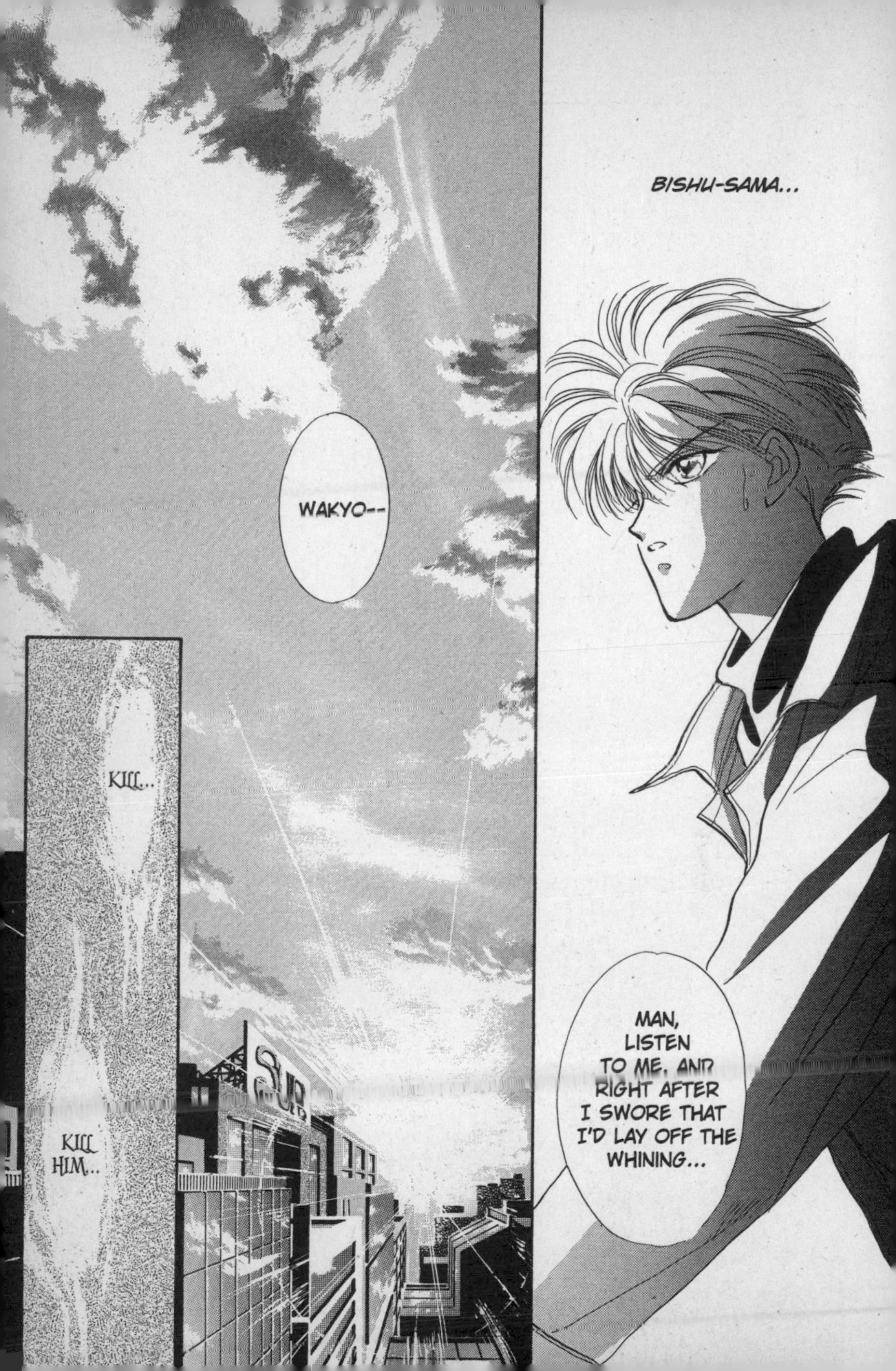
BISHU-SAMA...
MAN, LISTEN TO ME. AND RIGHT AFTER I SWORE THAT I'D LAY OFF THE WHINING...
WAKYO--
KILL...
KILL HIM...

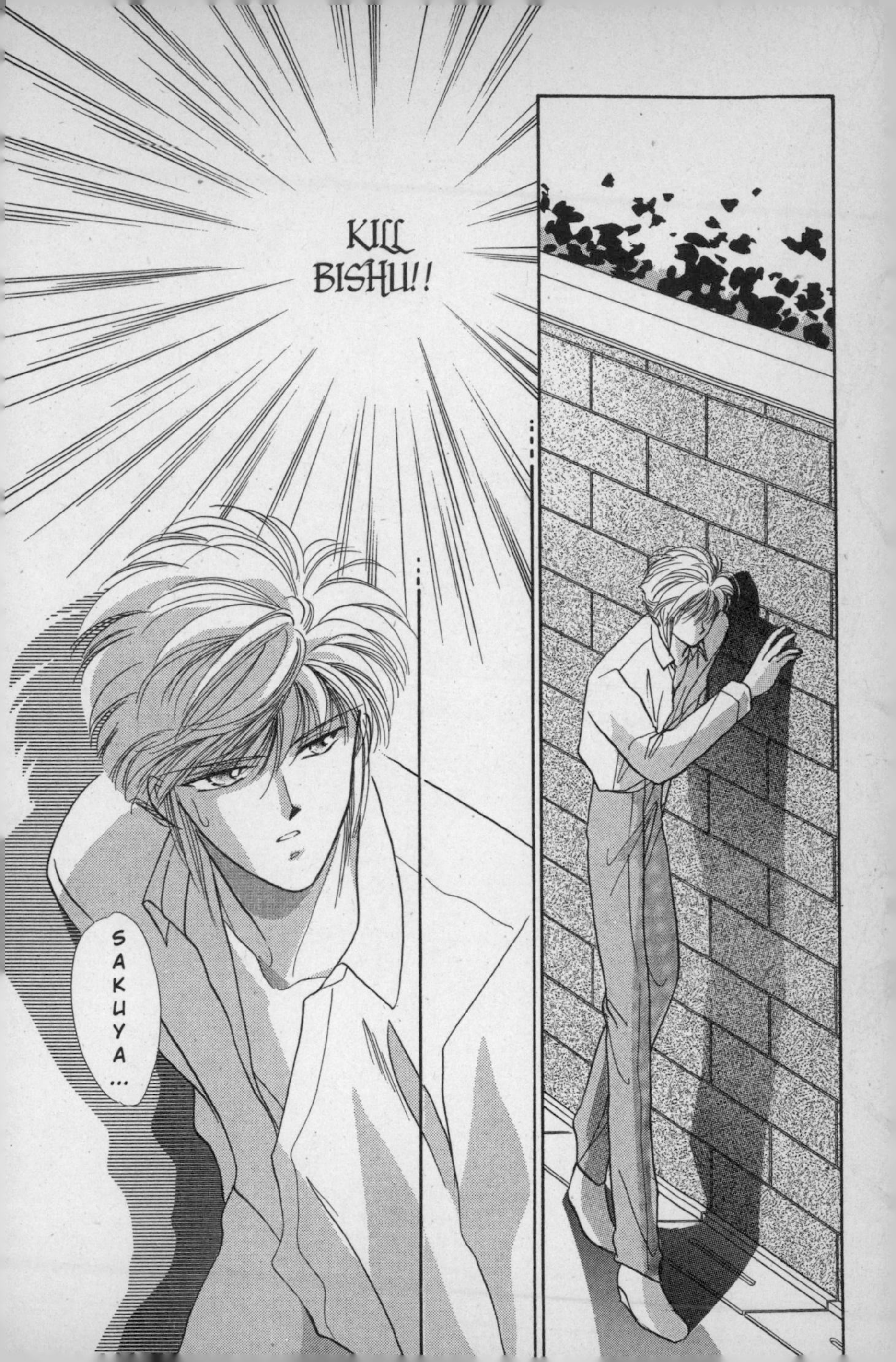
KILL BISHU!!
SAKUYA...

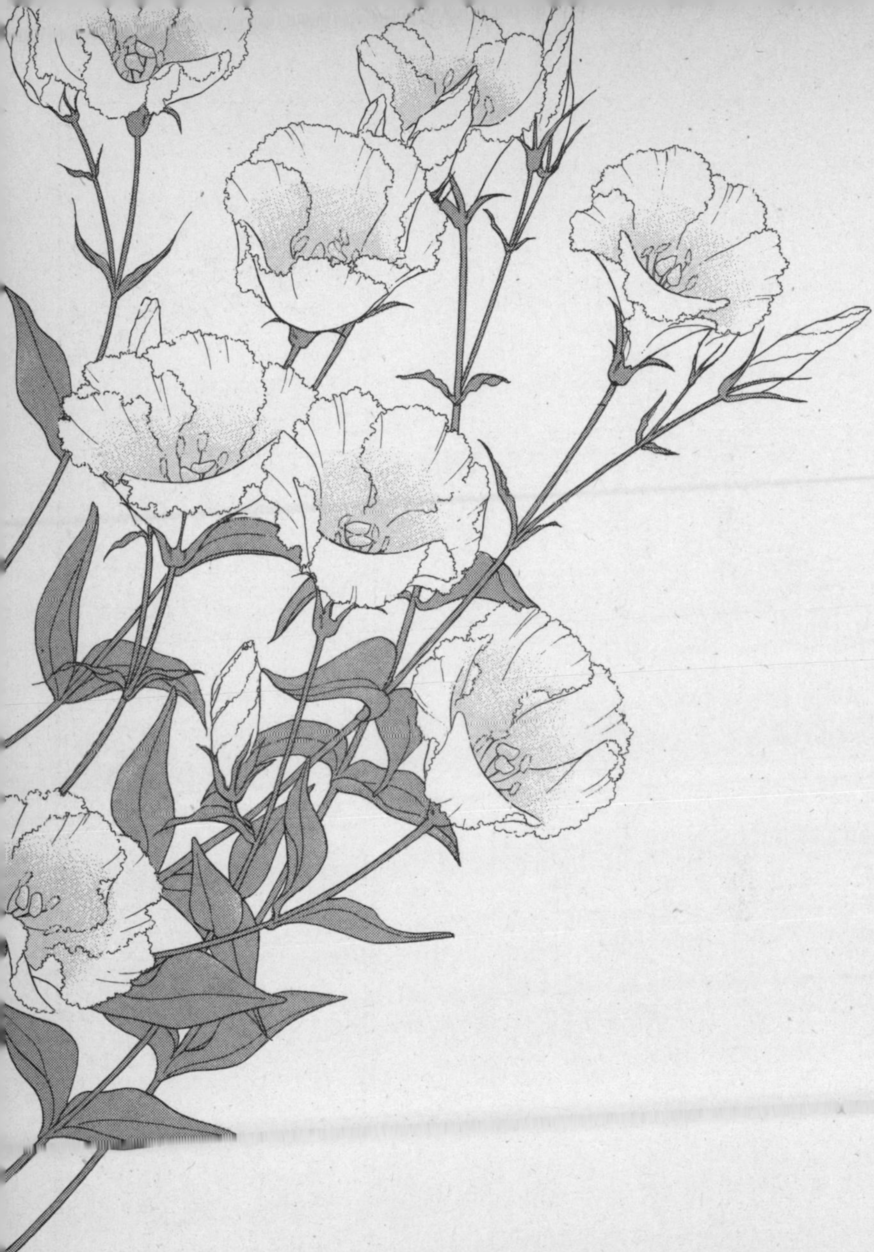

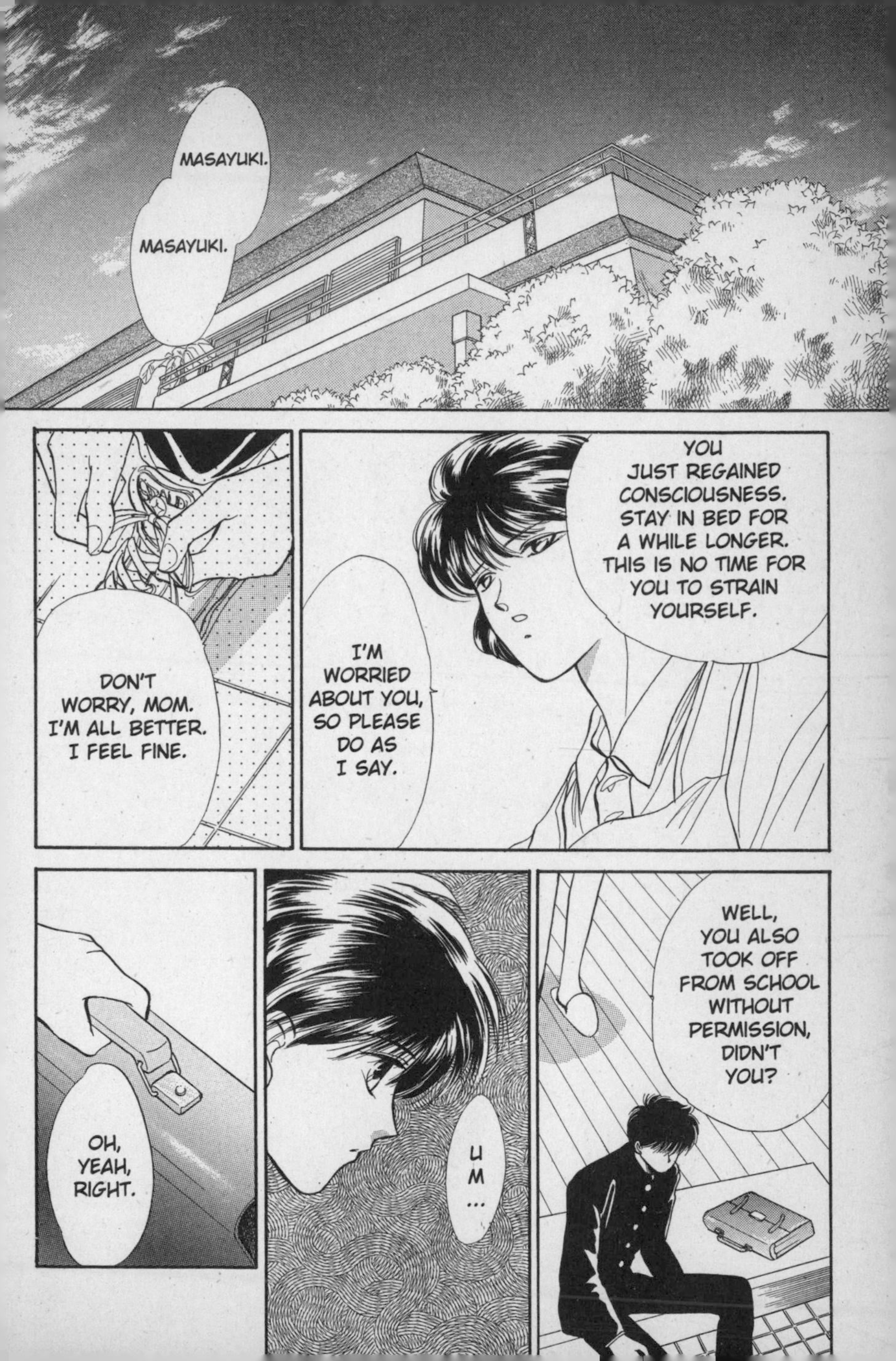
MASAYUKI.
MASAYUKI.
YOU JUST REGAINED CONSCIOUSNESS. STAY IN BED FOR A WHILE LONGER. THIS IS NO TIME FOR YOU TO STRAIN YOURSELF.
I'M WORRIED ABOUT YOU, SO PLEASE DO AS I SAY.
DON'T WORRY, MOM. I'M ALL BETTER. I FEEL FINE.
WELL, YOU ALSO TOOK OFF FROM SCHOOL WITHOUT PERMISSION, DIDN'T YOU?
UM ...
OH, YEAH, RIGHT.

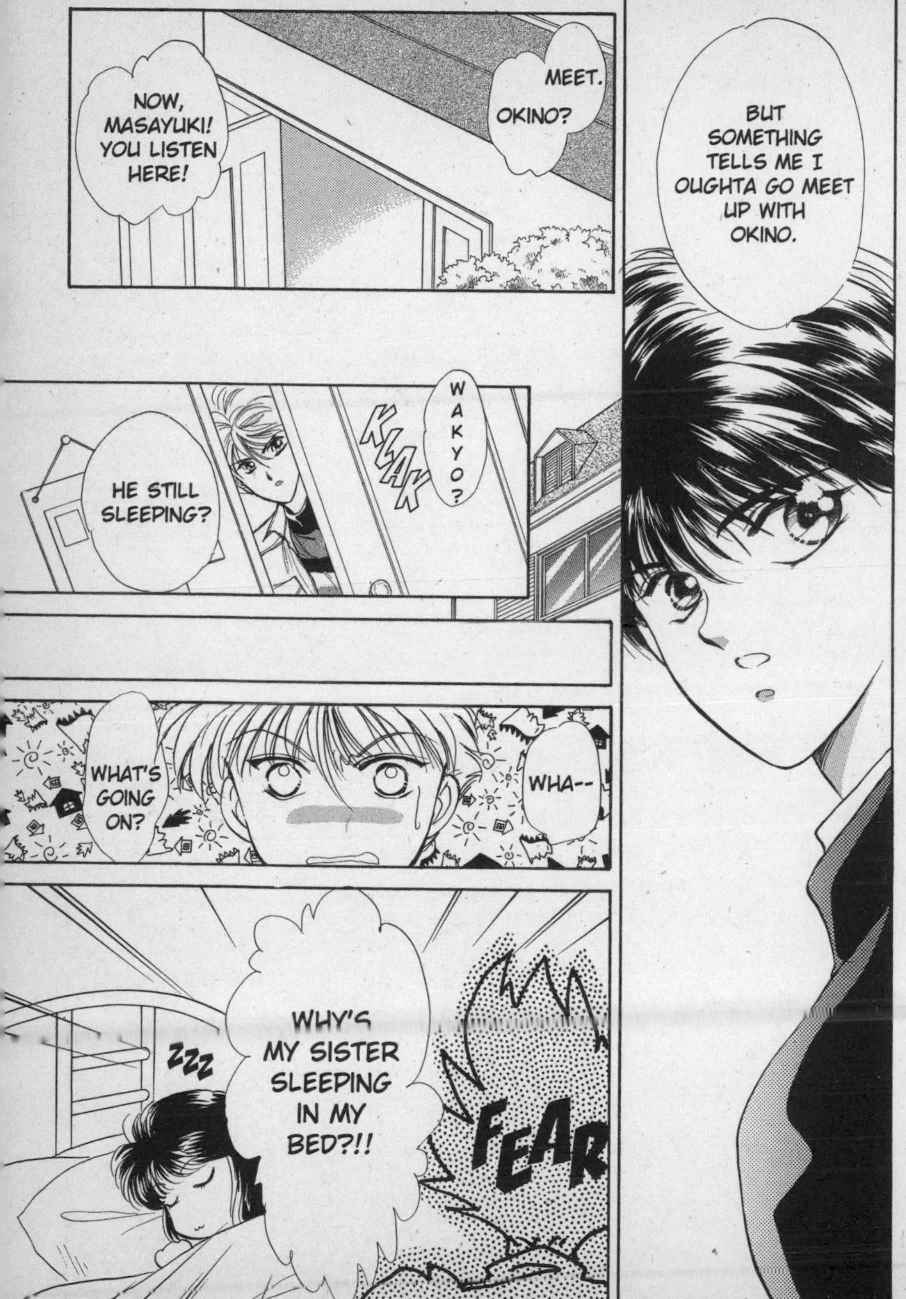
BUT SOMETHING TELLS ME I OUGHTA GO MEET UP WITH OKINO.
MEET.
OKINO?
NOW, MASAYUKI! YOU LISTEN HERE!
WAKYO?
KLAK
HE STILL SLEEPING?
WHA--
WHAT'S GOING ON?
WHY'S MY SISTER SLEEPING IN MY BED?!!
ZZZ
FEAR

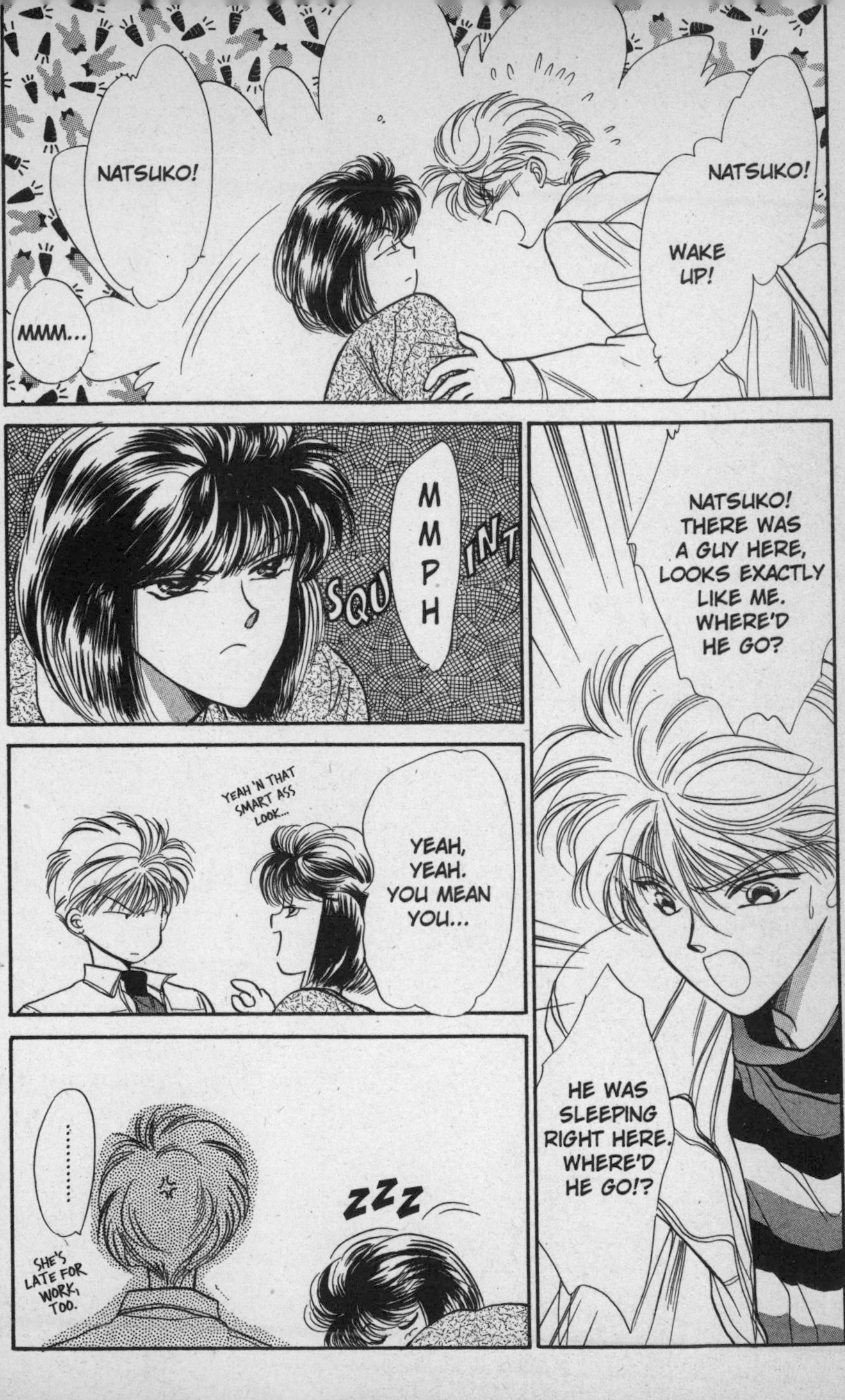
NATSUKO!
WAKE UP!
NATSUKO!
MMM...
NATSUKO! THERE WAS A GUY HERE, LOOKS EXACTLY LIKE ME. WHERE'D HE GO?
HE WAS SLEEPING RIGHT HERE. WHERE'D HE GO!?
MMMPH
SQUINT
YEAH, YEAH. YOU MEAN YOU...
YEAH 'N THAT SMART ASS LOOK...
......
ZZZ
SHE'S LATE FOR WORK, TOO.

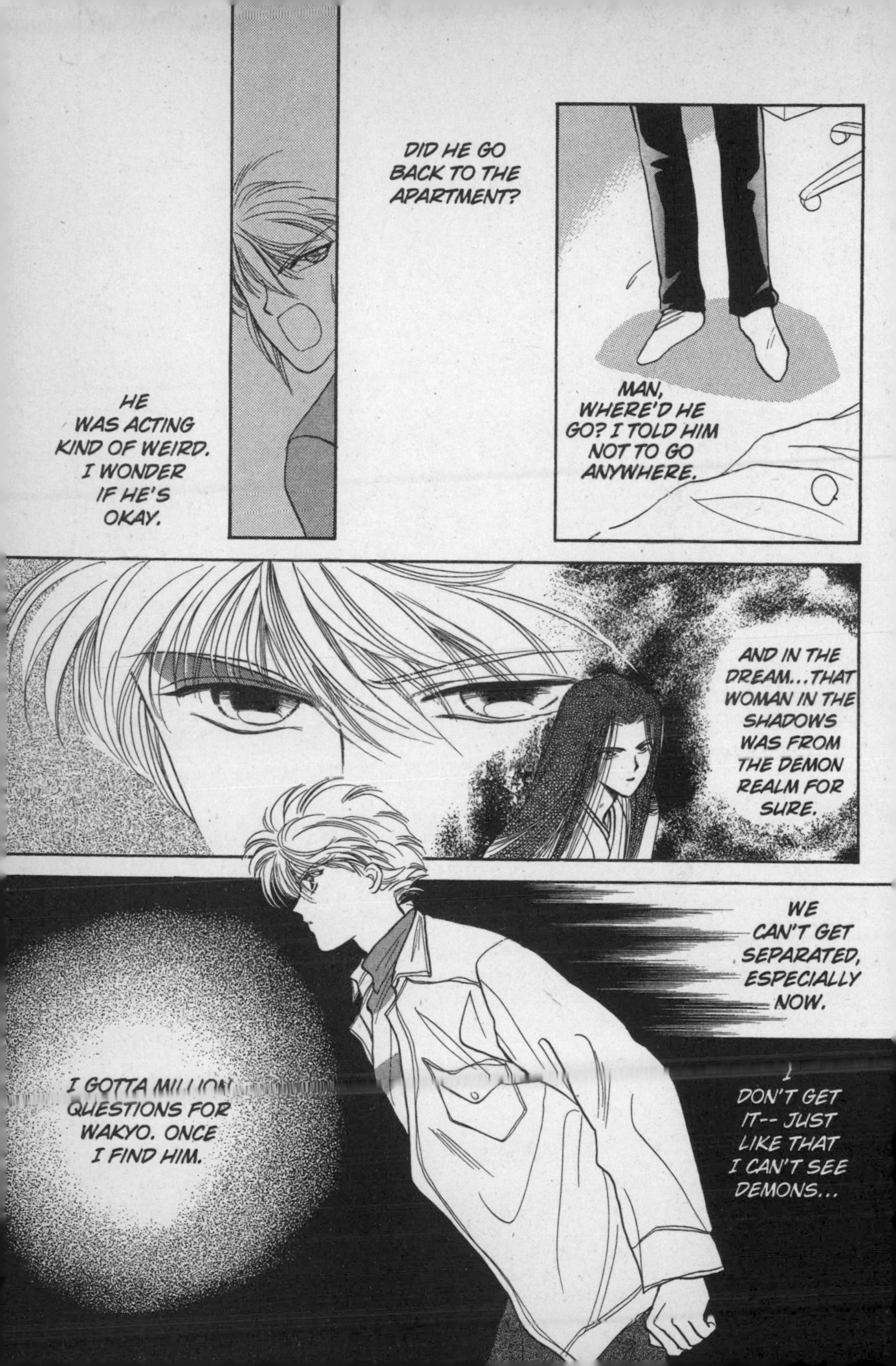
MAN, WHERE'D HE GO? I TOLD HIM NOT TO GO ANYWHERE.
DID HE GO BACK TO THE APARTMENT?
HE WAS ACTING KIND OF WEIRD. I WONDER IF HE'S OKAY.
AND IN THE DREAM...THAT WOMAN IN THE SHADOWS WAS FROM THE DEMON REALM FOR SURE.
WE CAN'T GET SEPARATED, ESPECIALLY NOW.
I DON'T GET IT-- JUST LIKE THAT I CAN'T SEE DEMONS...
I GOTTA MILLION QUESTIONS FOR WAKYO. ONCE I FIND HIM.

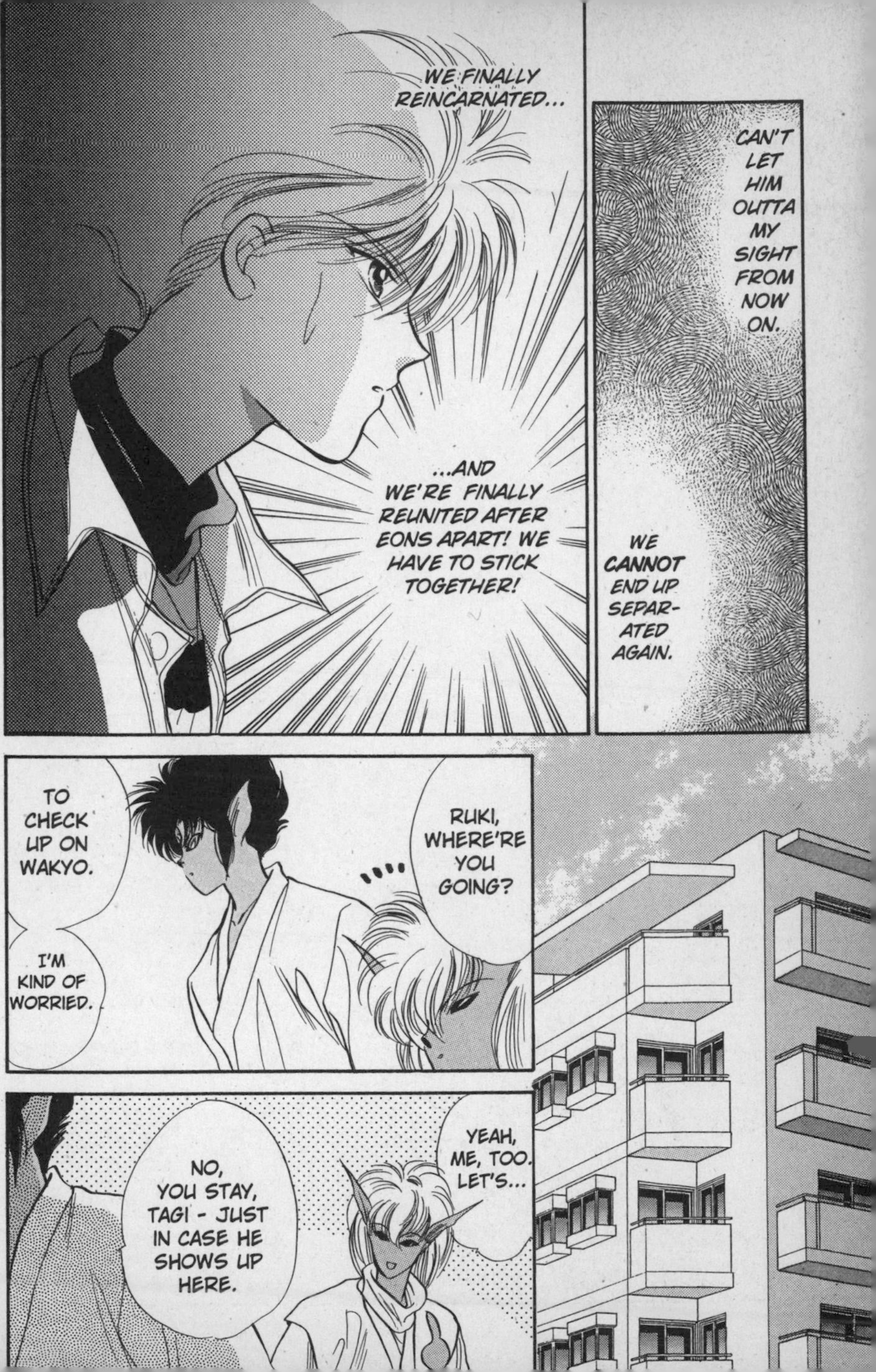
CAN'T LET HIM OUTTA MY SIGHT FROM NOW ON.
WE CANNOT END UP SEPAR-ATED AGAIN.
WE FINALLY REINCARNATED...
...AND WE'RE FINALLY REUNITED AFTER EONS APART! WE HAVE TO STICK TOGETHER!
RUKI, WHERE'RE YOU GOING?
TO CHECK UP ON WAKYO.
I'M KIND OF WORRIED.
YEAH, ME, TOO. LET'S...
NO, YOU STAY, TAGI - JUST IN CASE HE SHOWS UP HERE.

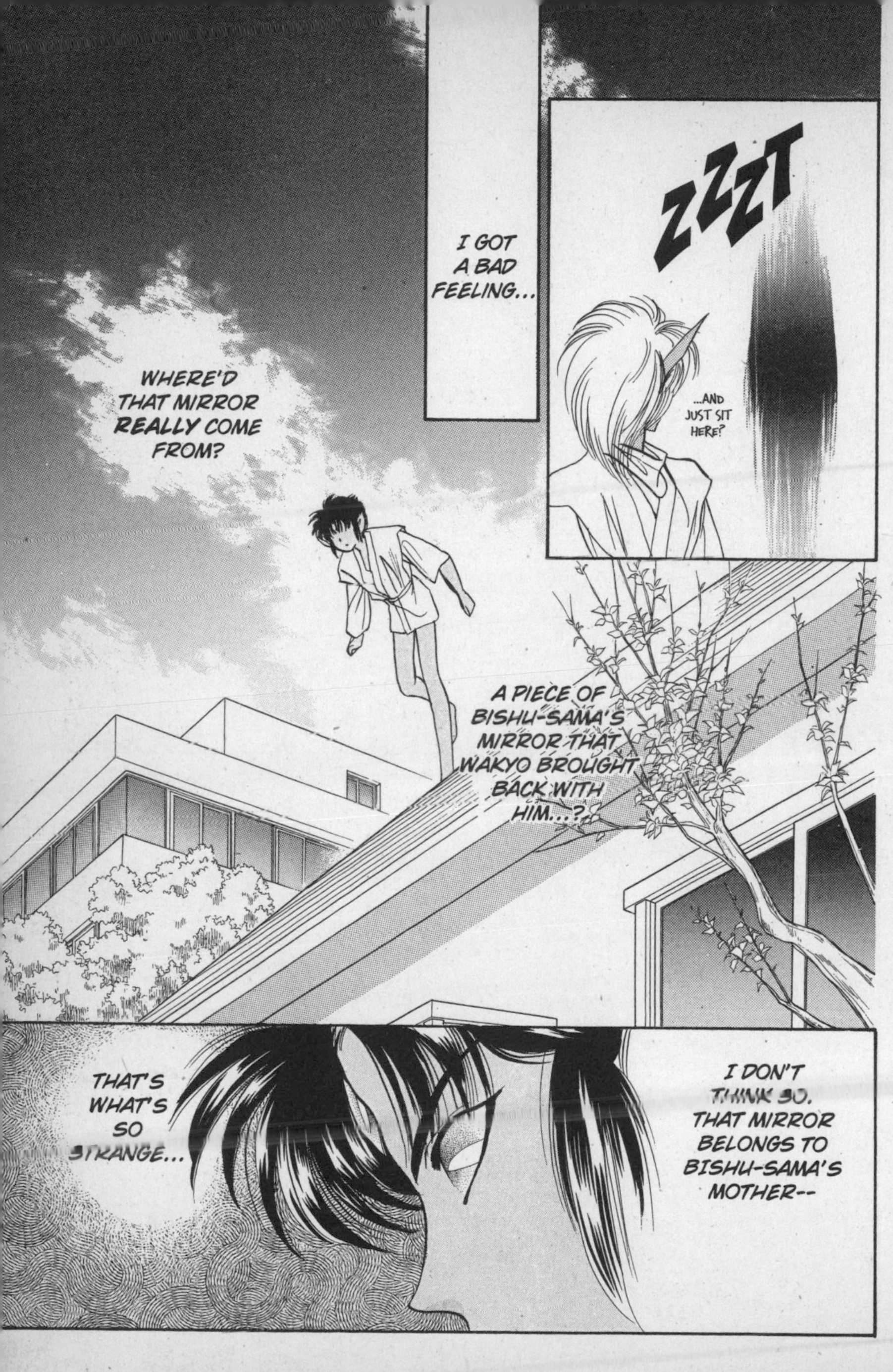

...AND JUST SIT HERE?
ZZZT
I GOT A BAD FEELING...
WHERE'D THAT MIRROR REALLY COME FROM?
A PIECE OF BISHU-SAMA'S MIRROR THAT WAKYO BROUGHT BACK WITH HIM...?
I DON'T THINK SO. THAT MIRROR BELONGS TO BISHU-SAMA'S MOTHER--
THAT'S WHAT'S SO STRANGE...

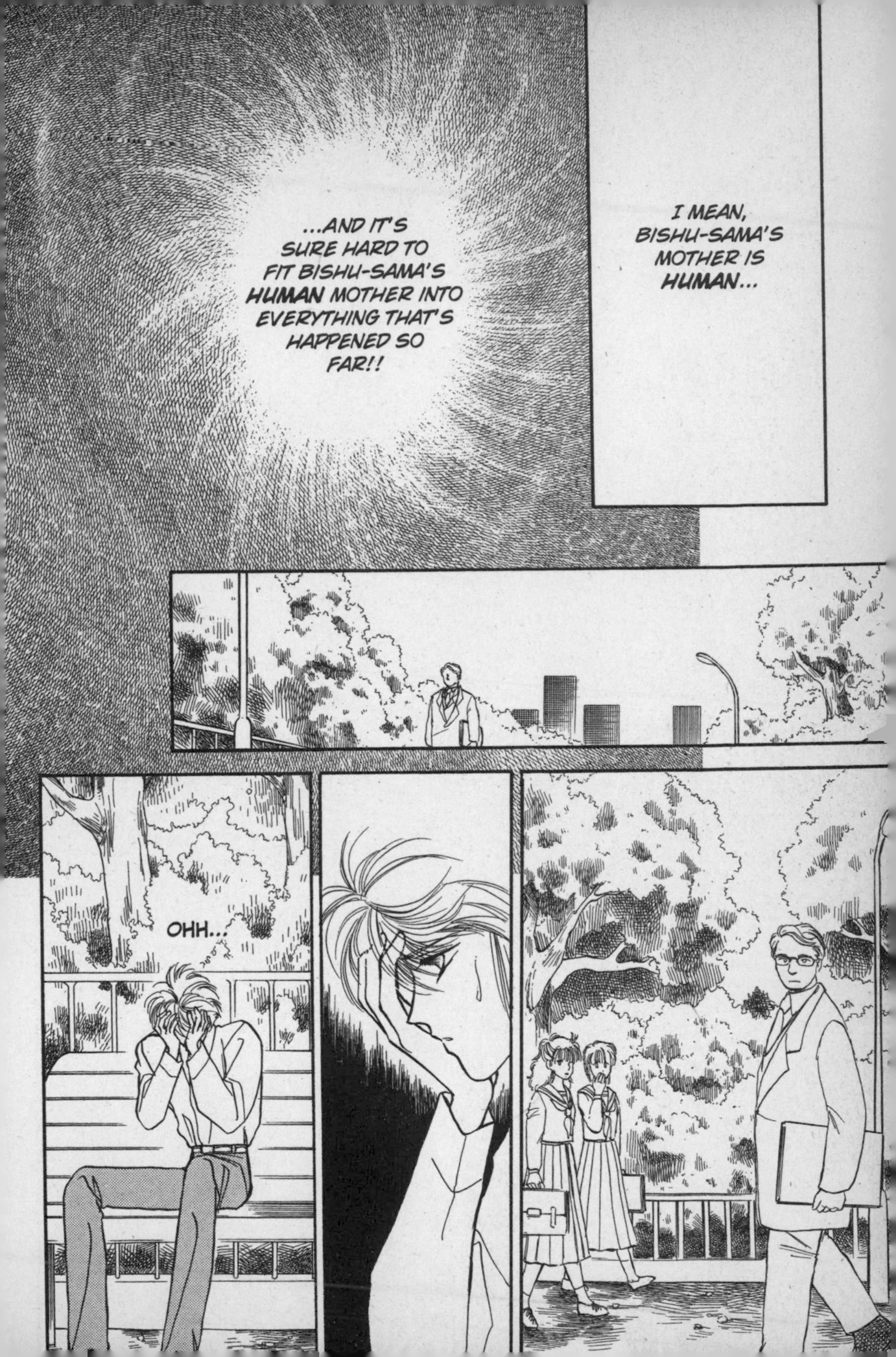
I MEAN, BISHU-SAMA'S MOTHER IS HUMAN...
...AND IT'S SURE HARD TO FIT BISHU-SAMA'S HUMAN MOTHER INTO EVERYTHING THAT'S HAPPENED SO FAR!!
OHH...

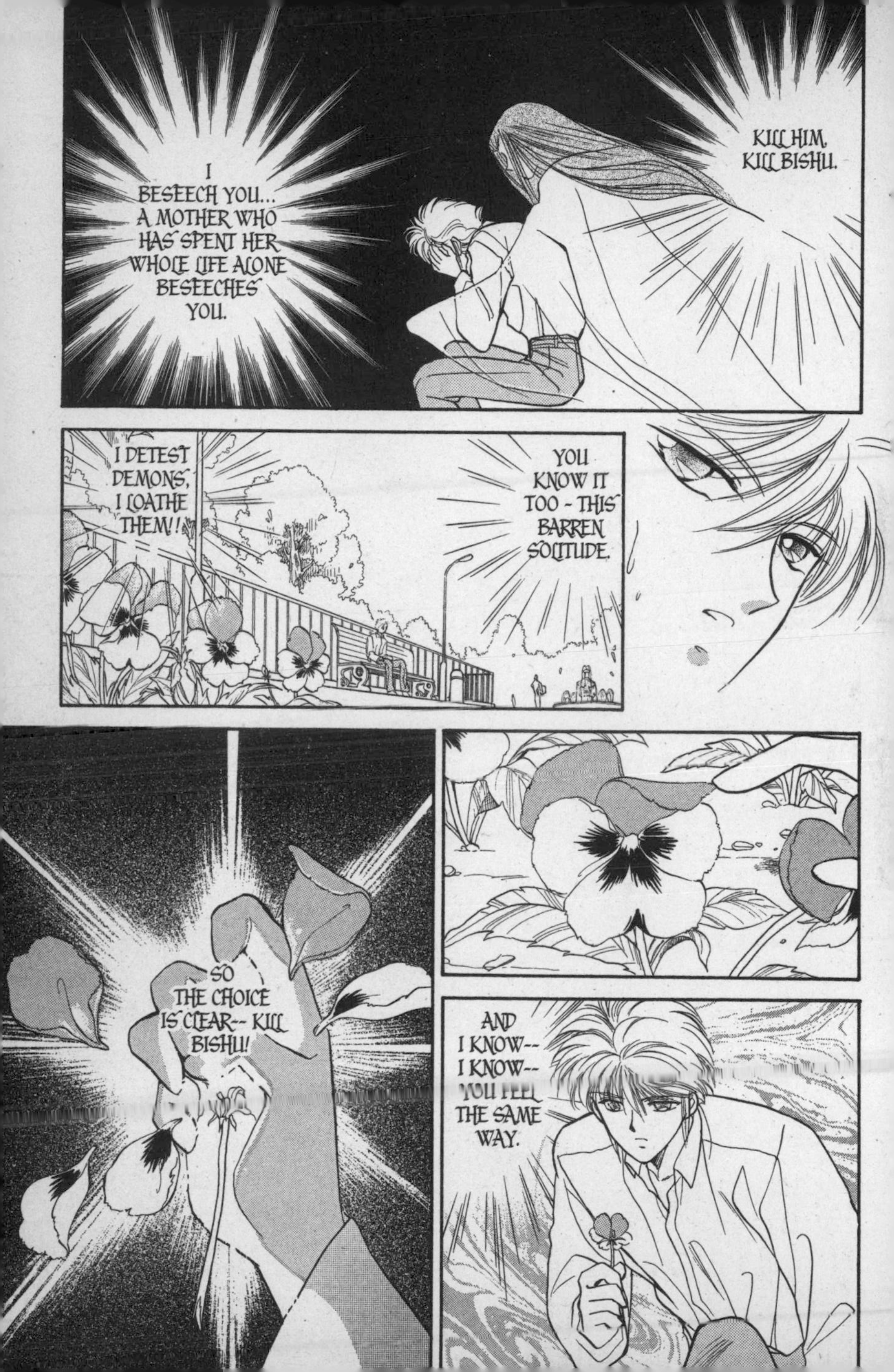
KILL HIM. KILL BISHU.
I BESEECH YOU... A MOTHER WHO HAS SPENT HER WHOLE LIFE ALONE BESEECHES YOU.
YOU KNOW IT TOO - THIS BARREN SOLITUDE.
I DETEST DEMONS, I LOATHE THEM!!
AND I KNOW-- I KNOW-- YOU FEEL THE SAME WAY.
SO THE CHOICE IS CLEAR-- KILL BISHU!

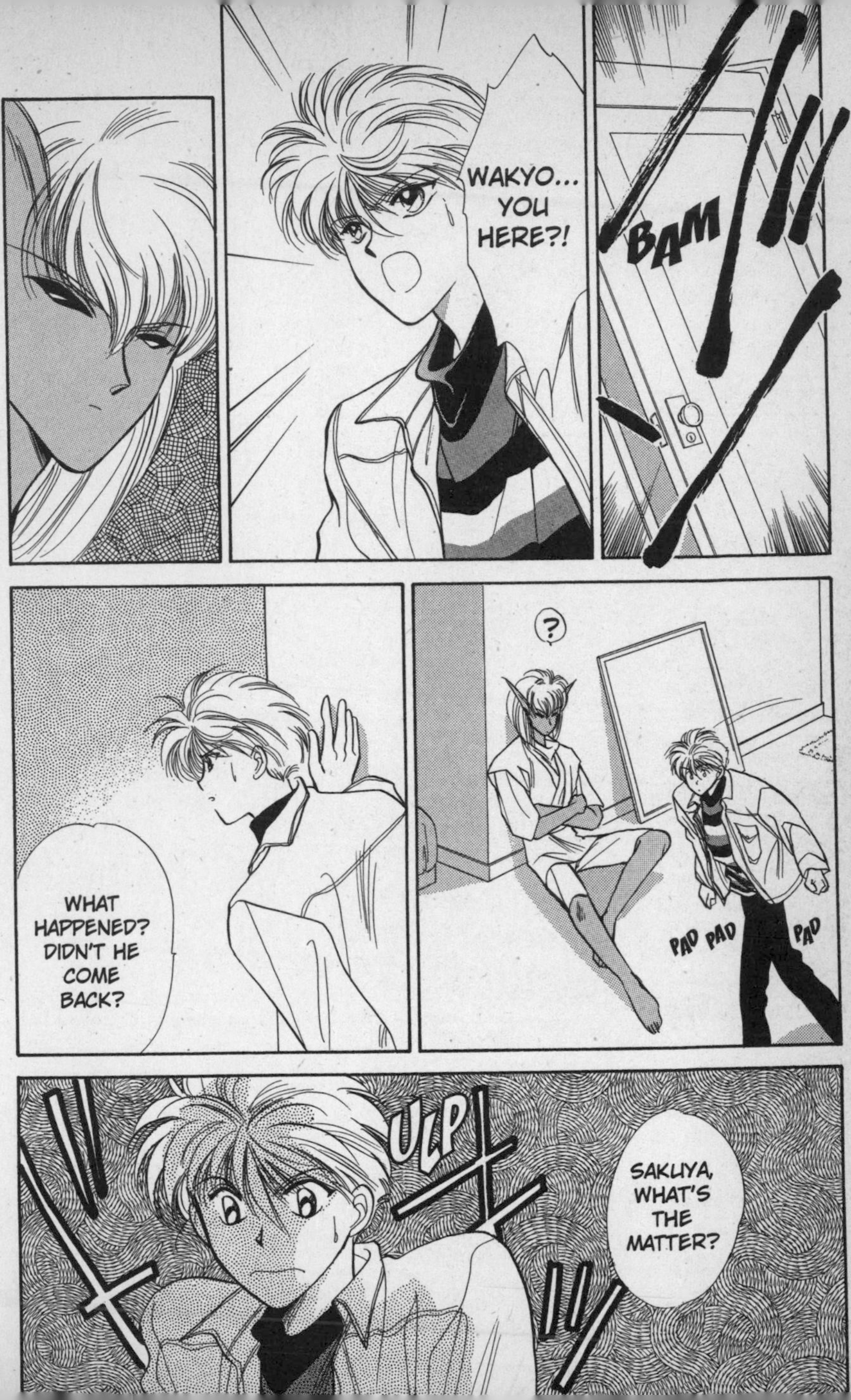
BAM
WAKYO... YOU HERE?!
?
PAD PAD
PAD
WHAT HAPPENED? DIDN'T HE COME BACK?
SAKUYA, WHAT'S THE MATTER?
ULP

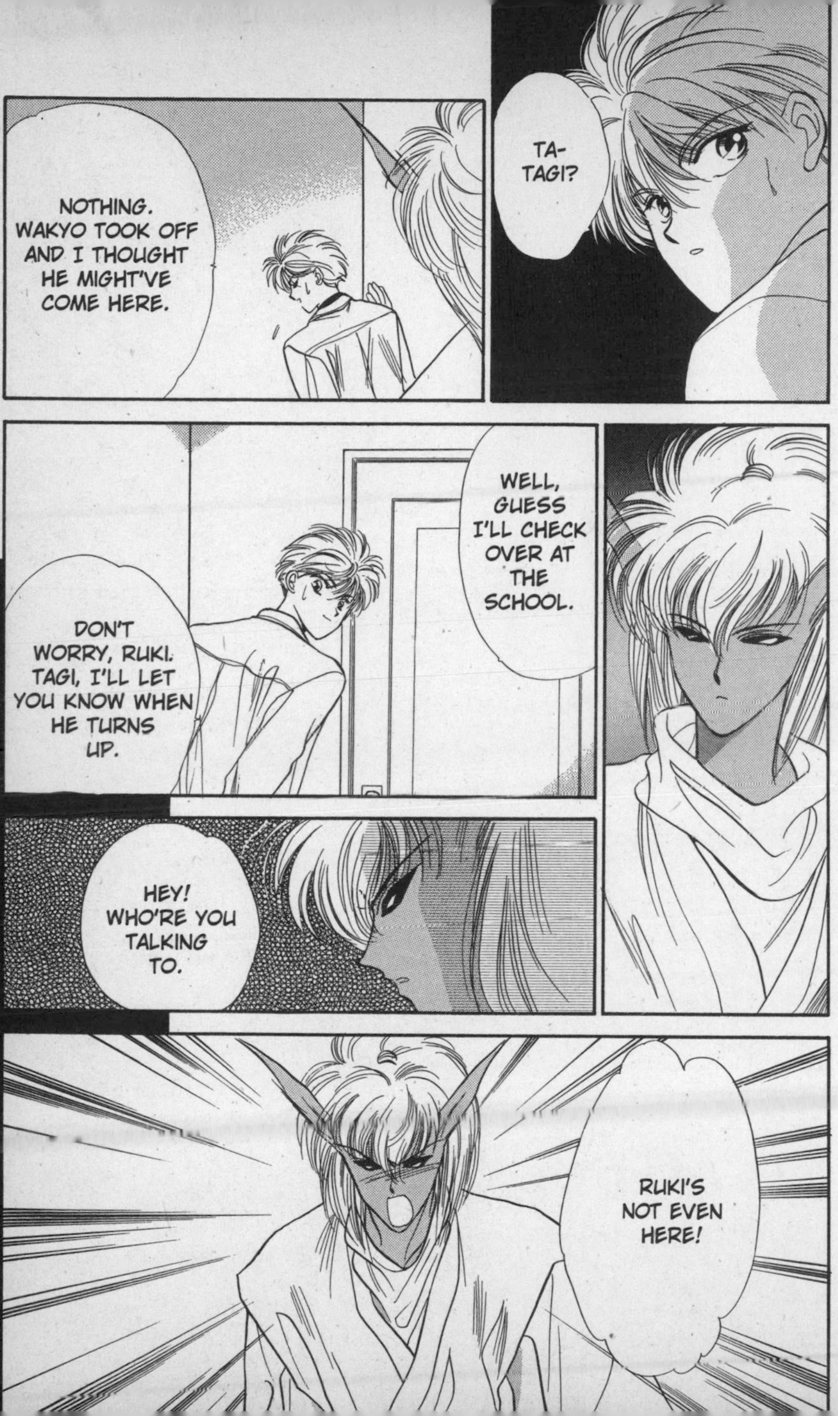
TA-TAGI?
NOTHING. WAKYO TOOK OFF AND I THOUGHT HE MIGHT'VE COME HERE.
WELL, GUESS I'LL CHECK OVER AT THE SCHOOL.
DON'T WORRY, RUKI. TAGI, I'LL LET YOU KNOW WHEN HE TURNS UP.
HEY! WHO'RE YOU TALKING TO.
RUKI'S NOT EVEN HERE!

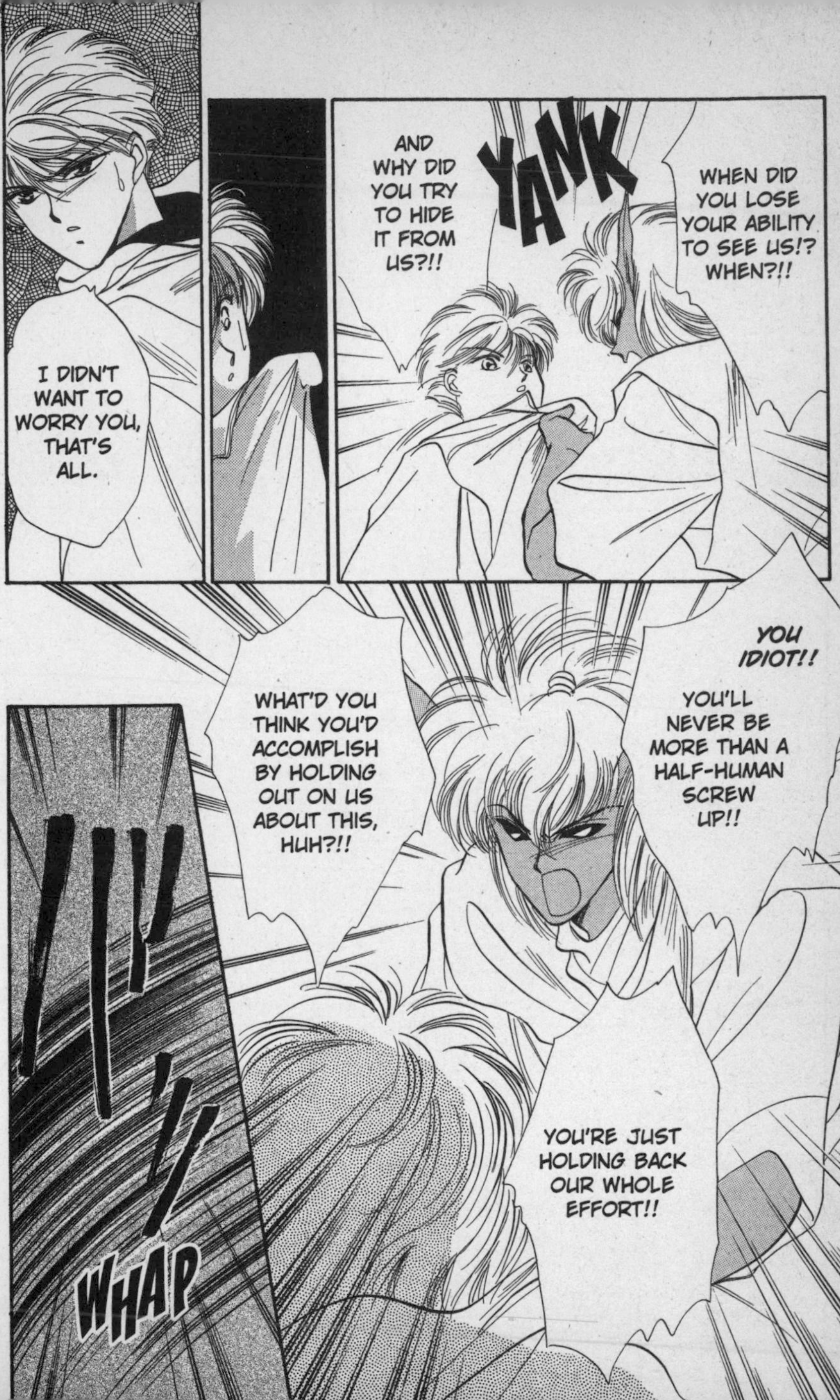
WHEN DID YOU LOSE YOUR ABILITY TO SEE US!? WHEN?!!
YANK
AND WHY DID YOU TRY TO HIDE IT FROM US?!!
I DIDN'T WANT TO WORRY YOU, THAT'S ALL.
YOU IDIOT!!
YOU'LL NEVER BE MORE THAN A HALF-HUMAN SCREW UP!!
WHAT'D YOU THINK YOU'D ACCOMPLISH BY HOLDING OUT ON US ABOUT THIS, HUH?!!
YOU'RE JUST HOLDING BACK OUR WHOLE EFFORT!!
WHAP

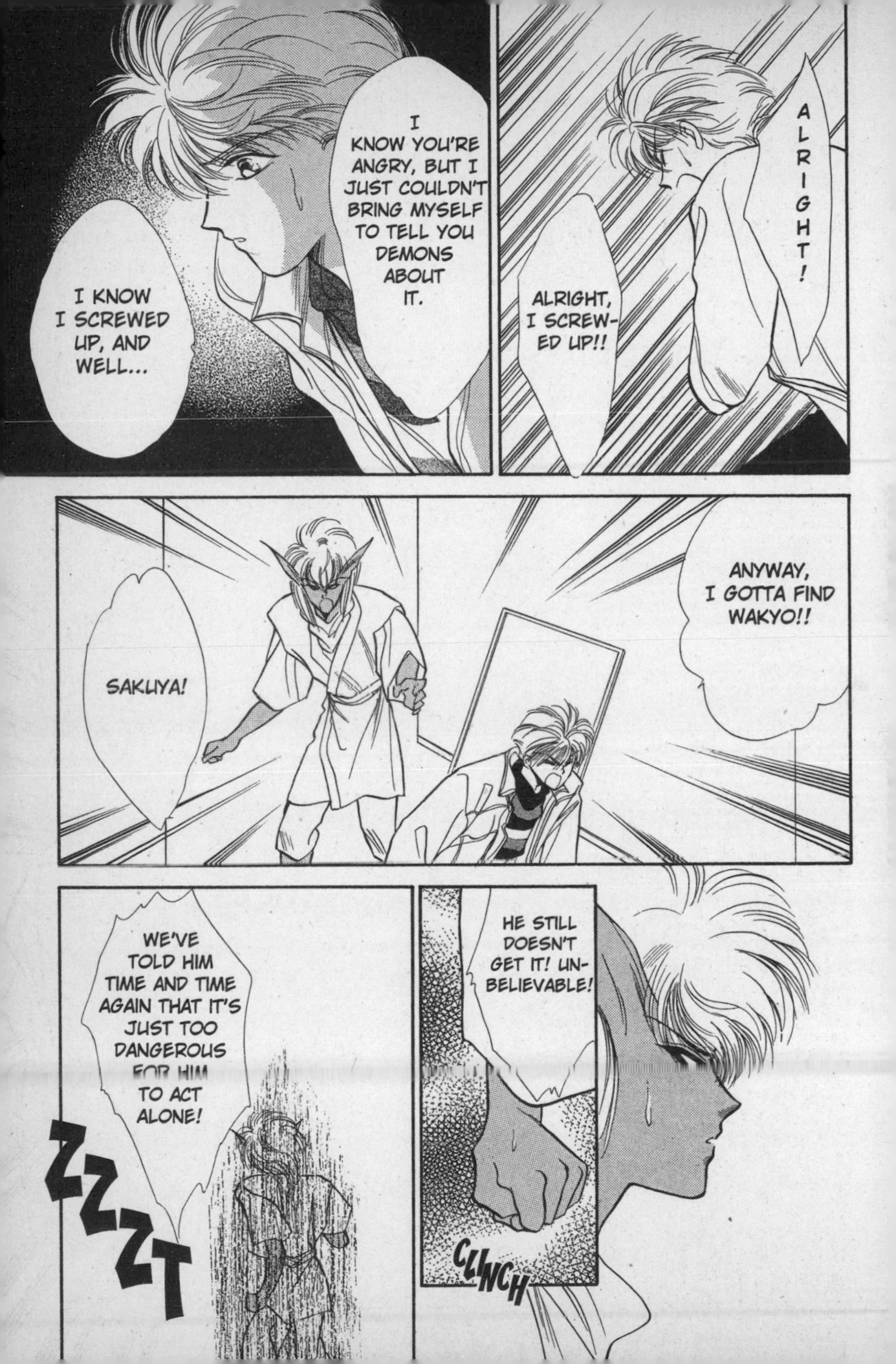
ALRIGHT!
ALRIGHT, I SCREWED UP!!
I KNOW YOU'RE ANGRY, BUT I JUST COULDN'T BRING MYSELF TO TELL YOU DEMONS ABOUT IT.
I KNOW I SCREWED UP, AND WELL...
ANYWAY, I GOTTA FIND WAKYO!!
SAKUYA!
HE STILL DOESN'T GET IT! UNBELIEVABLE!
CLINCH
WE'VE TOLD HIM TIME AND TIME AGAIN THAT IT'S JUST TOO DANGEROUS FOR HIM TO ACT ALONE!
ZZZZT

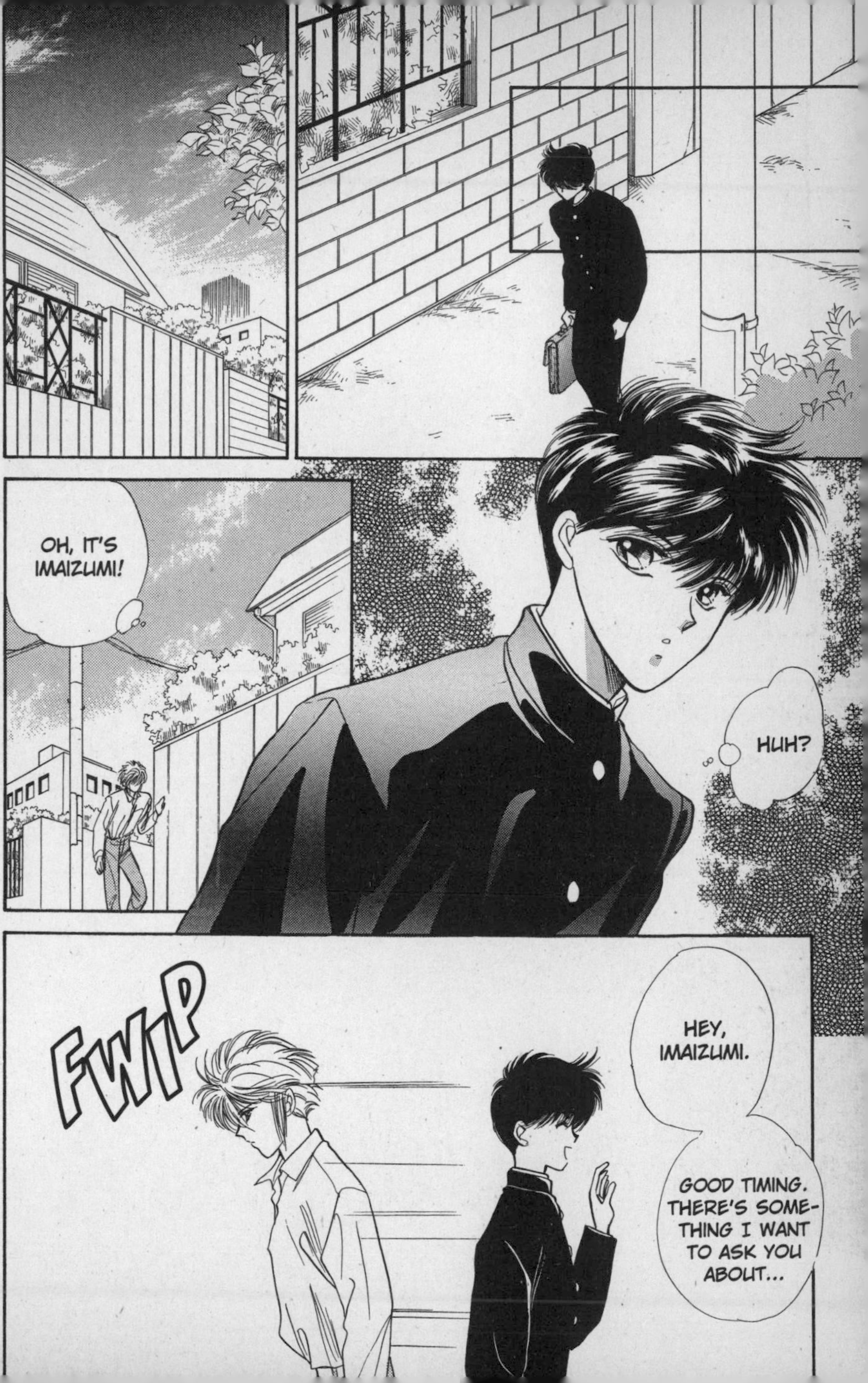
HUH?
OH, IT'S IMAIZUMI!
HEY, IMAIZUMI.
GOOD TIMING. THERE'S SOMETHING I WANT TO ASK YOU ABOUT...
FWIP

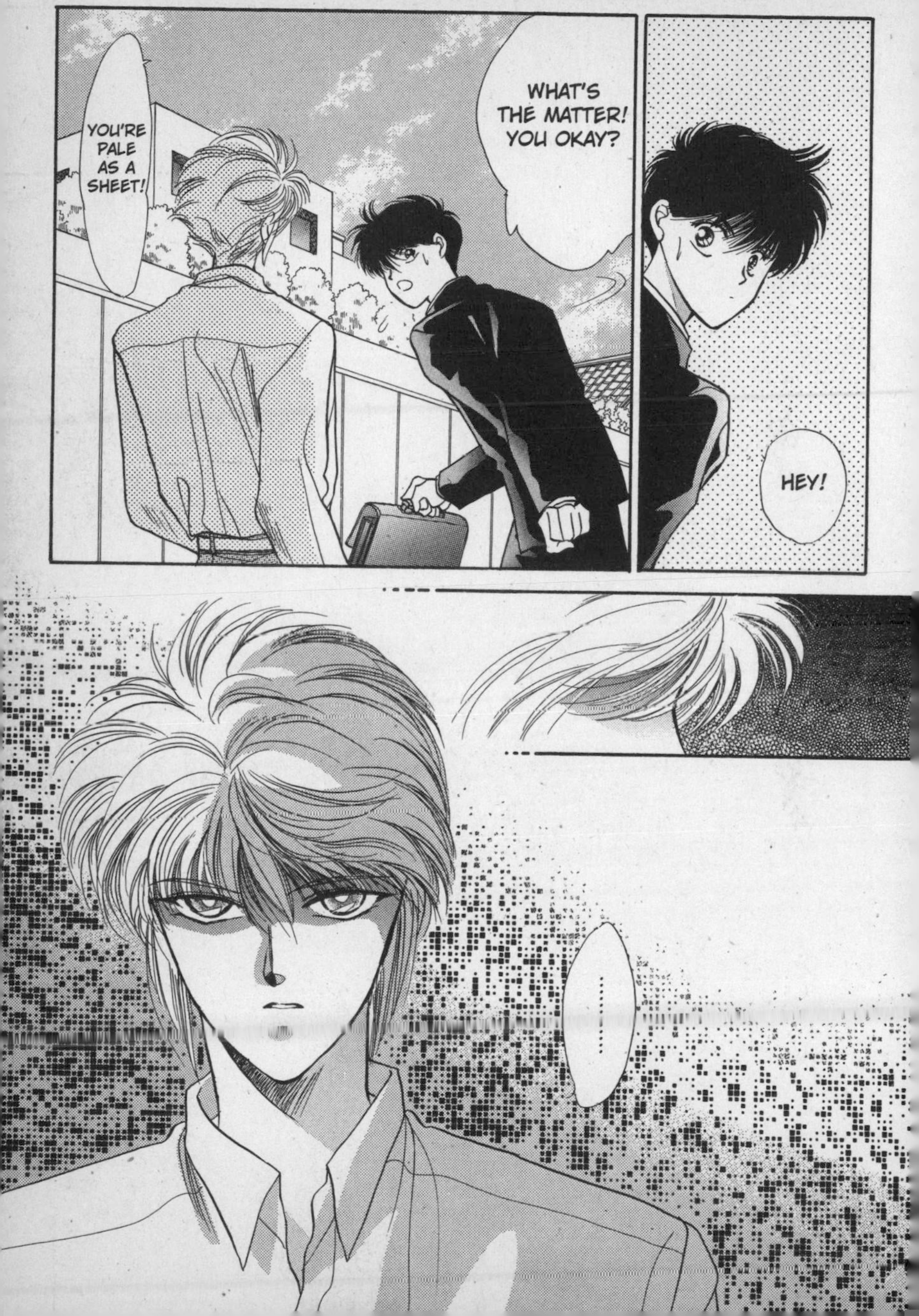
HEY!
WHAT'S THE MATTER! YOU OKAY?
YOU'RE PALE AS A SHEET!
......

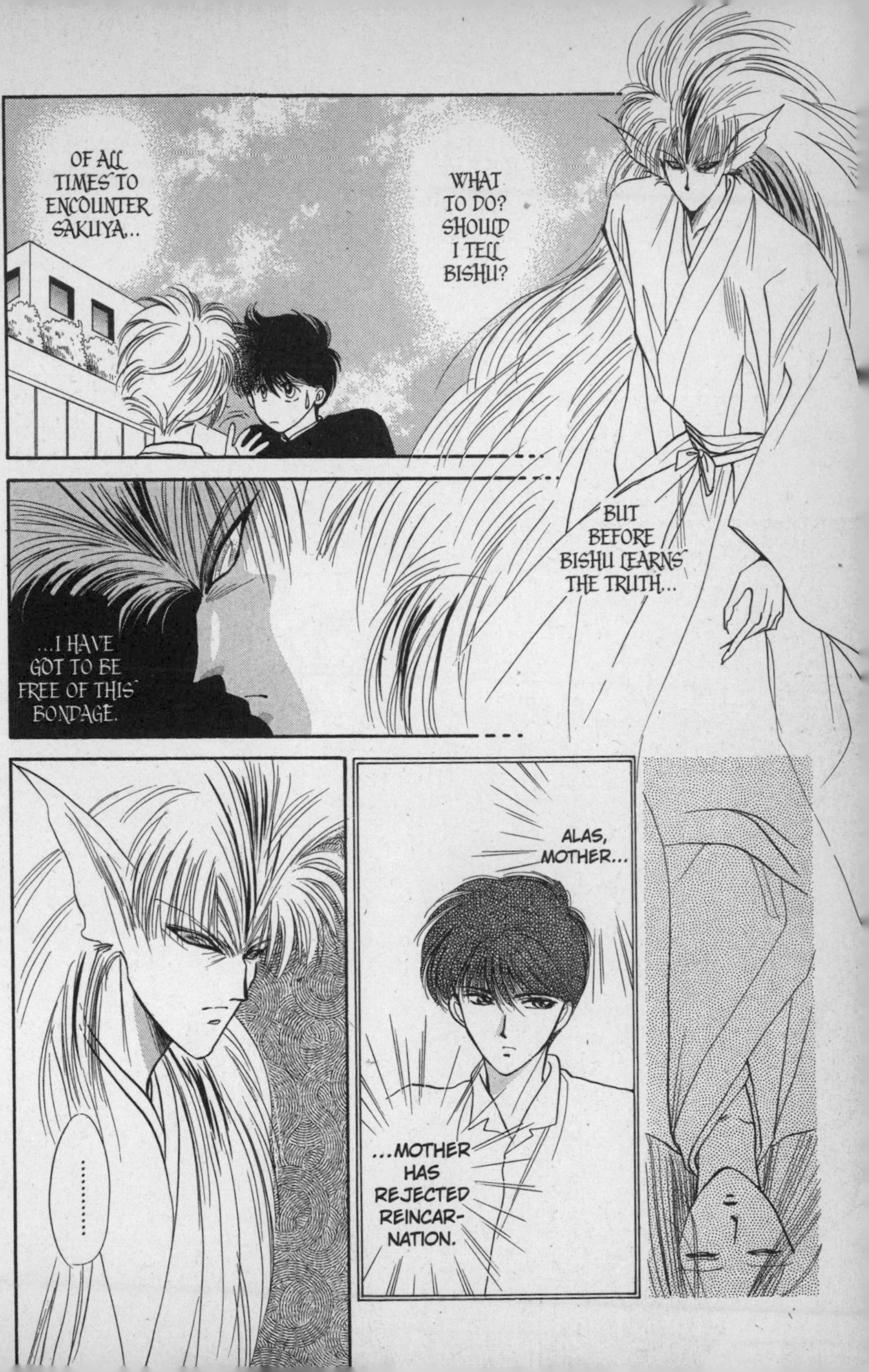
WHAT TO DO? SHOULD I TELL BISHU?
OF ALL TIMES TO ENCOUNTER SAKUYA...
BUT BEFORE BISHU LEARNS THE TRUTH...
...I HAVE GOT TO BE FREE OF THIS BONDAGE.
ALAS, MOTHER...
...MOTHER HAS REJECTED REINCARNATION.
......

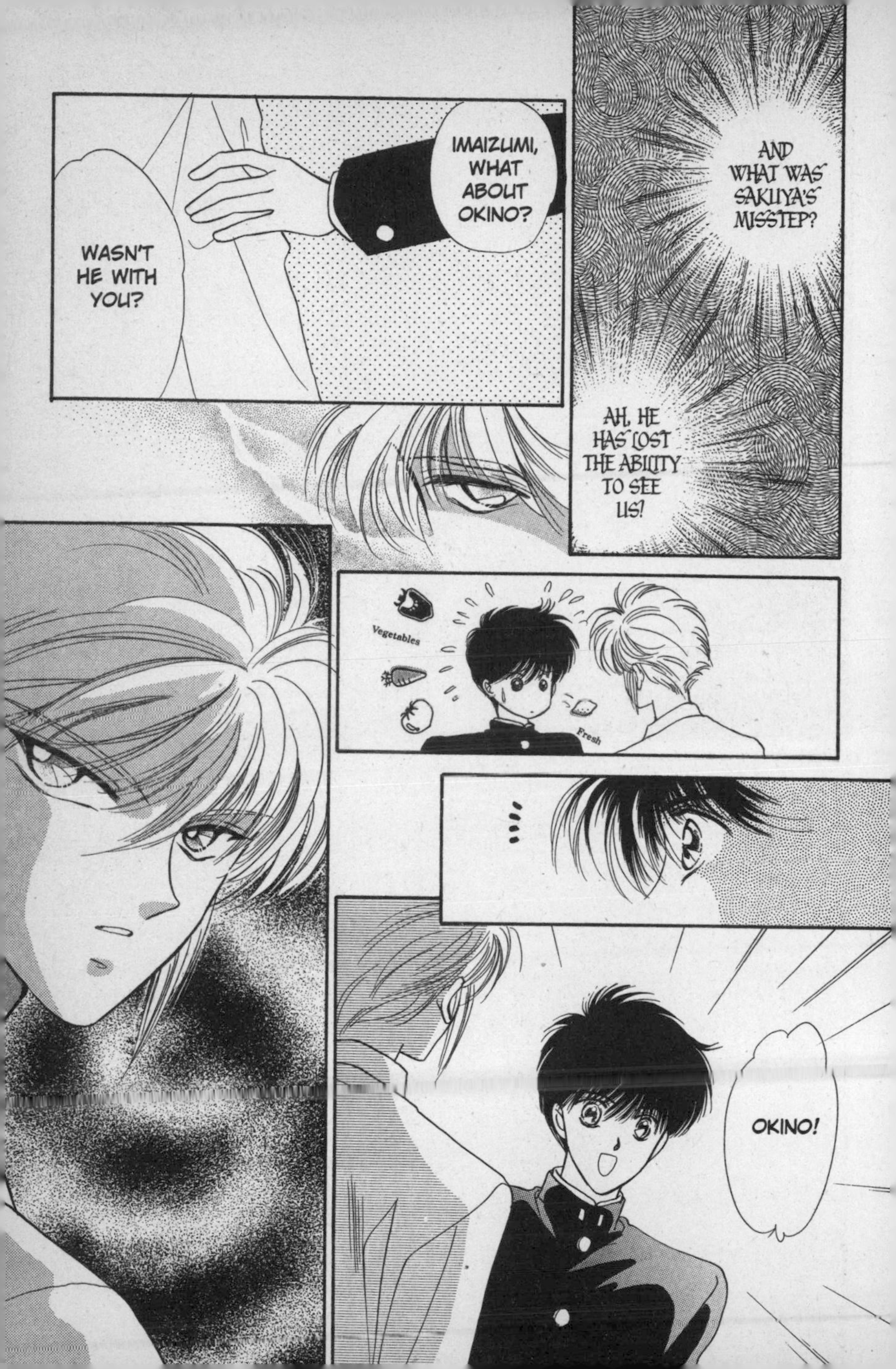
AND WHAT WAS SAKUYA'S MISSTEP?
AH, HE HAS LOST THE ABILITY TO SEE US!
IMAIZUMI, WHAT ABOUT OKINO?
WASN'T HE WITH YOU?
Vegetables
Fresh
...
OKINO!

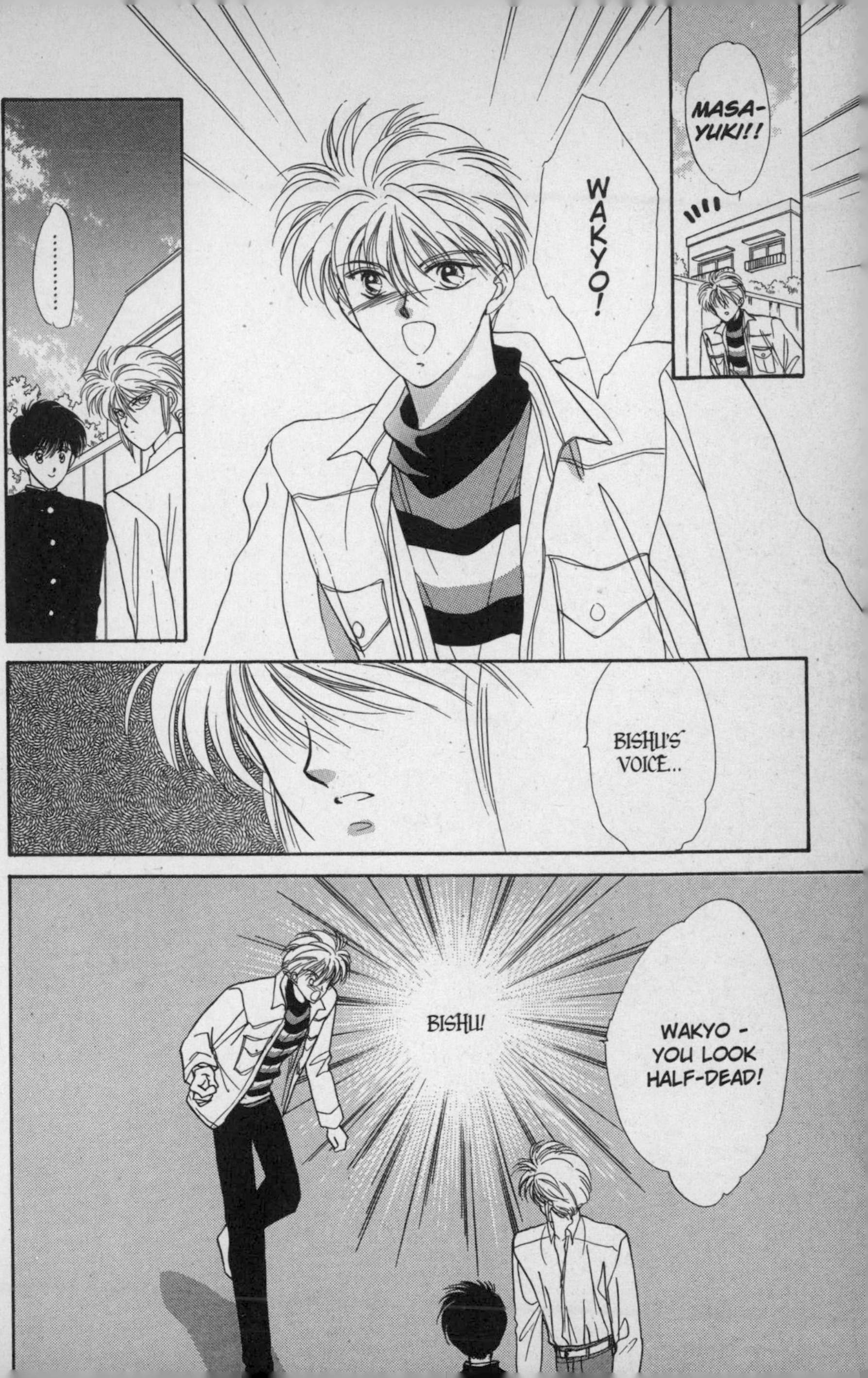
MASA-YUKI!!
WAKYO!
......
BISHU'S VOICE...
WAKYO - YOU LOOK HALF-DEAD!
BISHU!

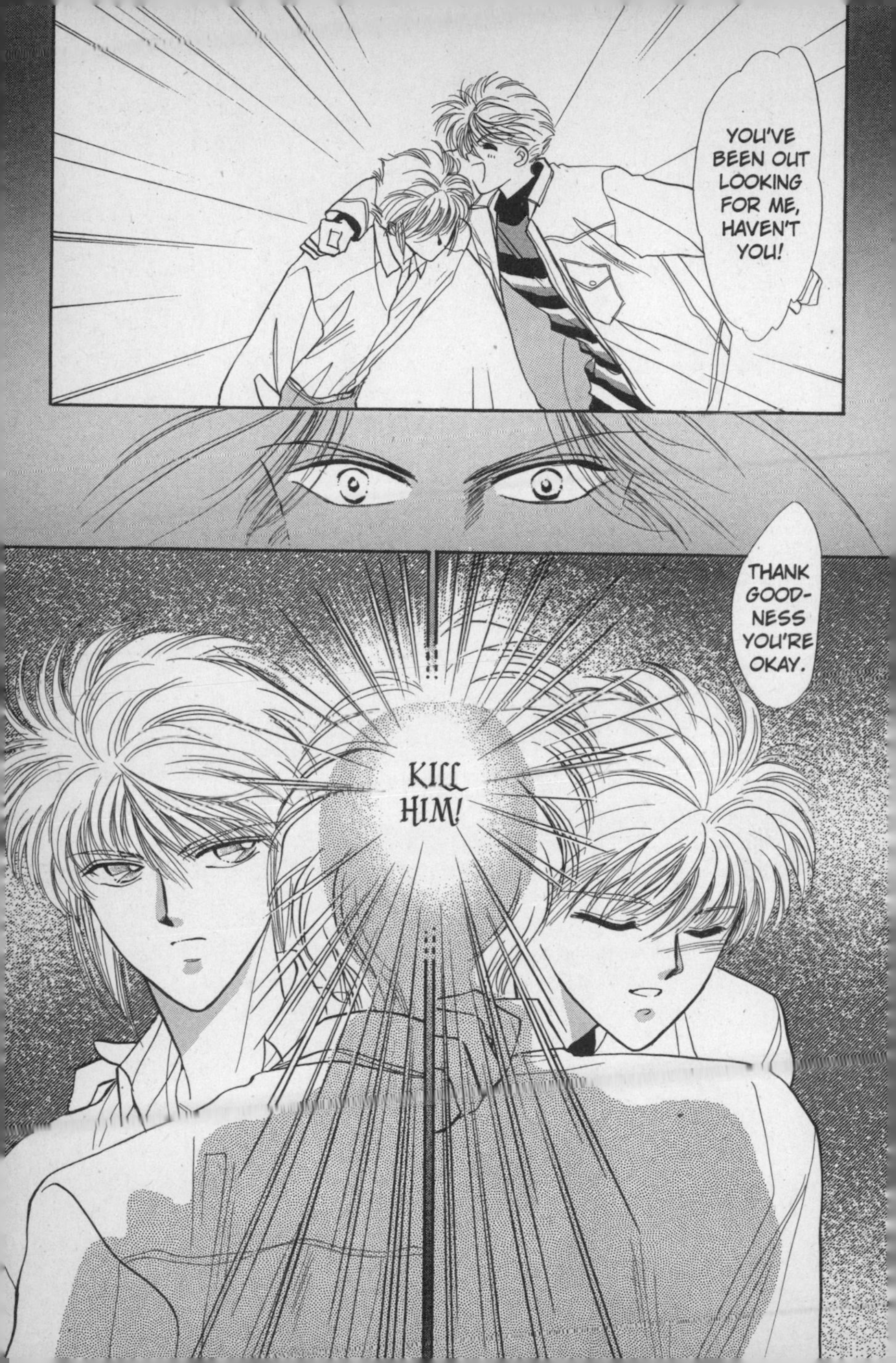
YOU'VE BEEN OUT LOOKING FOR ME, HAVEN'T YOU!
THANK GOOD-NESS YOU'RE OKAY.
KILL HIM!

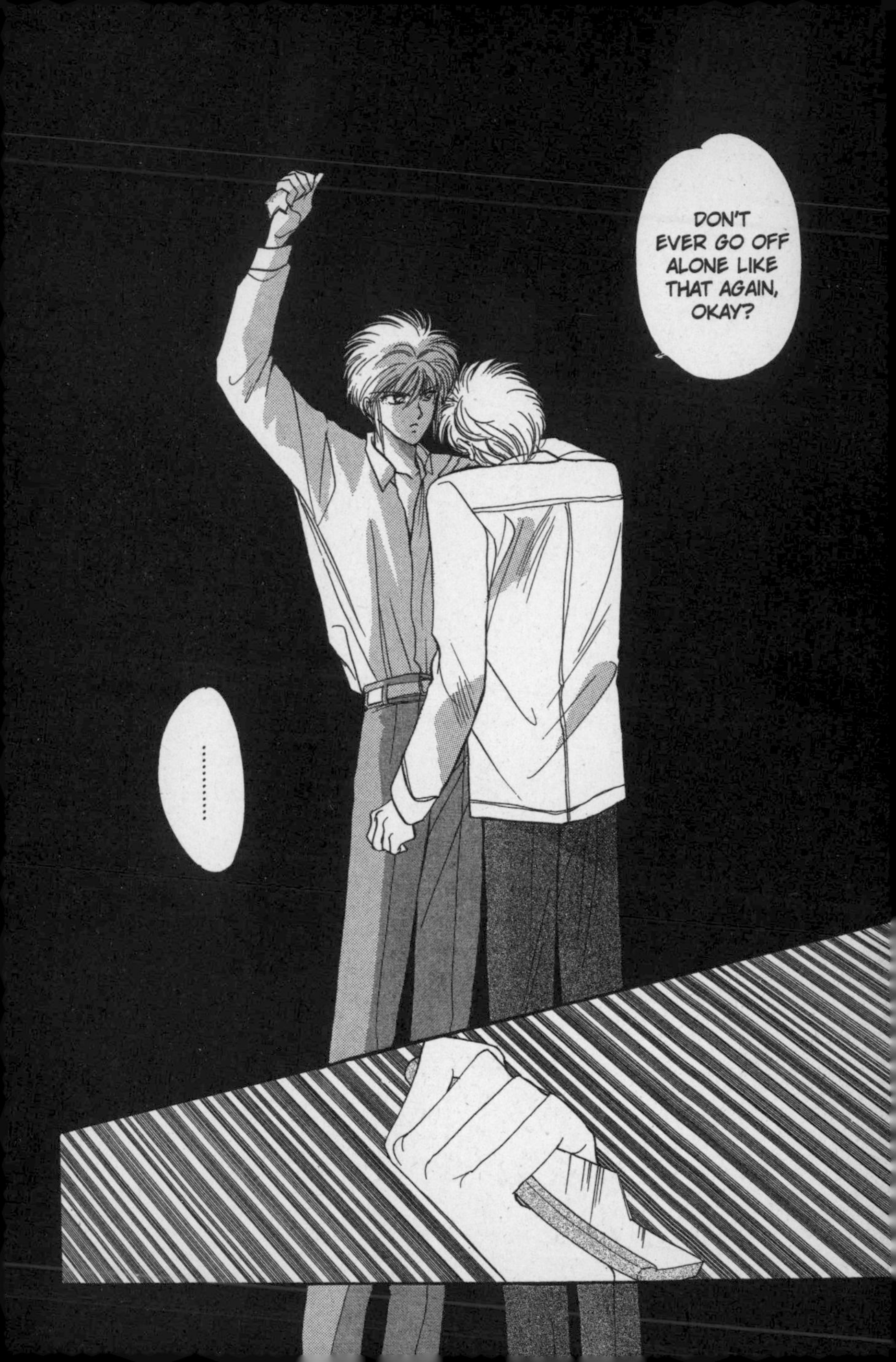
DON'T EVER GO OFF ALONE LIKE THAT AGAIN, OKAY?
......

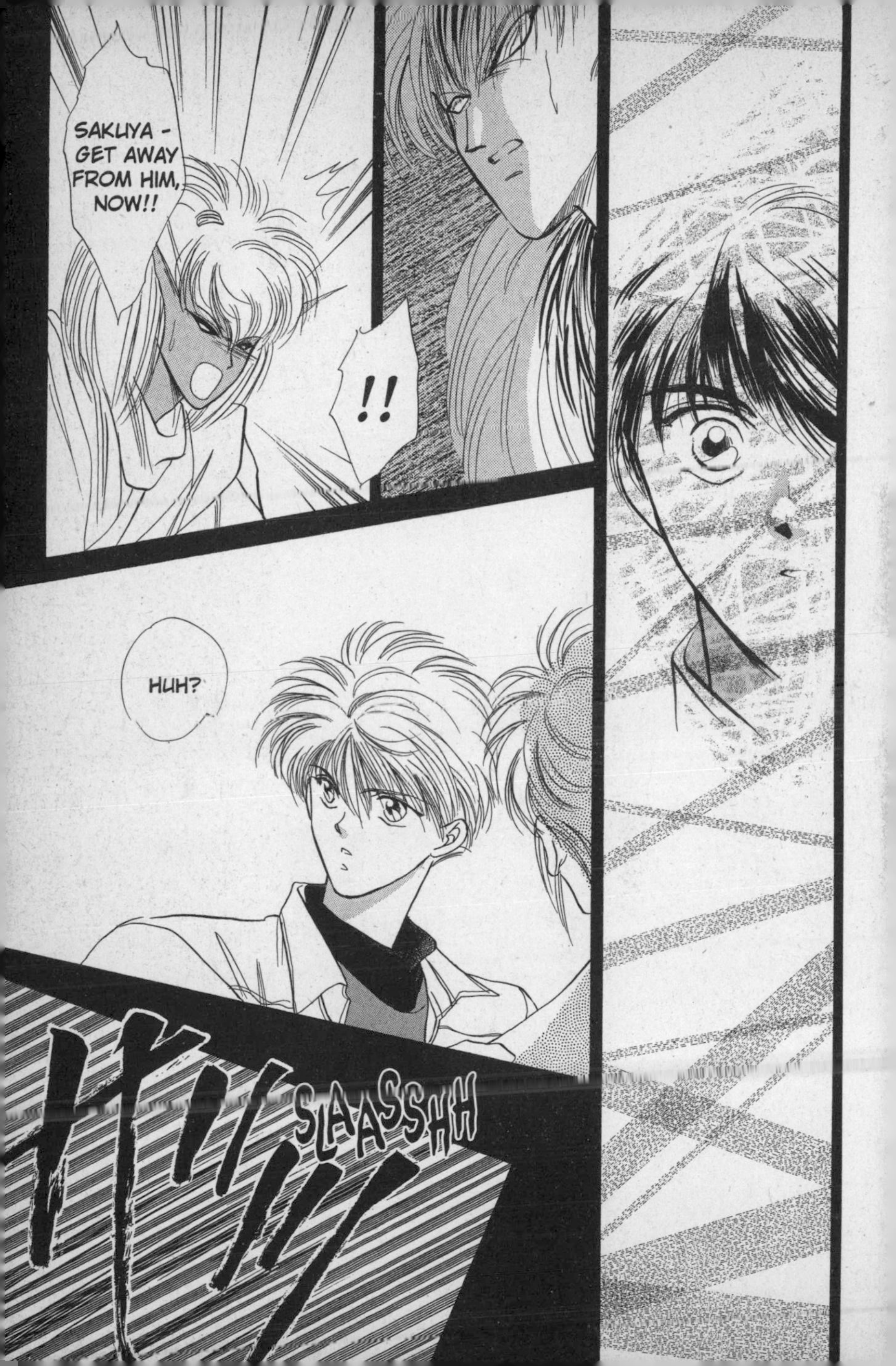
SAKUYA - GET AWAY FROM HIM, NOW!!
!!
HUH?
SLAASSHH

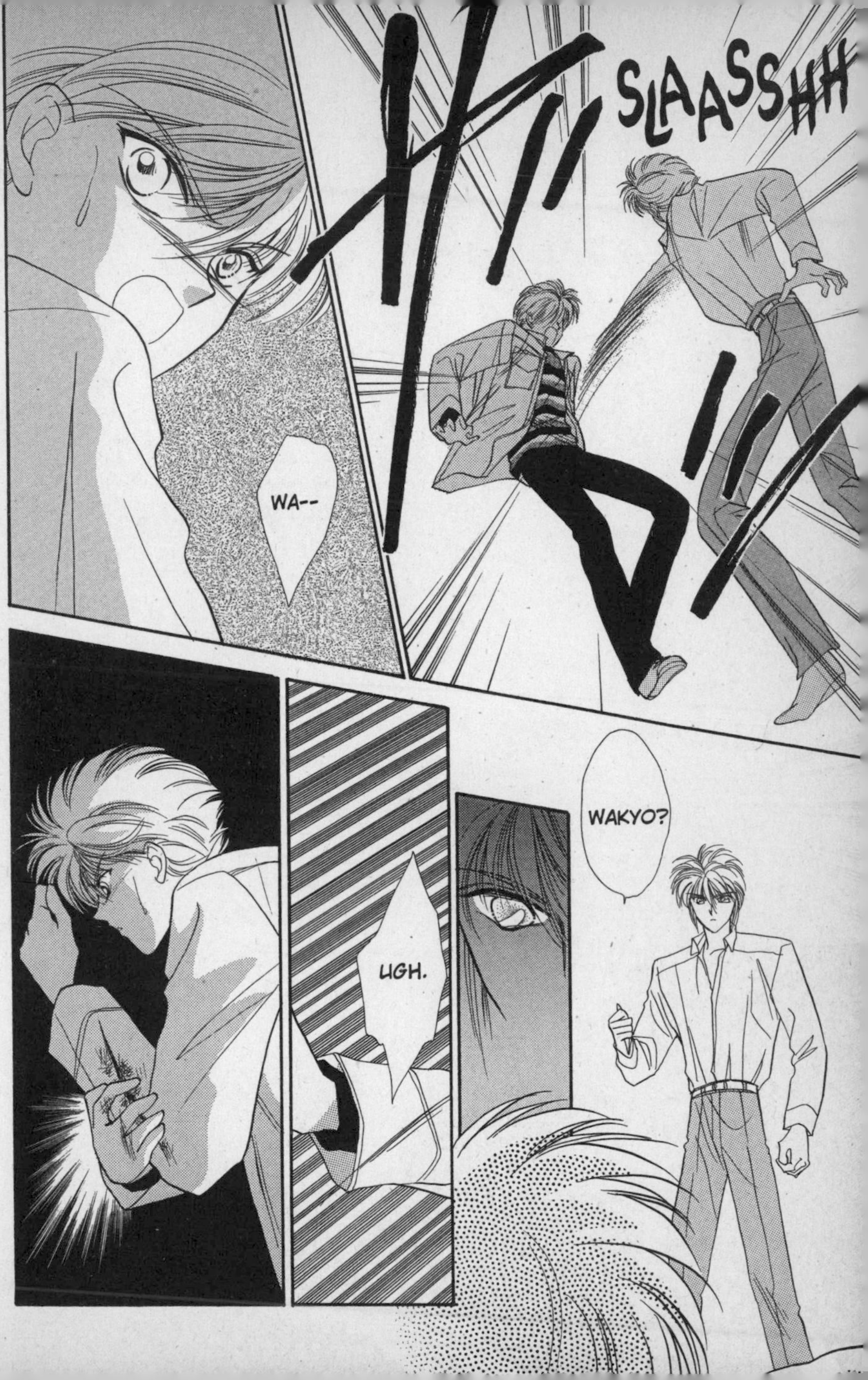

SLAASSHH
WA--
WAKYO?
UGH.

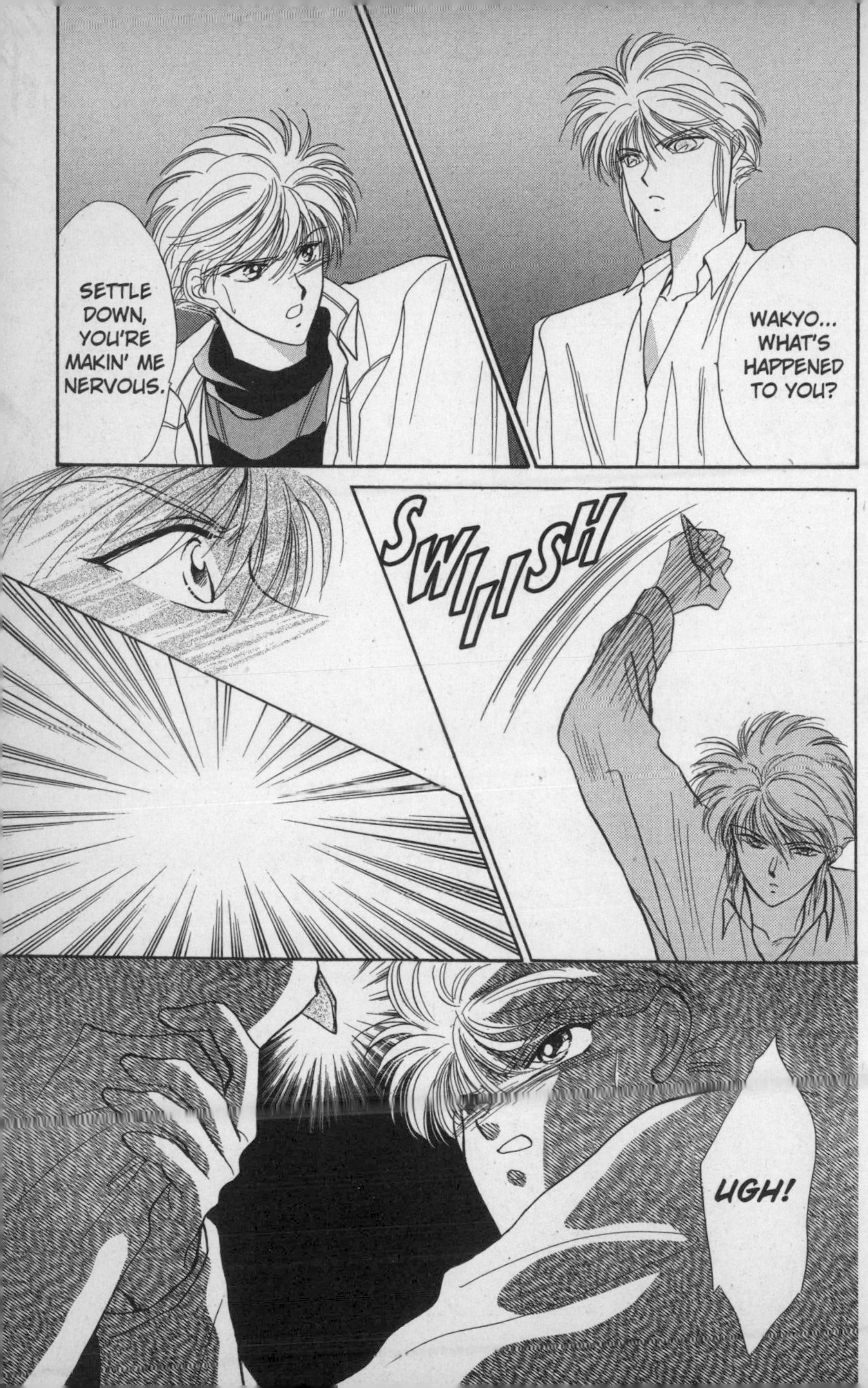
WAKYO... WHAT'S HAPPENED TO YOU?
SETTLE DOWN, YOU'RE MAKIN' ME NERVOUS.
SWIIISH
UGH!

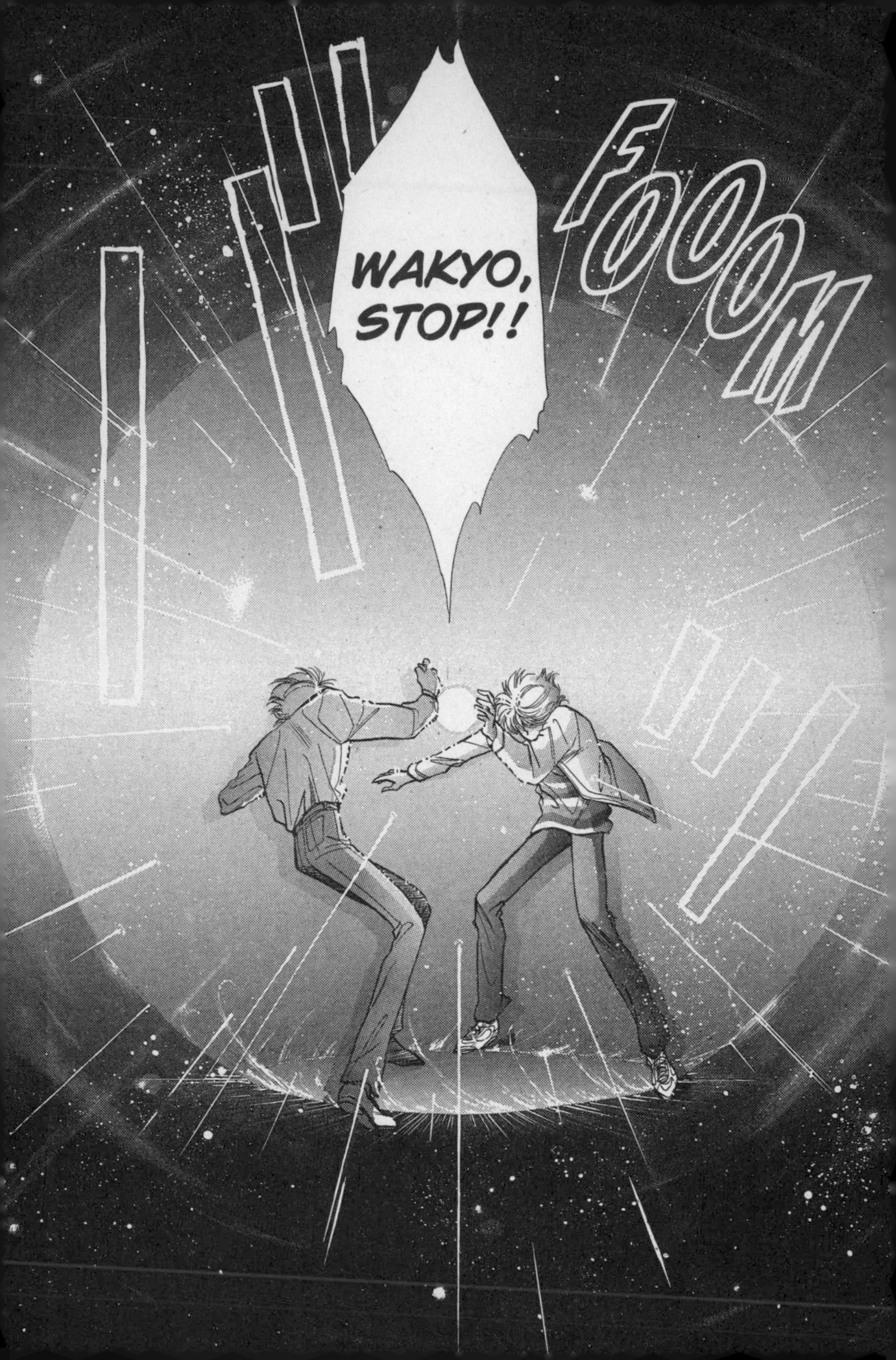
FOOOM
WAKYO, STOP!!

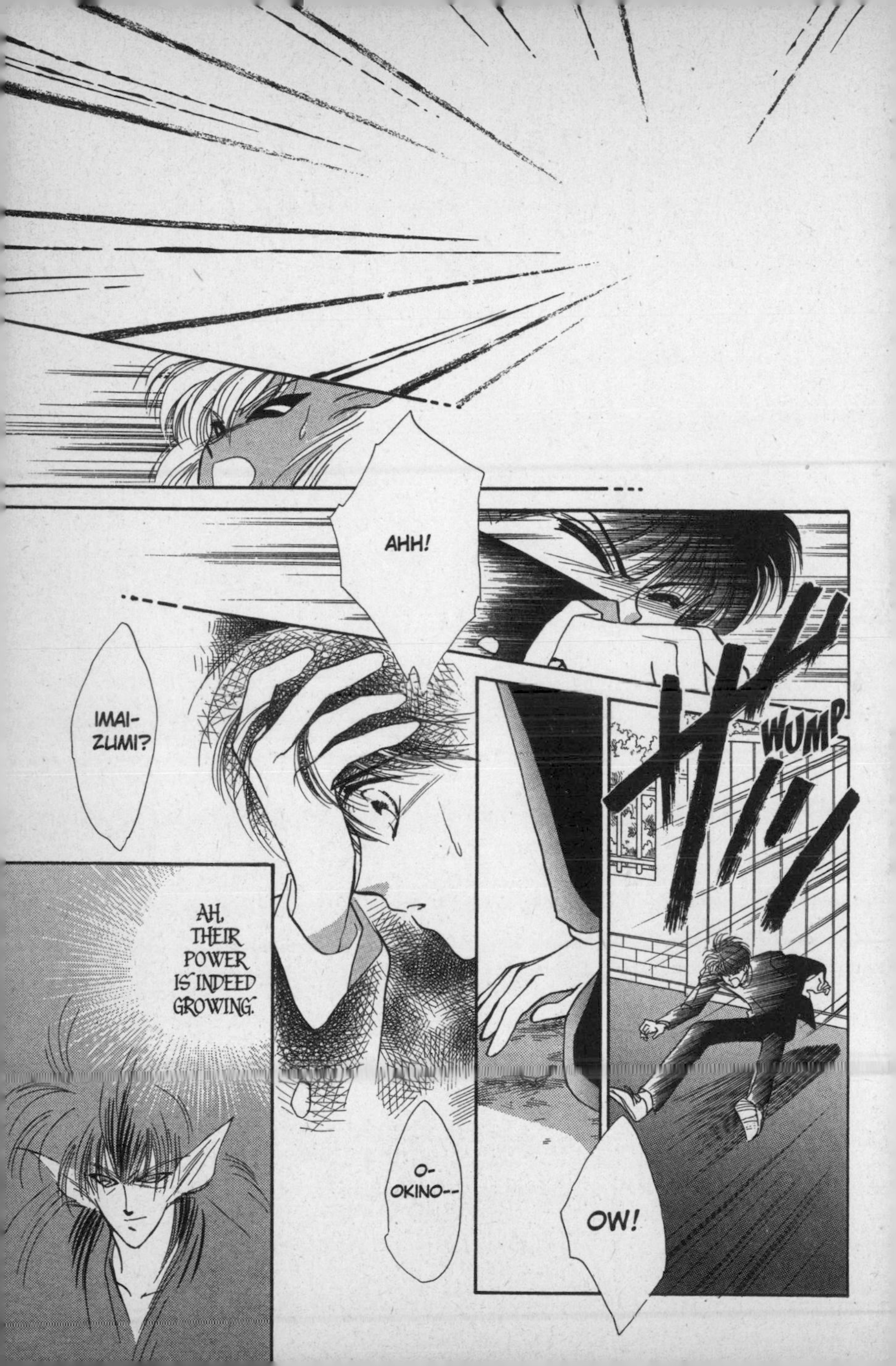
AHH!
WUMP
OW!
IMAI-ZUMI?
O-OKINO--
AH, THEIR POWER IS INDEED GROWING.

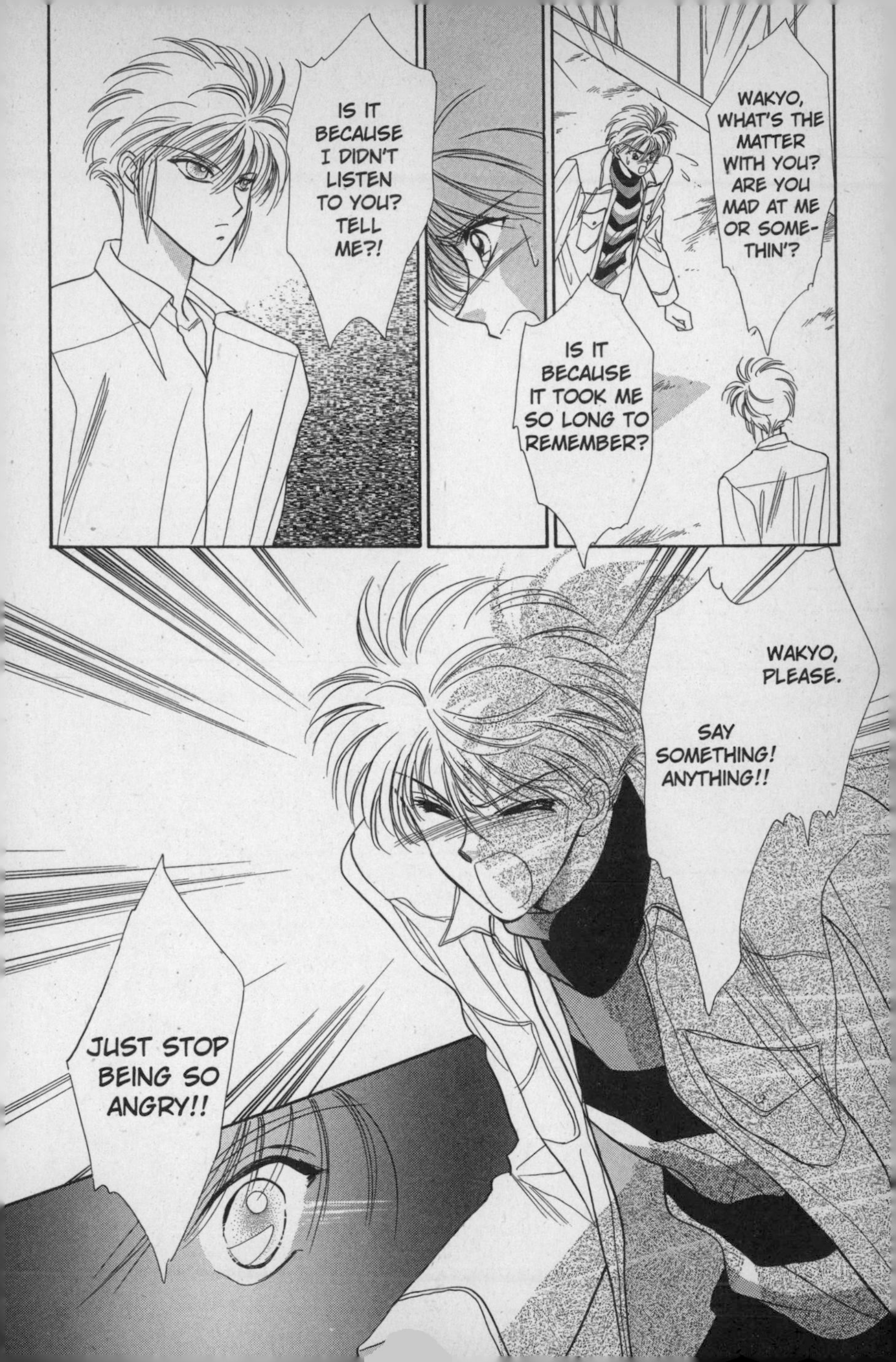

WAKYO, WHAT'S THE MATTER WITH YOU? ARE YOU MAD AT ME OR SOME-THIN'?
IS IT BECAUSE I DIDN'T LISTEN TO YOU? TELL ME?!
IS IT BECAUSE IT TOOK ME SO LONG TO REMEMBER?
WAKYO, PLEASE.
SAY SOMETHING! ANYTHING!!
JUST STOP BEING SO ANGRY!!

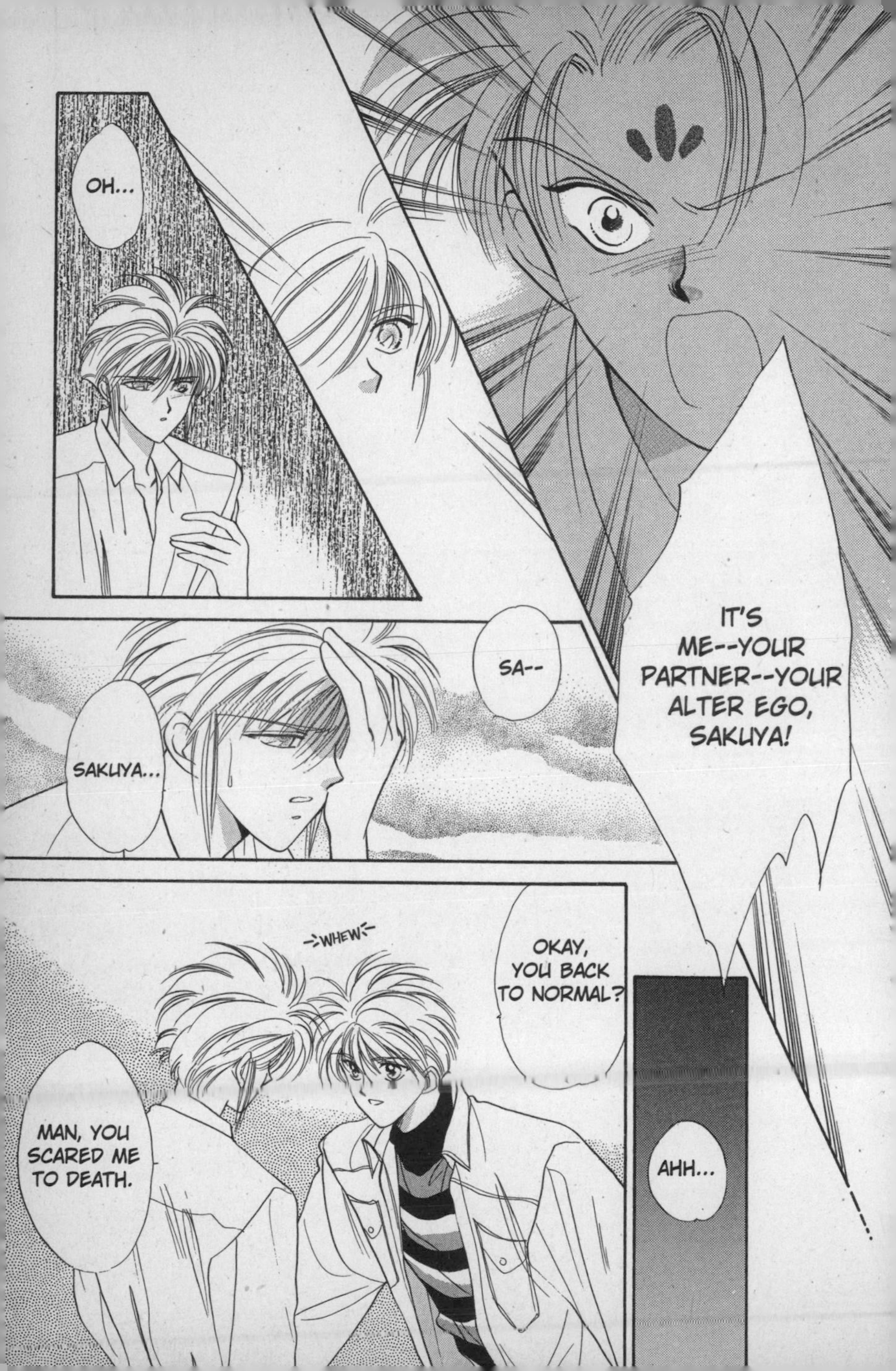
IT'S ME--YOUR PARTNER--YOUR ALTER EGO, SAKUYA!
OH...
SA--
SAKUYA...
AHH...
OKAY, YOU BACK TO NORMAL?
WHEW
MAN, YOU SCARED ME TO DEATH.

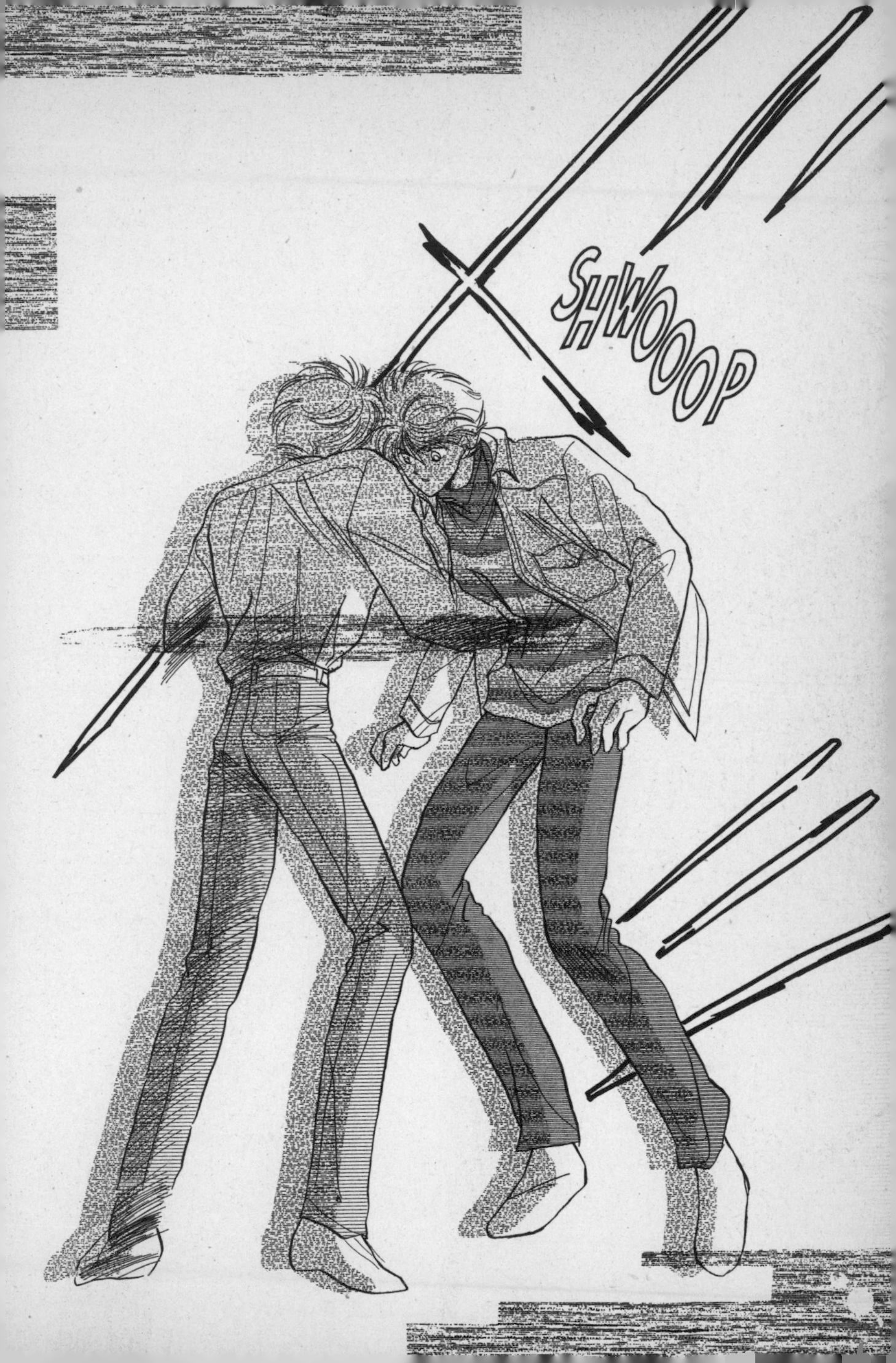
SHWOOOP

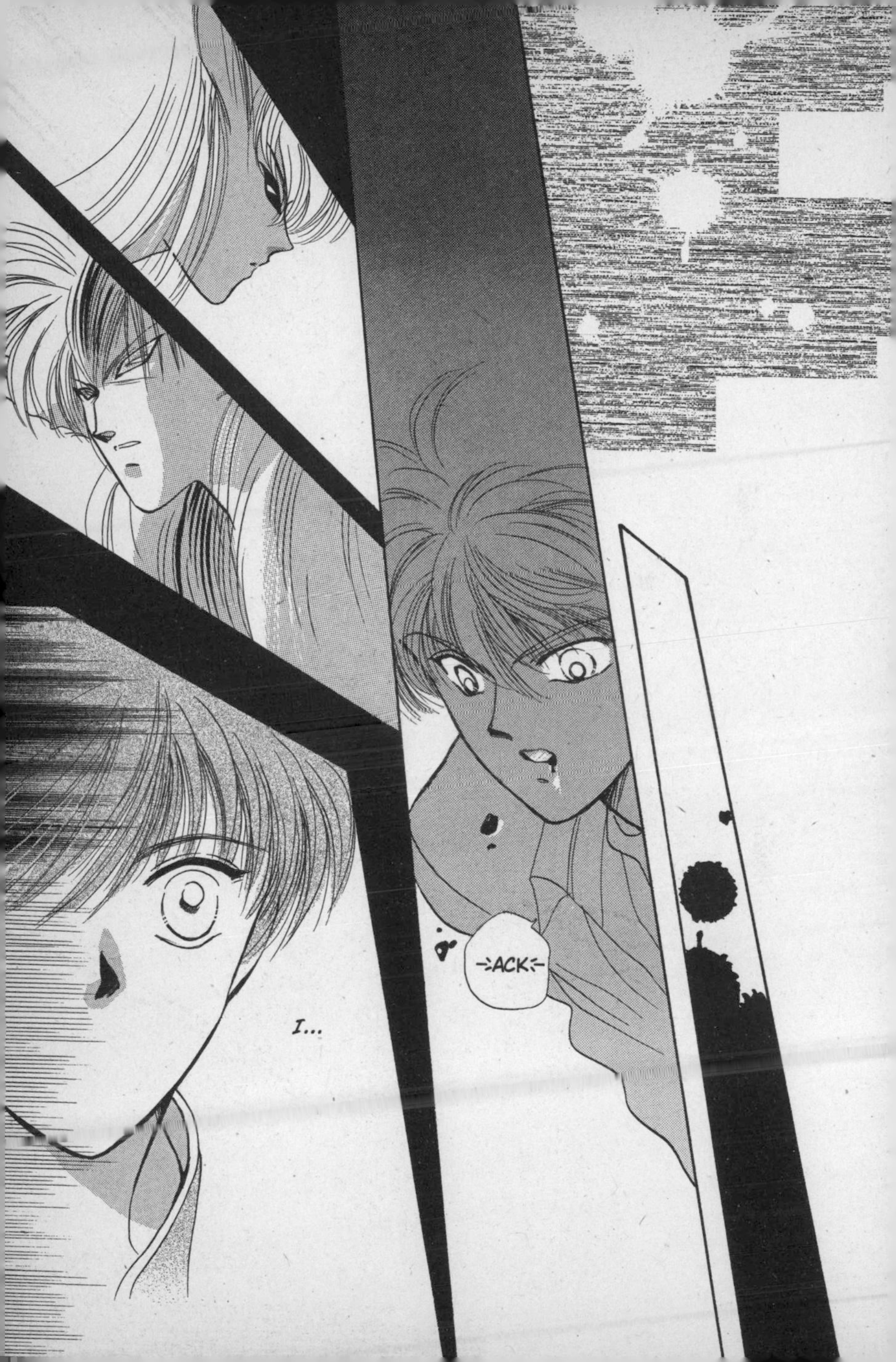
-ACK-
I...

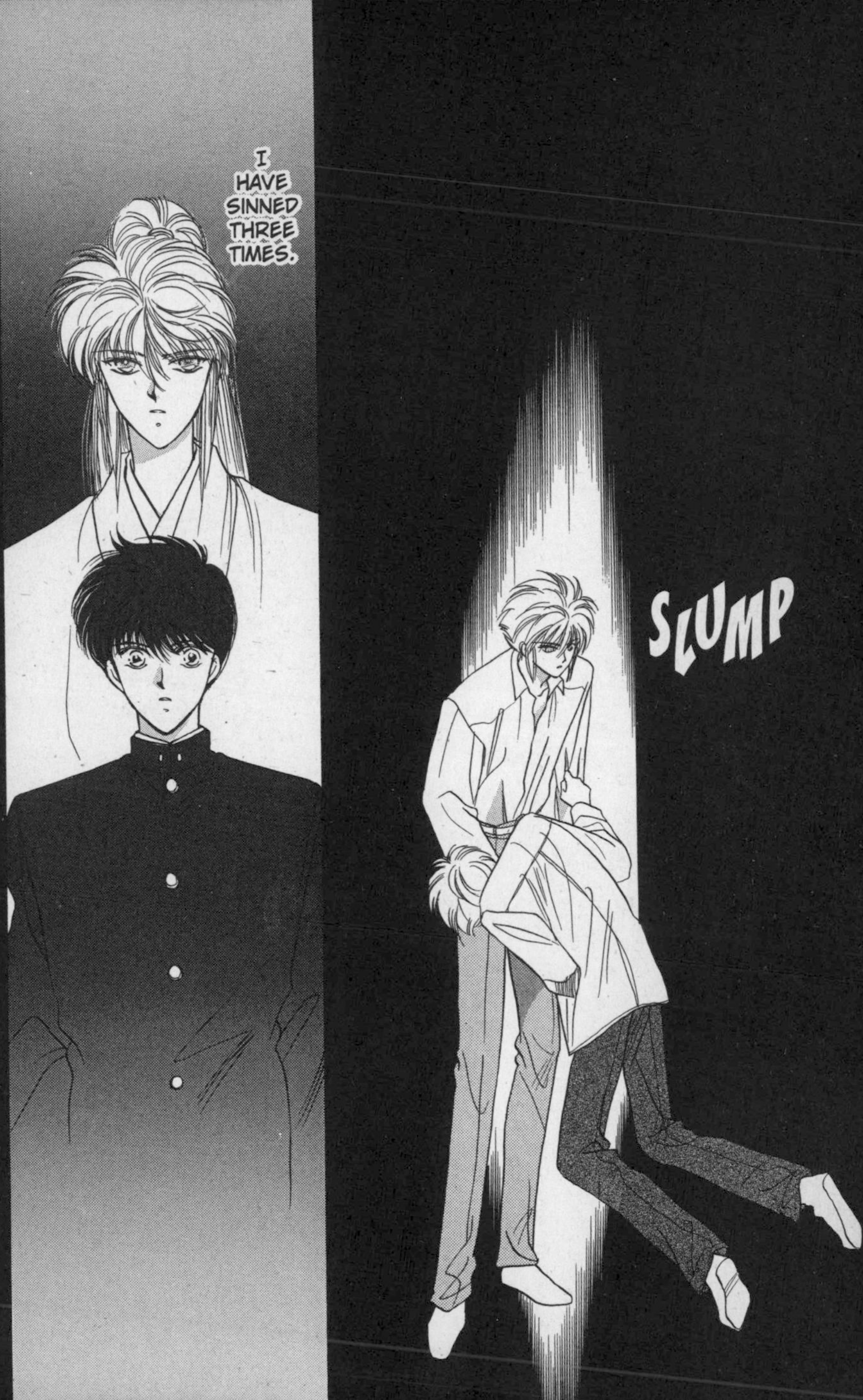
SLUMP
I HAVE SINNED THREE TIMES.

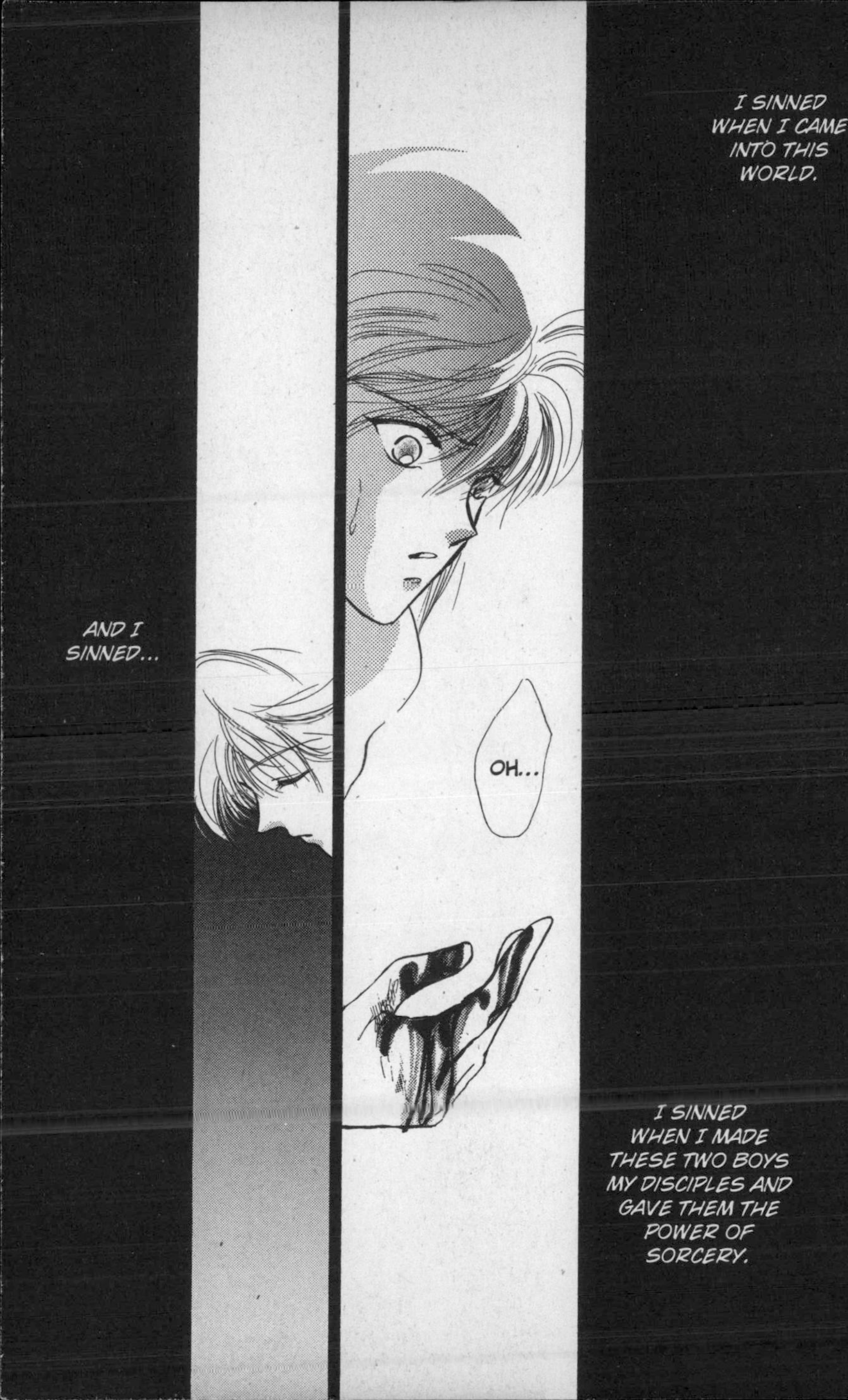
I SINNED WHEN I CAME INTO THIS WORLD.
OH...
AND I SINNED...
I SINNED WHEN I MADE THESE TWO BOYS MY DISCIPLES AND GAVE THEM THE POWER OF SORCERY.

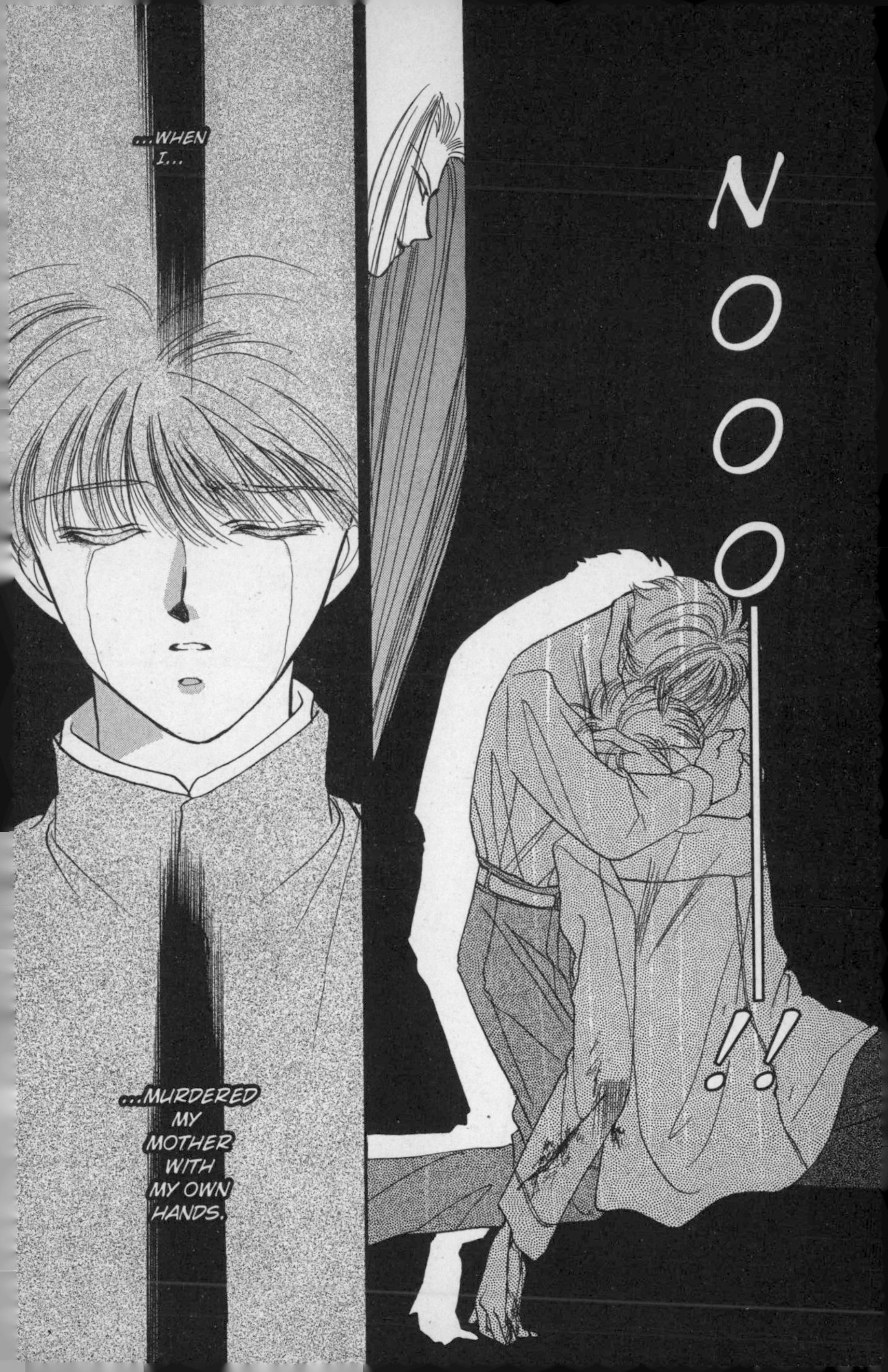
NOOO—!!
...WHEN I...
...MURDERED MY MOTHER WITH MY OWN HANDS.

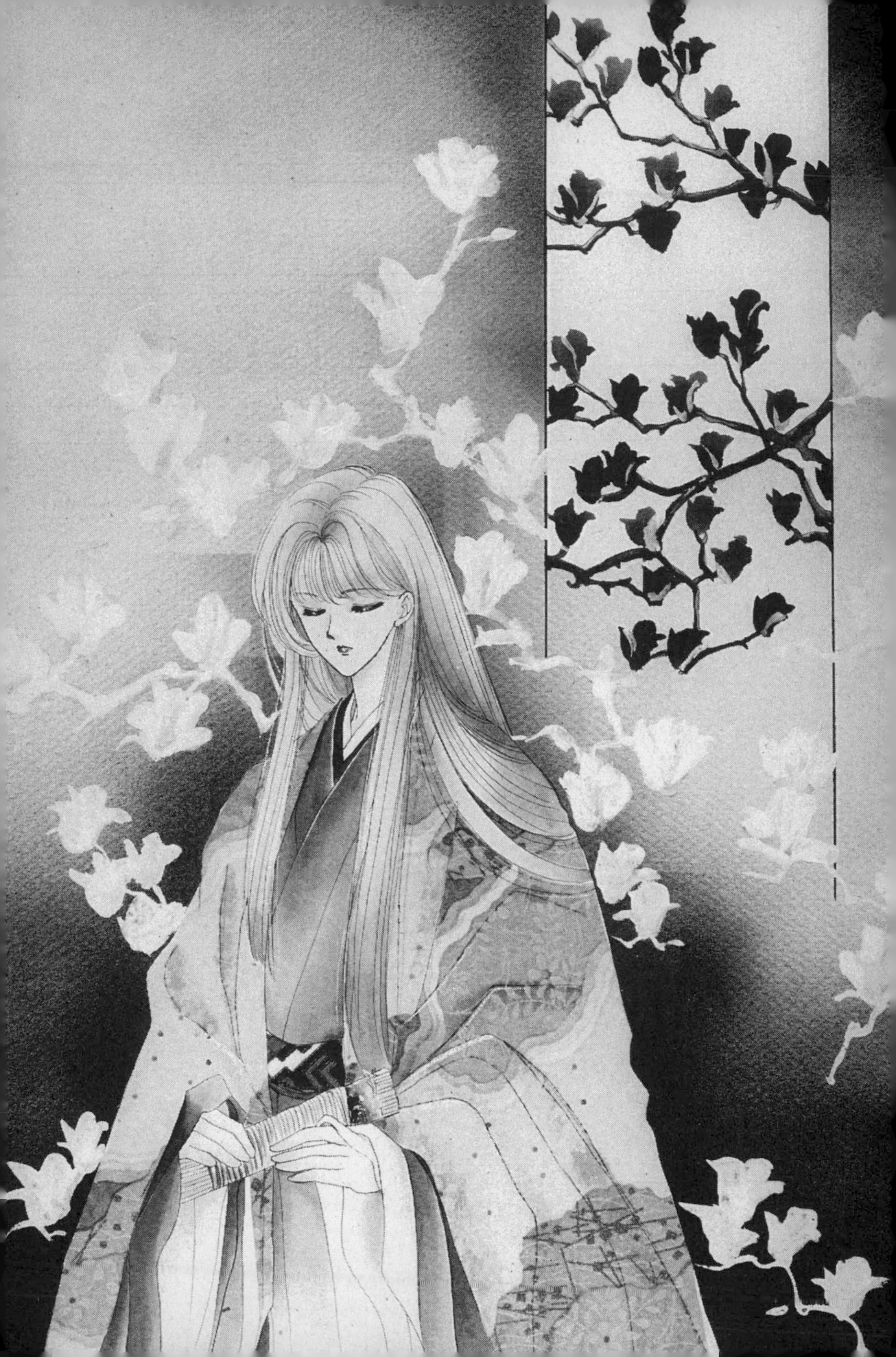

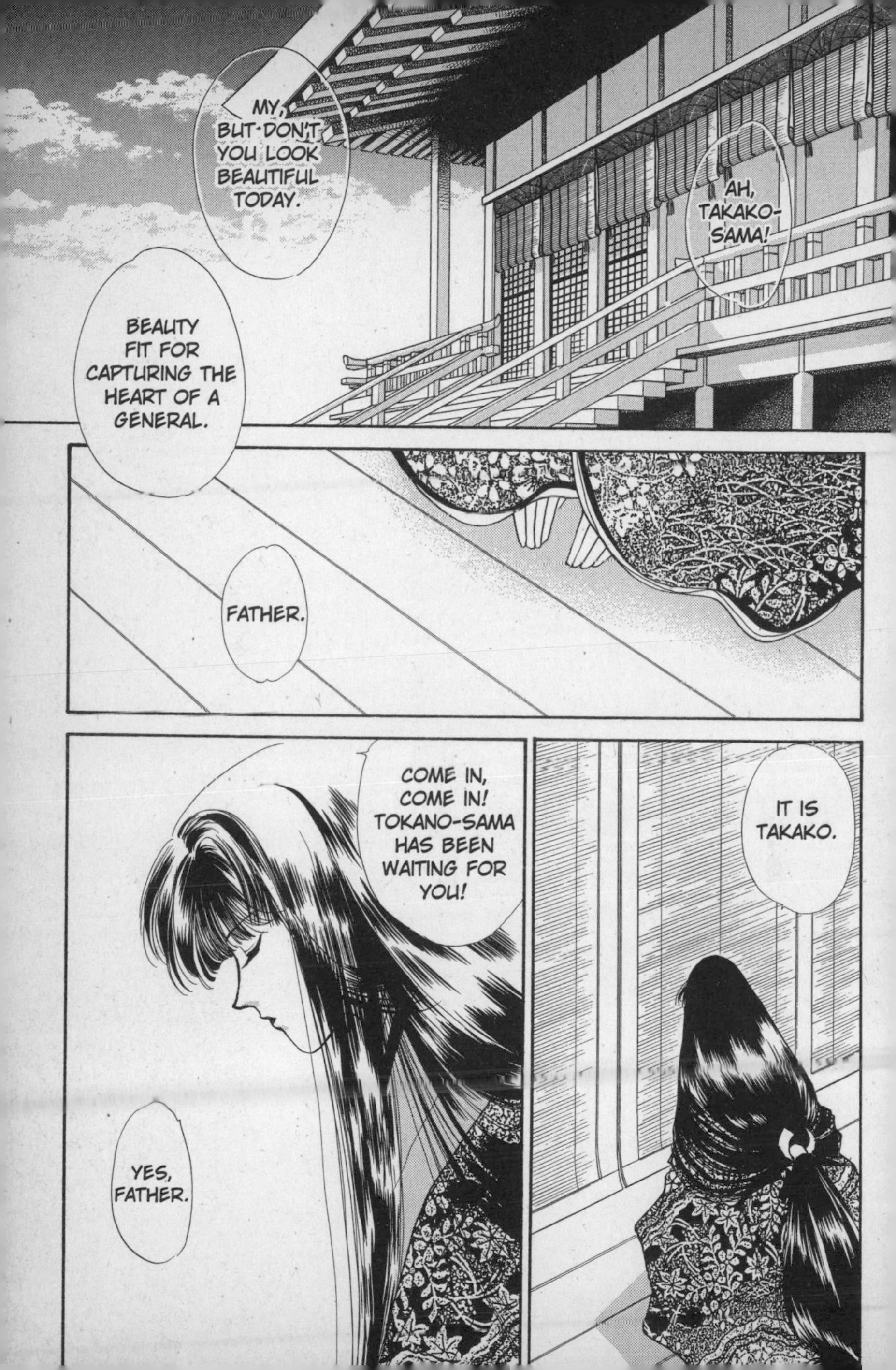
AH, TAKAKO-SAMA!
MY, BUT DON'T YOU LOOK BEAUTIFUL TODAY.
BEAUTY FIT FOR CAPTURING THE HEART OF A GENERAL.
FATHER.
IT IS TAKAKO.
COME IN, COME IN! TOKANO-SAMA HAS BEEN WAITING FOR YOU!
YES, FATHER.

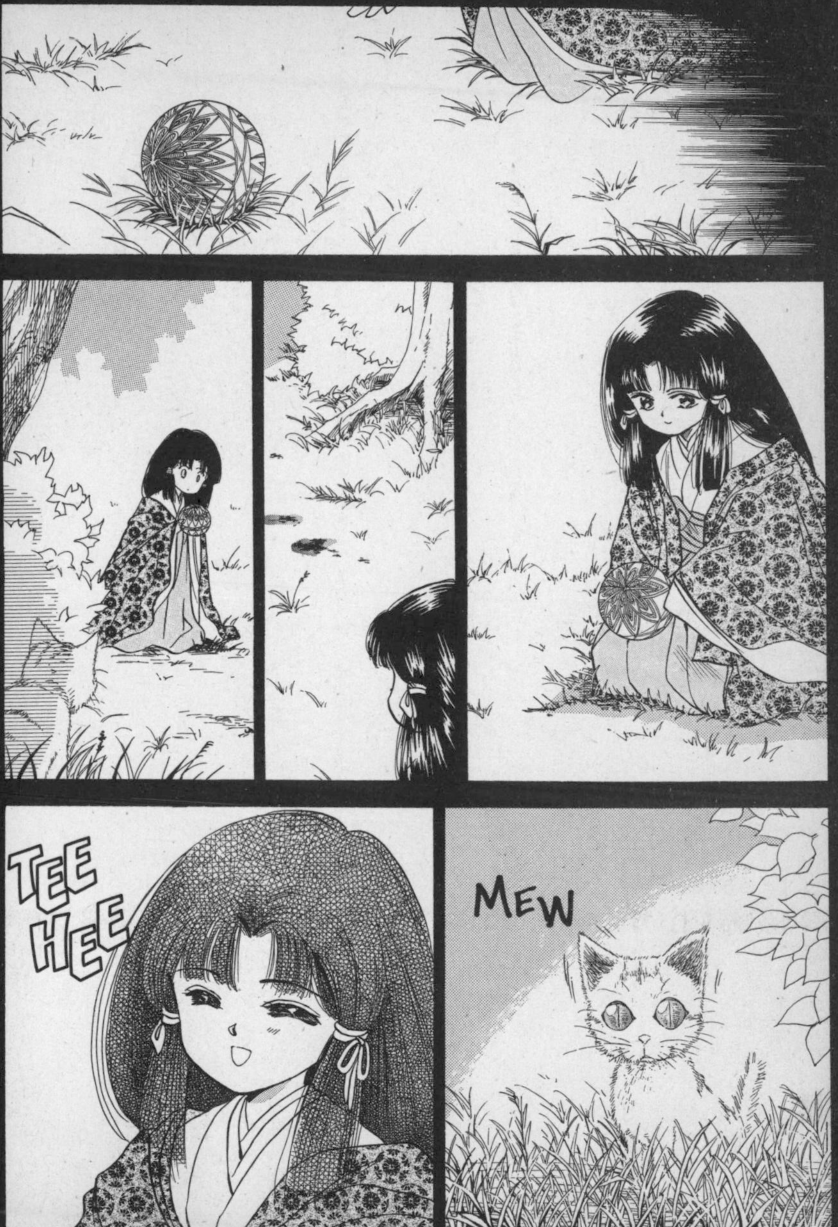
MEW
TEE HEE

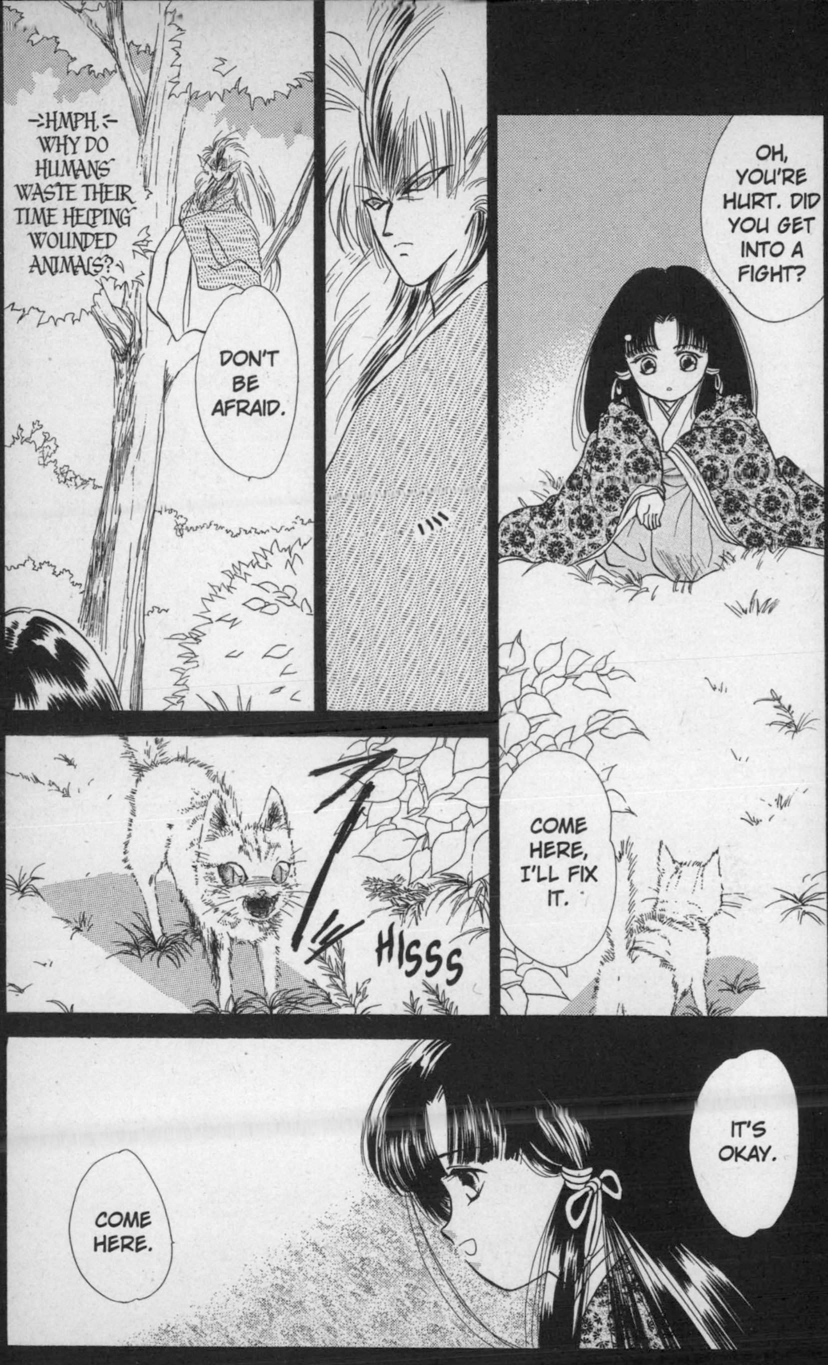

OH, YOU'RE HURT. DID YOU GET INTO A FIGHT?
HMPH. WHY DO HUMANS WASTE THEIR TIME HELPING WOUNDED ANIMALS?
DON'T BE AFRAID.
COME HERE, I'LL FIX IT.
HISSS
IT'S OKAY.
COME HERE.

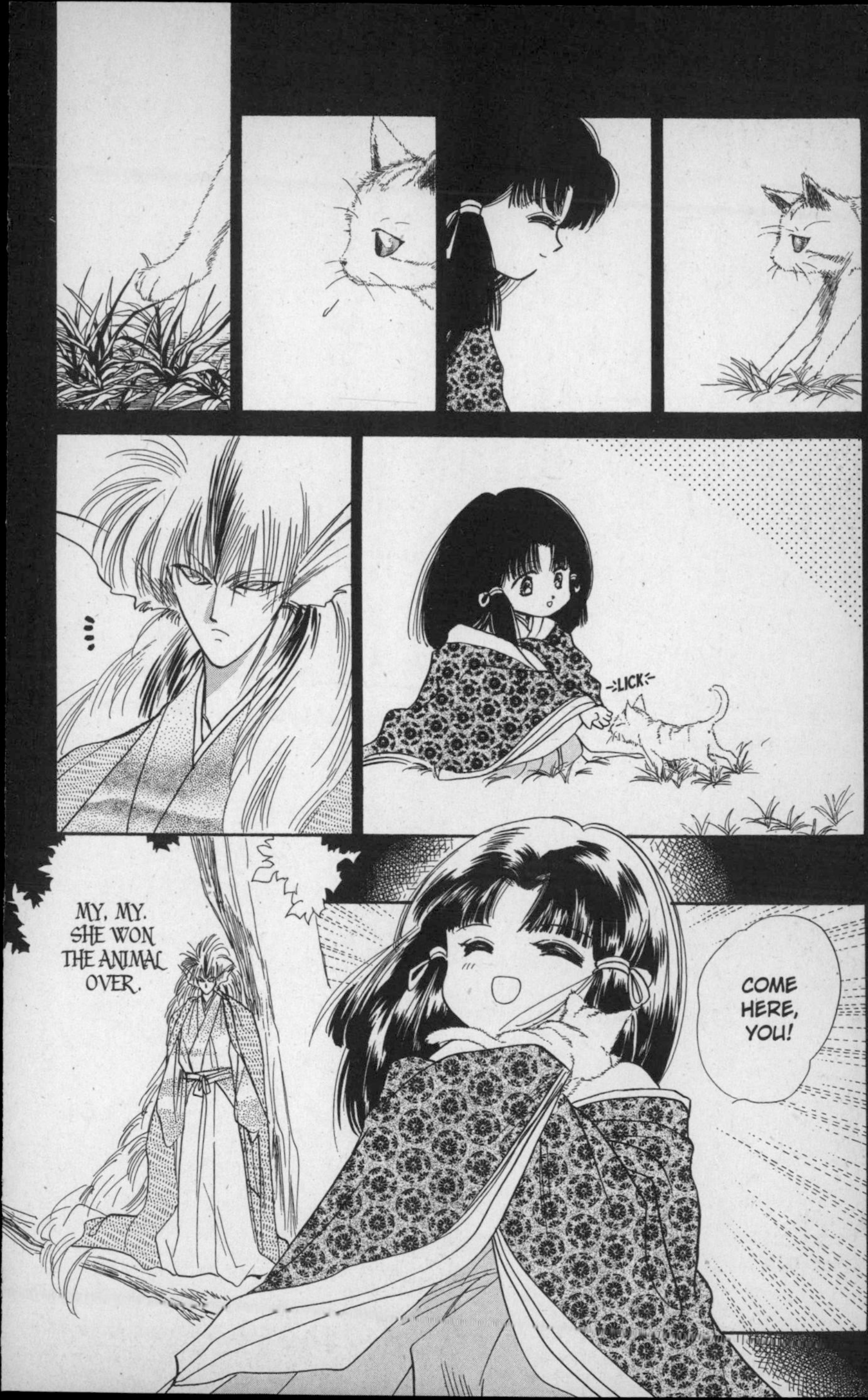
LICK
COME HERE, YOU!
MY, MY. SHE WON THE ANIMAL OVER.

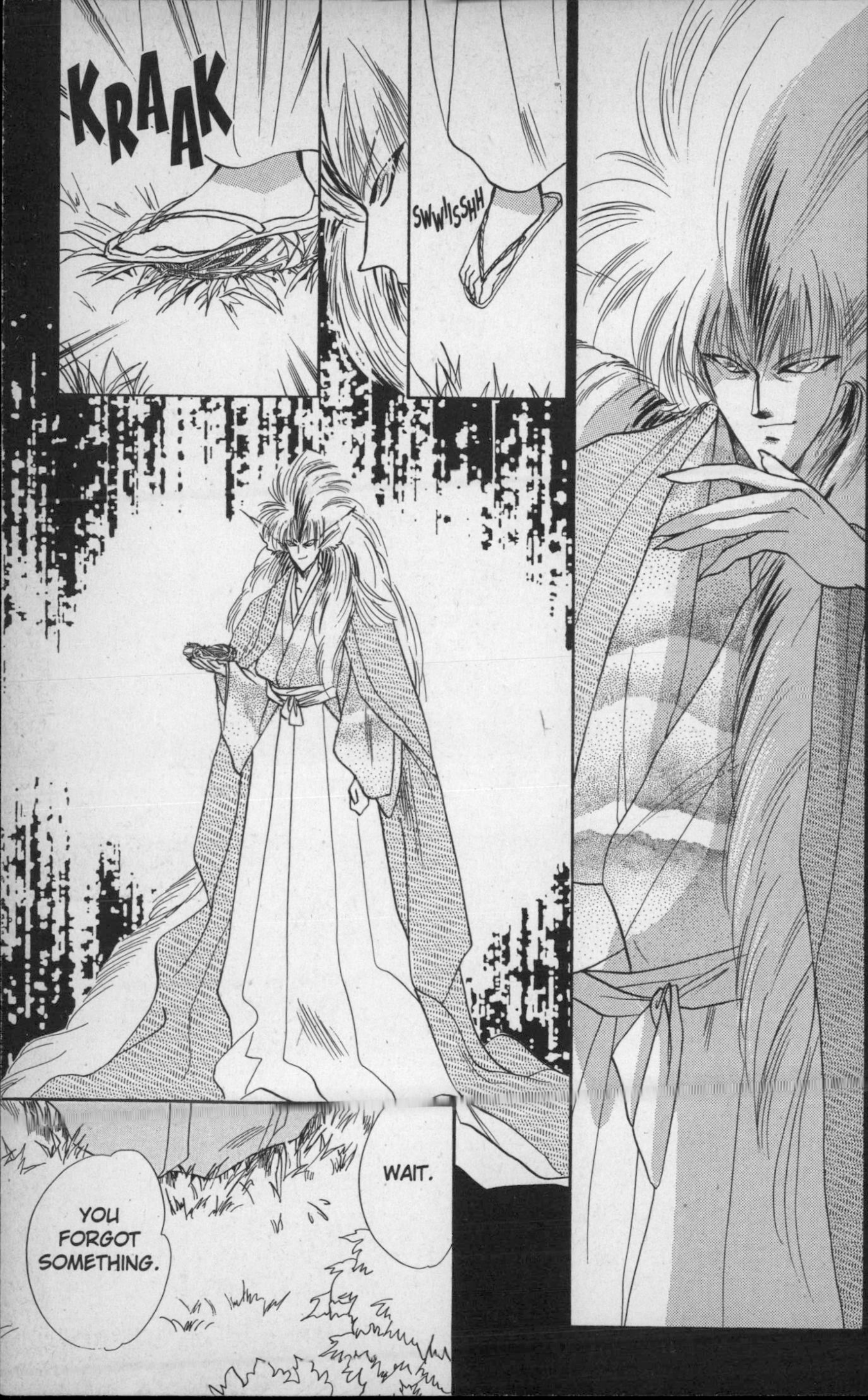
SWWIISSHH
KRAAK
WAIT.
YOU FORGOT SOMETHING.

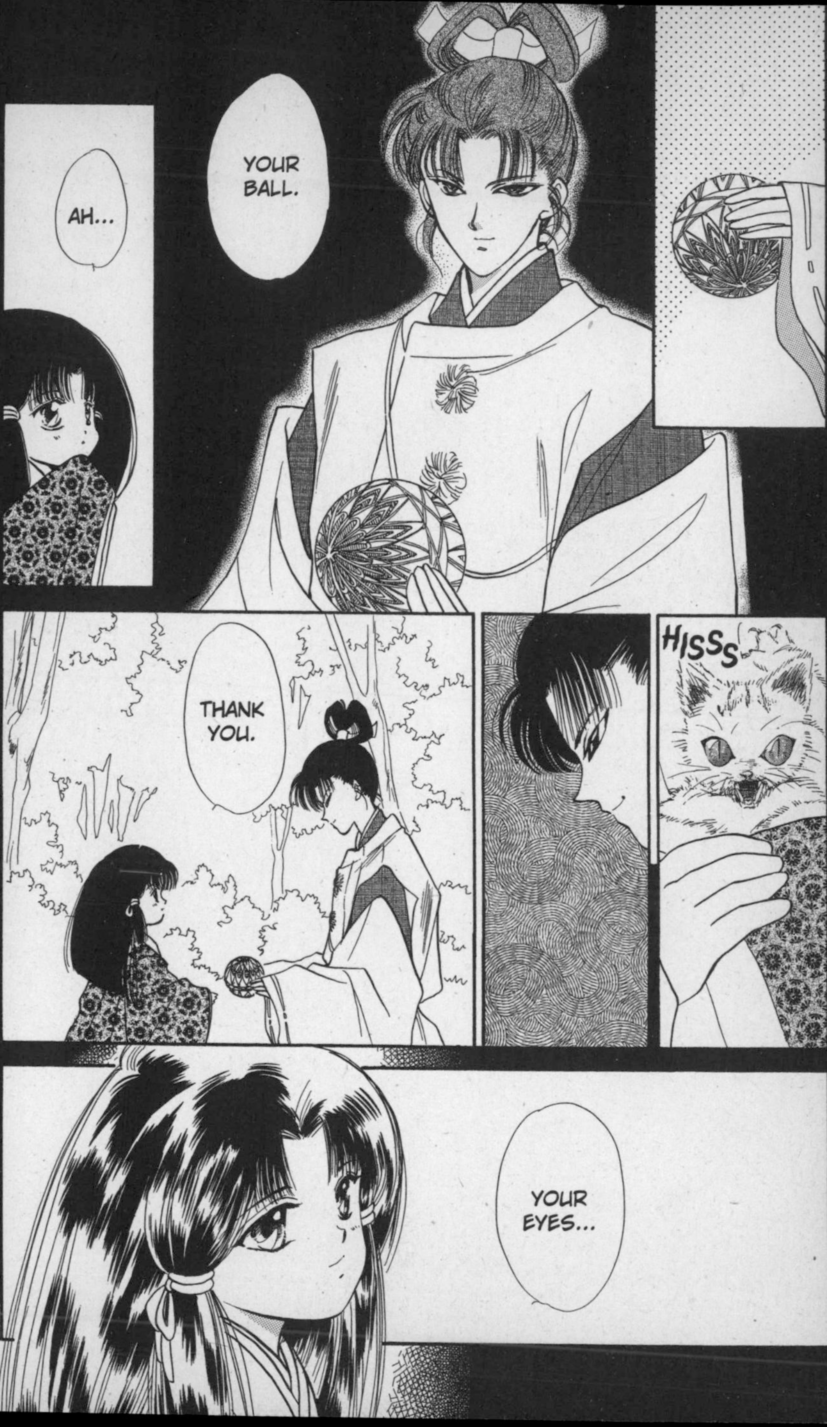
YOUR BALL.
AH...
HISSS
THANK YOU.
YOUR EYES...

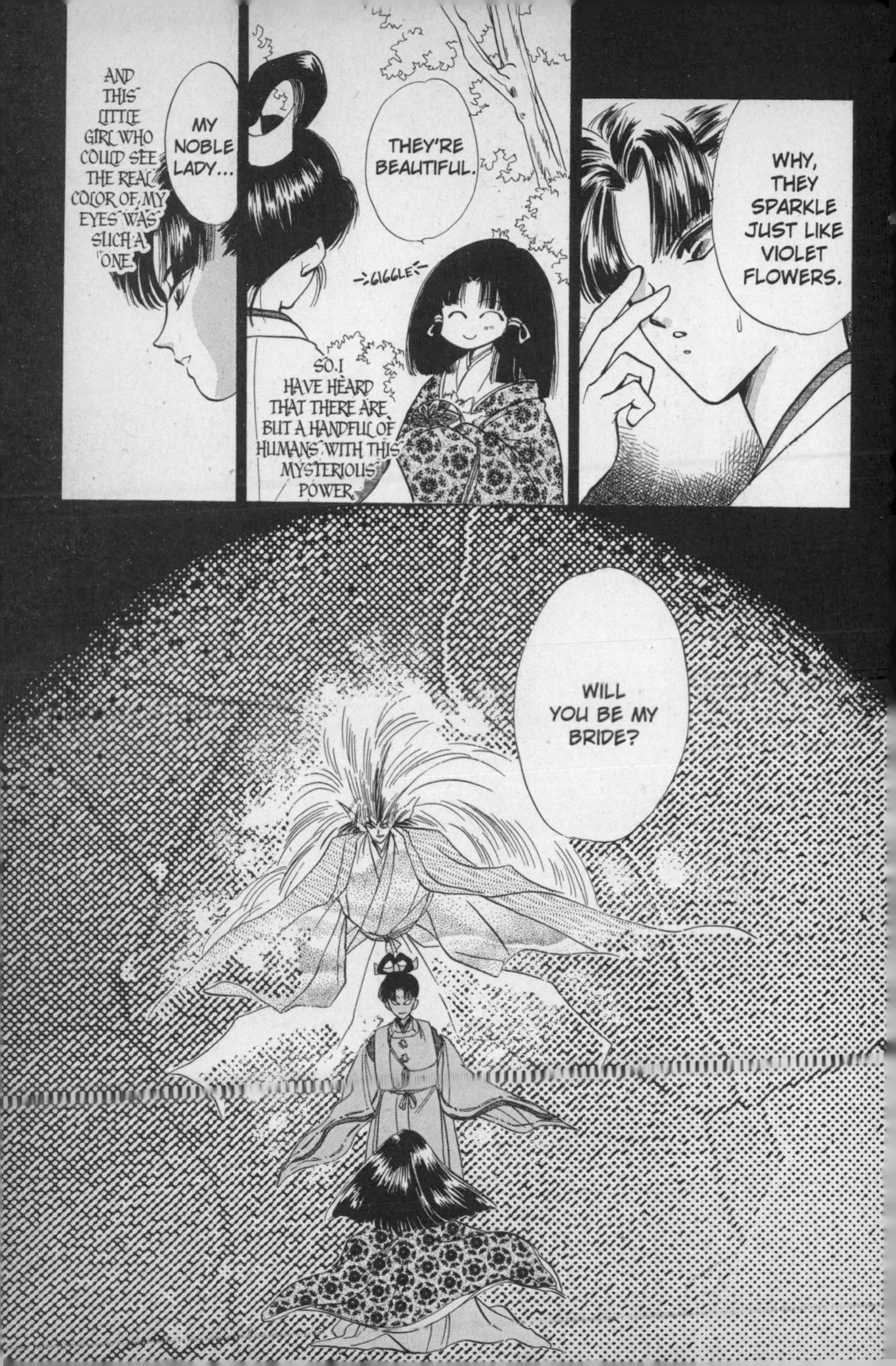
WHY, THEY SPARKLE JUST LIKE VIOLET FLOWERS.
THEY'RE BEAUTIFUL.
~GIGGLE~
SO, I HAVE HEARD THAT THERE ARE BUT A HANDFUL OF HUMANS WITH THIS MYSTERIOUS POWER.
MY NOBLE LADY...
AND THIS LITTLE GIRL WHO COULD SEE THE REAL COLOR OF MY EYES WAS SUCH A ONE.
WILL YOU BE MY BRIDE?

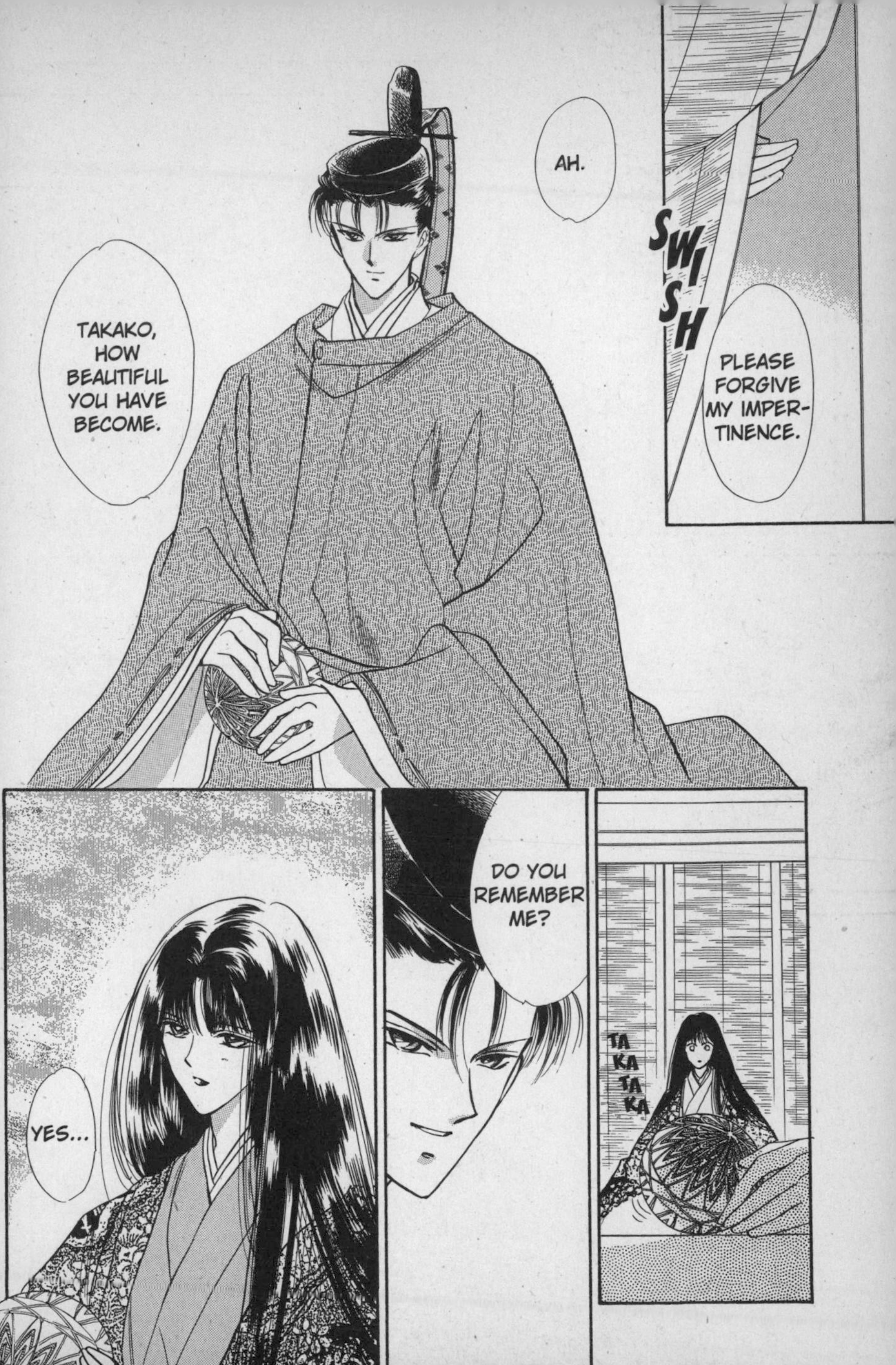
SWISH
PLEASE FORGIVE MY IMPER-TINENCE.
AH.
TAKAKO, HOW BEAUTIFUL YOU HAVE BECOME.
TA KA TA KA
DO YOU REMEMBER ME?
YES...

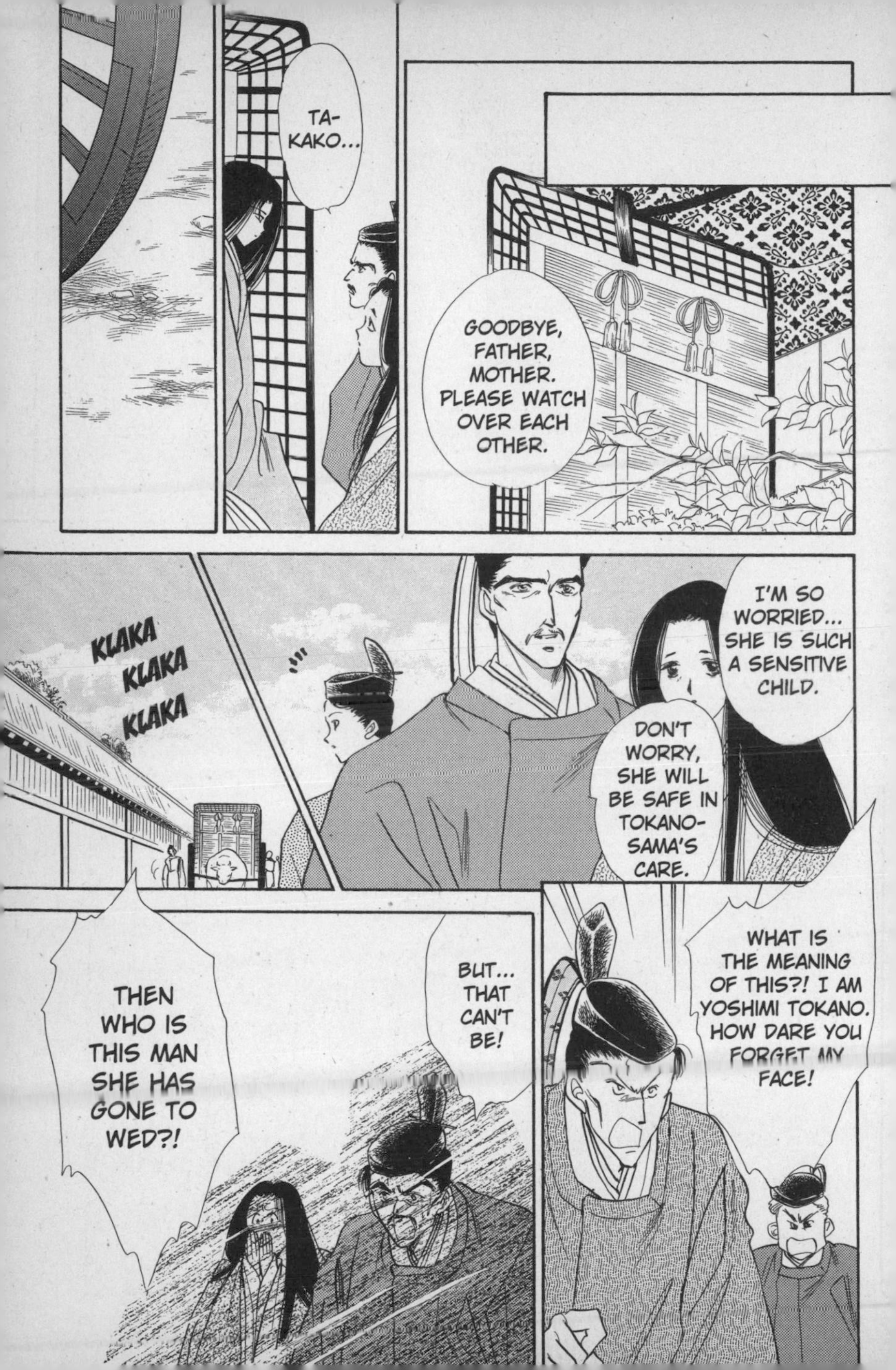
GOODBYE, FATHER, MOTHER. PLEASE WATCH OVER EACH OTHER.
TA-KAKO...
I'M SO WORRIED... SHE IS SUCH A SENSITIVE CHILD.
DON'T WORRY, SHE WILL BE SAFE IN TOKANO-SAMA'S CARE.
KLAKA KLAKA KLAKA
WHAT IS THE MEANING OF THIS?! I AM YOSHIMI TOKANO. HOW DARE YOU FORGET MY FACE!
BUT... THAT CAN'T BE!
THEN WHO IS THIS MAN SHE HAS GONE TO WED?!

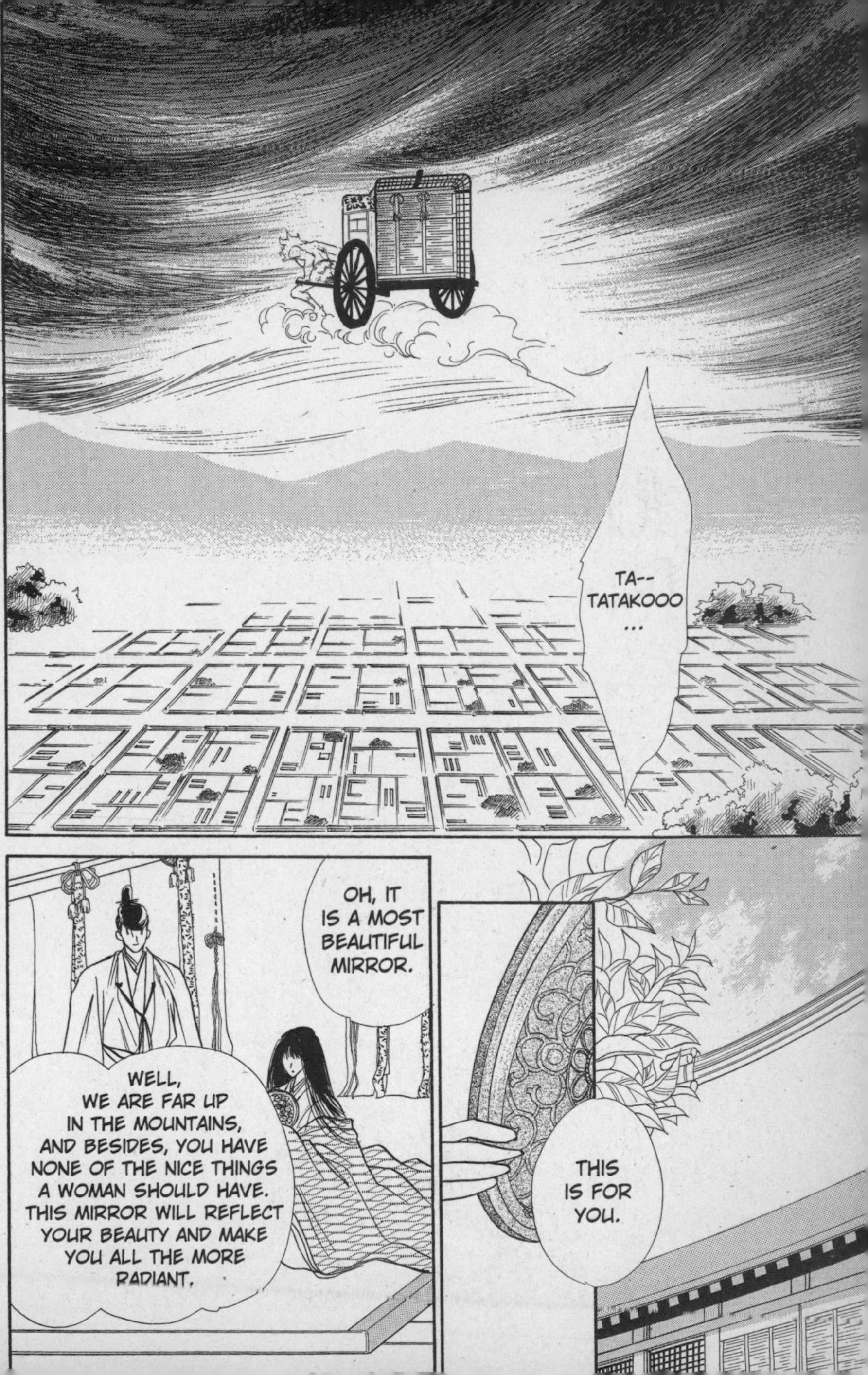
TA-- TATAKOOO ...
THIS IS FOR YOU.
OH, IT IS A MOST BEAUTIFUL MIRROR.
WELL, WE ARE FAR UP IN THE MOUNTAINS, AND BESIDES, YOU HAVE NONE OF THE NICE THINGS A WOMAN SHOULD HAVE. THIS MIRROR WILL REFLECT YOUR BEAUTY AND MAKE YOU ALL THE MORE RADIANT.

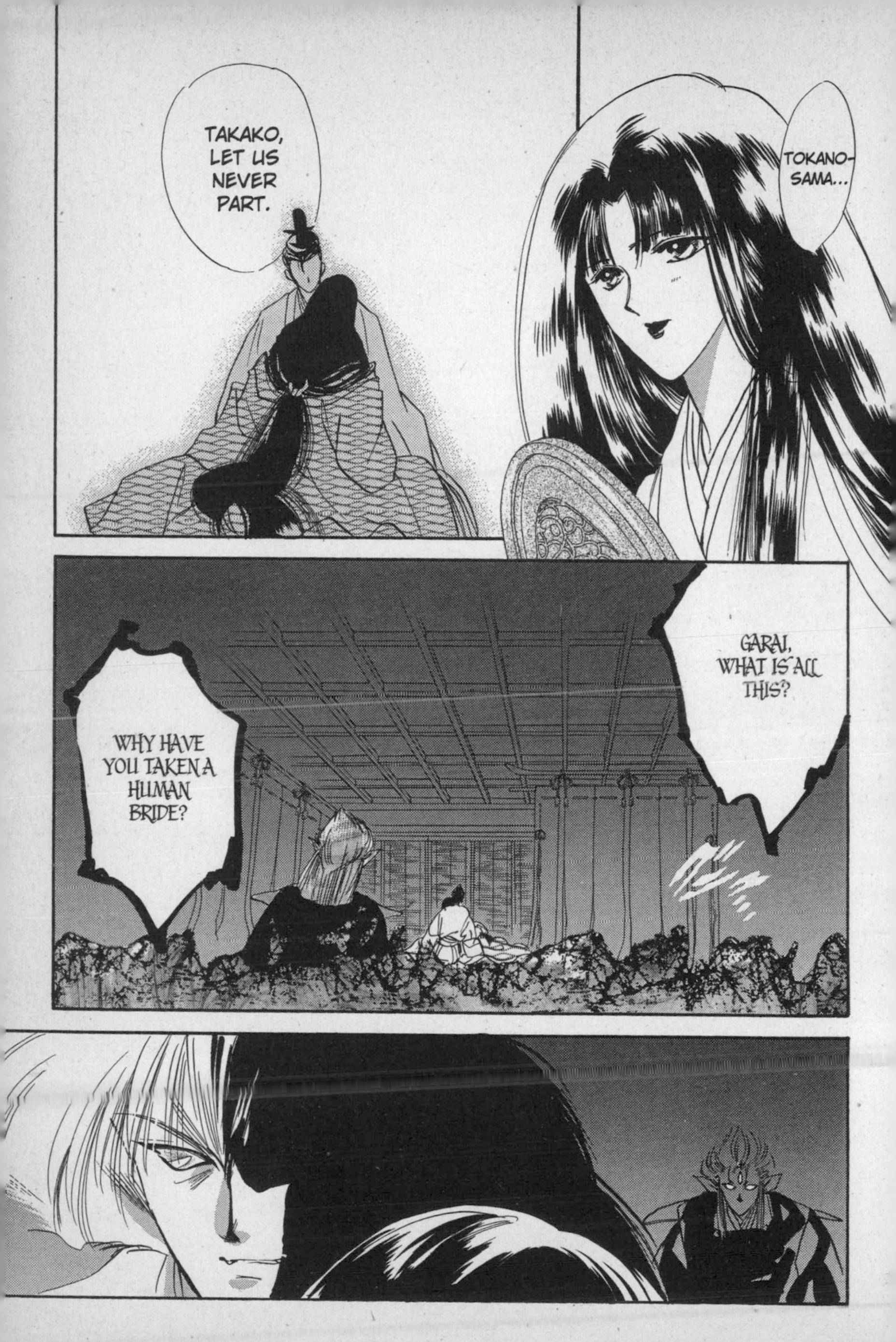
TOKANO-SAMA...
TAKAKO, LET US NEVER PART.
GARAI, WHAT IS ALL THIS?
WHY HAVE YOU TAKEN A HUMAN BRIDE?

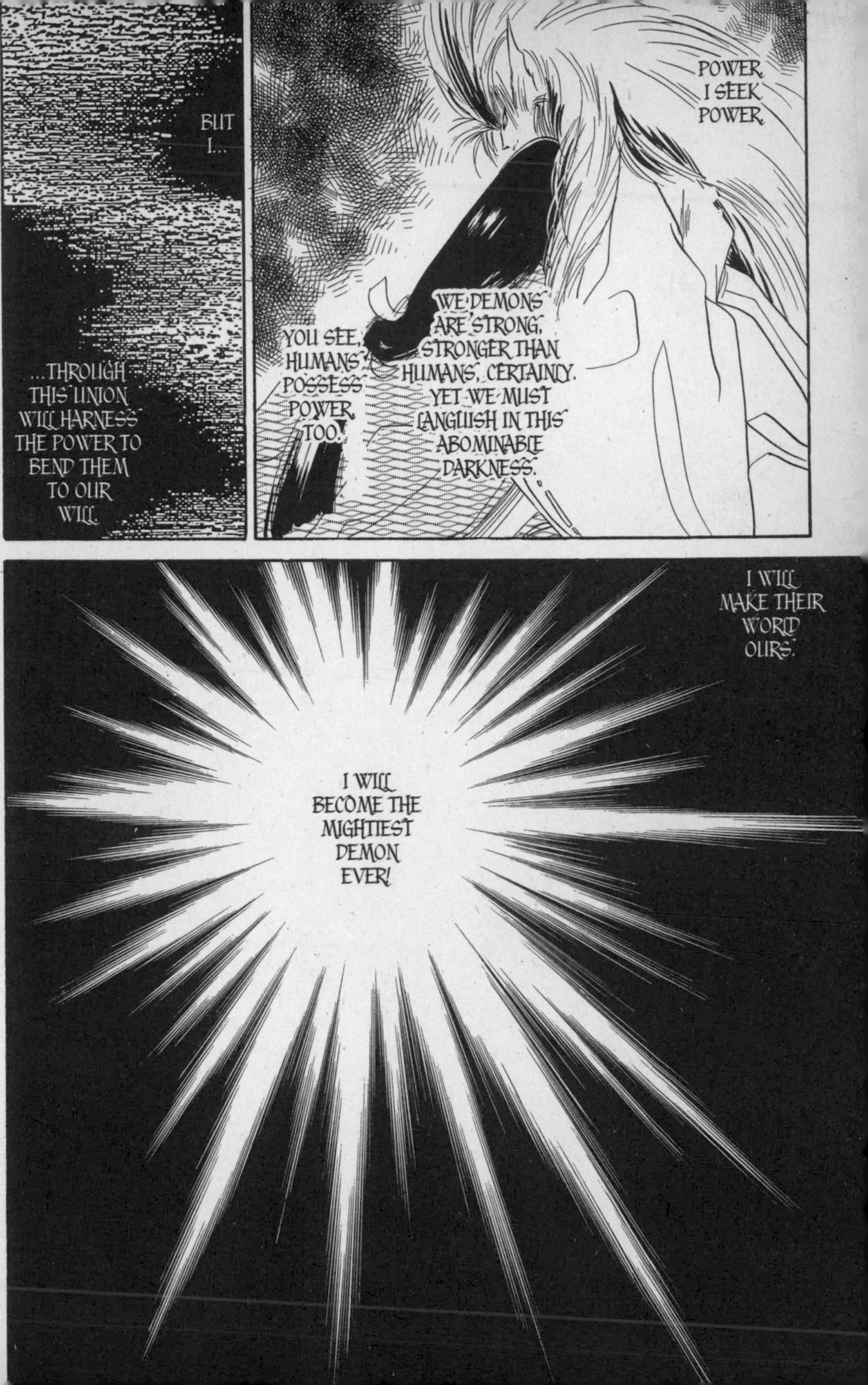
POWER. I SEEK POWER.
WE DEMONS ARE STRONG, STRONGER THAN HUMANS, CERTAINLY. YET WE MUST LANGUISH IN THIS ABOMINABLE DARKNESS.
YOU SEE, HUMANS POSSESS POWER, TOO.
BUT I...
...THROUGH THIS UNION WILL HARNESS THE POWER TO BEND THEM TO OUR WILL.
I WILL MAKE THEIR WORLD OURS.
I WILL BECOME THE MIGHTIEST DEMON EVER!

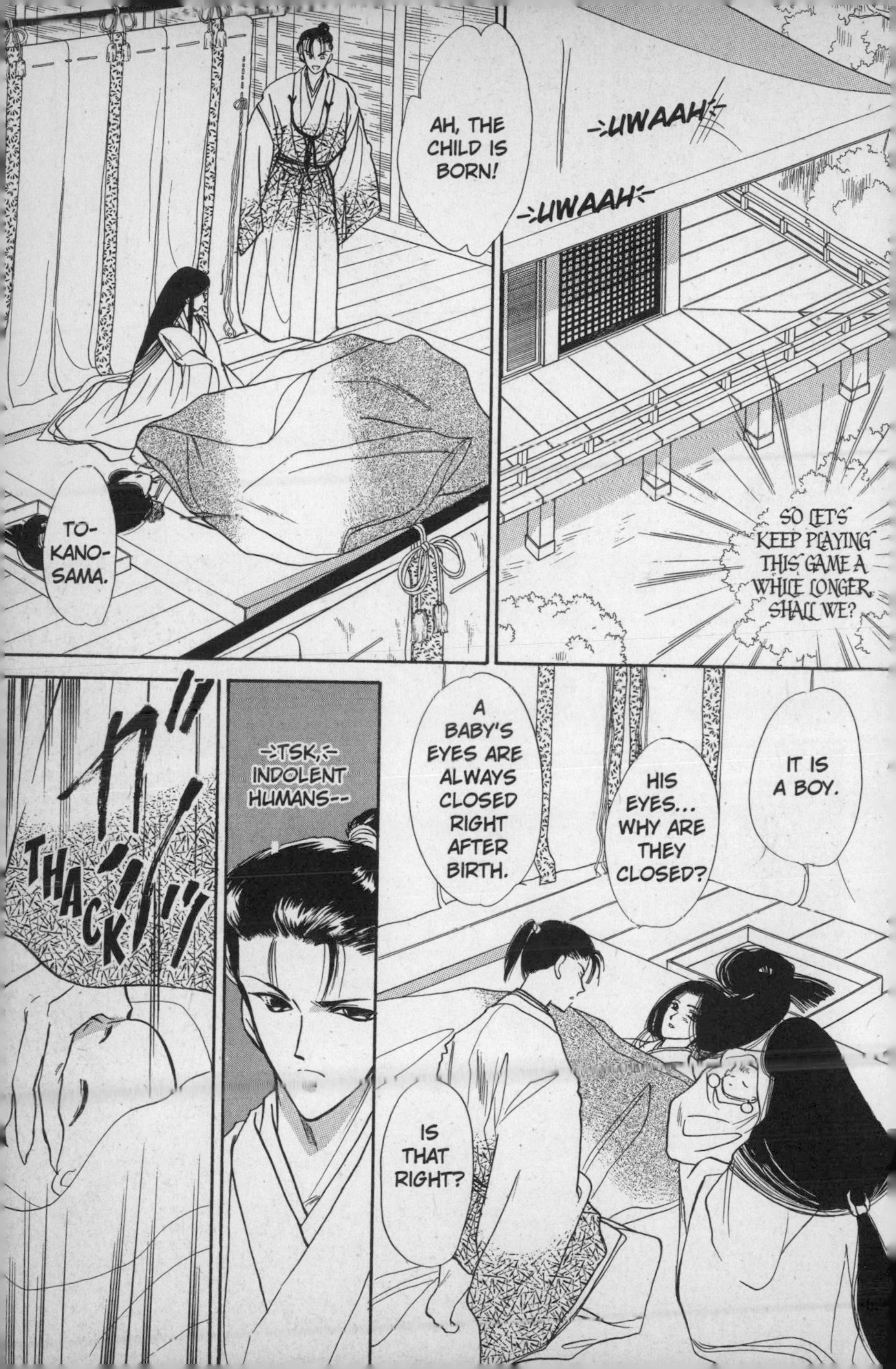

UWAAH
UWAAH
SO LET'S KEEP PLAYING THIS GAME A WHILE LONGER, SHALL WE?
AH, THE CHILD IS BORN!
TO-KANO-SAMA.
IT IS A BOY.
HIS EYES... WHY ARE THEY CLOSED?
A BABY'S EYES ARE ALWAYS CLOSED RIGHT AFTER BIRTH.
IS THAT RIGHT?
TSK, INDOLENT HUMANS--
THACK

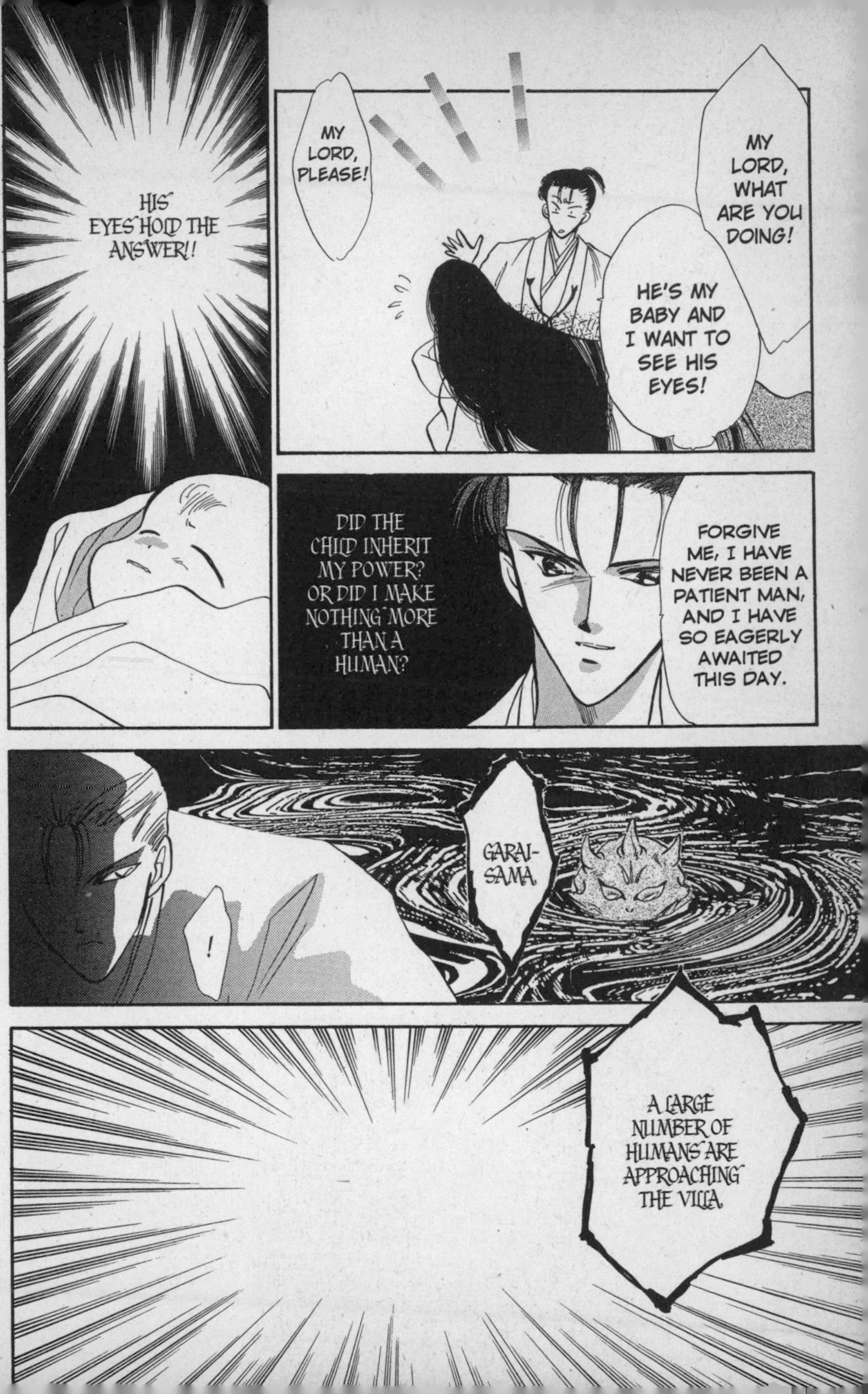
MY LORD, WHAT ARE YOU DOING!
HE'S MY BABY AND I WANT TO SEE HIS EYES!
MY LORD, PLEASE!
FORGIVE ME, I HAVE NEVER BEEN A PATIENT MAN, AND I HAVE SO EAGERLY AWAITED THIS DAY.
DID THE CHILD INHERIT MY POWER? OR DID I MAKE NOTHING MORE THAN A HUMAN?
HIS EYES HOLD THE ANSWER!!
GARAI-SAMA.
!
A LARGE NUMBER OF HUMANS ARE APPROACHING THE VILLA.

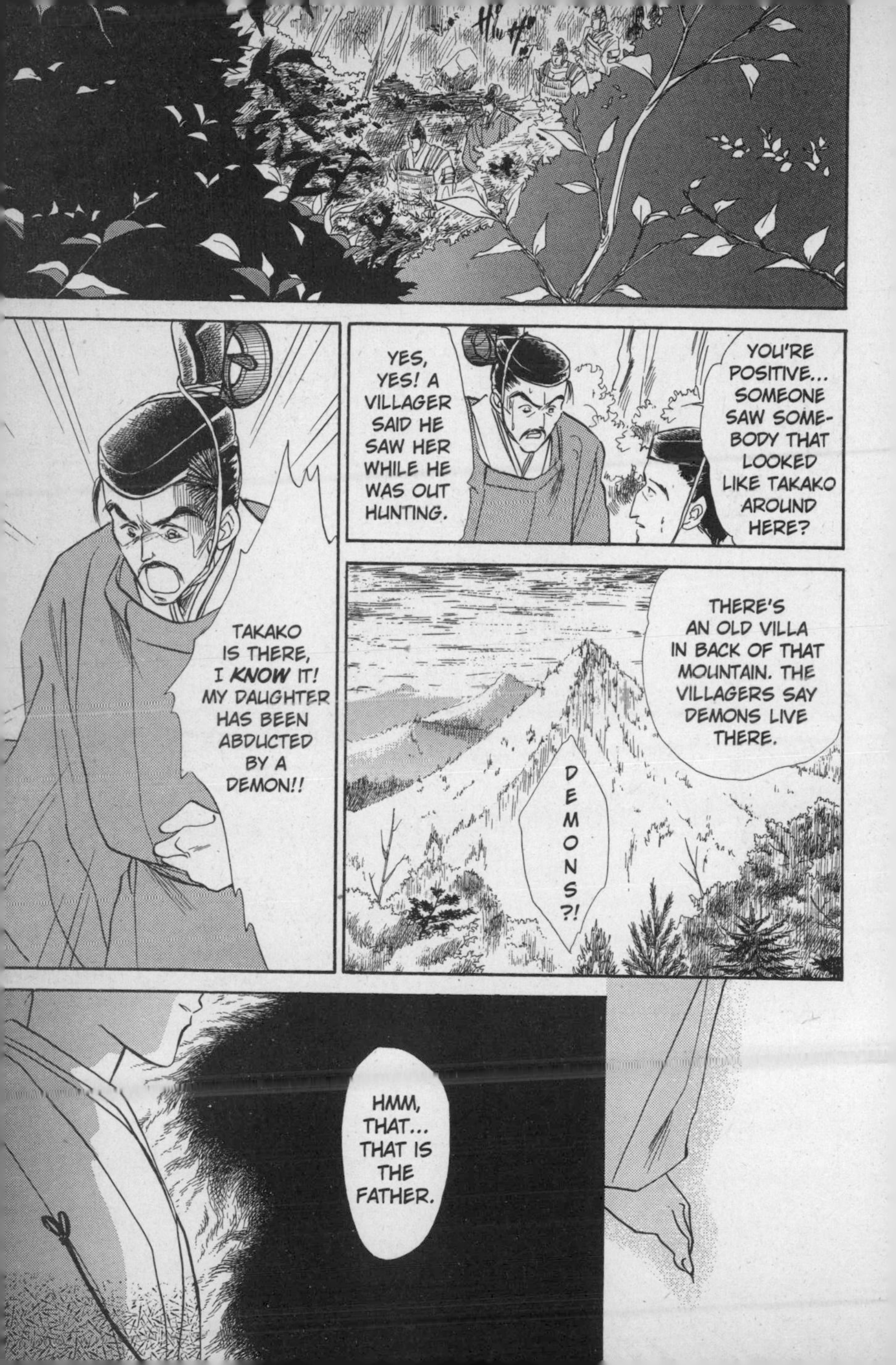

YOU'RE POSITIVE... SOMEONE SAW SOMEBODY THAT LOOKED LIKE TAKAKO AROUND HERE?
YES, YES! A VILLAGER SAID HE SAW HER WHILE HE WAS OUT HUNTING.
THERE'S AN OLD VILLA IN BACK OF THAT MOUNTAIN. THE VILLAGERS SAY DEMONS LIVE THERE.
DEMONS?!
TAKAKO IS THERE, I *KNOW* IT! MY DAUGHTER HAS BEEN ABDUCTED BY A DEMON!!
HMM, THAT... THAT IS THE FATHER.

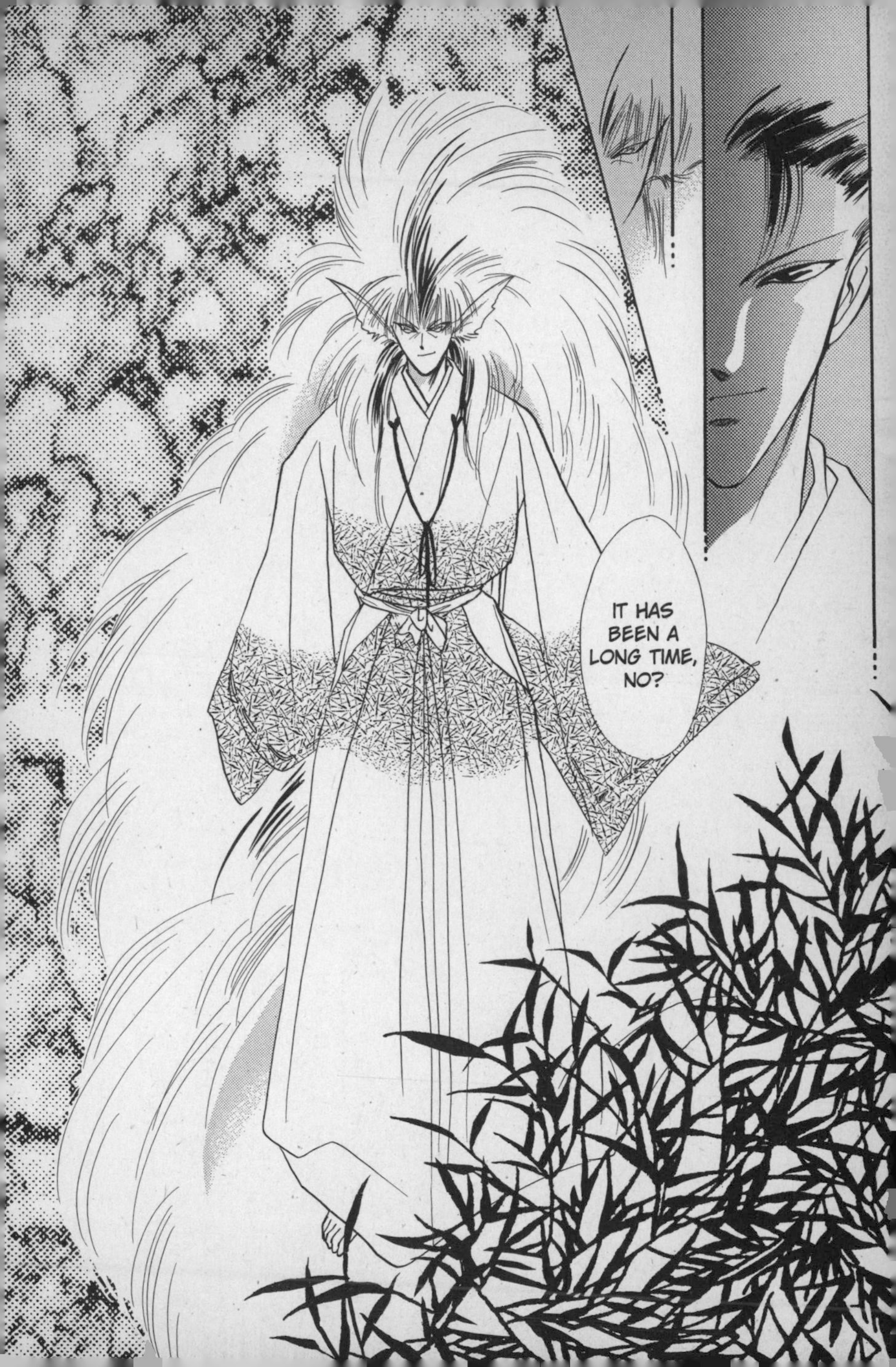
IT HAS BEEN A LONG TIME, NO?

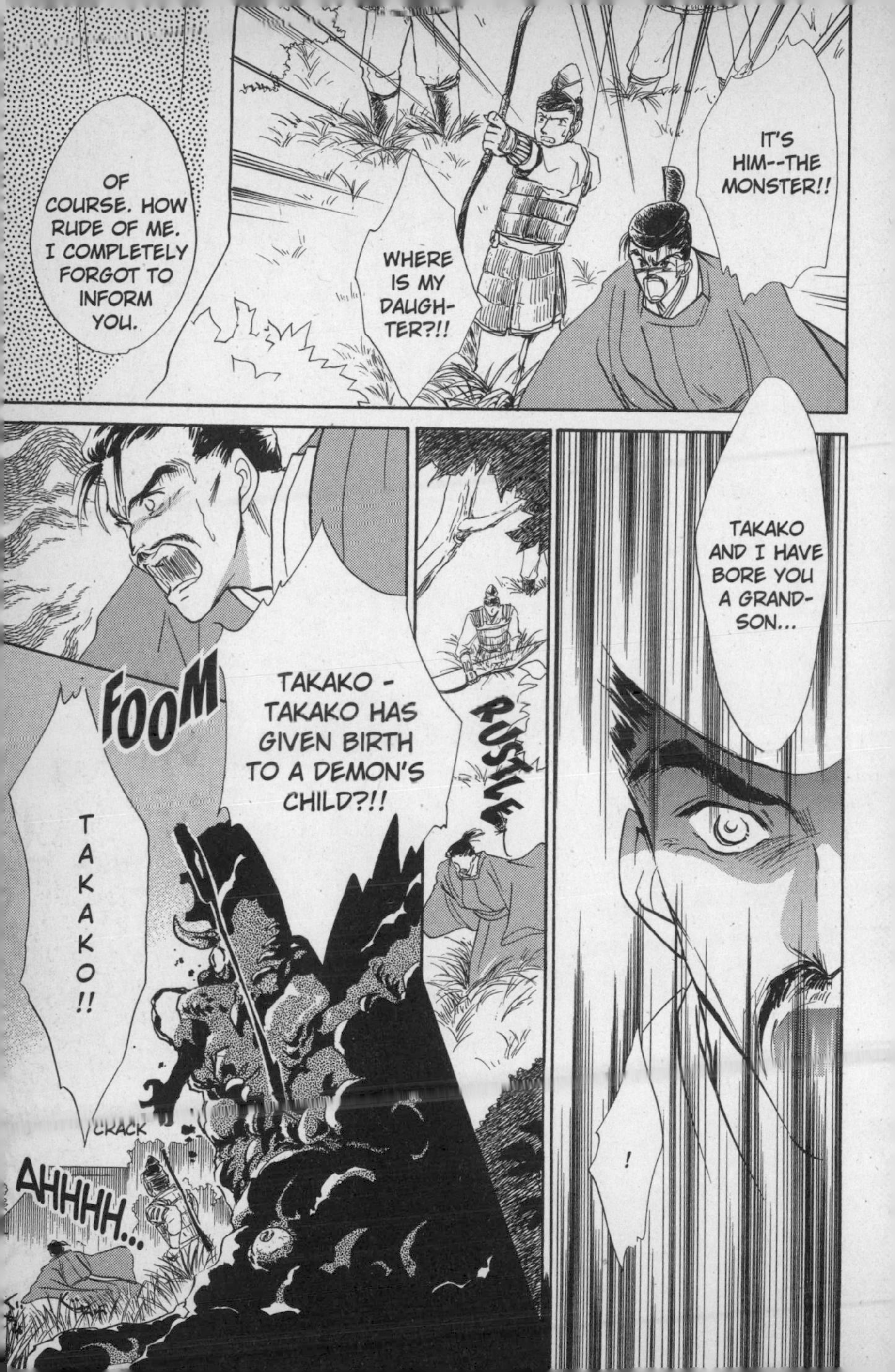
IT'S HIM--THE MONSTER!!
WHERE IS MY DAUGHTER?!!
OF COURSE. HOW RUDE OF ME. I COMPLETELY FORGOT TO INFORM YOU.
TAKAKO AND I HAVE BORE YOU A GRANDSON...
!
RUSTLE
TAKAKO - TAKAKO HAS GIVEN BIRTH TO A DEMON'S CHILD?!!
FOOM
TAKAKO!!
CRACK
AHHHH...

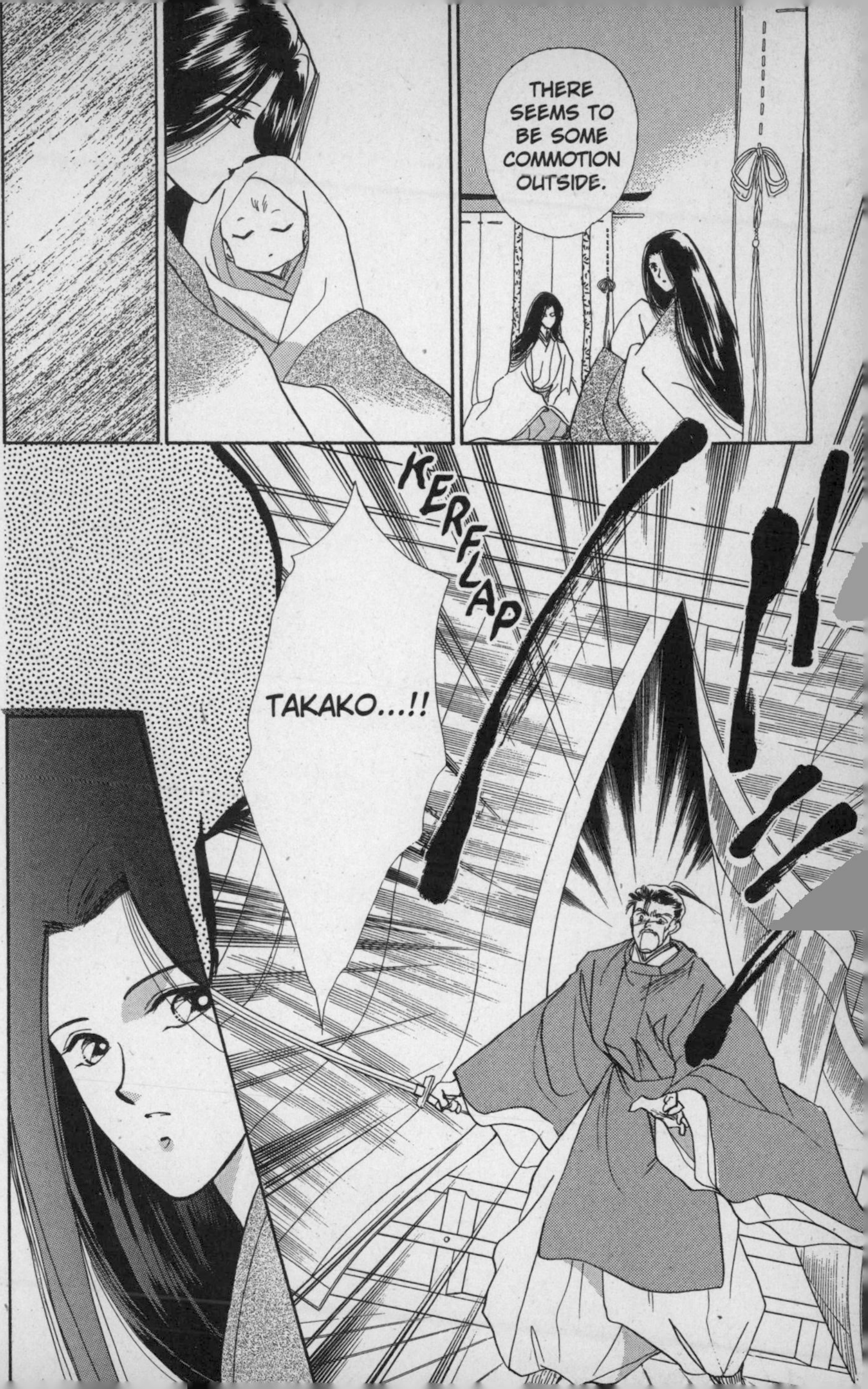
THERE SEEMS TO BE SOME COMMOTION OUTSIDE.
KERFLAP
TAKAKO...!!

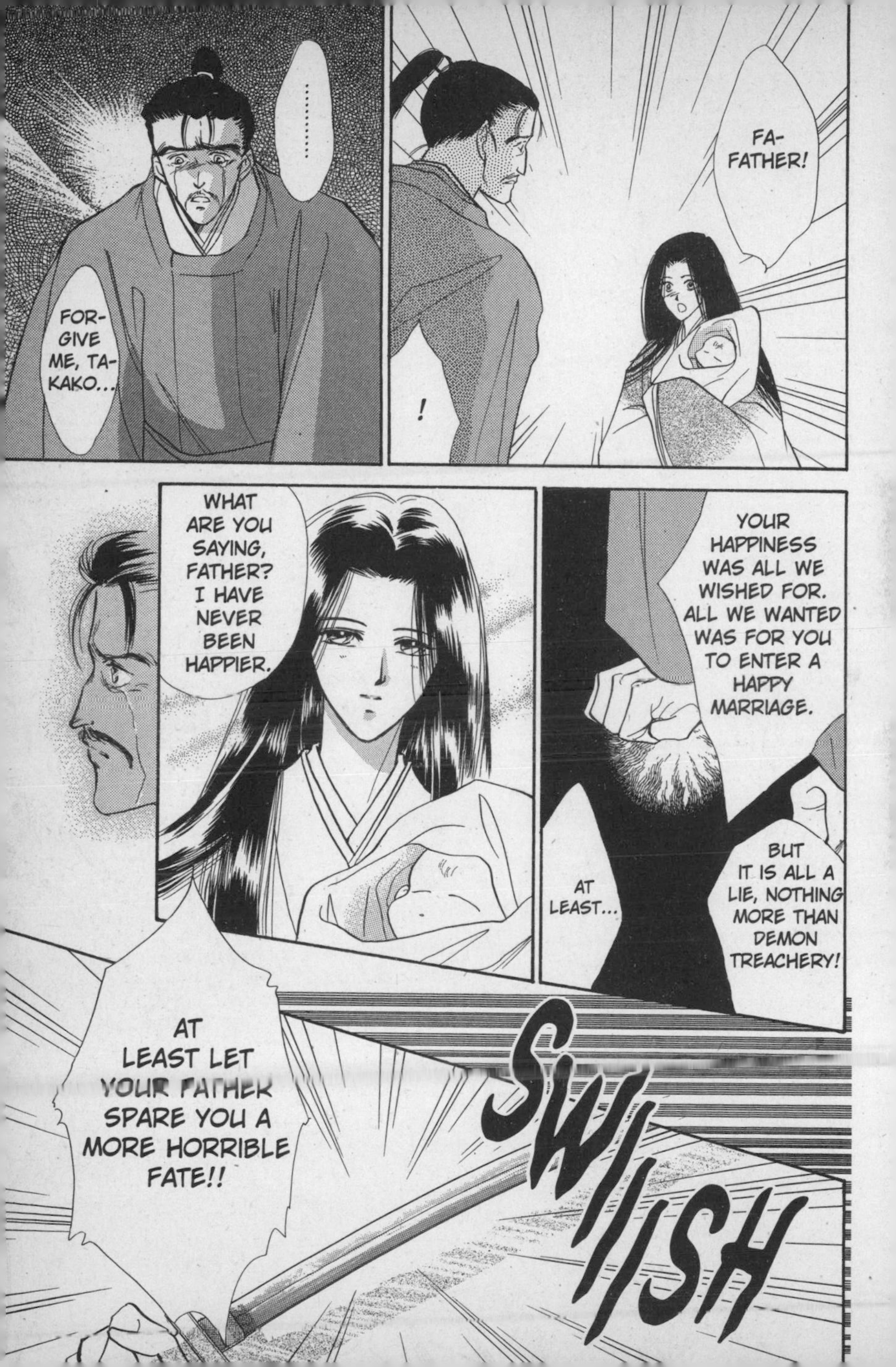
FA-
FATHER!
!
......
FOR-
GIVE
ME, TA-
KAKO...
YOUR HAPPINESS WAS ALL WE WISHED FOR. ALL WE WANTED WAS FOR YOU TO ENTER A HAPPY MARRIAGE.
BUT IT IS ALL A LIE, NOTHING MORE THAN DEMON TREACHERY!
AT LEAST...
WHAT ARE YOU SAYING, FATHER? I HAVE NEVER BEEN HAPPIER.
SWIISH
AT LEAST LET YOUR FATHER SPARE YOU A MORE HORRIBLE FATE!!

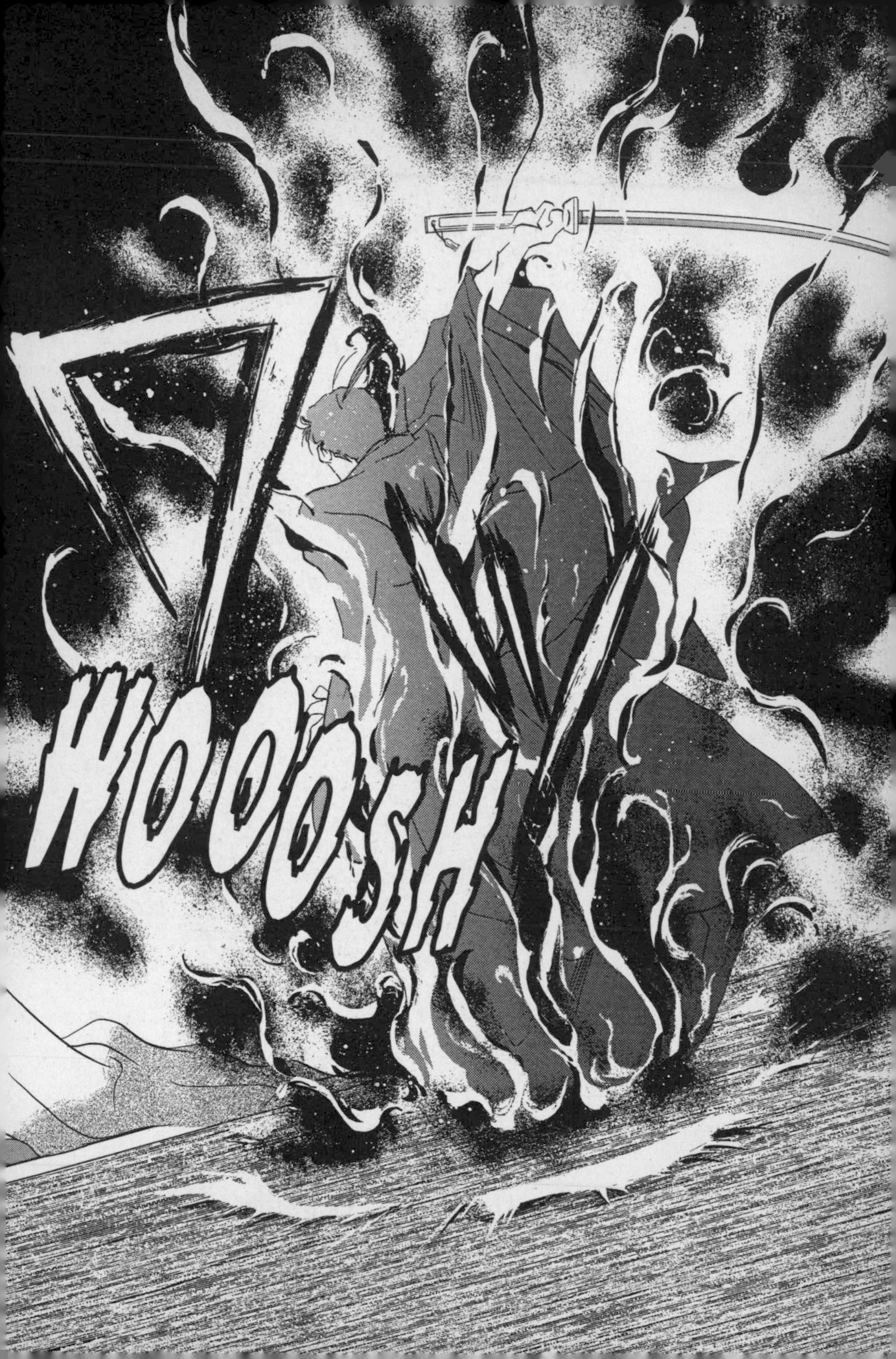
WHOOSH

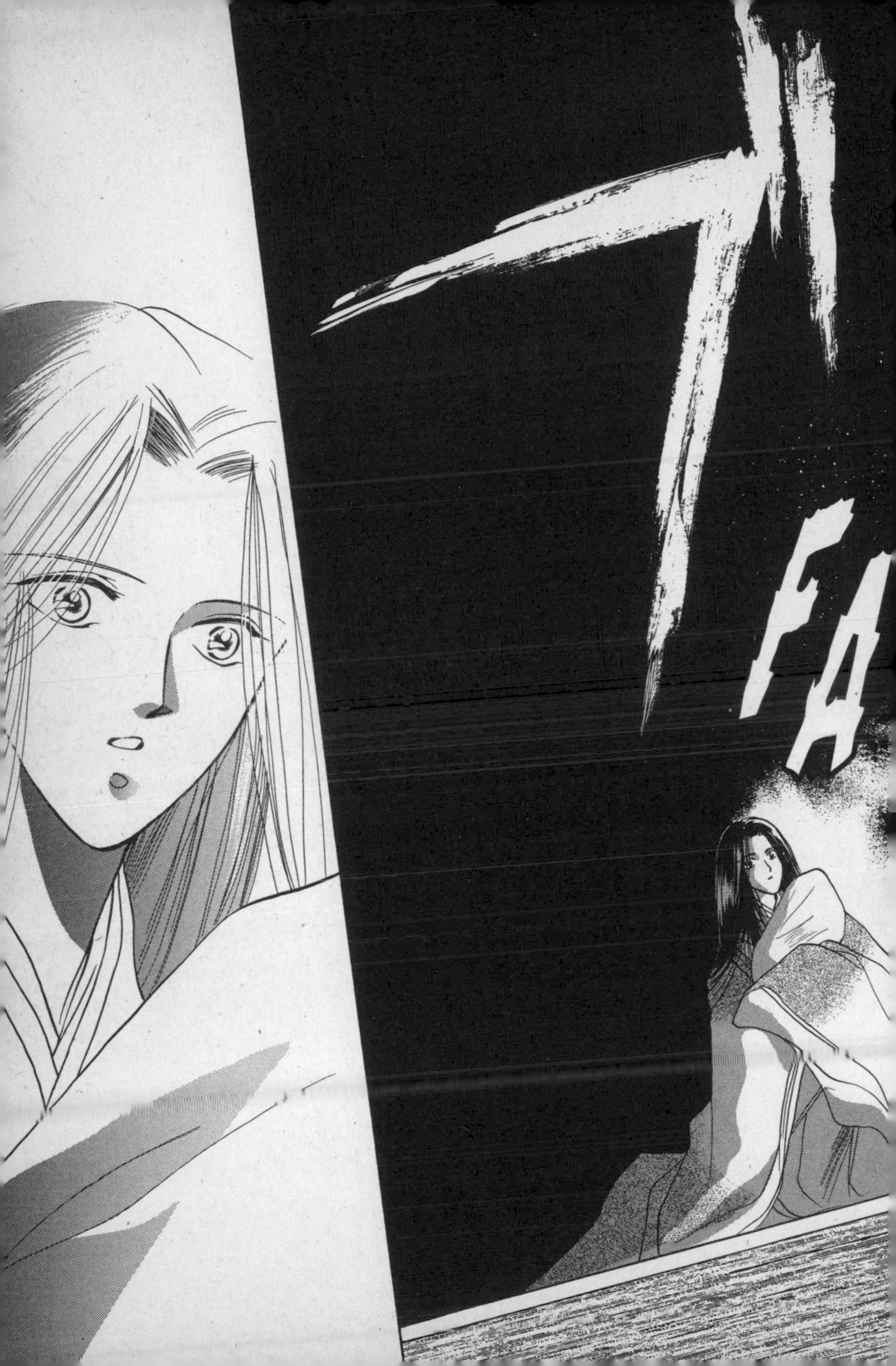
FA

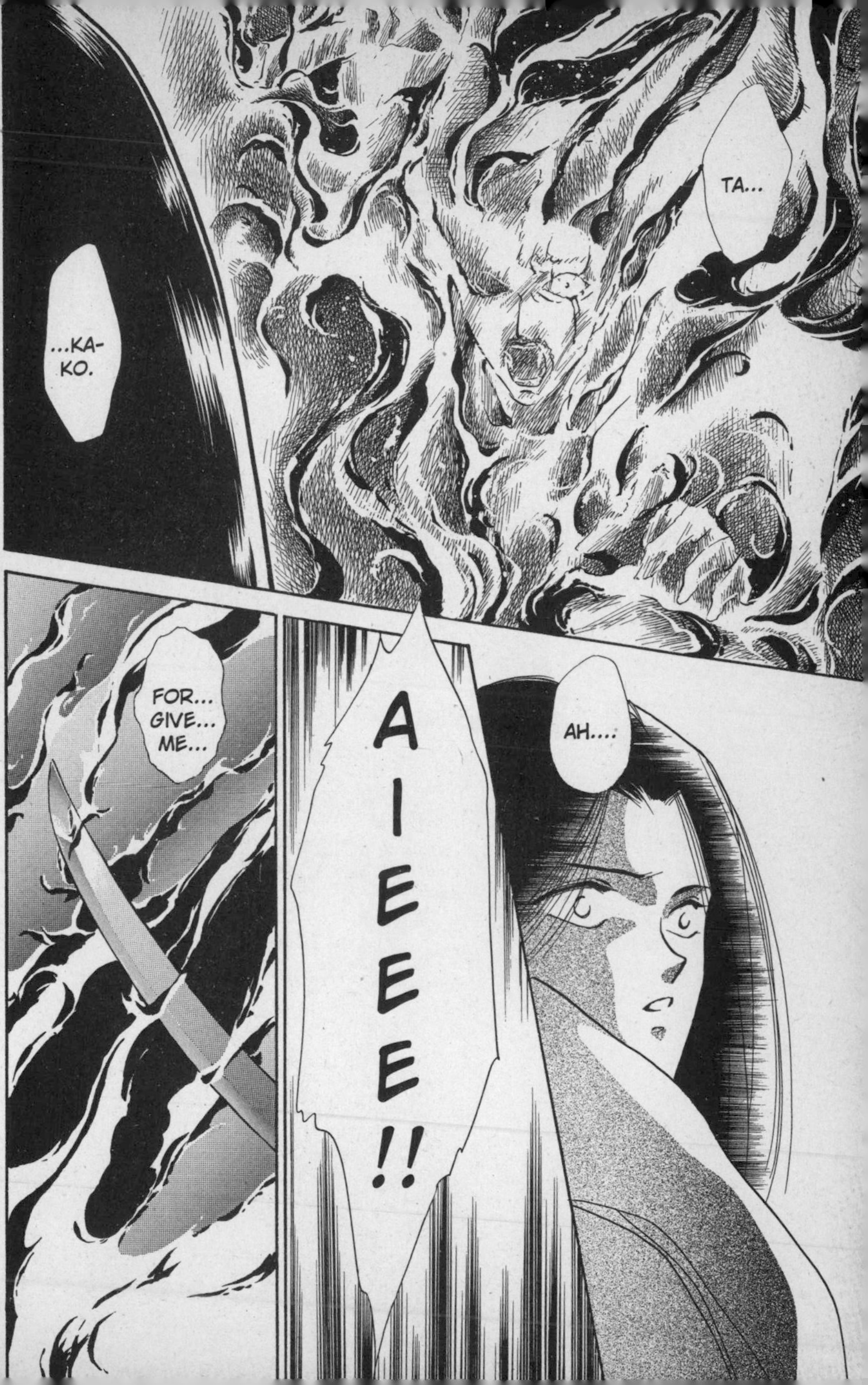
TA...
...KA-KO.
AH....
AIEEE!!
FOR... GIVE... ME...

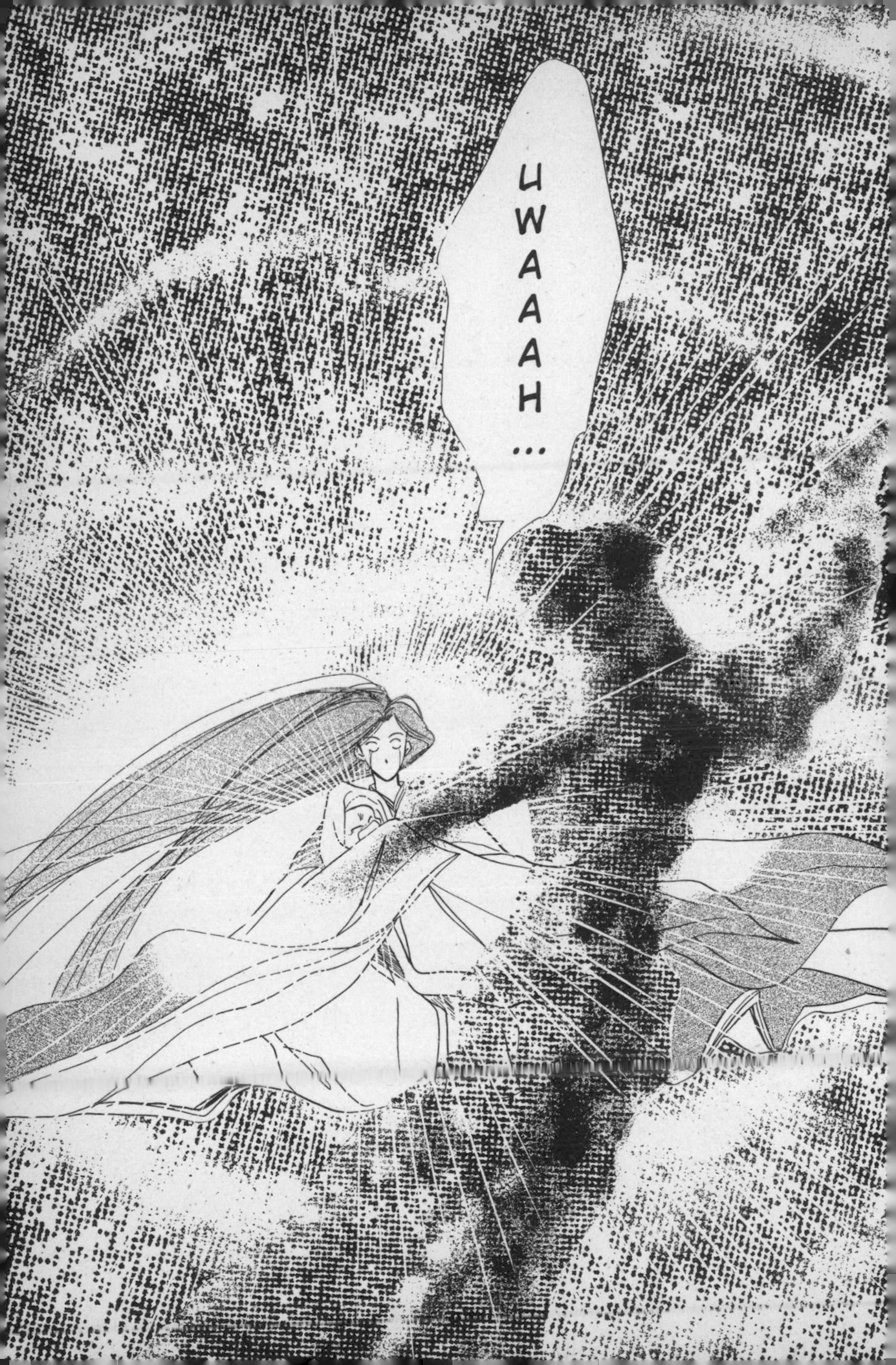
UWAAAH...

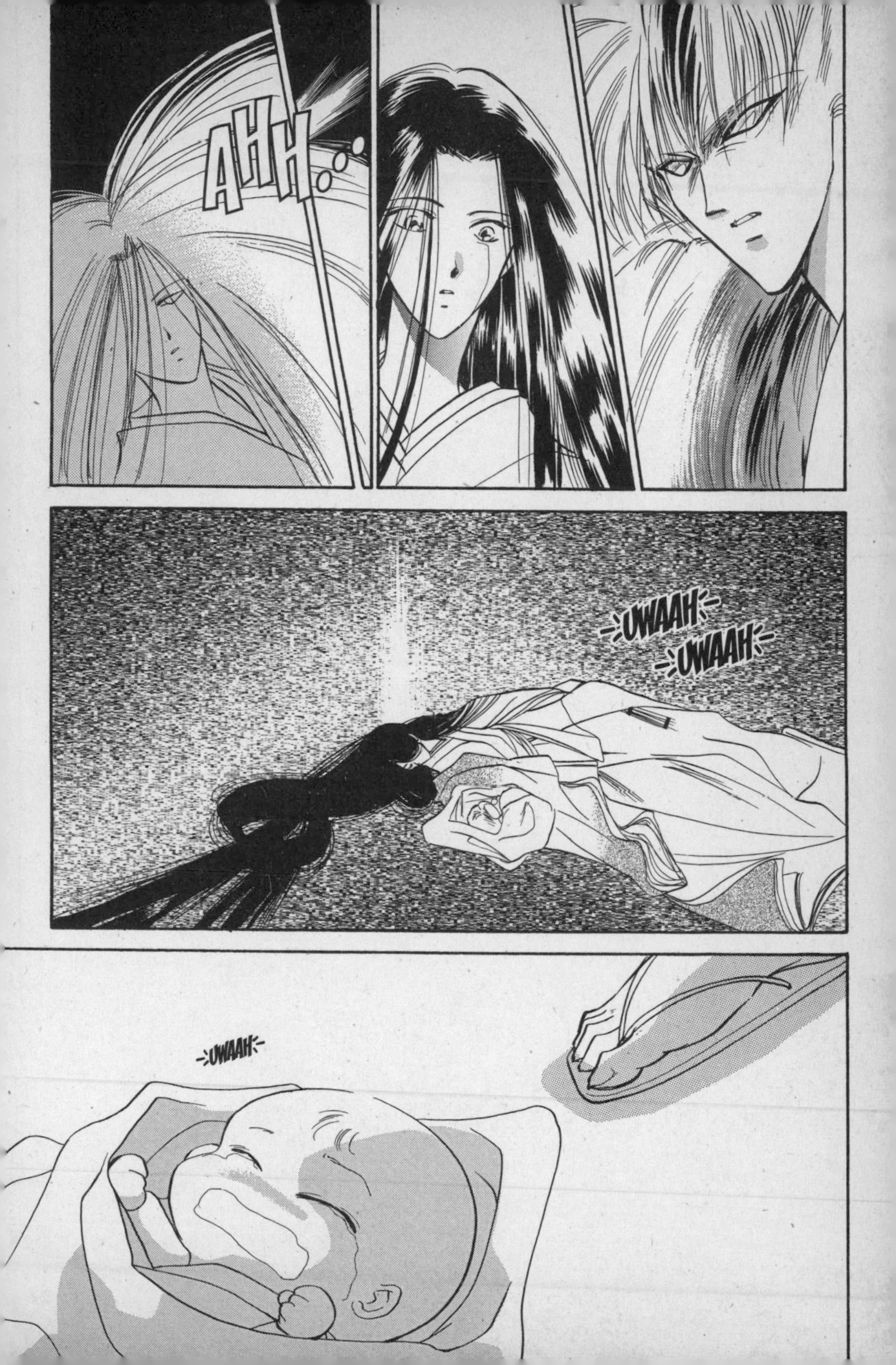
AHH...
UWAAH
UWAAH
UWAAH

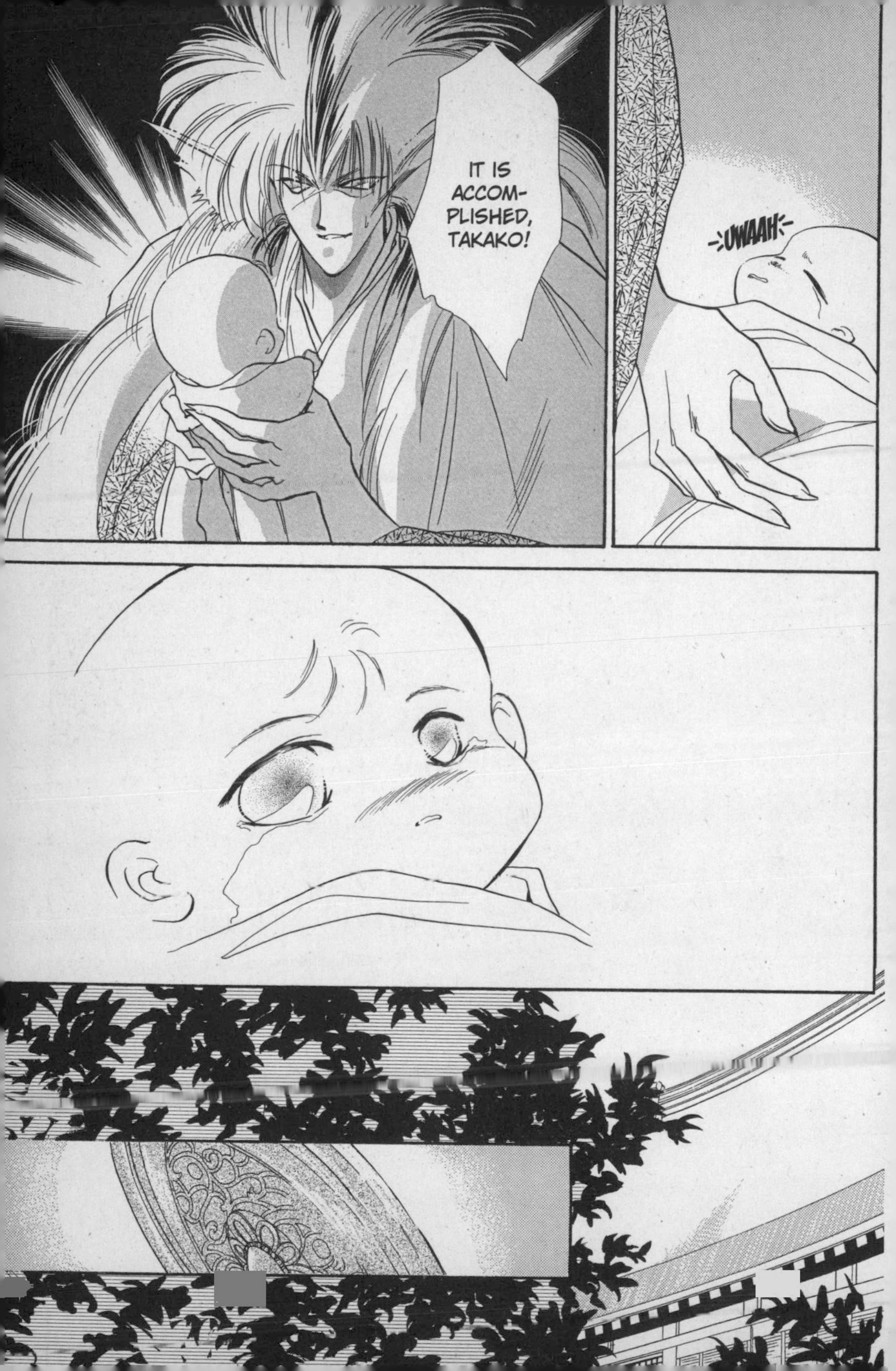
UWAAH
IT IS ACCOMPLISHED, TAKAKO!

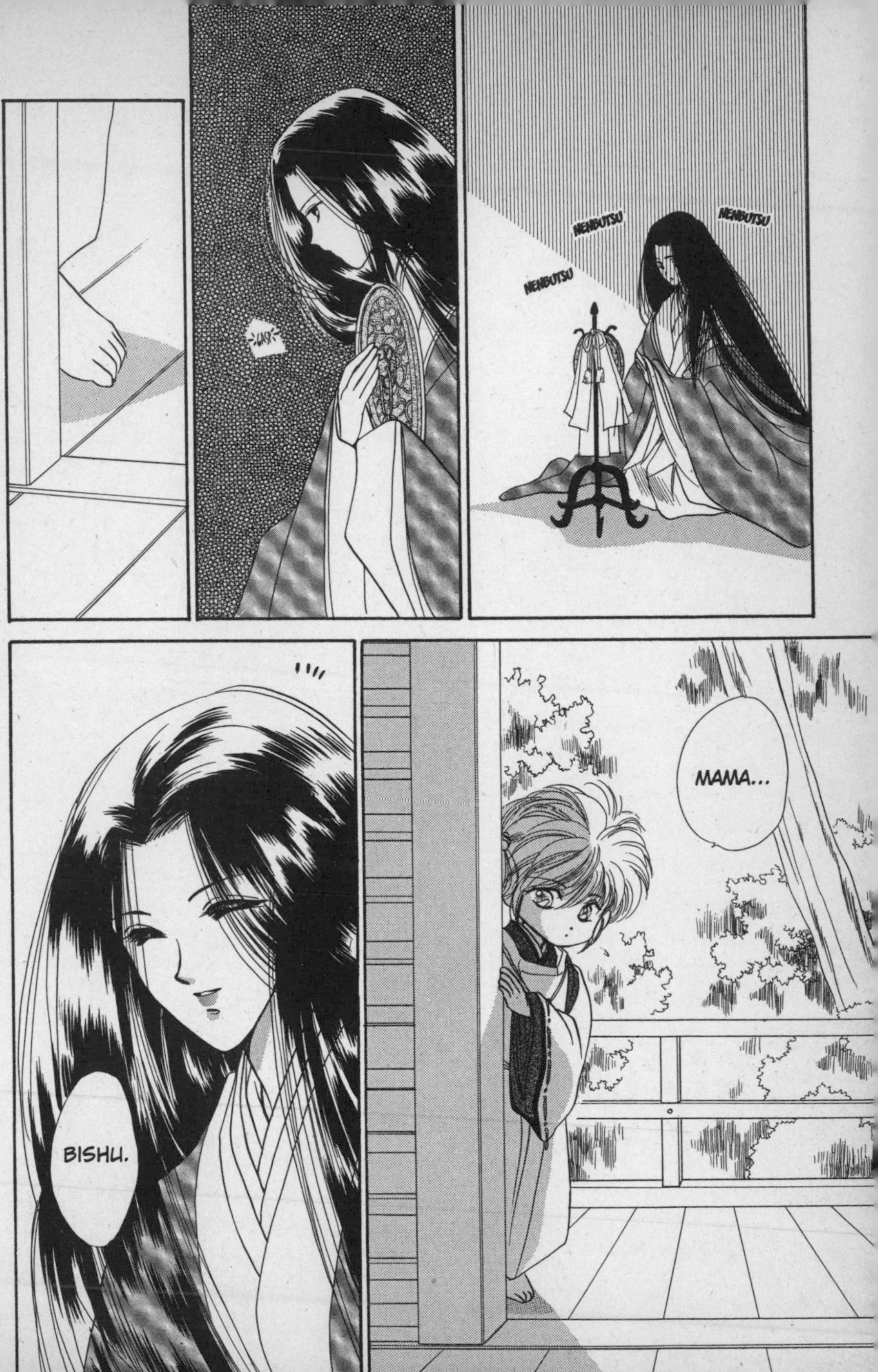
NENBUTSU
NENBUTSU
NENBUTSU
GASP
MAMA...
BISHU.

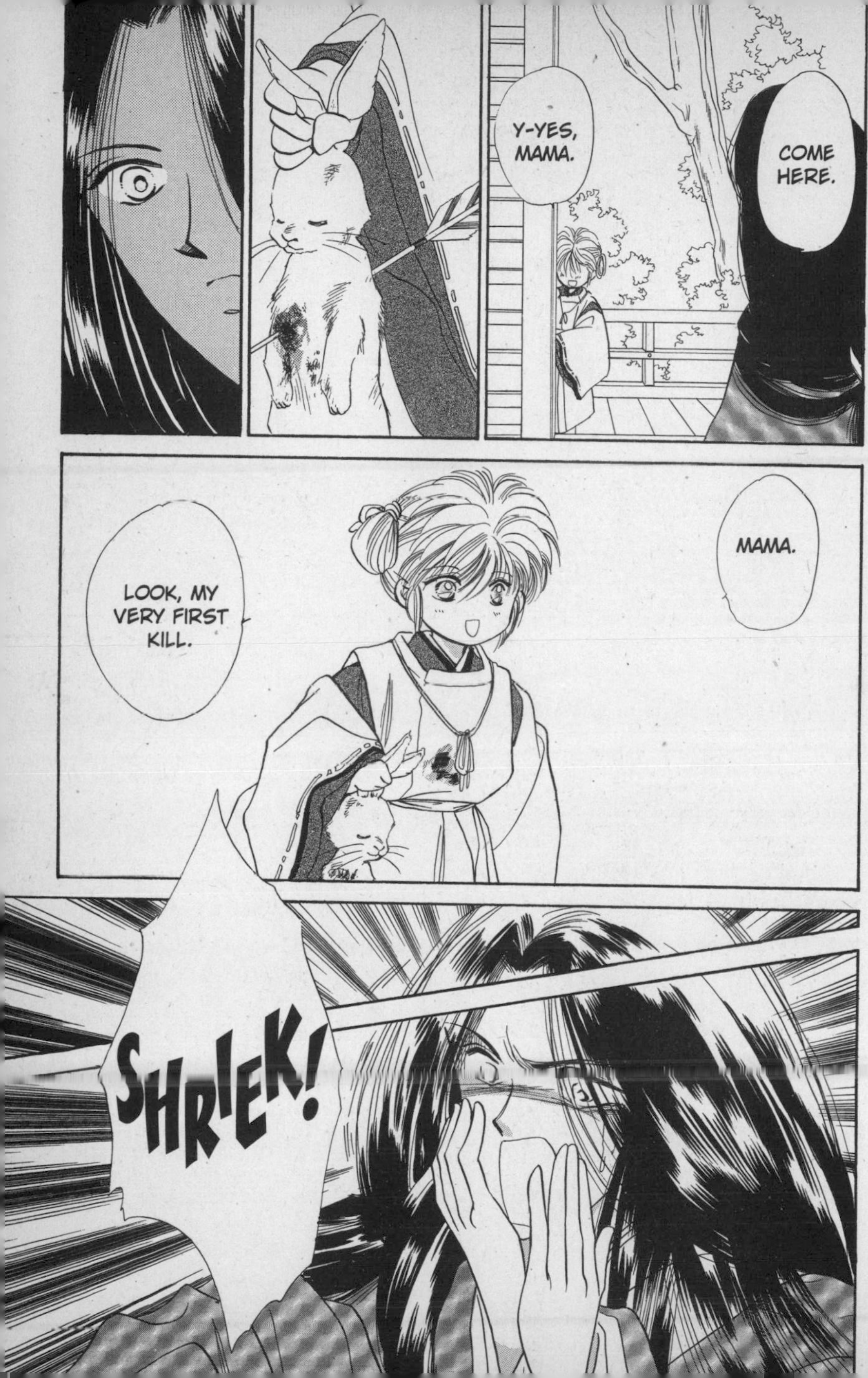
COME HERE.
Y-YES, MAMA.
MAMA.
LOOK, MY VERY FIRST KILL.
SHRIEK!

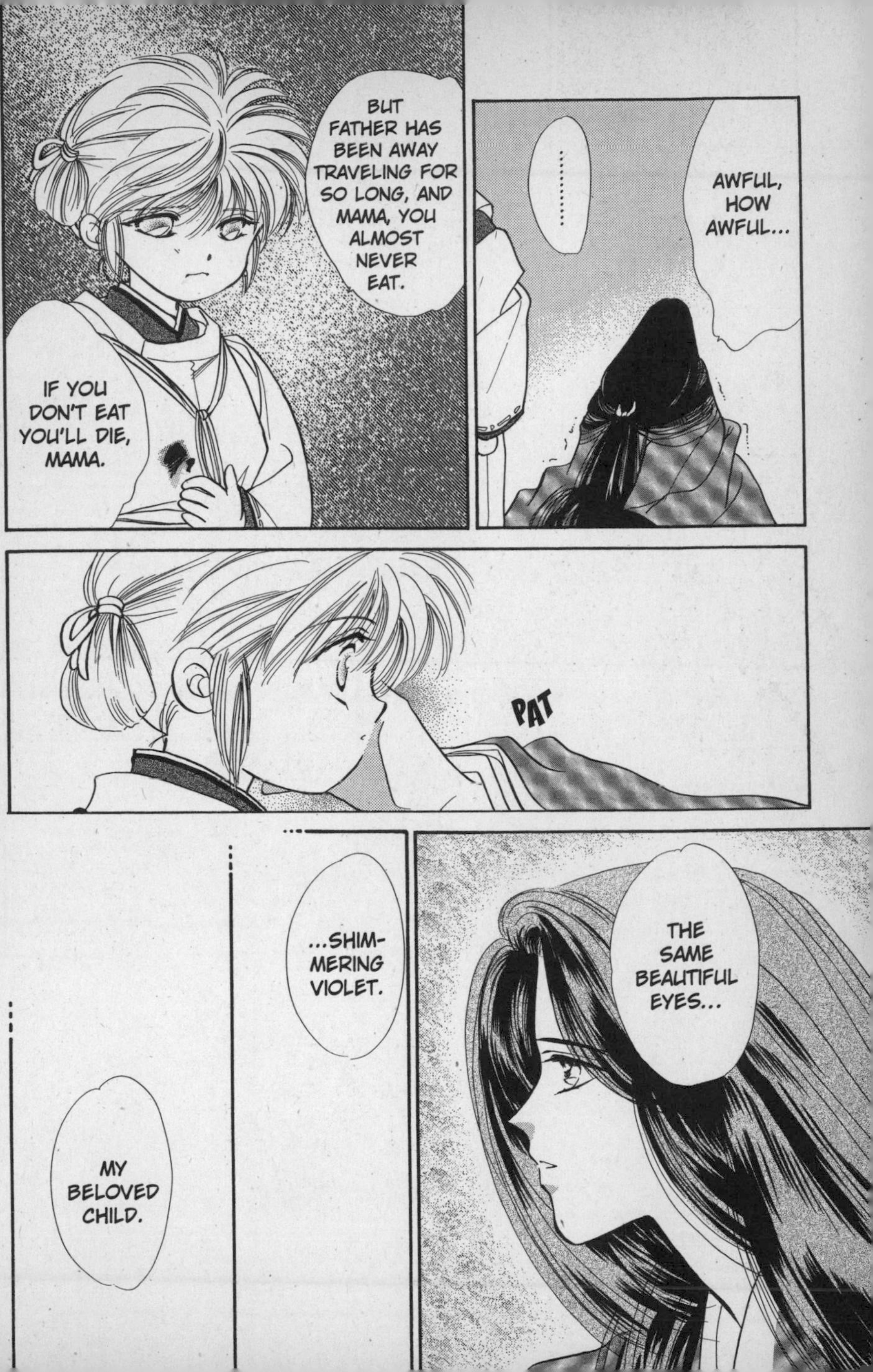
AWFUL, HOW AWFUL...
......
BUT FATHER HAS BEEN AWAY TRAVELING FOR SO LONG, AND MAMA, YOU ALMOST NEVER EAT.
IF YOU DON'T EAT YOU'LL DIE, MAMA.
PAT
THE SAME BEAUTIFUL EYES...
...SHIM-MERING VIOLET.
MY BELOVED CHILD.

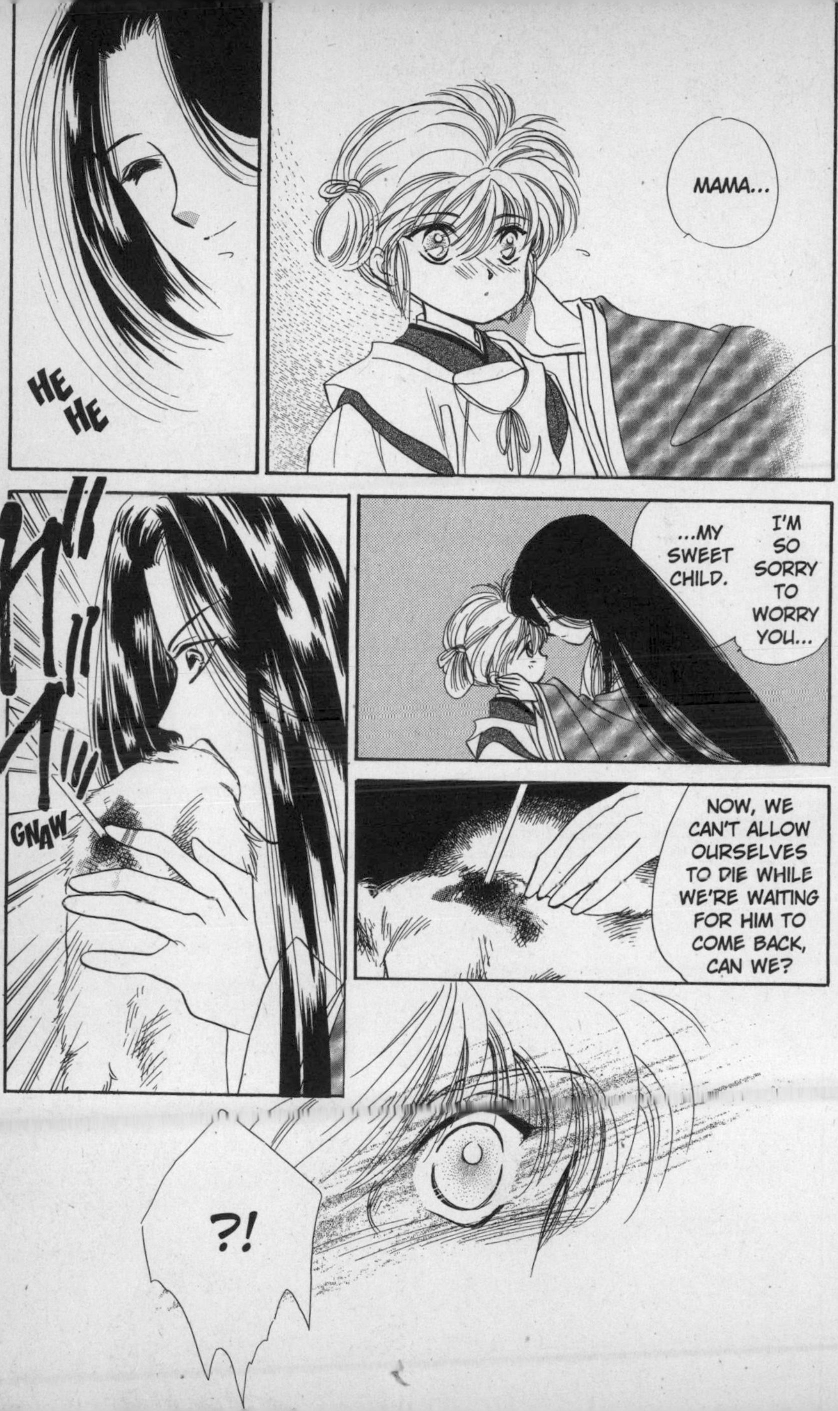
MAMA...
HE HE
I'M SO SORRY TO WORRY YOU...
...MY SWEET CHILD.
NOW, WE CAN'T ALLOW OURSELVES TO DIE WHILE WE'RE WAITING FOR HIM TO COME BACK, CAN WE?
GNAW
?!

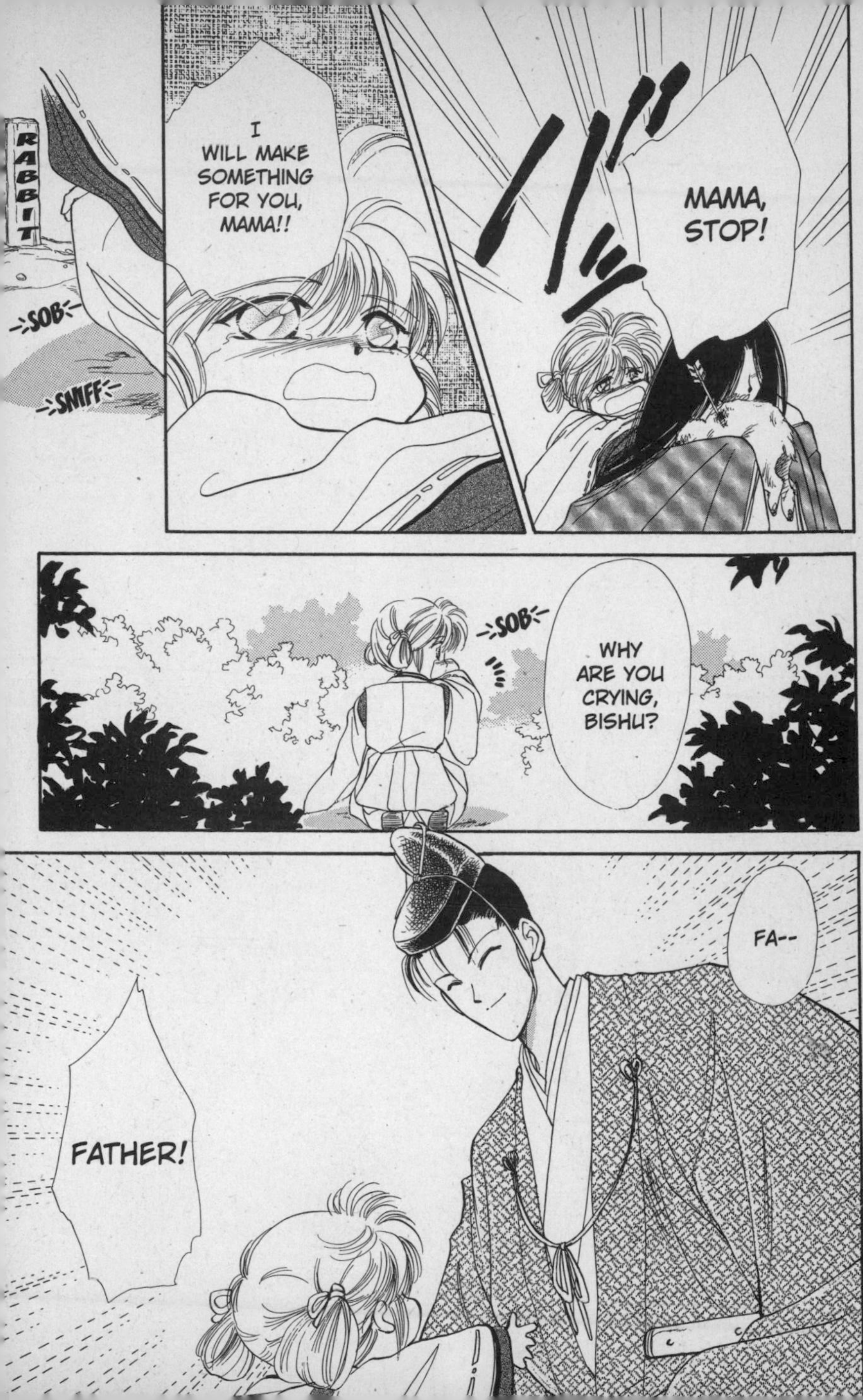
MAMA, STOP!
I WILL MAKE SOMETHING FOR YOU, MAMA!!
RABBIT
SOB
SNIFF
WHY ARE YOU CRYING, BISHU?
SOB
FA--
FATHER!

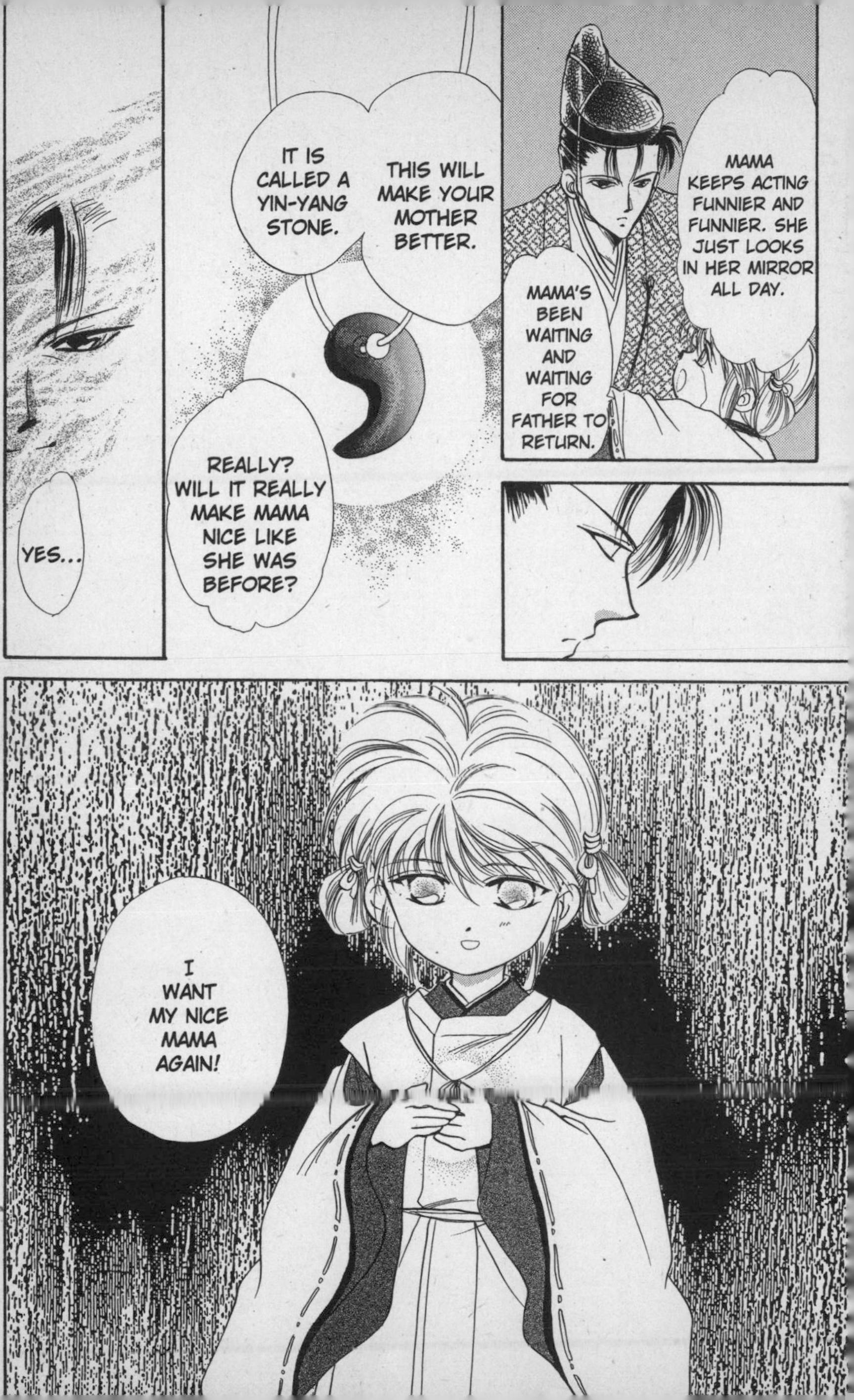
MAMA KEEPS ACTING FUNNIER AND FUNNIER. SHE JUST LOOKS IN HER MIRROR ALL DAY.
MAMA'S BEEN WAITING AND WAITING FOR FATHER TO RETURN.
THIS WILL MAKE YOUR MOTHER BETTER.
IT IS CALLED A YIN-YANG STONE.
REALLY? WILL IT REALLY MAKE MAMA NICE LIKE SHE WAS BEFORE?
YES...
I WANT MY NICE MAMA AGAIN!

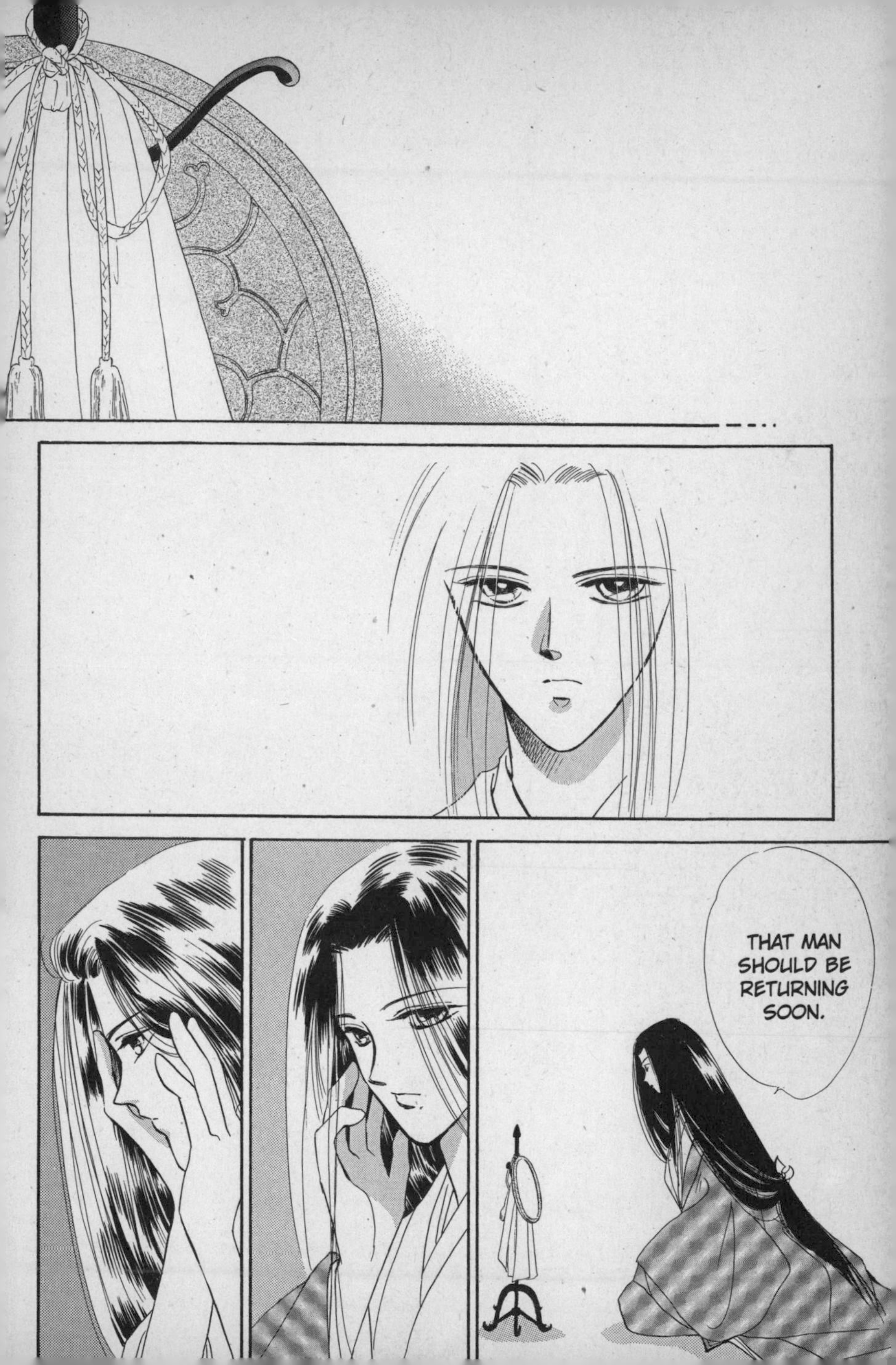
THAT MAN SHOULD BE RETURNING SOON.

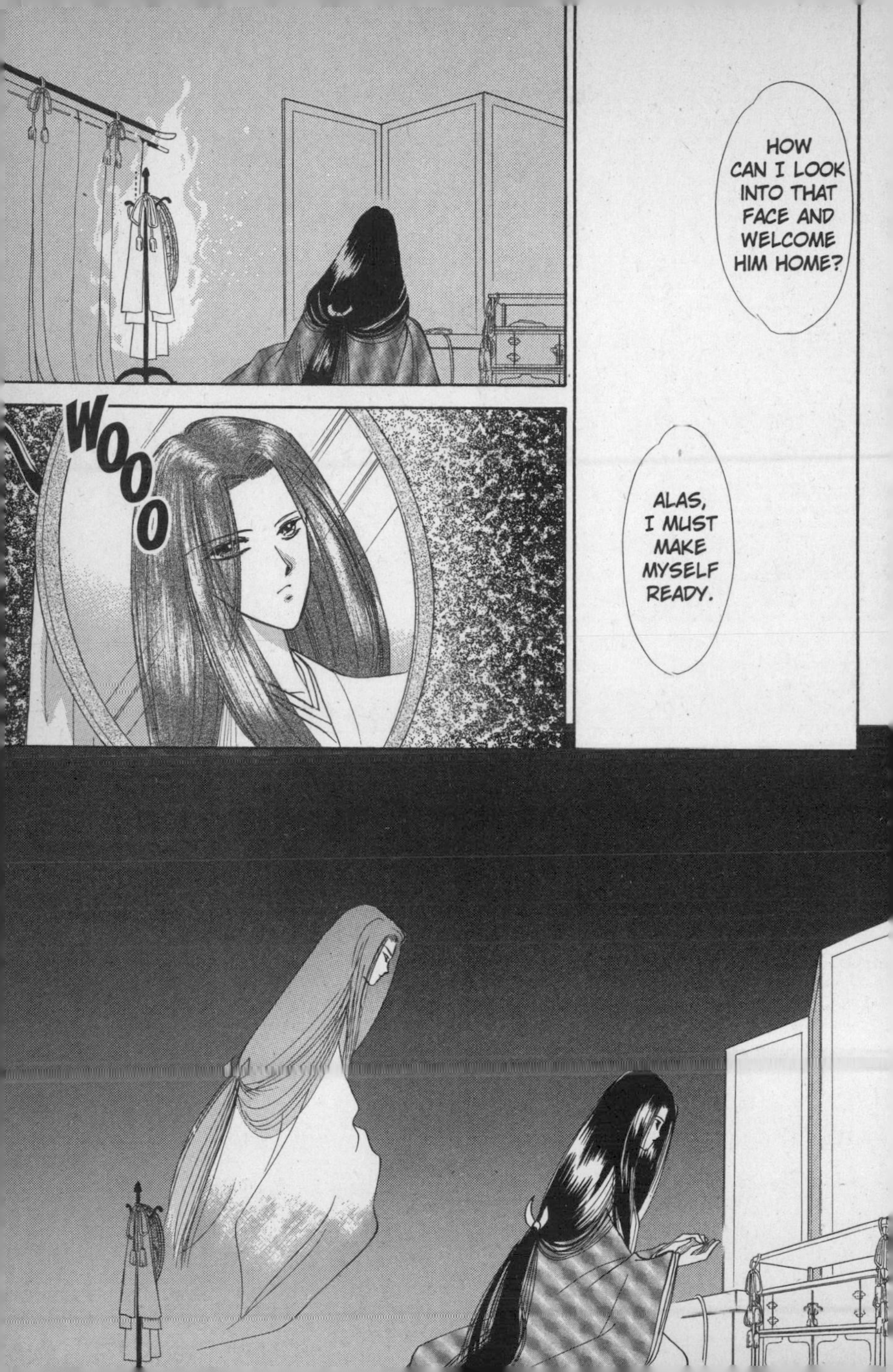
HOW CAN I LOOK INTO THAT FACE AND WELCOME HIM HOME?
ALAS, I MUST MAKE MYSELF READY.
WOOO

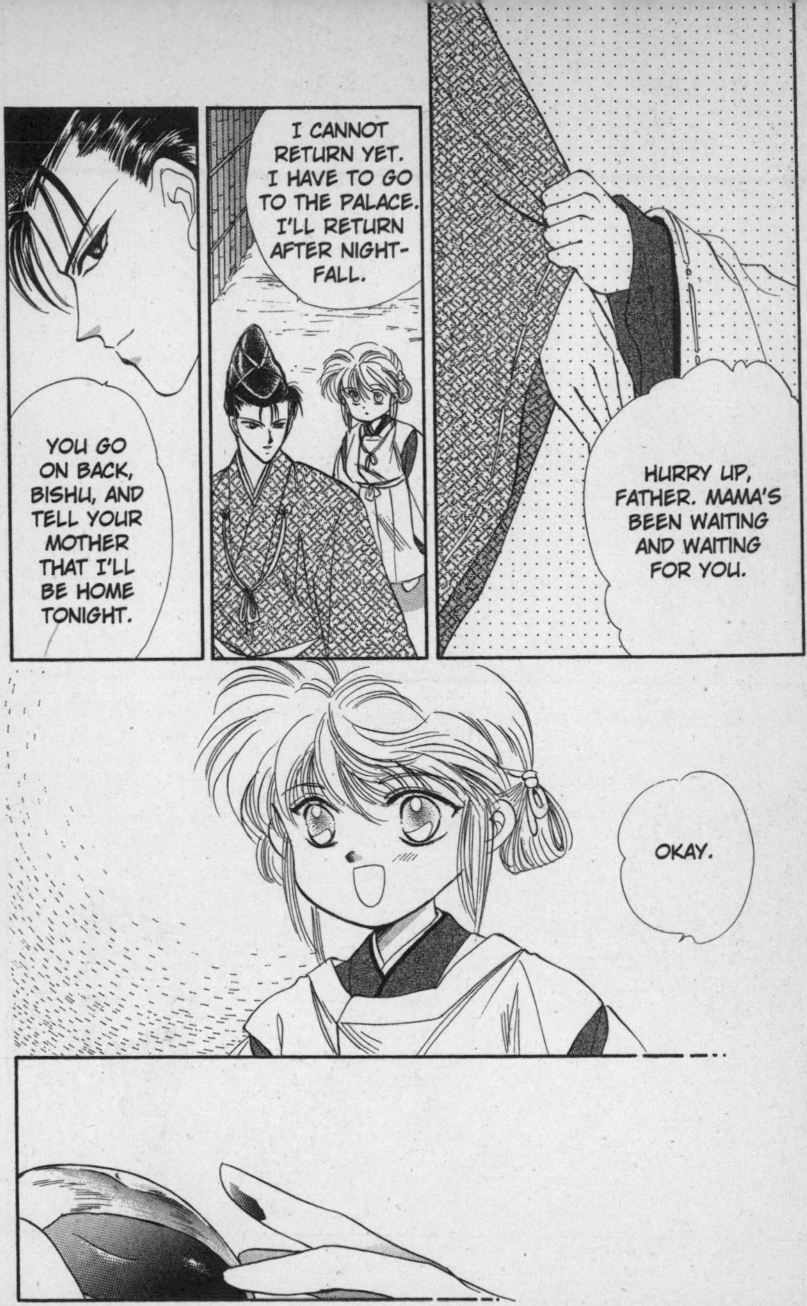
HURRY UP, FATHER. MAMA'S BEEN WAITING AND WAITING FOR YOU.
I CANNOT RETURN YET. I HAVE TO GO TO THE PALACE. I'LL RETURN AFTER NIGHT-FALL.
YOU GO ON BACK, BISHU, AND TELL YOUR MOTHER THAT I'LL BE HOME TONIGHT.
OKAY.

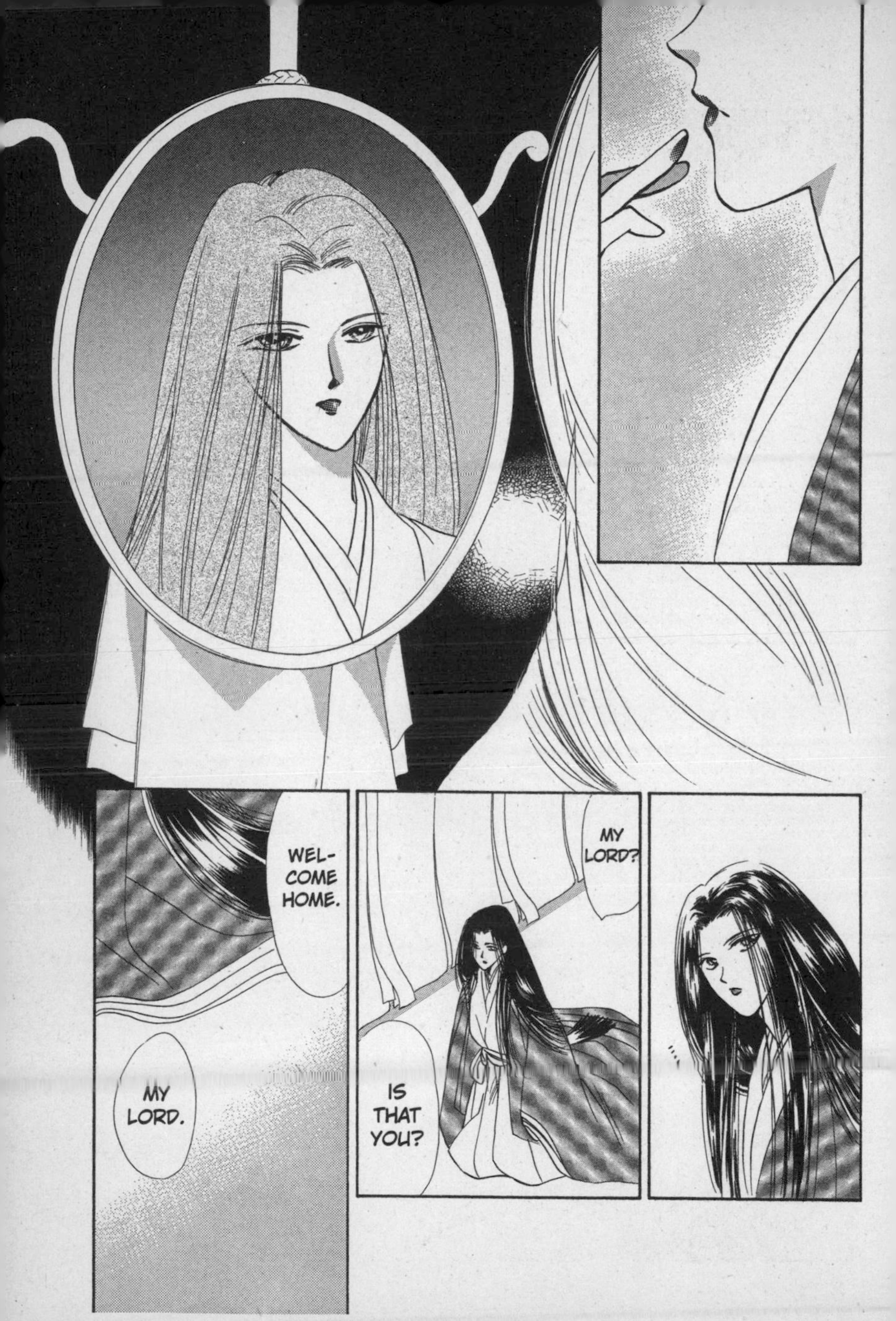
MY LORD?
IS THAT YOU?
WEL-COME HOME.
MY LORD.

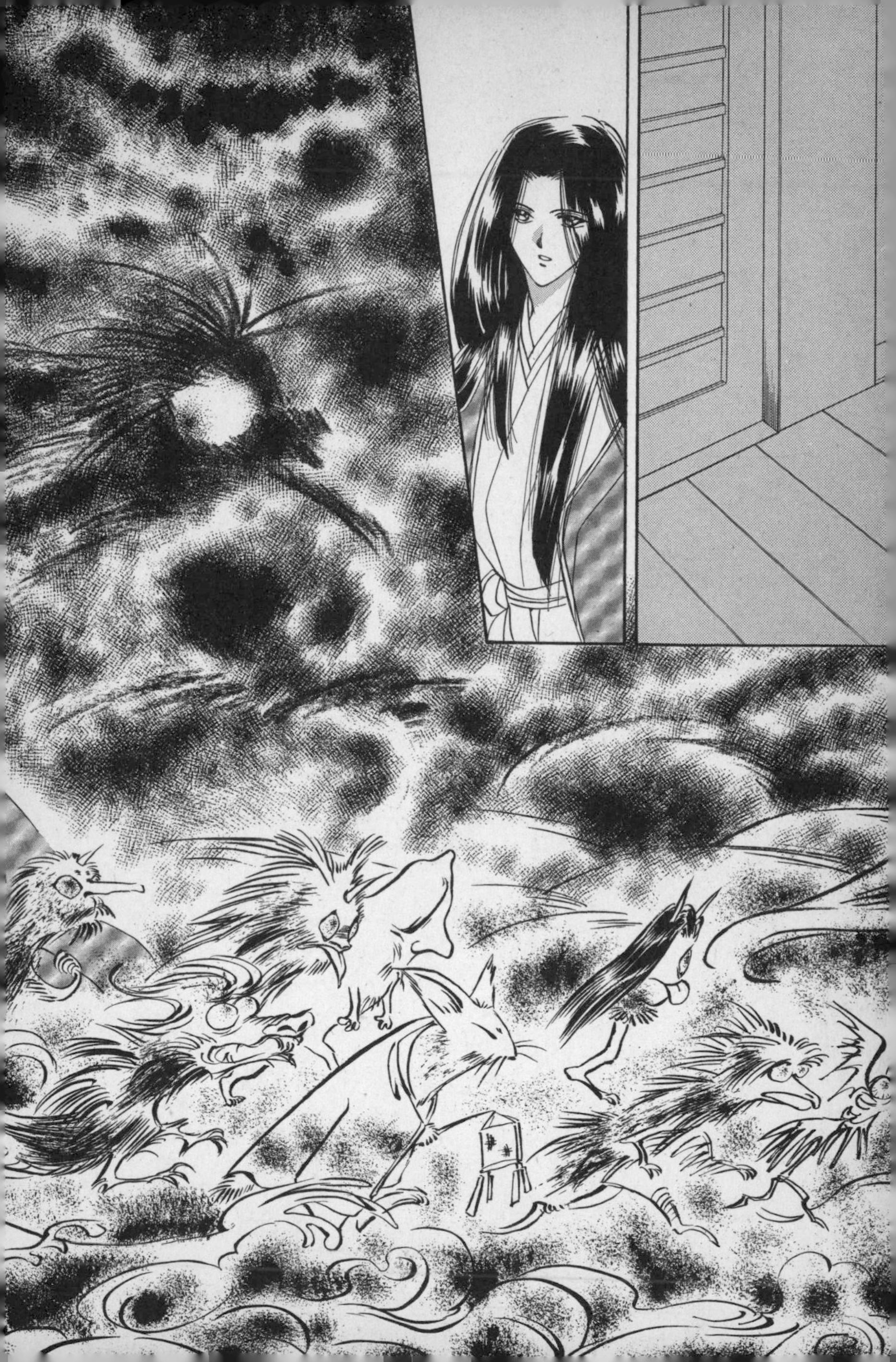

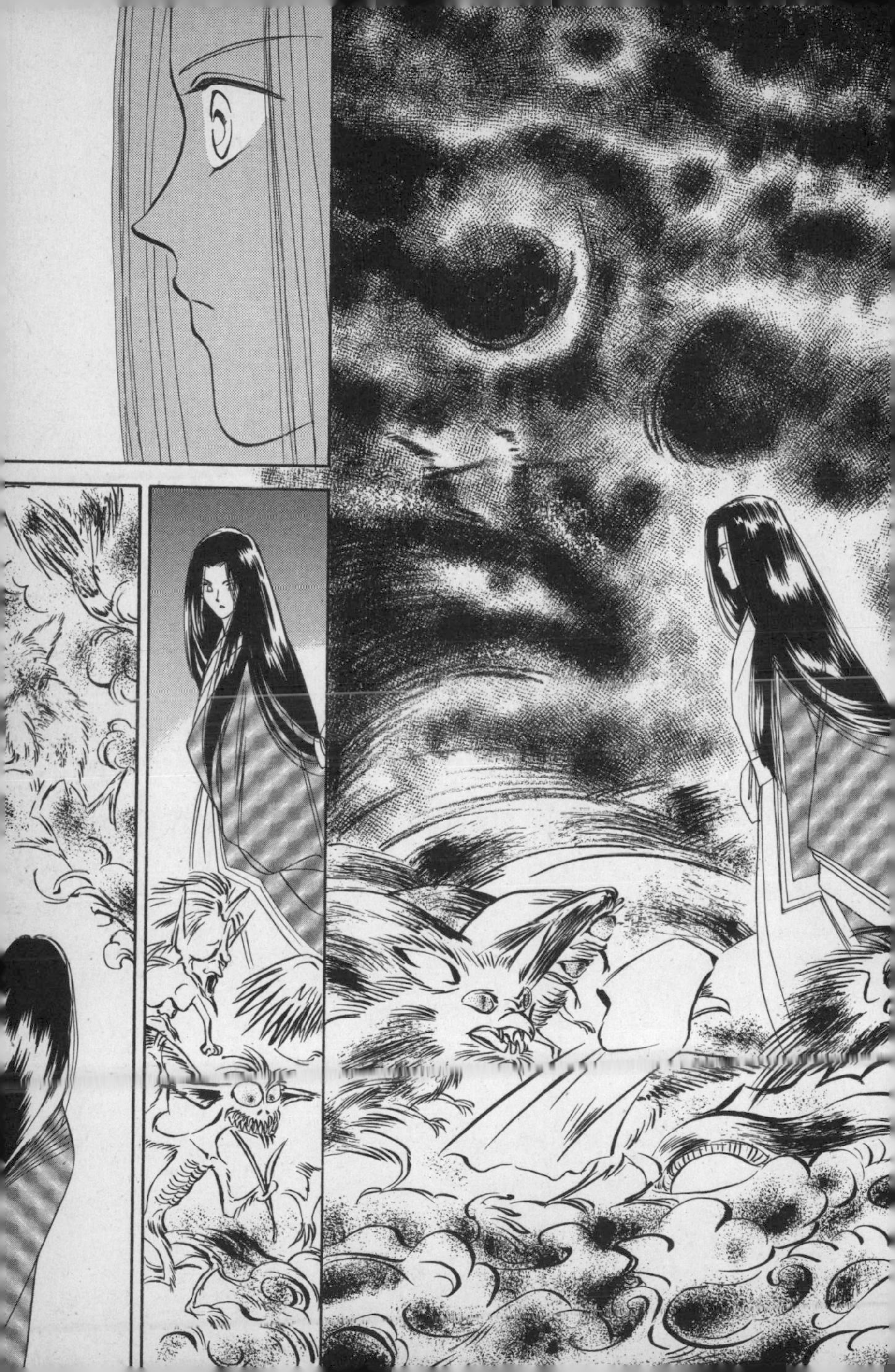

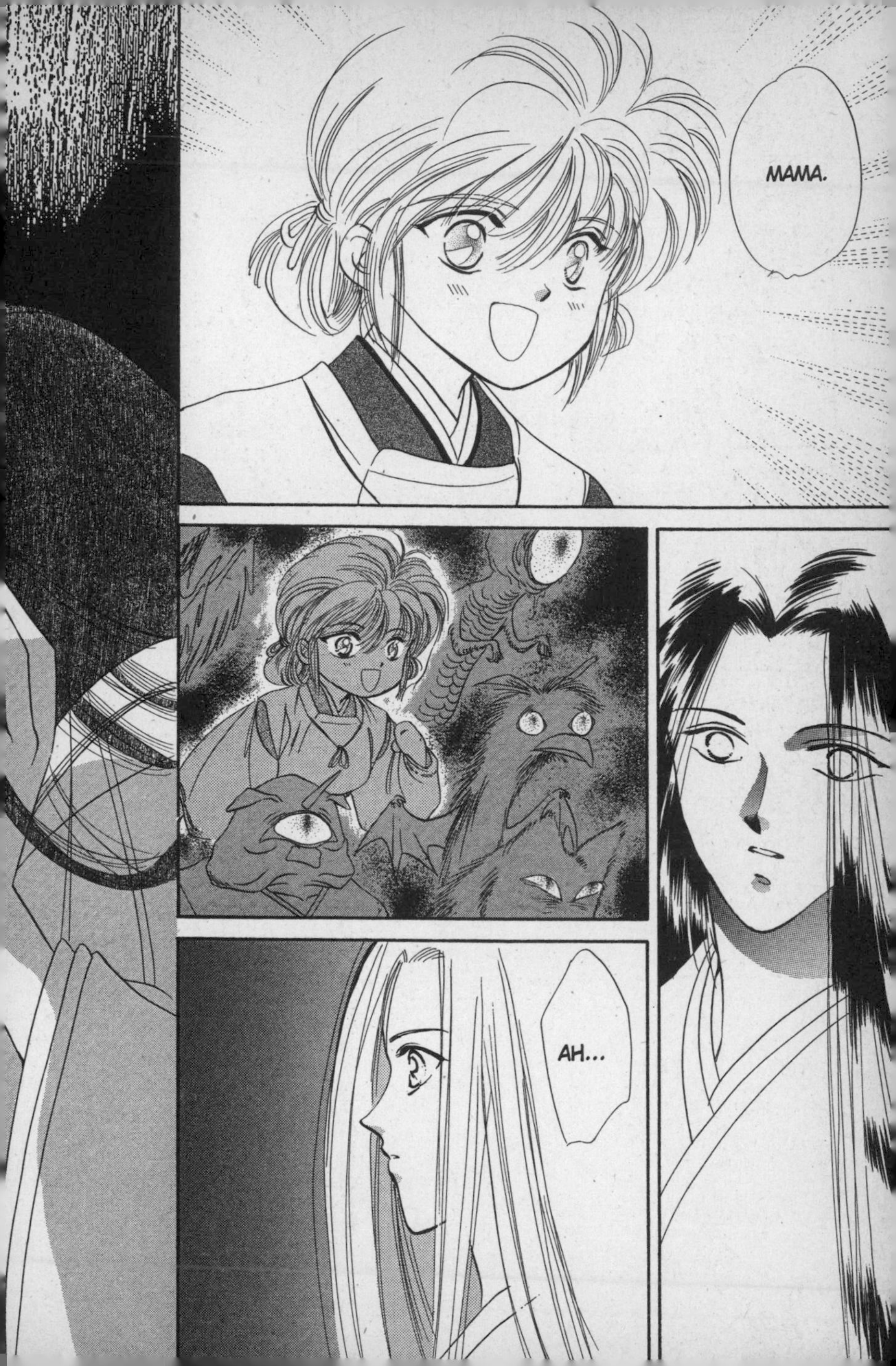
MAMA.
AH...

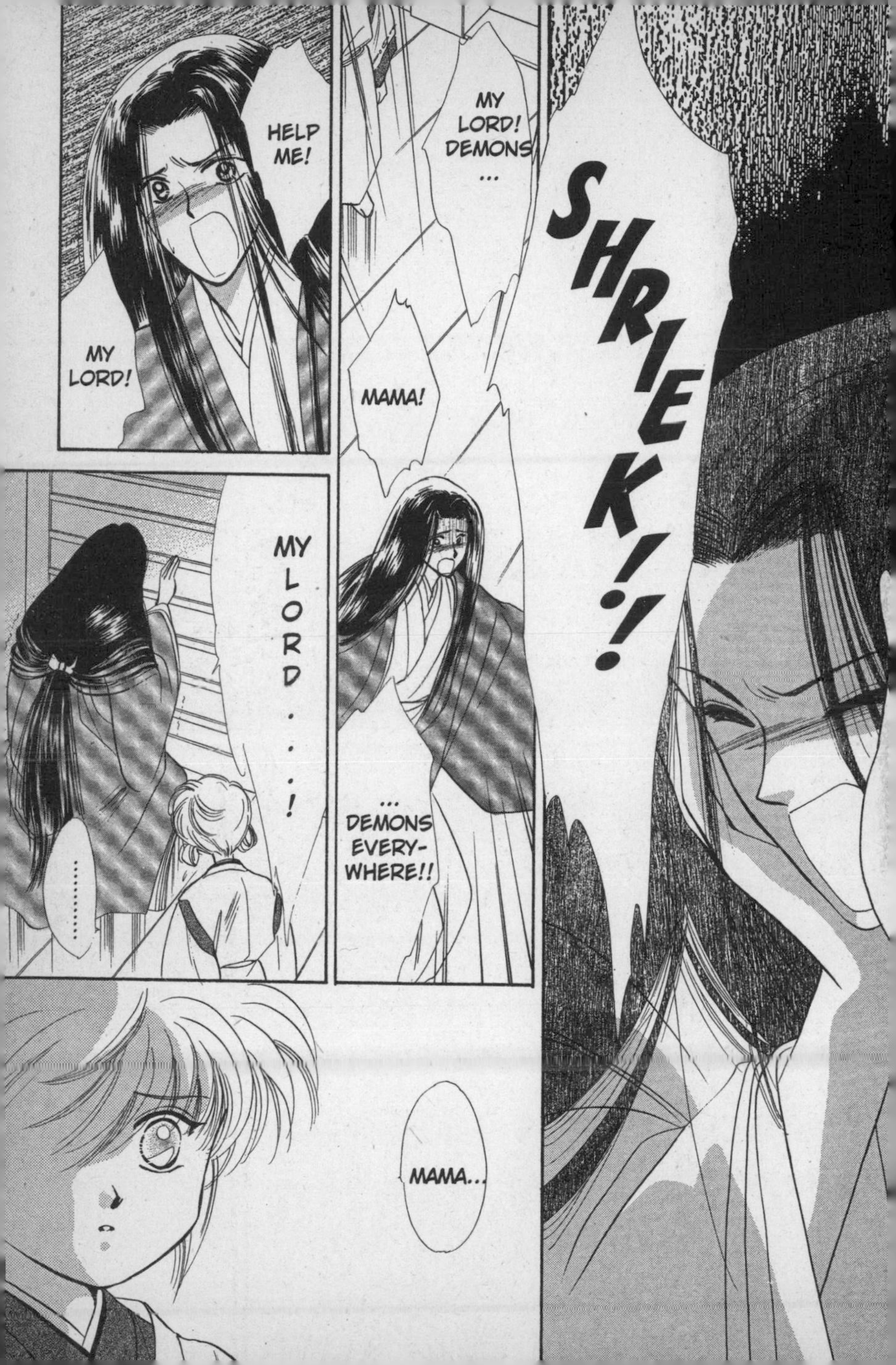
SHRIEK!!
MY LORD! DEMONS ...
MAMA!
... DEMONS EVERYWHERE!!
HELP ME!
MY LORD!
MY LORD . . . !
......
MAMA...

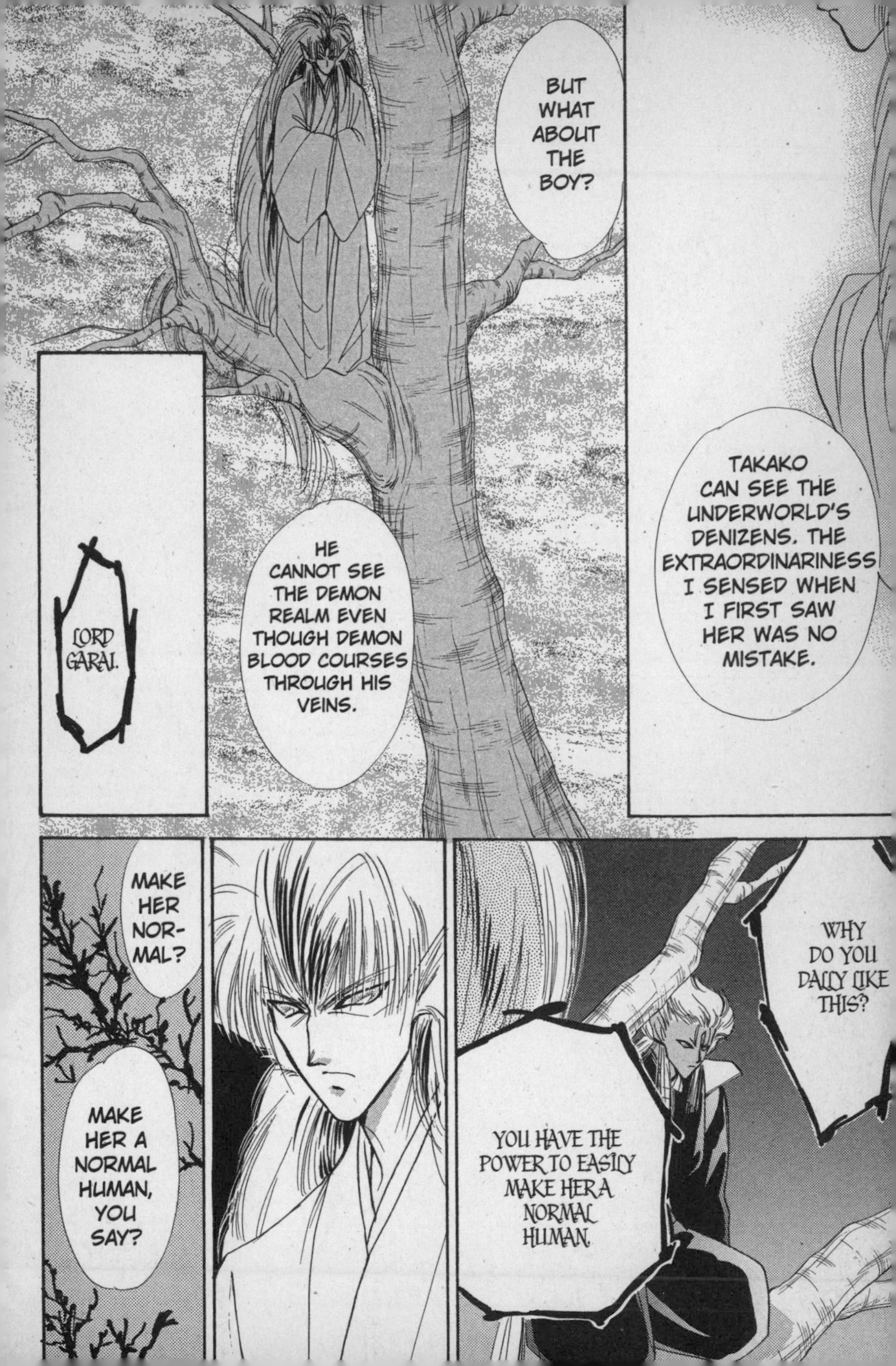
TAKAKO CAN SEE THE UNDERWORLD'S DENIZENS. THE EXTRAORDINARINESS I SENSED WHEN I FIRST SAW HER WAS NO MISTAKE.
BUT WHAT ABOUT THE BOY?
HE CANNOT SEE THE DEMON REALM EVEN THOUGH DEMON BLOOD COURSES THROUGH HIS VEINS.
LORD GARAI.
WHY DO YOU DALLY LIKE THIS?
YOU HAVE THE POWER TO EASILY MAKE HER A NORMAL HUMAN.
MAKE HER NOR-MAL?
MAKE HER A NORMAL HUMAN, YOU SAY?

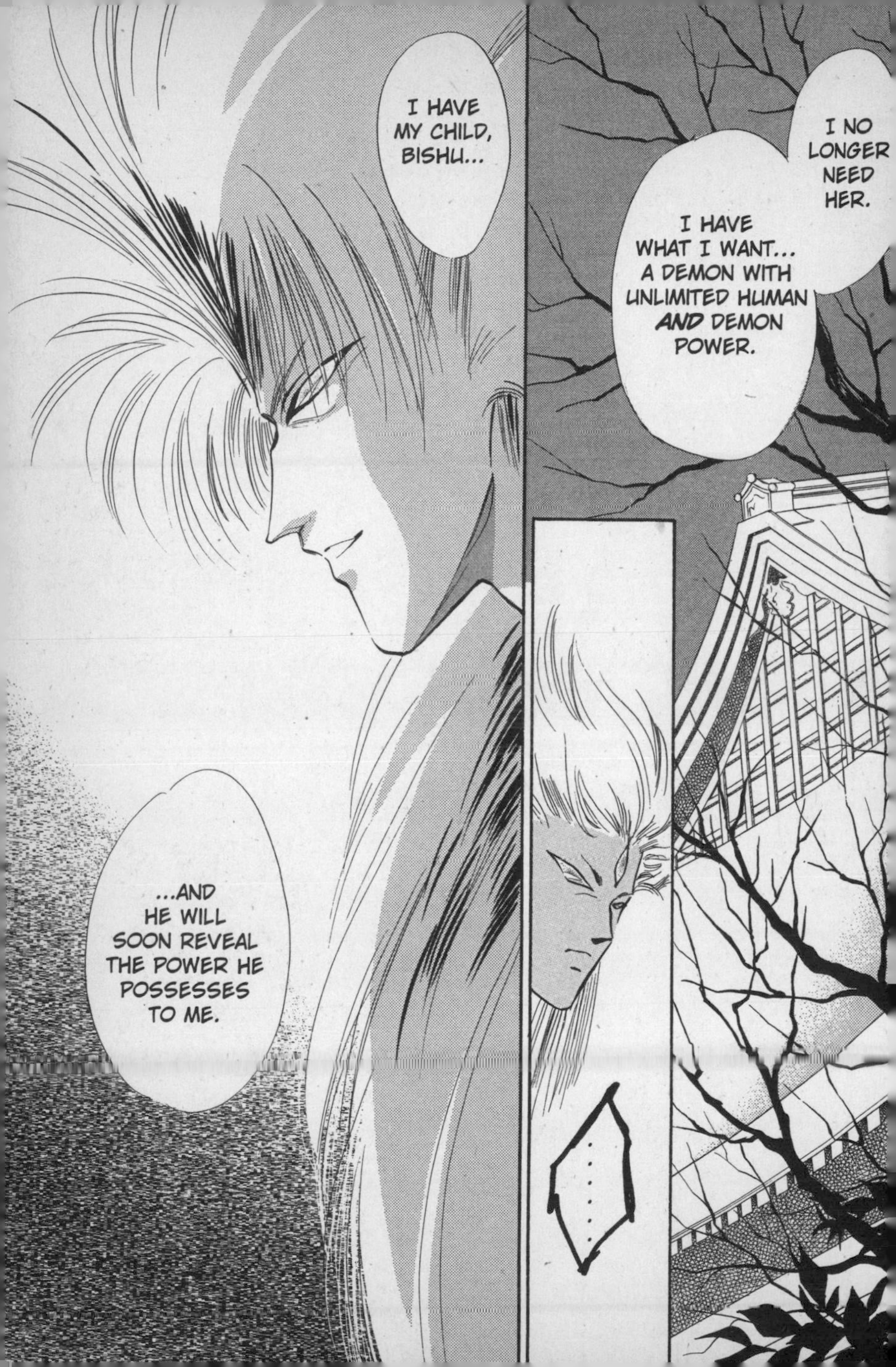
I NO LONGER NEED HER.
I HAVE WHAT I WANT... A DEMON WITH UNLIMITED HUMAN AND DEMON POWER.
......
I HAVE MY CHILD, BISHU...
...AND HE WILL SOON REVEAL THE POWER HE POSSESSES TO ME.

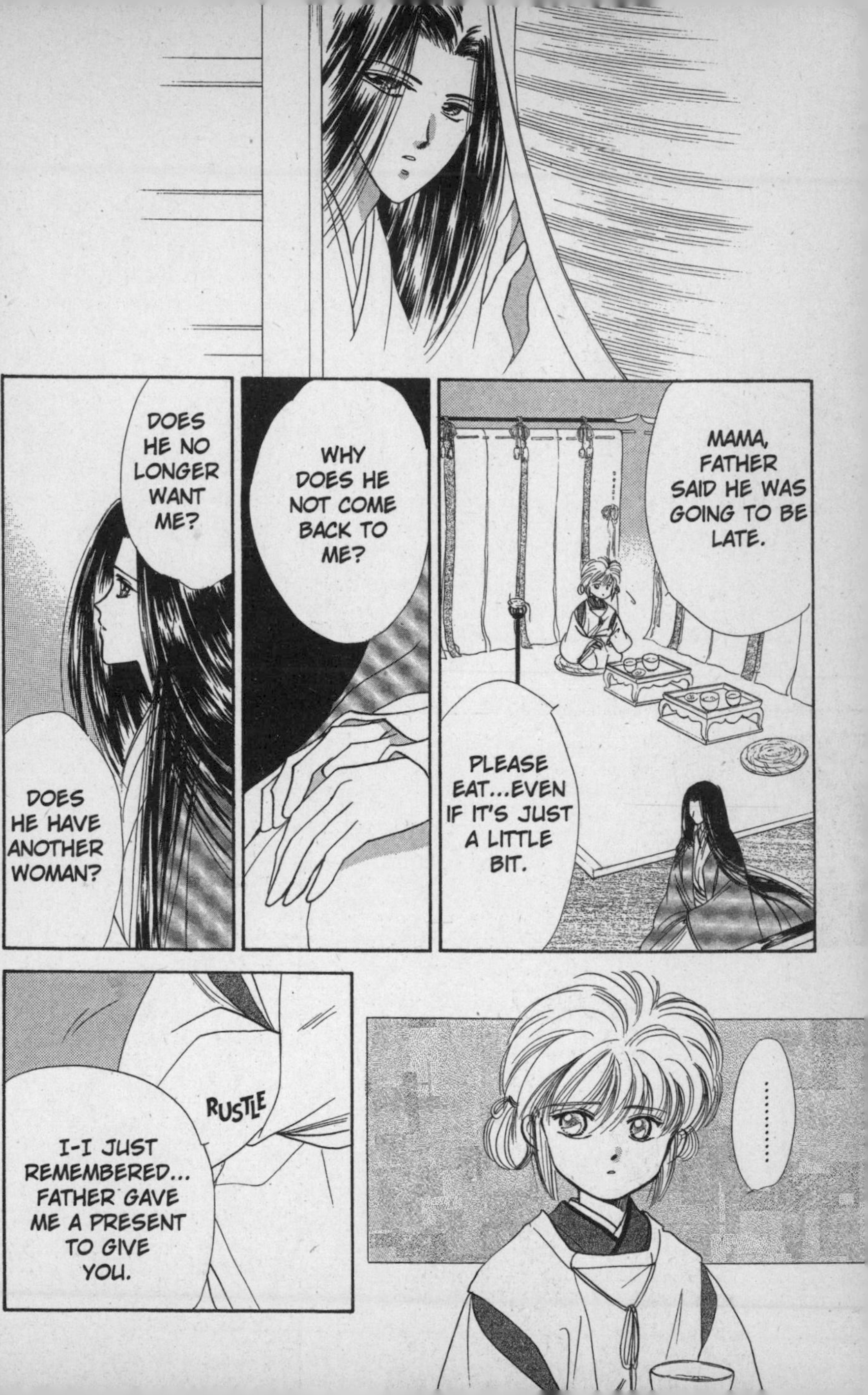
MAMA, FATHER SAID HE WAS GOING TO BE LATE.
PLEASE EAT...EVEN IF IT'S JUST A LITTLE BIT.
WHY DOES HE NOT COME BACK TO ME?
DOES HE NO LONGER WANT ME?
DOES HE HAVE ANOTHER WOMAN?
......
RUSTLE
I-I JUST REMEMBERED... FATHER GAVE ME A PRESENT TO GIVE YOU.

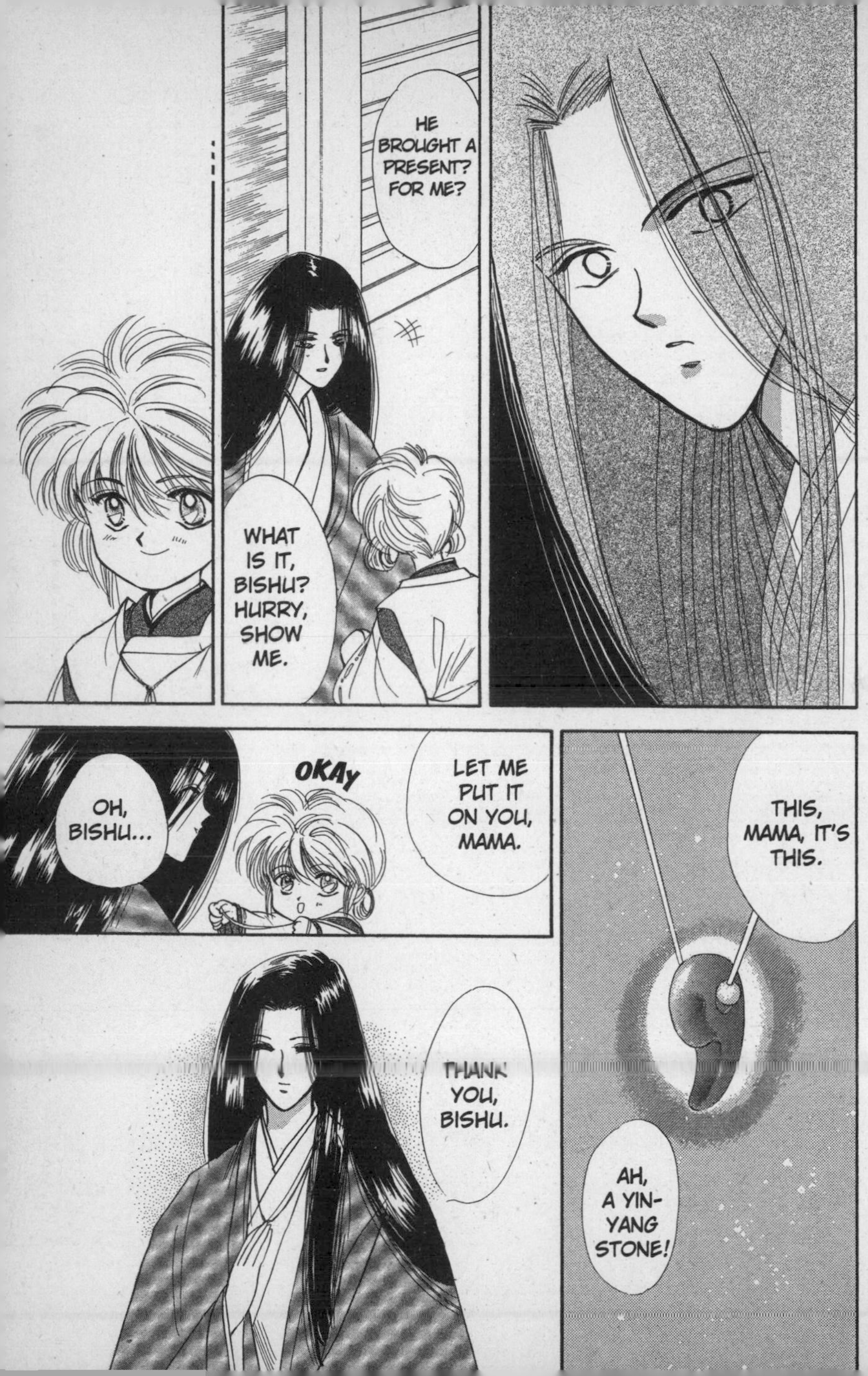
HE BROUGHT A PRESENT? FOR ME?
WHAT IS IT, BISHU? HURRY, SHOW ME.
THIS, MAMA, IT'S THIS.
AH, A YIN-YANG STONE!
LET ME PUT IT ON YOU, MAMA.
OKAY
OH, BISHU...
THANK YOU, BISHU.

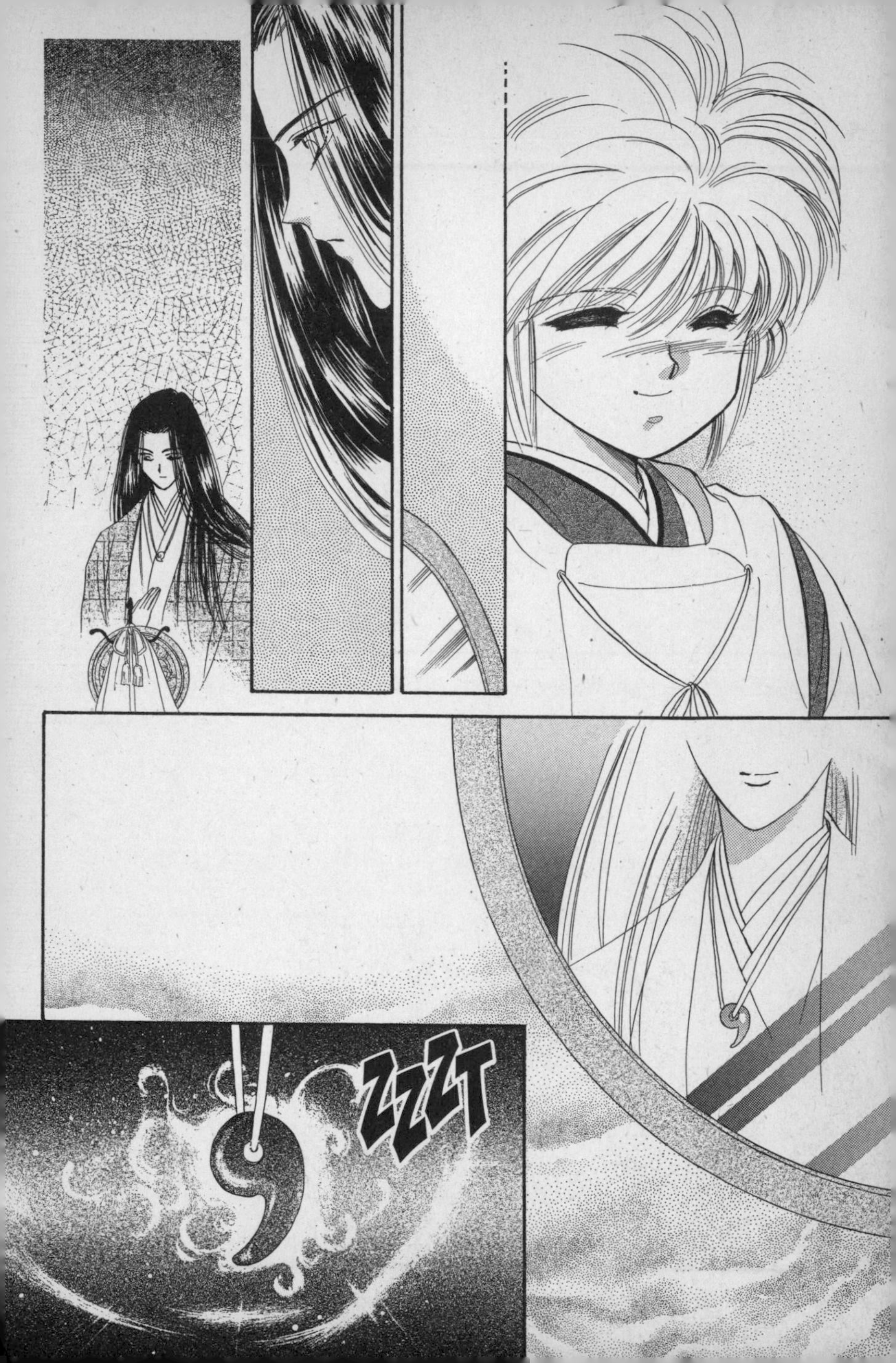
ZZZT

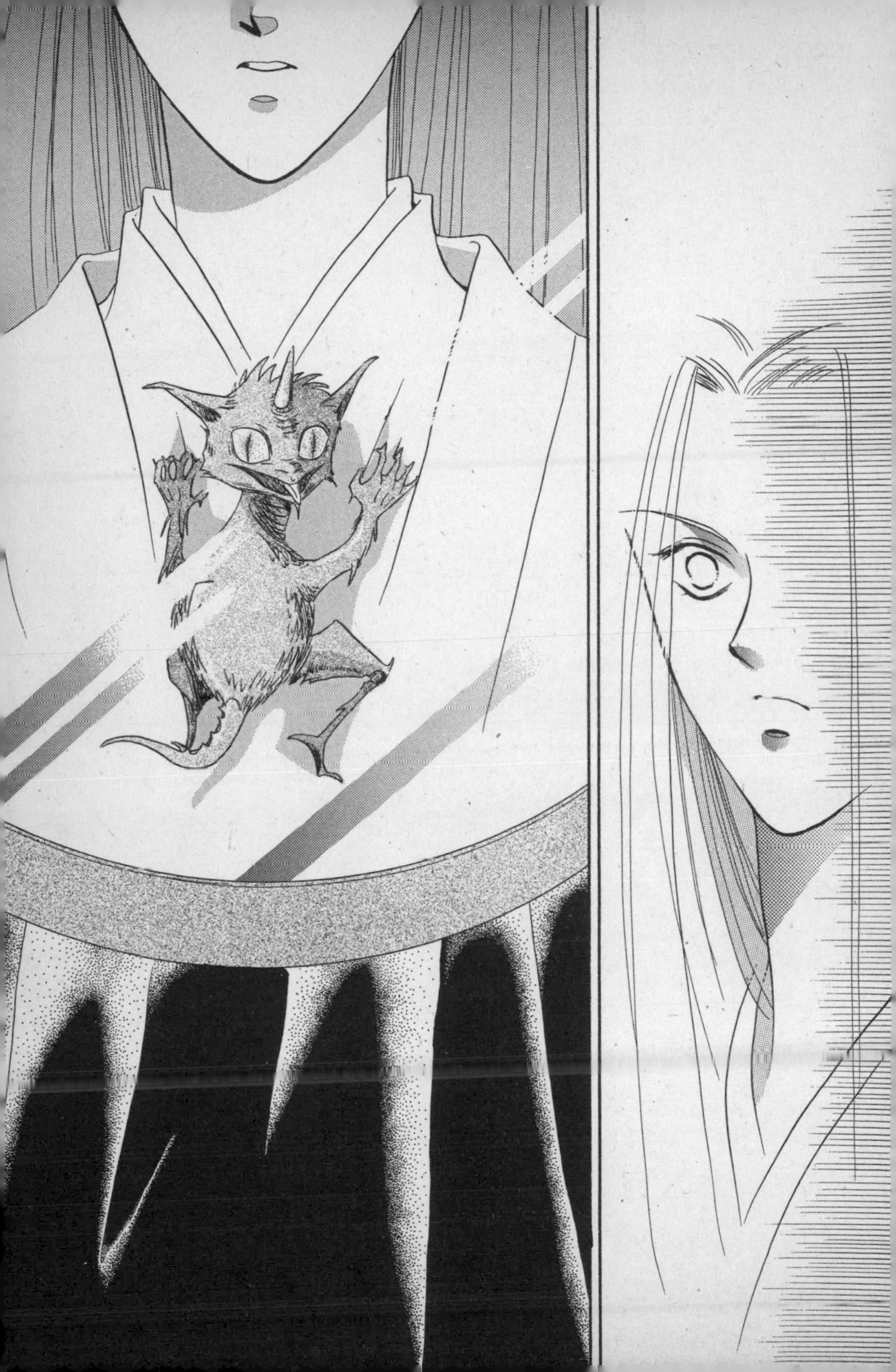

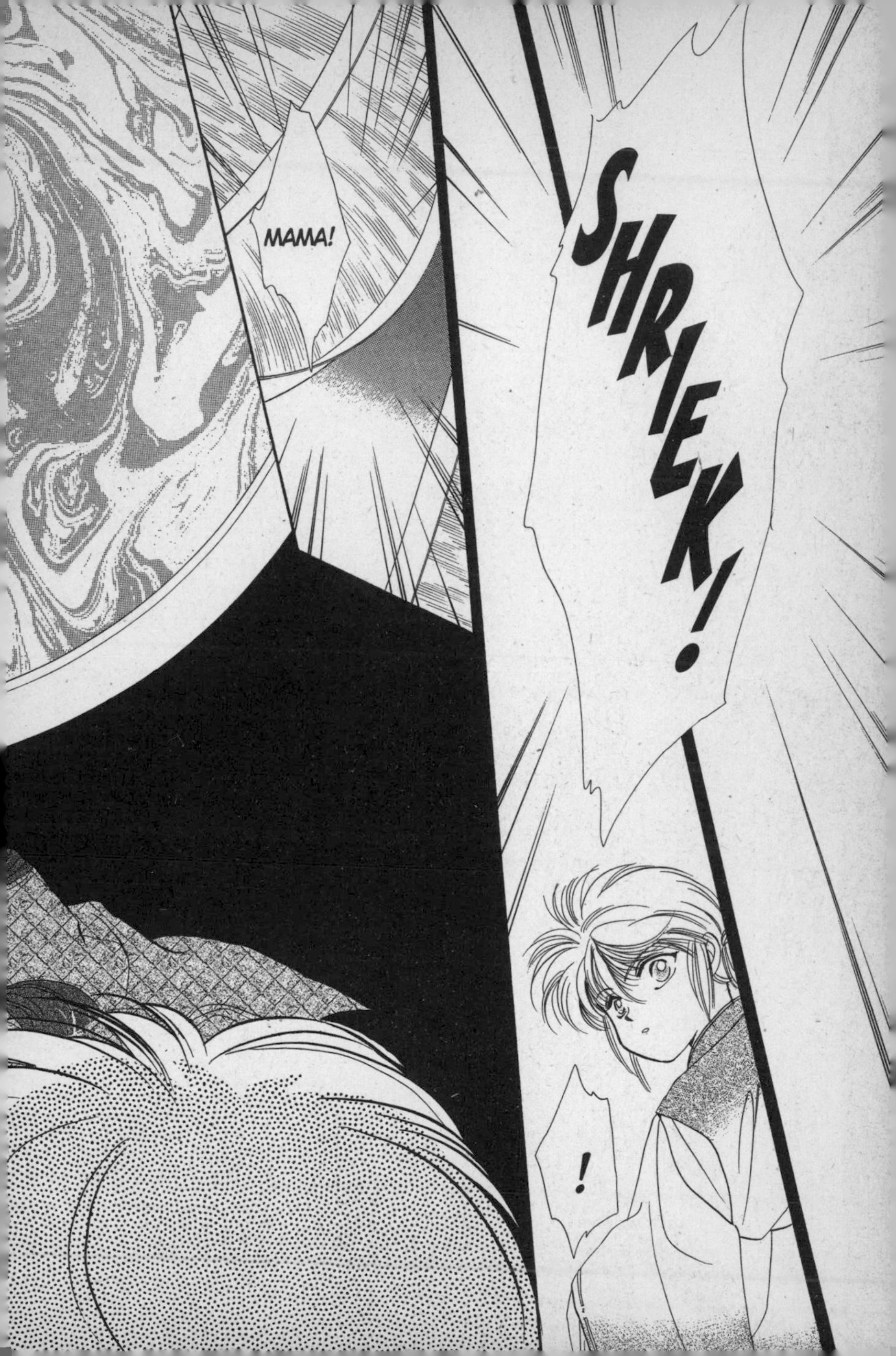
SHRIEK!
!
MAMA!

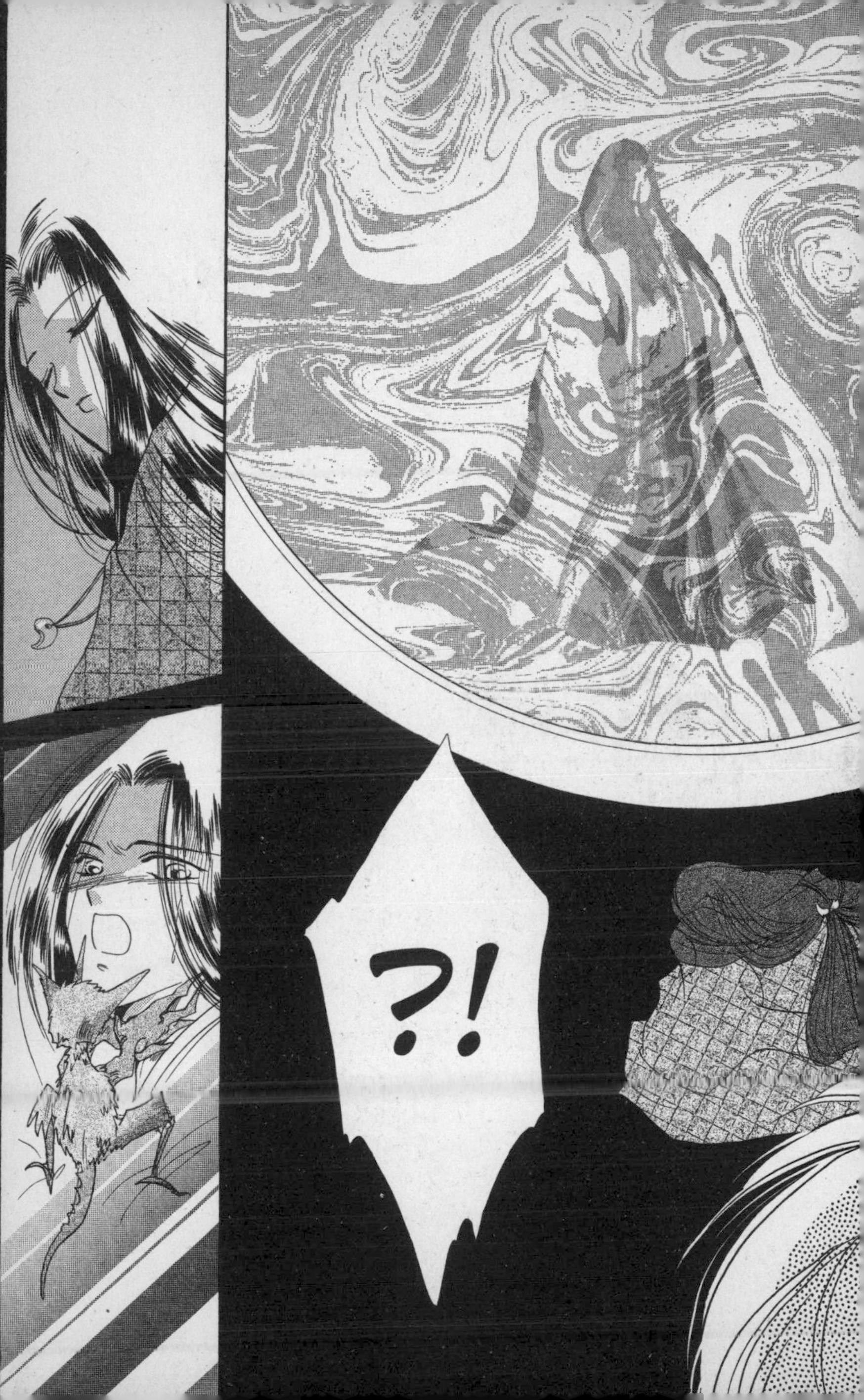
?!

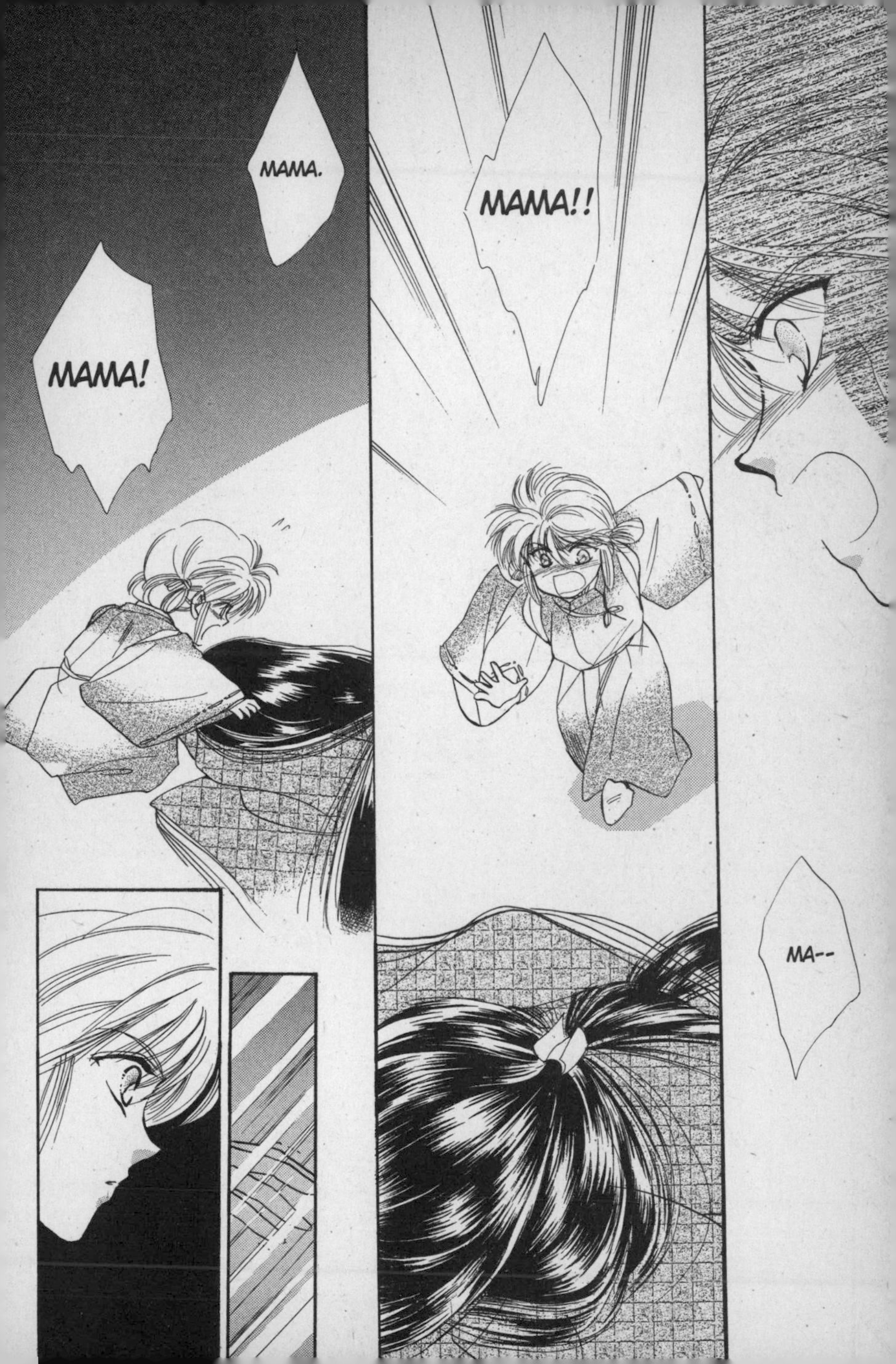
MAMA!!
MAMA.
MAMA!
MA--

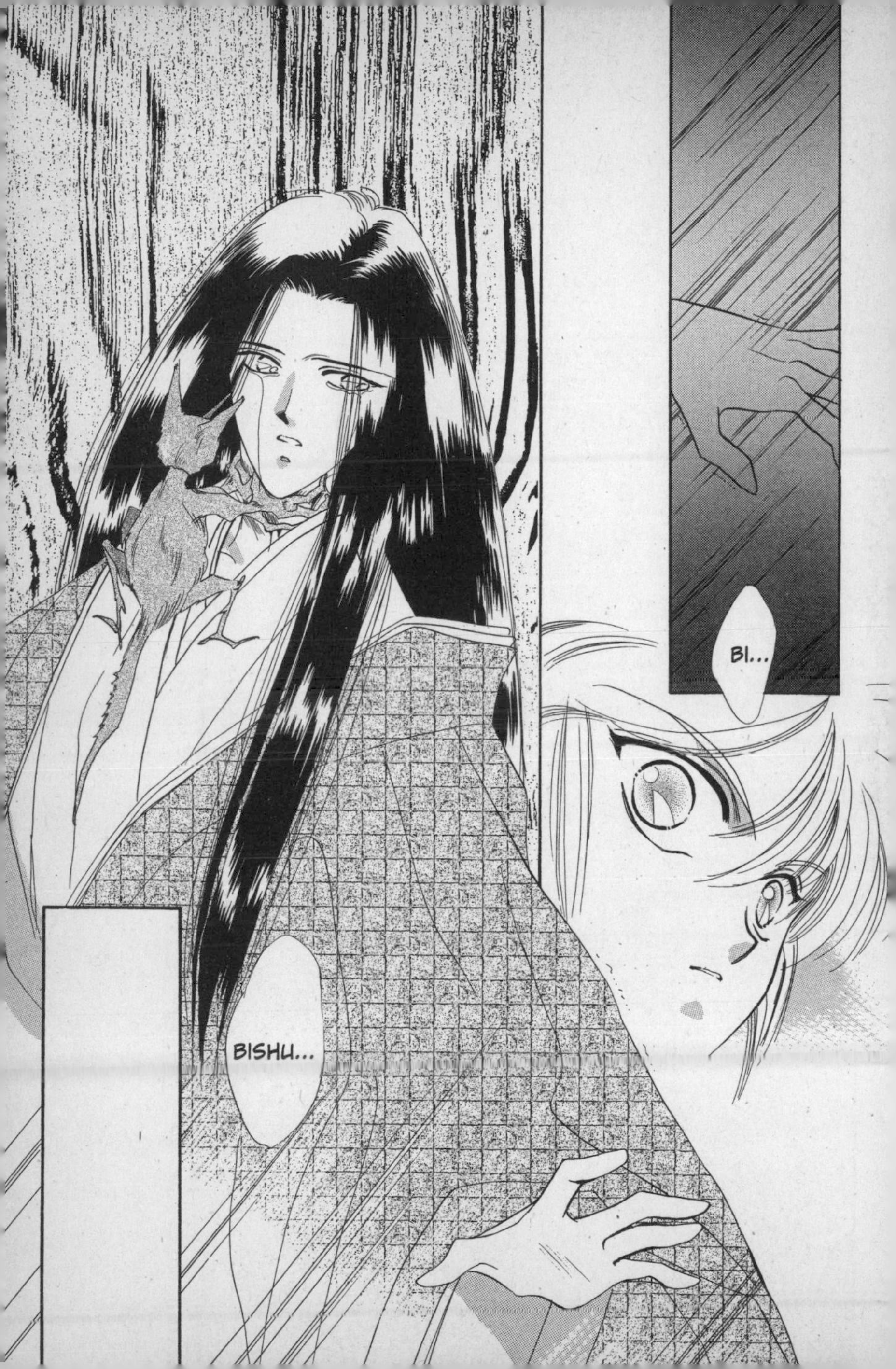
BI...
BISHU...

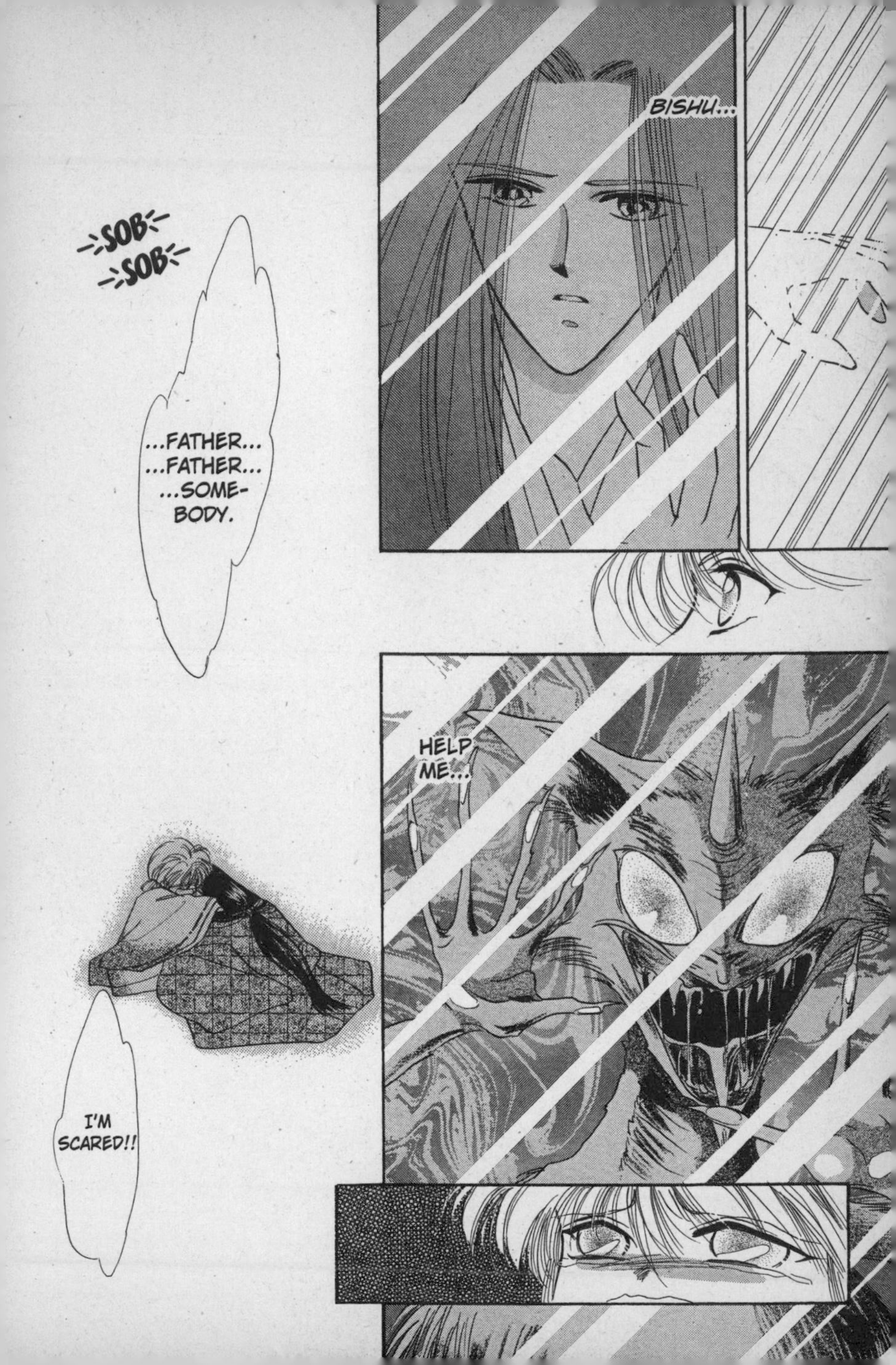
BISHU...
SOB SOB
...FATHER... ...FATHER... ...SOME-BODY.
HELP ME...
I'M SCARED!!

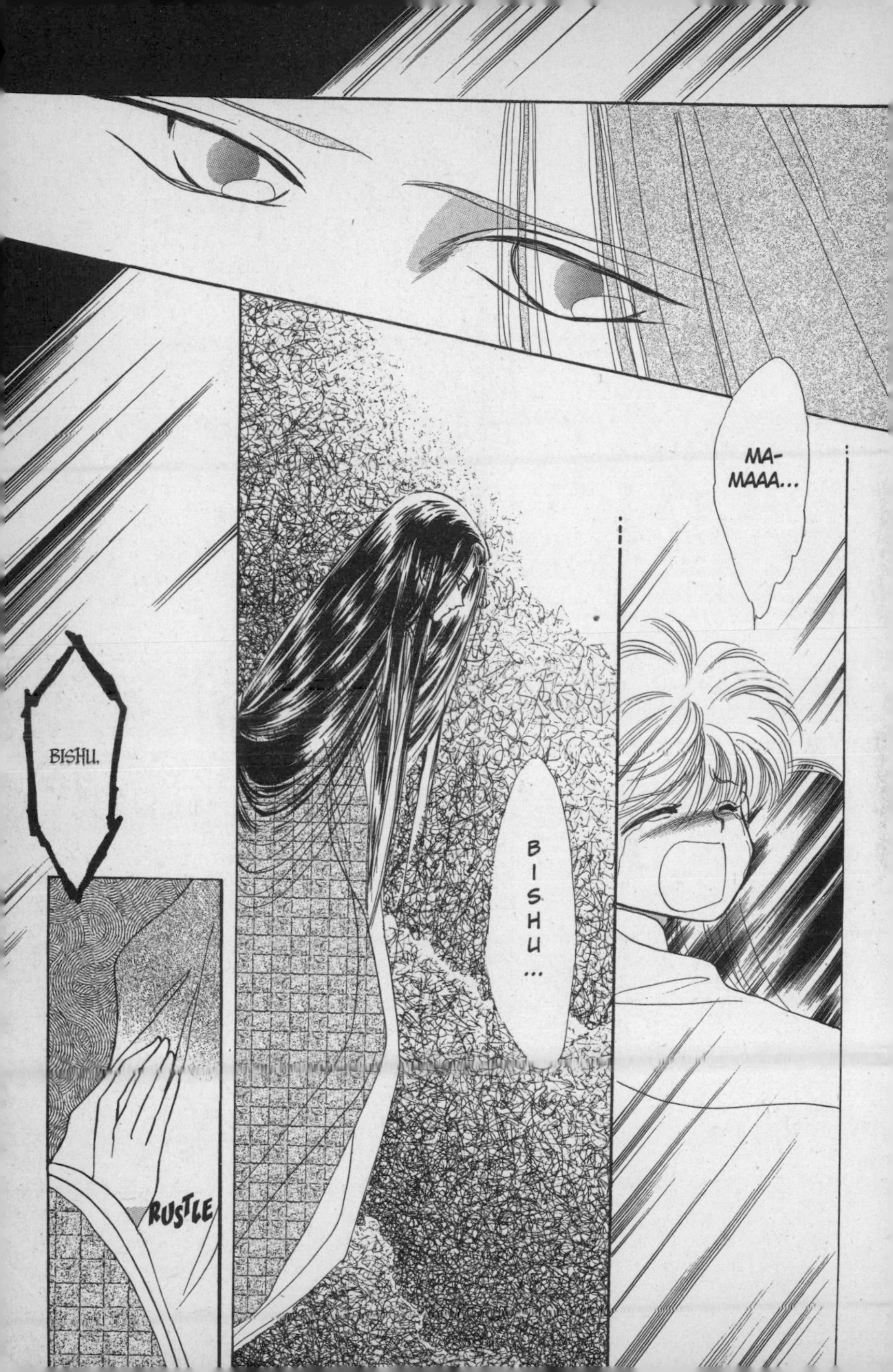
MA-
MAAA...
BISHU...
BISHU.
RUSTLE

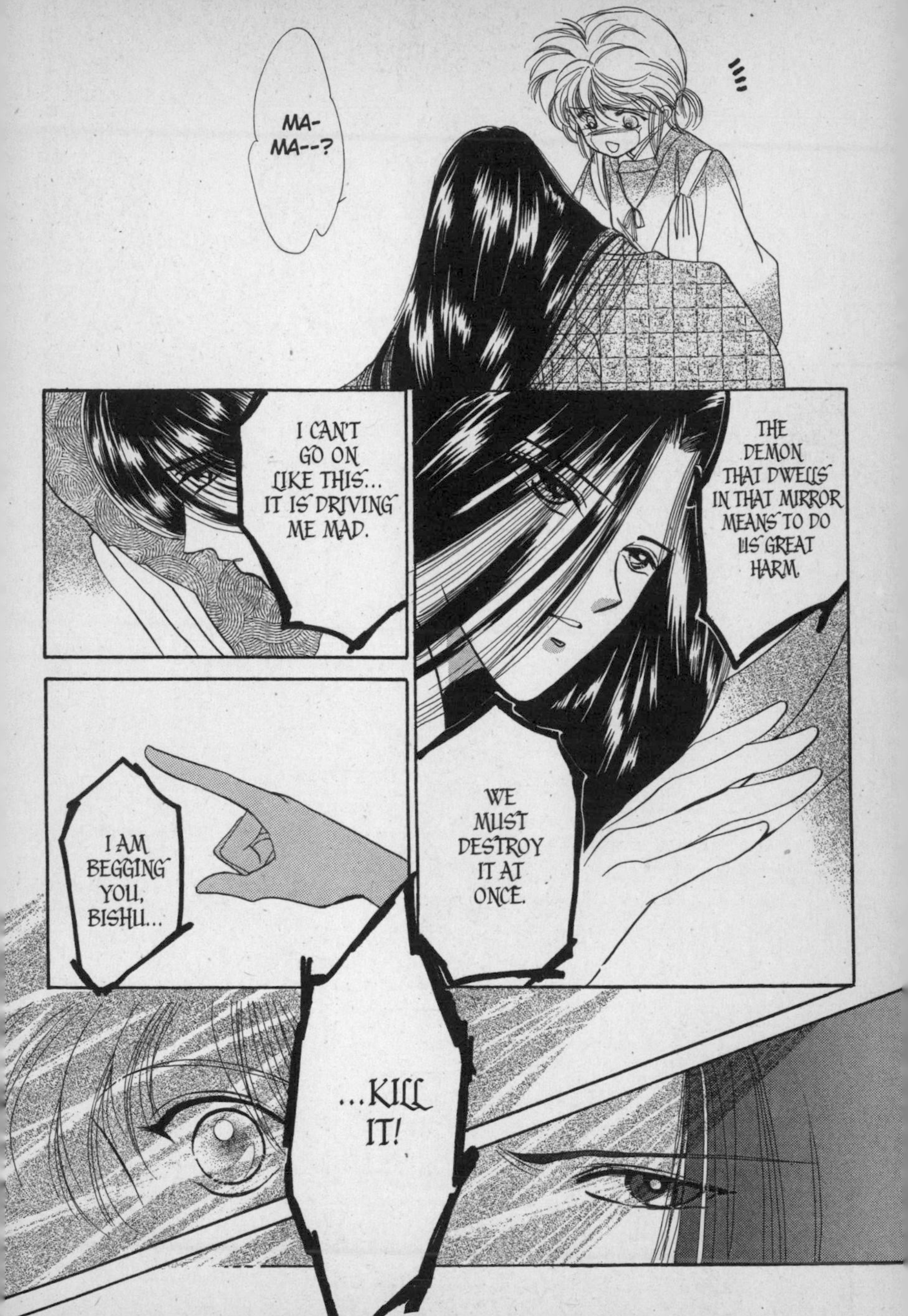
MA-MA--?
THE DEMON THAT DWELLS IN THAT MIRROR MEANS TO DO US GREAT HARM.
I CAN'T GO ON LIKE THIS... IT IS DRIVING ME MAD.
WE MUST DESTROY IT AT ONCE.
I AM BEGGING YOU, BISHU...
...KILL IT!

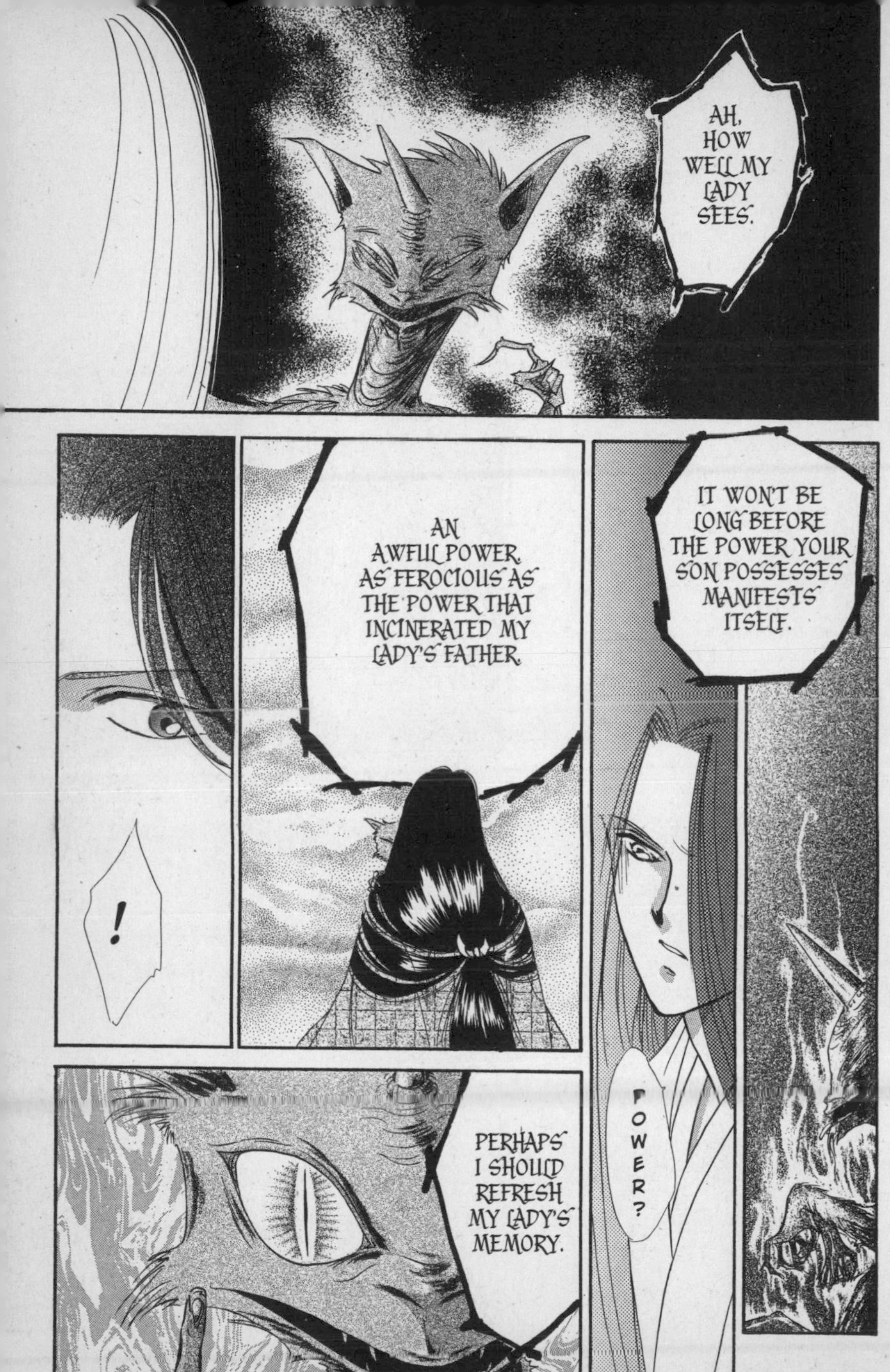

AH, HOW WELL MY LADY SEES.
IT WON'T BE LONG BEFORE THE POWER YOUR SON POSSESSES MANIFESTS ITSELF.
POWER?
AN AWFUL POWER. AS FEROCIOUS AS THE POWER THAT INCINERATED MY LADY'S FATHER.
!
PERHAPS I SHOULD REFRESH MY LADY'S MEMORY.

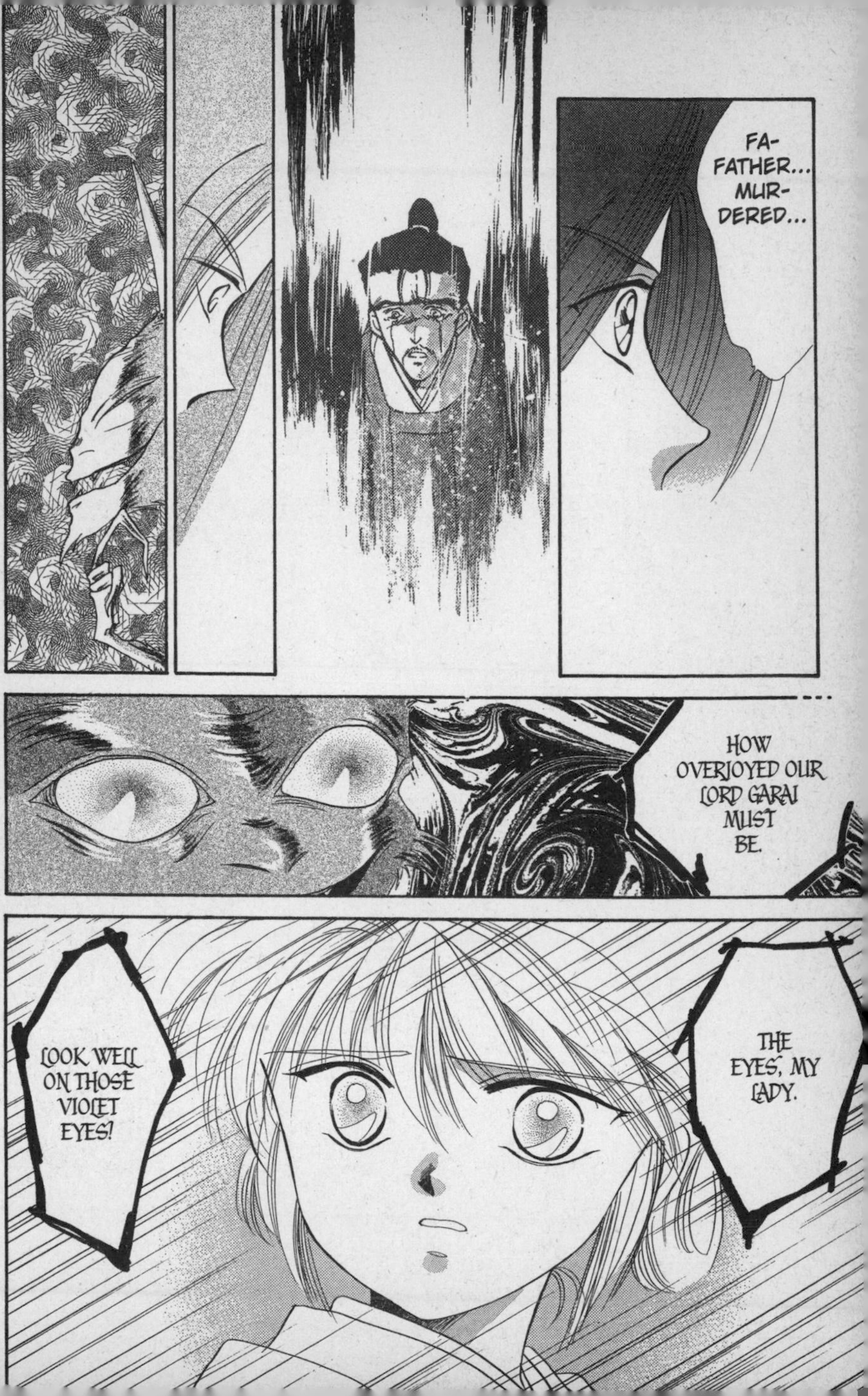
FA- FATHER... MUR- DERED...
HOW OVERJOYED OUR LORD GARAI MUST BE.
THE EYES, MY LADY.
LOOK WELL ON THOSE VIOLET EYES!

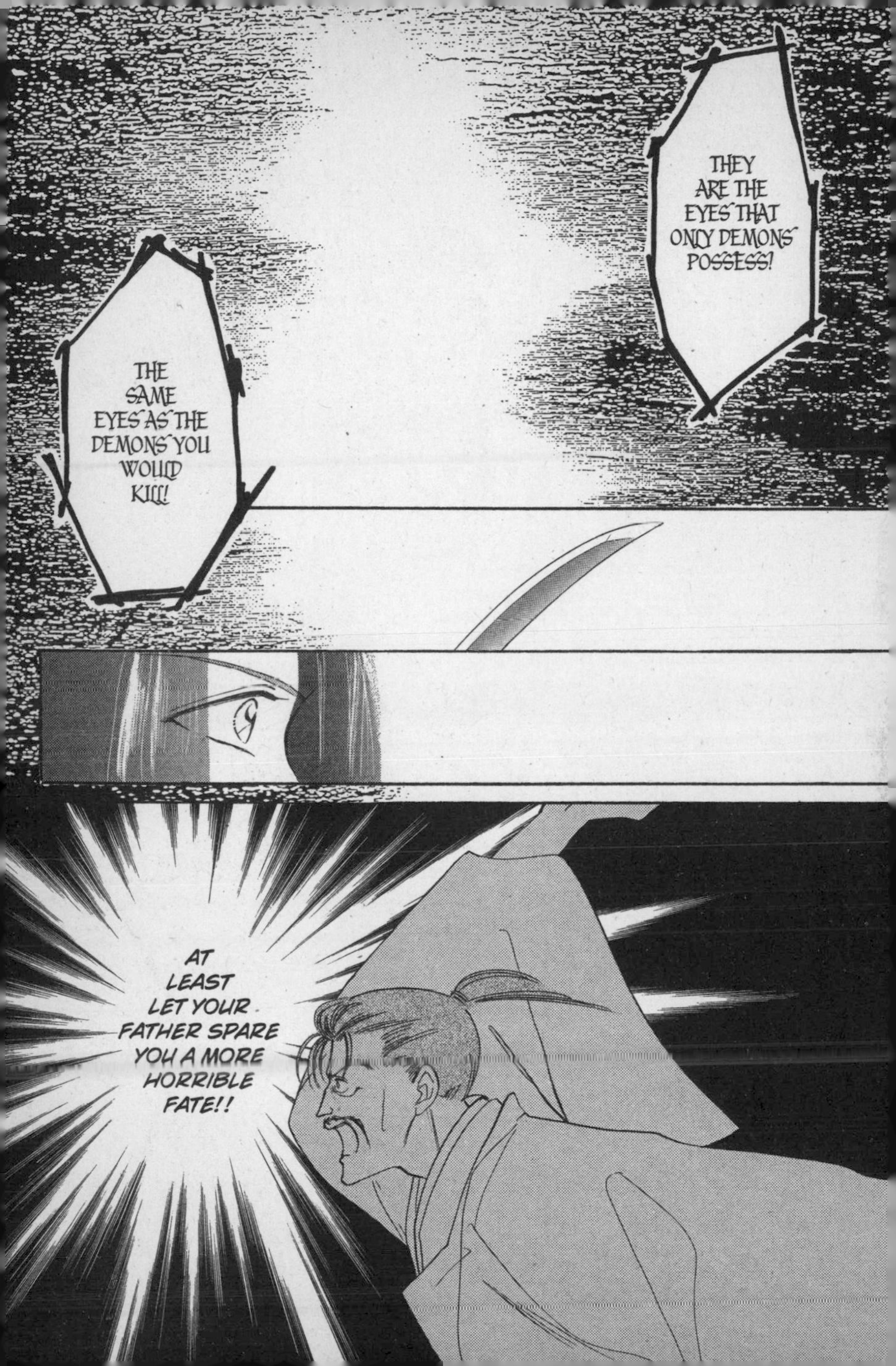
THEY ARE THE EYES THAT ONLY DEMONS POSSESS!
THE SAME EYES AS THE DEMONS YOU WOULD KILL!
AT LEAST LET YOUR FATHER SPARE YOU A MORE HORRIBLE FATE!!

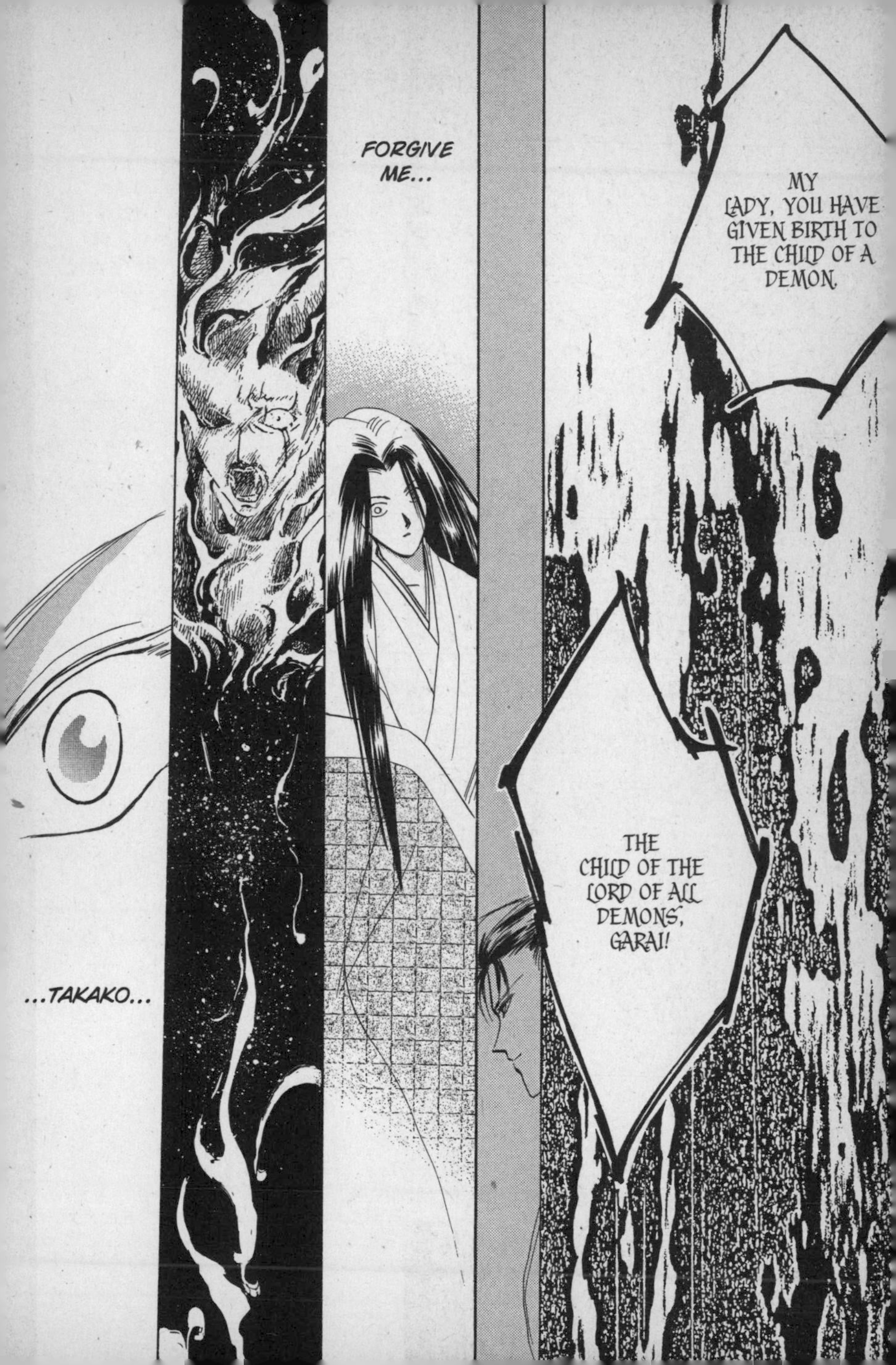
MY LADY, YOU HAVE GIVEN BIRTH TO THE CHILD OF A DEMON.
THE CHILD OF THE LORD OF ALL DEMONS, GARAI!
FORGIVE ME...
...TAKAKO...

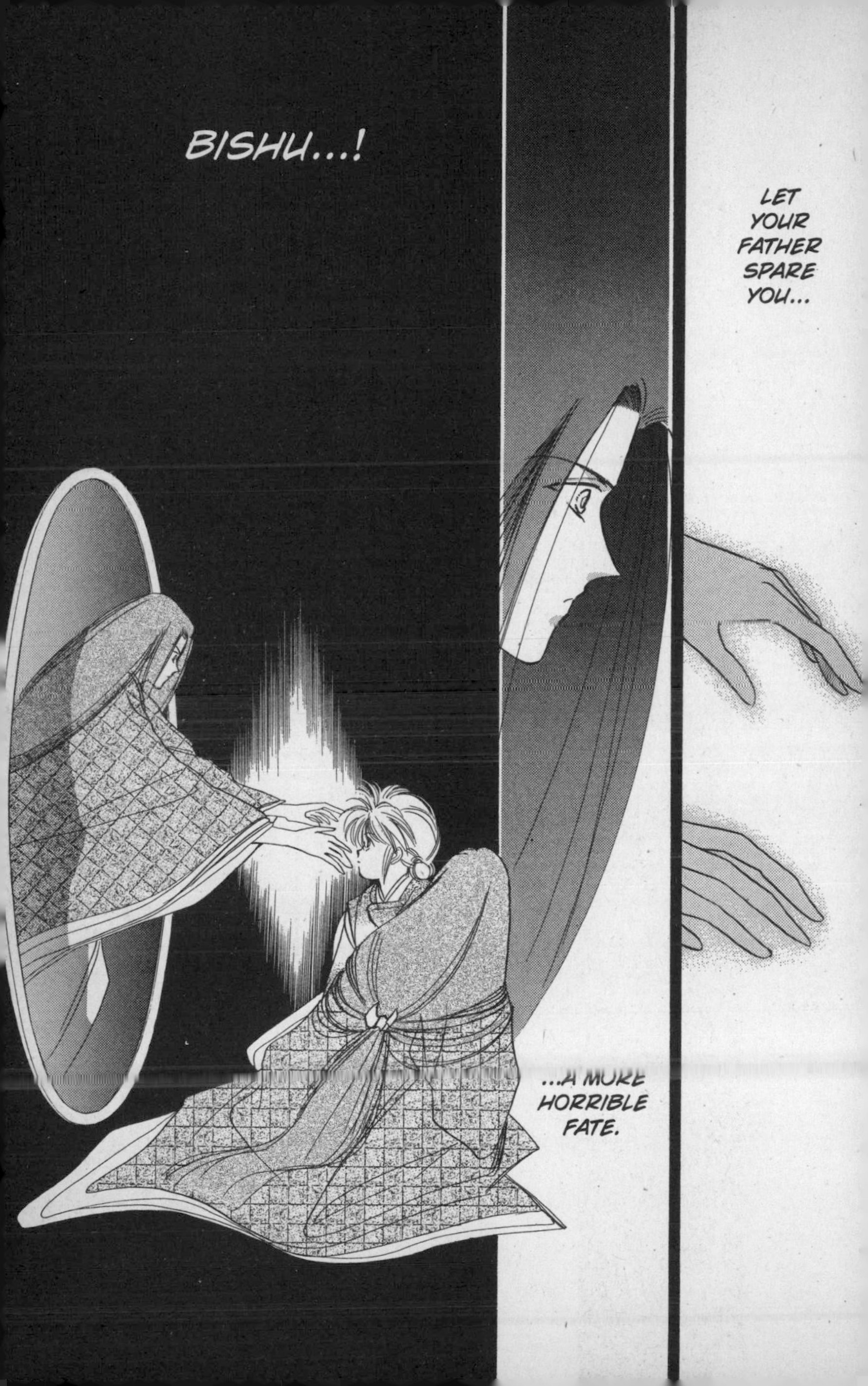
LET YOUR FATHER SPARE YOU...
...A MORE HORRIBLE FATE.
BISHU...!

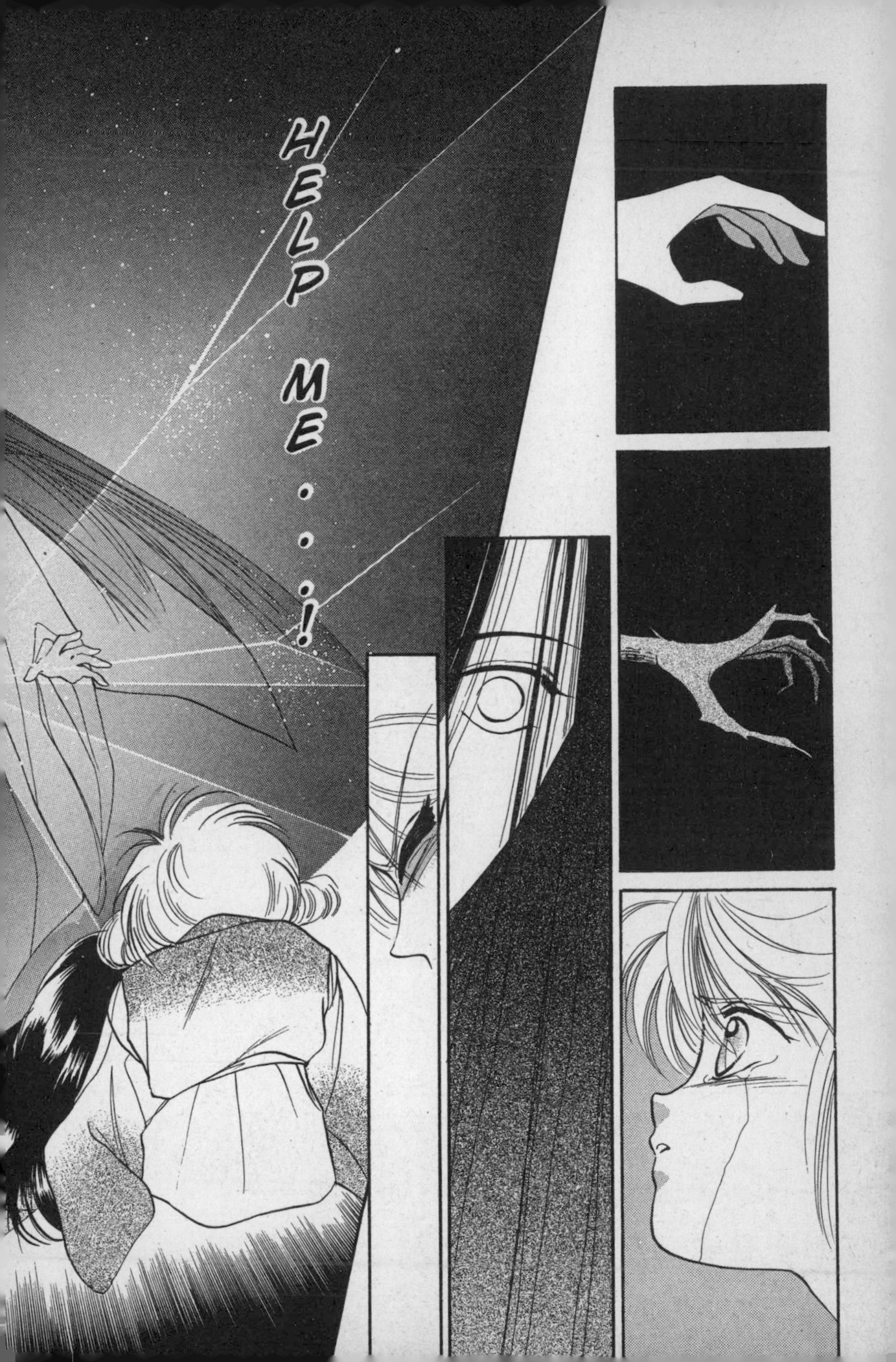

HELP ME...!

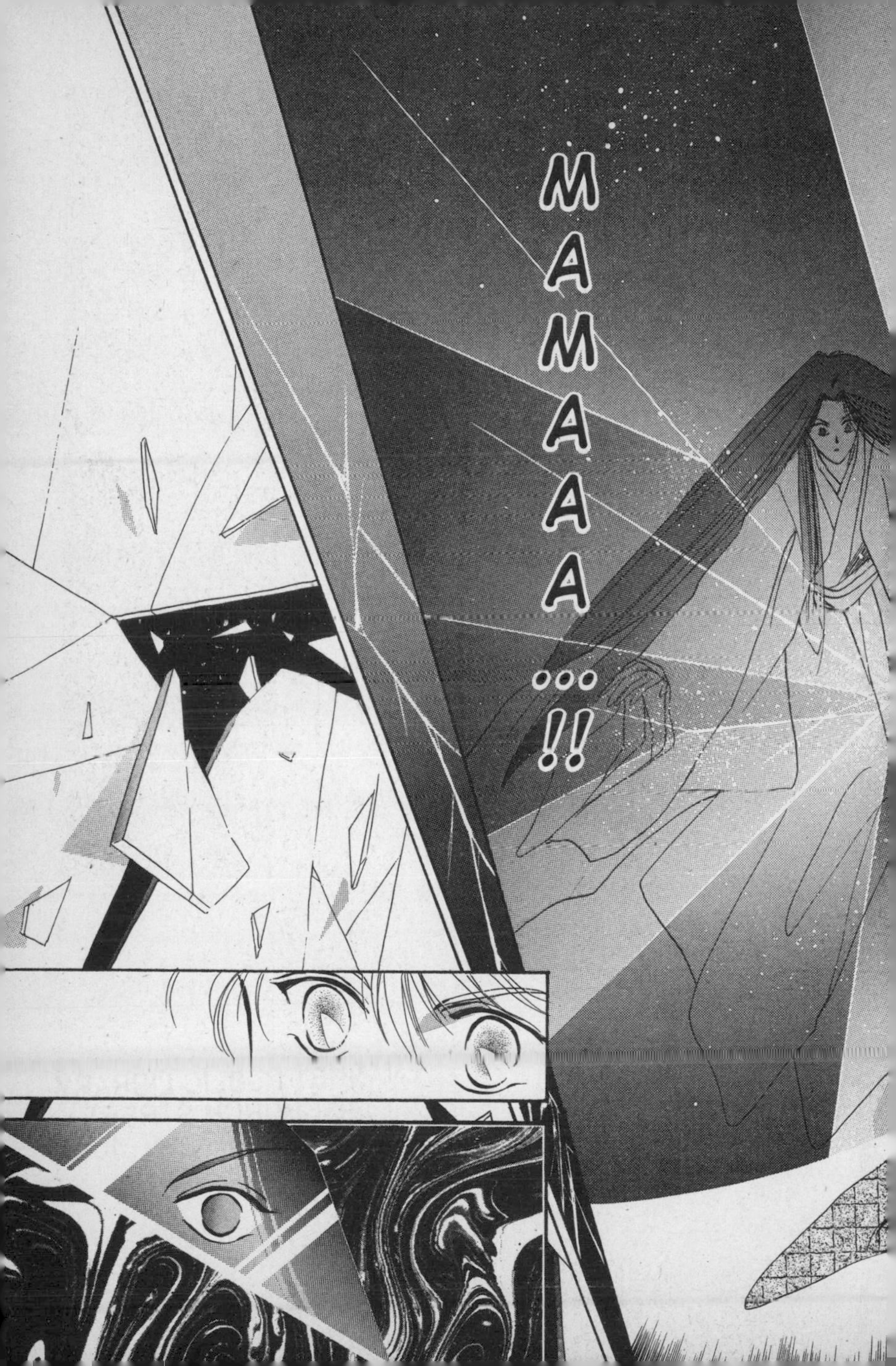
MAMAAAA...!!

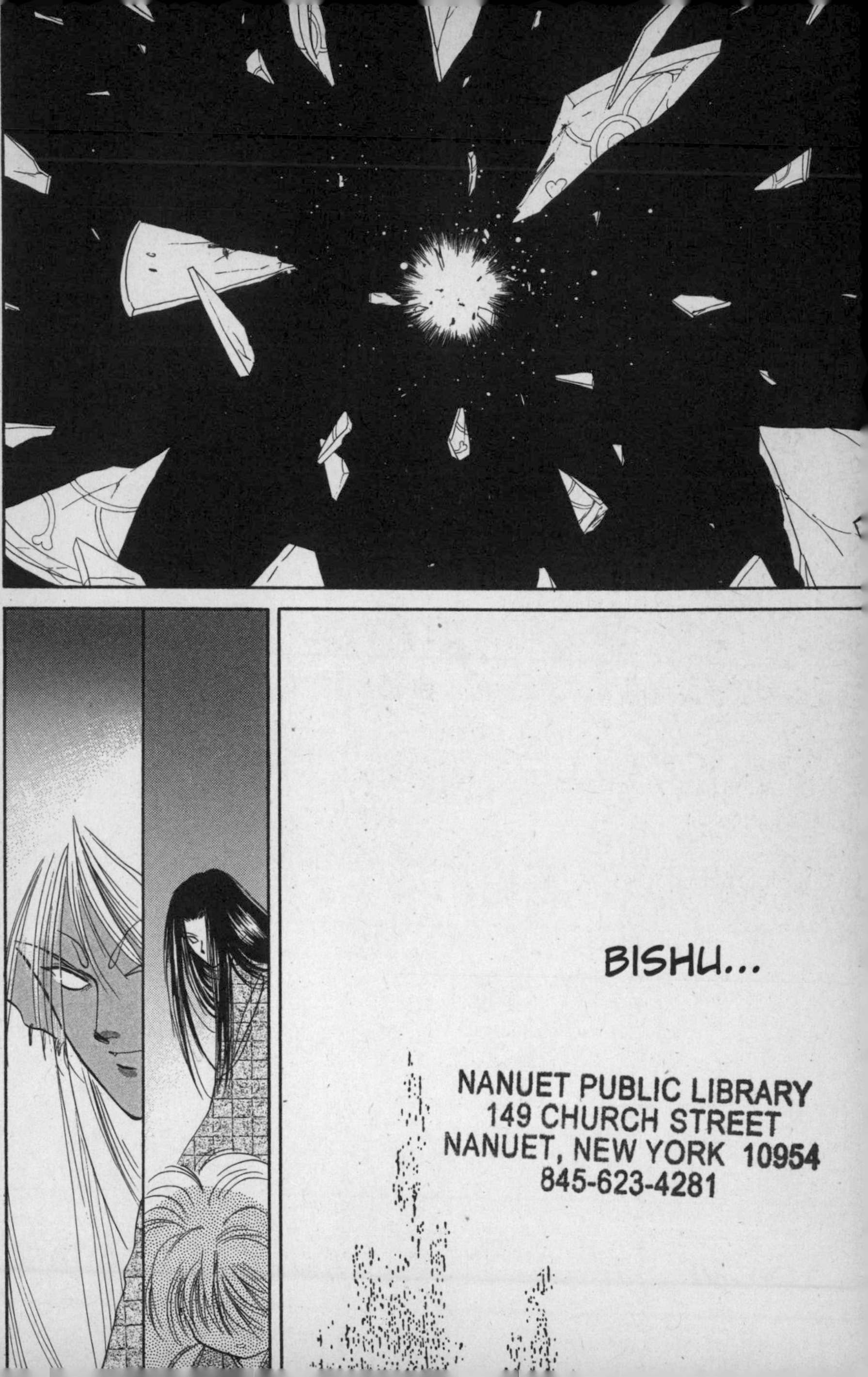
BISHU...

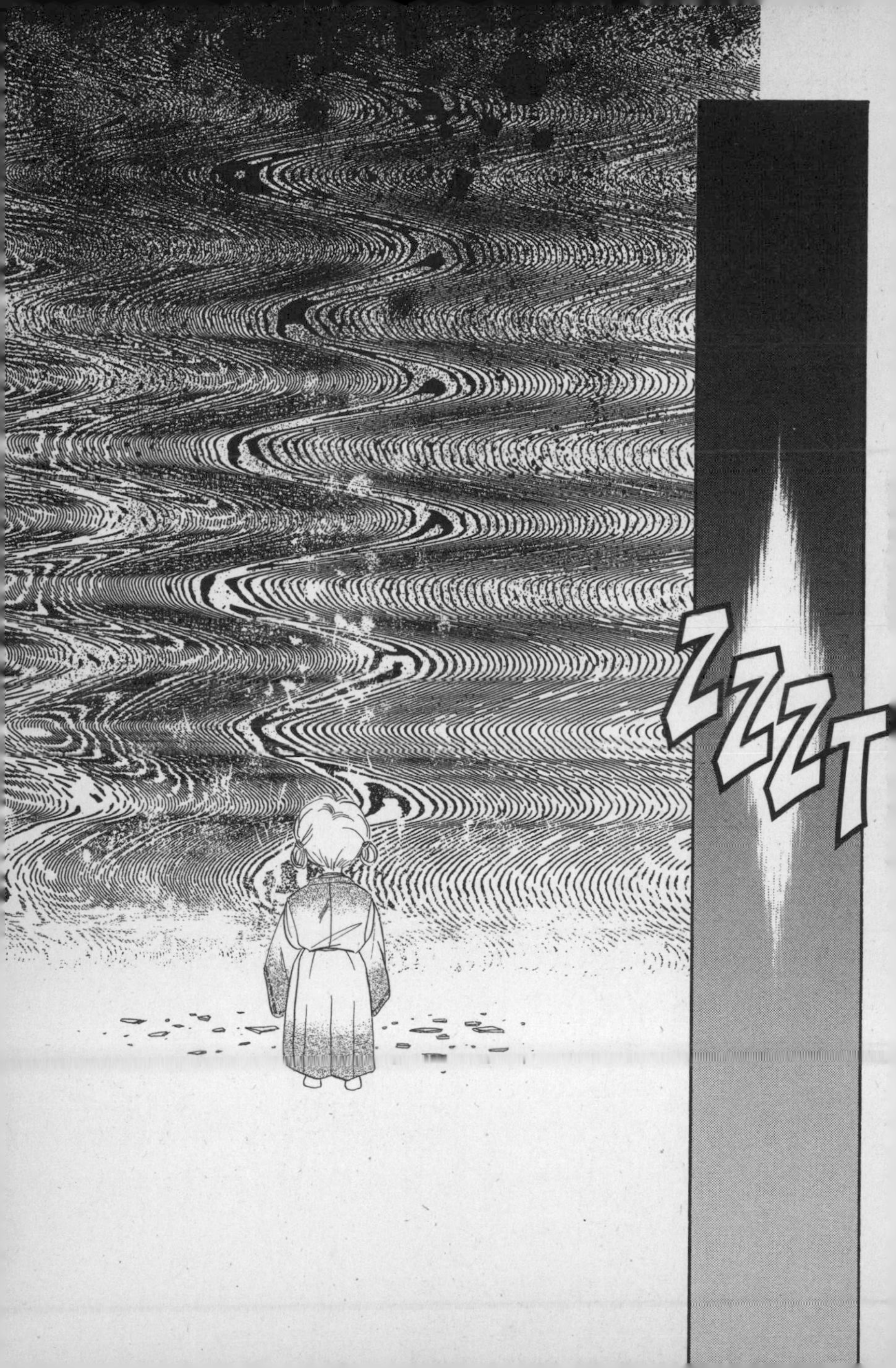
ZZZT

MO--
...MOTH-
ER?

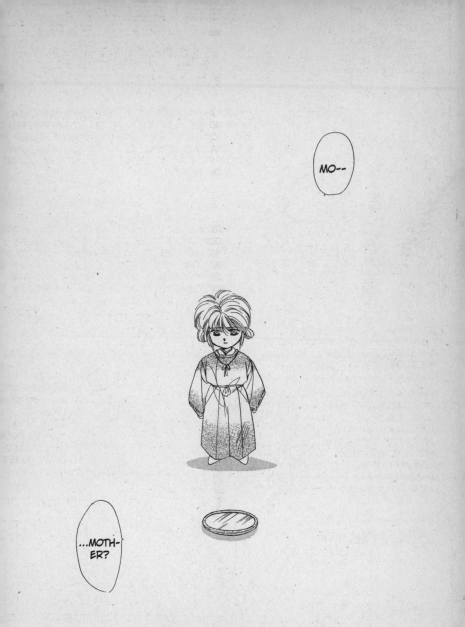

PIECES OF A SPIRAL V.3: END

AFTERWORD

♡ SPECIAL THANKS ♡ SAYURI.N. MIHARU.N
SANAE.E. RYOKUYA.S. TOMOMI.H

HELLO AGAIN, EVERYBODY. HOW HAVE YOU BEEN? SOMEHOW I MADE IT TO VOLUME 3. I FEEL GREAT, AND I COULDN'T HAVE DONE IT WITHOUT ALL OF YO I'M REALLY GRATEFUL TO ALL OF YOU WHO HAVE STUCK WITH THE STORY SO FAR, AND I HOPE YOU' KEEP ON READING.

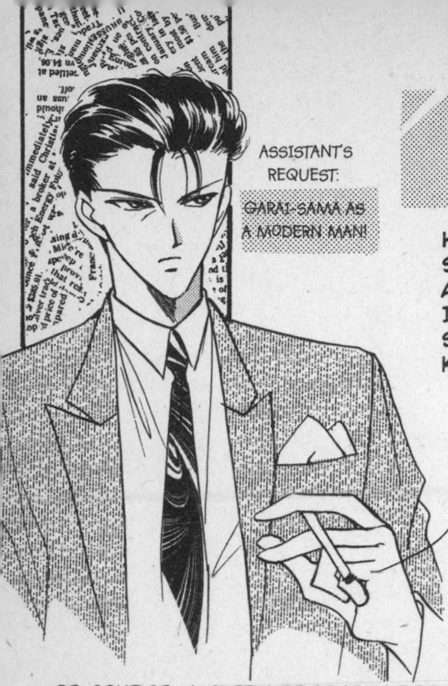

ASSISTANT'S REQUEST:
GARAI-SAMA AS A MODERN MAN!

■ RECENTLY I GOT A PHONE CALL FROM A DEA OLD FRIEND FROM JUNIOR HIGH AND HIGH SCHOOL TELLING ME SHE FOUND SOME OF MY BOOKS IN A BOOKSTORE AND SHE TOOK THE OFF THE SHELF AND PUT THEM OUT WHERE EVERYBODY COULD SEE THEM. EVERYBODY SHOULD HAVE FRIENDS LIKE THAT! THANKS FOR YOUR HELP!

OF COURSE, A CLERK PROBABLY RETURNED THEM TO THE SHELF AFTER SHE LEFT. OH WELL... BUT I'M REALLY BLESSED WITH ALL THE HELP FROM FAMILY AND FRIENDS ALIKE. THANK YOU SO MUCH, EVERYONE!!

I BOUGHT A FAN THE OTHER DAY. I MUST SAY TODAY'S FANS REALLY GET THE JOB DONE. THEY'RE LIGHT, COMPACT, COME WITH TIMERS - THEY HELP ME PUT IN A GOOD DAY'S WORK AND GET A GOOD NIGHT'S SLEEP!

WELL, THAT'S ALL FOR THIS TIME. TILL WE MEET AGAIN STAY IN GOO HEALTH AND GOOD CHEER.

1993.8. KAIM

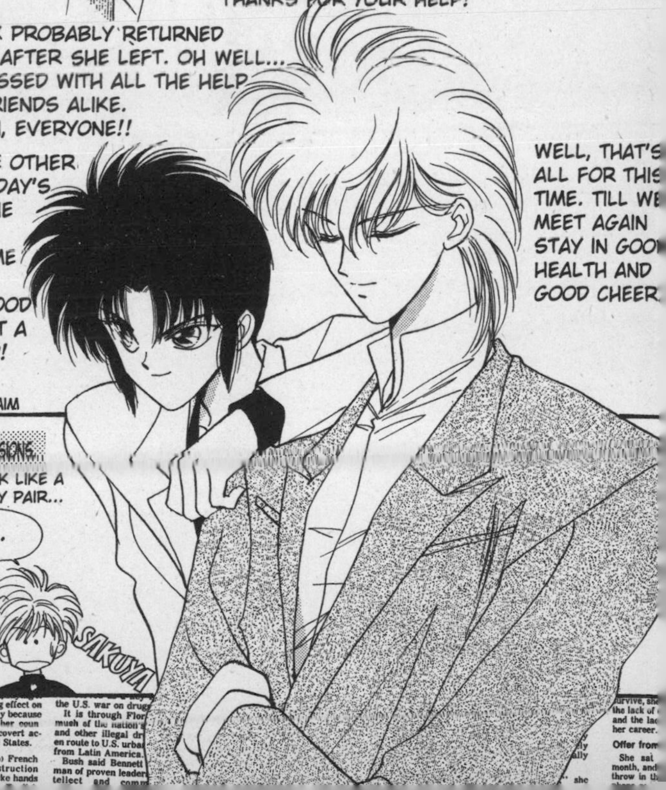

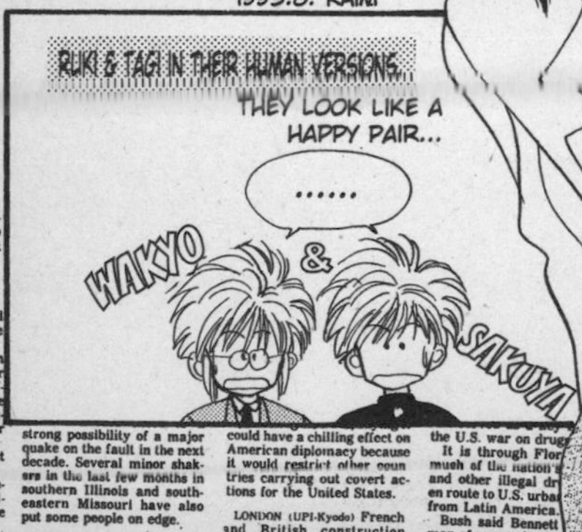

RUKI & TAGI IN THEIR HUMAN VERSIONS.
THEY LOOK LIKE A HAPPY PAIR...
......
WAKYO
&
SAKUYA

RASEN NO KAKERA Vol. 3 © 1993 Kaimu Tachibana. All rights reserved. First Published in Japan in 1993 by SHIN-SHOKAN CO., LTD.

Pieces of a Spiral Volume 3, published by WildStorm Productions, an imprint of DC Comics, 888 Prospect St. #240, La Jolla, CA 92037. English Translation © 2006. All Rights Reserved. English translation rights in U.S.A. arranged with SHINSHOKAN., LTD. and DC COMICS, through Tuttle-Mori Agency, Inc., Tokyo. The stories, characters, and incidents mentioned in this magazine are entirely fictional. Printed on recyclable paper. WildStorm does not read or accept unsolicited submissions of ideas, stories or artwork. Printed in Canada.

DC Comics, a Warner Bros. Entertainment Company.

Translation and Adaptation
by Glenn Rich

Wilson Ramos Jr. — Lettering
Larry Berry — Design
Jim Chadwick — Editor

ISBN: 1-4012-0748-0
ISBN-13: 978-1-4012-0748-9